THE IMPERATIVES OF SUSTAINABLE DEVELOPMENT

Thirty years ago, the UN report *Our Common Future* placed sustainable development firmly on the international agenda. *The Imperatives of Sustainable Development* takes the ethical foundations of *Our Common Future* and builds a model that emphasizes three equally important moral imperatives – satisfying human needs, ensuring social justice, and respecting environmental limits. This model suggests sustainability themes and assigns thresholds to them, thereby defining the space within which sustainable development can be achieved.

The authors accept that there is no single pathway to the sustainable development space. Different countries face different challenges and must follow different pathways. This perspective is applied to all countries to determine whether the thresholds of the sustainability themes selected have been met, now and in the past. The authors build on the extensive literature on needs, equity, justice, environmental science, ecology, and economics, and show how the three moral imperatives can guide policymaking. *The Imperatives of Sustainable Development* synthesizes past reasoning, summarizes the present debate, and provides a clear direction for future thinking.

This book will be essential reading for everyone interested in the future of sustainable development and in the complex environmental and social issues involved.

Erling Holden is Professor in the Renewable Energy Program at the Faculty of Engineering and Science, Western Norway University of Applied Sciences, Sogndal, Norway; and Professor at TIK Centre for Technology, Innovation and Culture, University of Oslo, Norway.

Kristin Linnerud is a Senior Research Fellow at CICERO, Center for International Climate and Environment Research, Oslo, Norway.

David Banister is Professor Emeritus of Transport Studies at the School of Geography and the Environment, University of Oxford, UK.

Valeria Jana Schwanitz is Associate Professor at the Faculty of Engineering and Science, Western Norway University of Applied Sciences, Sogndal, Norway.

August Wierling is Associate Professor at the Faculty of Engineering and Science, Western Norway University of Applied Sciences, Sogndal, Norway.

THE IMPERATIVES OF SUSTAINABLE DEVELOPMENT

Needs, Justice, Limits

Erling Holden, Kristin Linnerud, David Banister,
Valeria Jana Schwanitz, August Wierling

LONDON AND NEW YORK

from Routledge

First published 2018
by Routledge
2 Park Square, Milton Park, Abingdon, Oxon OX14 4RN

and by Routledge
711 Third Avenue, New York, NY 10017

Routledge is an imprint of the Taylor & Francis Group, an informa business

British Library Cataloguing-in-Publication Data
A catalogue record for this book is available from the British Library

Library of Congress Cataloging-in-Publication Data
A catalog record for this book has been requested

ISBN: 978-1-138-71424-3 (hbk)
ISBN: 978-1-138-71426-7 (pbk)
ISBN: 978-0-203-02217-7 (ebk)

Typeset in Bembo
by Saxon Graphics Ltd, Derby

We dedicate this book to the United Nations, which is unremittingly working to put sustainable development on the international agenda and in doing so never ceases to focus on the future of the people and the planet.

CONTENTS

List of figures   ix
List of tables   xi
Preface   xiii
Acknowledgements   xvii

Introduction   1

1   The moral imperatives of sustainable development   10

2   Satisfying human needs   35

3   Ensuring social justice   57

4   Respecting environmental limits   78

5   A normative model of sustainable development   105

6   Facts and figures   136

7   An analytic narrative for sustainable development   172

8   Lost in translation?   198

9   The next steps   221

Appendix   246
Index   252

FIGURES

1.1	The moral imperatives of sustainable development and the sustainable development space	18
1.2	Quantifying the sustainable development space	28
5.1	A normative model for sustainable development. Step 1: The moral imperatives of sustainable development	111
5.2	A normative model for sustainable development. Step 2: The theories fundamental to understanding sustainable development's moral imperatives	113
5.3	A normative model for sustainable development. Step 3: Identifying key sustainability themes	120
5.4	A normative model for sustainable development. Step 4: Identifying headline indicators	125
5.5	A normative model for sustainable development. Step 5: Assigning thresholds	127
5.6	Quantifying the sustainable development space	129
6.1	Share of three poverty dimensions in the multidimensional poverty index (MPI) for the 20 poorest countries (sorted according to the international poverty line)	141
6.2	Human development index compared with the happy life years in 2012	144
6.3	The participatory democracy index of the Varieties of Democracy Project versus *The Economist*'s democracy index (EIUDI) for 2010	147
6.4	Share of women in national parliaments versus the participatory democracy index of the Varieties of Democracy Project for 2010	148

6.5   Annual growth of a country's average income compared to growth for the poorest 40 per cent for the most recent available combination of years   150

6.6   Change in the Gini coefficient with time compared to the shared prosperity index for the most recently available combination of years   151

6.7   Distribution of world income in 1988 with regional contribution (stacked)   153

6.8   Distribution of world income in 2008 with regional contribution (stacked)   154

6.9   Greenhouse gas emission pathways compatible with a 2°C target.   157

6.10   Per-capita greenhouse gas emissions in 2010 for 190 countries   158

6.11   Global ecological footprint versus global biocapacity from 1000 to 2012   161

6.12   Ecological footprint in 2012 for different world regions   161

6.13   Share of natural intact vegetation (NIV), species abundance, and species richness in per cent across 35 biodiversity hotspots   163

6.14   Current land use in selected countries   164

7.1   Human development index against the participatory democracy index of the Varieties of Democracy Project for 2010   176

7.2   Per-capita greenhouse gas emissions against the human development index for 2010   177

7.3   Cluster membership changes between 2000 and 2010 (based on a joint intersection of 79 countries)   179

7.4   Dynamic trends 2000–2010 with respect to the key themes 'eradicating extreme poverty' and 'ensuring fair distribution' for countries of clusters A, D, F, and G   185

8.1   Approaches to sustainable development at different scales   215

TABLES

1.1	Key sustainability themes for the three moral imperatives	26
6.1	Final choices of indicators and thresholds for key themes and their links to sustainable development agenda goals	165
7.1	Performance of different clusters of countries across the six key themes.	181
7.2	Key characteristics across clusters, taken from various 2010 background data sources	182
9.1	Growth in cities and in urban population	233

PREFACE

In September 2015, the UN General Assembly launched the 2030 Agenda for Sustainable Development, a promising achievement, consisting of 17 sustainable development goals. The goals provided an important first step towards a world with less poverty, fewer environmental problems, and reduced inequalities. However, the UN's formulation of the goals was problematic: the goals focus too much on what we can and want to do and too little on what we must and should do. This book focuses on what we must and should do to achieve sustainable development, and in doing so draws on knowledge and inspiration presented three decades ago.

Thirty years have passed since the head of the UN World Commission on Environment and Development, Gro Harlem Brundtland, presented the report *Our Common Future*, which made three important contributions to the international agenda. First, it stated that fighting poverty and protecting the environment could no longer be separate tasks. Rather, the two tasks were intertwined. Second, it urged the world community to ensure that future generations could meet their rightful needs. Third, it launched a concept that links poverty, environmental protection, and future generations' needs: 'sustainable development'. *Our Common Future* still provides the authoritative definition of the concept, acknowledged by the 2012 UN Conference on Sustainable Development's political outcome document, *The Future We Want*, and by the UN 2030 Agenda.

Thirty years ago I delivered my master's thesis and started my academic career. Encouraged by *Our Common Future*, I started rather ambitiously by pondering how to achieve sustainable development. First, as a mechanical engineer, I favoured the role of new technology. Later, as a PhD student in planning, I favoured the roles of institutional and land-use changes. Even later, as a postdoctoral student in sociology, I favoured the roles of individual and societal changes. Today I embrace all these perspectives – technological change, institutional change, land-use change, individual change, and social change. I am, however, increasingly attracted by the role of individuals. In individuals we find the seeds that can lead to changes necessary to achieve sustainable development. This attraction is fundamental in my research on sustainable development.

The sustainable development concept heavily influences the international agenda three decades after *Our Common Future*. However, I am concerned that three of the concept's original imperatives have been weakened since 1987. First, the ethical and moral imperatives of sustainable development have been weakened. Sustainable development should be understood as a normative goal, but this goal has been replaced by a practical goal that reflects what we can and want to do. In rhetoric and action, we have moved from 'our common future' to 'the future we want'. Second, justice as a central imperative of sustainable development has been weakened. Ensuring justice was a central message from *Our Common Future*: justice for the poor, justice for future generations, and justice for nature and non-humans. Third, *Our Common Future* reminded us that there are environmental limits we cannot cross and that crossing them would endanger global welfare. The UN sustainable development goals, I would argue, do not pay sufficient attention to these imperatives.

The aim of this book is to reintroduce ethics, justice, and environmental limits to the academic (and hopefully political) definition and understanding of sustainable development.

I planned to write this book alone. I quickly realized – like most sustainability researchers eventually do – that I needed knowledge from more perspectives and disciplines than I possess. The solution was to increase the number of contributing authors. To address the need to say something insightful about the link between the economy – including economic growth – and sustainable development, I asked Kristin Linnerud, an economist, to contribute. To address the need to analyse, assess, and interpret data from many disciplines, I asked Valeria Jana Schwanitz, a physicist and economist, and August Wierling, a physicist, to contribute. Finally, to address the need to say something about the political implications of our sustainable development model, I asked David Banister, a geographer specializing in environmental issues, to contribute. The team writing approach improved the book substantially, and demonstrated how interdisciplinarity can be creatively harnessed in understanding the complex debates on sustainable development, and in taking those debates forward.

It should come as no surprise that the concept of sustainable development has been defined and understood differently over time, for the world changes and our conception of it changes, too. Such is especially the case when important concepts emerge and influence the international agenda. The *idea* of sustainable development remains, however: We must not destroy the natural environment on which we, nature itself, and future generations depend.

This is a powerful idea. In *The Worldly Philosophers*, the American economist Robert Heilbroner claims that when ideas enter our minds, they are a greater force for change than presidents, armies, and laws. Those who presently think that the prospect of achieving sustainable development is bleak and that the world is heading in the wrong direction could perhaps find comfort in Martin Luther King Jr's words: 'The arc of the moral universe is long, but it bends towards justice.' Those hopeful words give encouragement for the chances of achieving sustainable development too.

Erling Holden
Sogndal, 21 February 2017

ACKNOWLEDGEMENTS

This book is an outcome from the Release Project (Renewable Energy Projects: Local Impacts and Sustainability). Release is funded by The Research Council of Norway's Strategic Projects – University Colleges (SHP), Sogn and Fjordane Energi, Sparebankstiftinga Sogn and Fjordane, Sogn and Fjordane County, and Hydro Energi.

INTRODUCTION

> But the 'environment' is where we all live; and 'development' is what we all do
> in attempting to improve our lot within that abode. The two are inseparable.
> Chairperson Gro Harlem Brundtland (WCED, 1987, p. xi)

In May 1983, the United Nations General Assembly (UNGA) established the
World Commission on Environment and Development (WCED) and tasked it
with formulating a 'global agenda for change' (ibid., p. ix). The need to formulate
an agenda was part of an urgent call by the UNGA to propose long-term
environmental strategies for achieving sustainable development, including the need
to define sustainable development goals for the world community. On 19 October
1987, Chairperson Gro Harlem Brundtland officially presented the Commission's
report, *Our Common Future*, to the UNGA.[1] Though the report neither formulated
an agenda nor defined the goals, it nevertheless provided the world community
with the sustainable development concept that has structured international debate
about the environment and development ever since (Lafferty & Meadowcroft,
2000; Bernstein, 2013). Moreover, the report provided the world community with
the authoritative definition of sustainable development: 'Sustainable development
is development that meets the needs of the present without compromising the
ability of future generations to meet their own needs' (WCED, 1987, p. 43).

The authoritative definition did not come easily though. It was the result of
years of discussion within the Commission – a discussion that started with deciding
on the Commission's name. Its original name, given by the UNGA on 19
December 1983, was a 'Special Commission on the Environment for the Year
2000 and Beyond'. However, early in 1984 Chairperson Gro Harlem Brundtland,
Vice Chairperson Mansour Khalid, and Secretary General Jim MacNeill agreed to
change the name. They saw that their central task would be to overcome the

conventional view that the environment could be addressed separately from the overall social and economic set-up of the world, and that economic development and environmental protection were two distinct and incompatible goals. Rather, they soon came to realize that the links between poverty, inequality, and environmental degradation must form a major theme in their analysis and recommendations. Thus, they changed the name of the Commission, first to 'World Commission on Environmental Development', and then to 'World Commission on Environment and Development' (Borowy, 2014). Indeed, those changes were important. They influenced the wording in the authoritative definition and made it much easier to overcome the tensions between commissioners representing low-income countries in the South and those representing high-income countries in the North.

It would take almost three decades before the world community formulated and agreed an agenda and defined sustainable development goals. On 25 September 2015, the UNGA adopted the 2030 Agenda for Sustainable Development, *Transforming Our World*, which included 17 global sustainable development goals (SDGs) and 169 targets to guide world development towards 2030 (UN, 2015). It is promising that 'the Heads of States and Government and High Representatives' on behalf of the people commit themselves 'to working tirelessly for the full implementation of this Agenda by 2030' (ibid., p. 3). On 1 January 2016, the SDGs officially came into force. While the SDGs are not legally binding, governments are expected to take ownership and establish national frameworks for the achievement of the 17 goals. Countries have the primary responsibility for follow-up and review of the progress made in implementing the goals, which will require high-quality, accessible data and timely data collection. It is fair to say that the 2030 Agenda and its accompanying SDGs constitute an impressive achievement. The mere fact that the world community has finally agreed upon common sustainable development goals and committed themselves to work tirelessly in implementing them is a success in itself. Nevertheless, we believe that there is considerable room for improving the SDGs. This book suggests some improvements.

Formulating the 2030 Agenda and defining the SDGs would have been much easier if the world community had already reached a consensus on how to define and operationalize sustainable development. Alas, the 2030 Agenda has not received much help from academia in reaching such consensus. The ink was not dry in the *Our Common Future* report before critics queued up to express their scepticism about the sustainable development concept. O'Riordan (1988) described it as a potentially meaningless concept. Jacobs (1991), and later Giddings *et al.* (2002), called it a contested concept randomly shaped by people's preferences and worldviews. Daly and Townsend (1992) famously commented that sustainable development was an oxymoron.[2] Hopwood *et al.* (2005) saw it as an unclear concept that did not provide sufficient meaning to guide policy. More recently, Stafford-Smith (2014) and Stokstad (2015) have described it as vague, weak, and fragmented.[3] And indeed, these examples represent just a tiny fraction of the critique.

We think the critique is unfair. The definition of sustainable development provided by *Our Common Future* expresses anything but a vague, weak idea – meeting basic needs, recognizing environmental limits, and acknowledging the principle of justice within and between generations. This idea endures because it captures the essence of the problems of environmental protection and development confronting the modern world. It resonates with people's sense of sustainability. We agree, however, with the critique that sustainable development is difficult to define and hard to operationalize. Nevertheless, it is important to have such a definition and a model that operationalizes it, and achieving these two aims provides the rationale for this book.

The authoritative definition is elegant and quotable, but it does not really tell us what sustainable development is. What are 'the needs of the present generation'? Are we merely looking at satisfying basic needs to prevent extreme poverty or are we looking at some sort of enhanced needs that take into account people's aspirations for a better life? And what can possibly be the needs of future generations? Do we know what they are? We do not. Only future generations themselves, not the present one, will know what their needs will be. To what extent can we sacrifice the needs of the present generation for the uncertain needs of future generations? Equally puzzling, what does 'compromise the ability' mean? Apparently, that has something to do with the environmental state of the planet. Although we struggle to say anything specific about the needs of future generations, it is probably safe to say that maintaining a healthy planet is high on that list. Admittedly, *Our Common Future* gives some clues, but these are indeed open to interpretation. As early as 1992, only five years after the report was launched, the report's lead author Jim MacNeill wrote that 'a new way to define infinity was the ever-expanding number of self-serving definitions of sustainable development' (Borowy, 2014, p. ix). So, what exactly *is* sustainable development? Sustainable development says something about what we should do. But exactly what is it that we should do? To guide us further, we need a *normative definition* of sustainable development.

Ultimately, sustainability needs to be addressed globally. However, although national territories, economies, and societies constitute only one level of system organization, it is perhaps the most significant level because governance is presently strongest at the national level (Dahl, 2012). National governments possess the most significant means and the capacity to use them to address all relevant imperatives of global sustainable development. Thus, our model presented in chapter 5, though globally rooted, manifests itself primarily on a national level. This does not mean that local sustainability, for example in cities, communities, firms, and households, is unimportant. Local unsustainable behaviour can trigger global unsustainability. Moreover, the local level possesses many of the measures and means by which to promote global sustainability. Also, the necessary debate about sustainable development's normative foundation takes place locally. Therefore, we need a multilevel approach in pursuing sustainable development. Nevertheless, local sustainability must be rooted in the global imperatives too, though differently than at the national level (see chapter 8).

This book has three main messages.

- We claim that sustainable development is an ethical statement, from which we can derive three equally important moral imperatives: satisfying human needs, ensuring social justice, and respecting environmental limits. Sustainable development's key themes must come from theories that are fundamental to the understanding of those imperatives, not merely reflecting stakeholders' parochial preferences or a short-term political consensus. Since *Our Common Future*, the ethical importance has seemingly waned. Thus, the book is part of, we believe, a much needed ethical (re)turn in defining and operationalizing sustainable development.
- We claim that the moral imperatives define a sustainable development space that constitutes constraints on human behaviour. Different countries will choose different pathways to get into that space, thereby reflecting the sustainability challenges they face (e.g., reducing poverty or mitigating greenhouse gas emissions) or the means they prefer (e.g., economic measures, or command and control measures). Within the sustainable development space, countries are free to pursue the pathways they prefer and value, and different countries and different regions will likely follow different paths.
- We claim that we need numbers to assess where countries stand in relation to the sustainable development space and, consequently, to state the challenges they face to enter that space. Moreover, we must develop positive narratives to see how different countries can find inspiration and useful illustrations to enter the sustainable development space. In doing so, we need to understand what the main challenges are that countries face and we need to understand the similarities and differences in their chosen development paths.

The book has two parts. The first part (chapters 1–5) is strictly normative, and presents concepts, theories, the model, and the sustainable development space. Chapters 2–4 present theories that are fundamental to understanding the imperatives of human needs, social justice, and environmental limits. These chapters serve as an introduction to the theoretical foundations of sustainable development. Those who are more interested in the sustainable development model, or those who already are familiar with specific parts of the theoretical foundation could jump directly to chapter 5. The second part (chapters 6–9) is more applied, and presents country data, describes narratives, discusses local sustainability, and points at some overall policy implications of the book.

The content of the individual chapters is as follows:

Chapter 1 starts by asserting that sustainable development is an ethical statement, from which we can derive three equally important moral imperatives of sustainable development: satisfying human needs, ensuring social justice, and respecting environmental limits. These moral imperatives constitute a sustainable development space that establishes constraints on human development. The chapter continues with a discussion about what sustainable development is not. We argue that economic growth is not one of the imperatives of sustainable development. Thus, economic growth is neither inherently sustainable nor inherently unsustainable. Likewise, we argue that deploying new technology is neither inherently sustainable nor inherently unsustainable. The chapter also presents a critique of the three-pillar model of sustainable development and of the UN's SDGs. The chapter ends by presenting the six key sustainability themes (which come from dominant theories of the moral imperatives) and some thoughts on local sustainability.

Chapter 2 presents some influential theories on human needs. A proper theoretical understanding of what human needs are and how they can be satisfied is a prerequisite for identifying the key sustainability themes in our model presented in chapter 5. This chapter has three sections. The first briefly presents *Our Common Future*'s take on human needs. The second section presents Max-Neef's, Maslow's, and Doyal and Gough's theories on basic needs, all of which provide a natural starting point in satisfying human needs. The third section presents Sen's capability approach, which acknowledges that satisfying human needs is more than merely satisfying basic needs. Overall, a theory of human needs can be seen as a two-stage process. First, people must be provided with the means and opportunities to avoid poverty and deprivations. Second, people must be provided with an enhanced set of capabilities to do things they have reason to value.

Chapter 3 presents some influential theories on social justice. A proper theoretical understanding of what social justice is, and how the concept can be encapsulated, forms a prerequisite for identifying the key sustainability themes in our sustainable development model. This chapter has three sections. The first briefly presents *Our Common Future*'s take on social justice, including justice between generations as well as justice within generations. The second section presents John Rawls' theory of justice (1999), including a short introduction of utilitarianism, which he strongly rejects. The third section presents Sen's idea of justice (2009). Rawls' two principles of justice constitute the basis for the two key sustainability themes related to social justice: democratic participation and fair distribution of primary goods. Sen's comparative approach to justice serves as the basis for our discussion of local sustainability.

Chapter 4 gives an account of the status of the global natural capital, how human activities interact with and depend on these resources, and how we can define thresholds for critical natural capital in order to sustain the services of nature. An important message in the chapter is that there are planetary boundaries that we must respect in order to ensure a safe operating space for humans over time, and the two most important (out of a total of nine) are planetary boundaries related to climate change and biosphere integrity (Steffen *et al.*, 2015). Respecting these boundaries leads to a discussion of what part of natural capital should be sustained for the future − all, or part of it − resulting in the notions of weak and strong sustainability. We conclude the chapter by comparing various contributions in economics and showing how they can help us understand, measure, and deal with environmental limits.

Chapter 5 presents a five-step, normative model of sustainable development. The first step acknowledges that sustainable development is a normative value system, which consists of three moral imperatives. The second step presents relevant theories that give weight to those imperatives. The third step derives key themes from those theories. The fourth step suggests headline indicators for each key theme. The fifth step assigns thresholds to the indicators and thus completes the model. The six thresholds form a six-dimensional space within which we find the sustainable development space. Simply speaking, being inside the sustainable development space means that a country has achieved sustainable development, whereas being outside it means that a country is in an unsustainable state. Importantly, each country faces specific challenges in its pursuit of sustainable development. Thus, low-income countries face different challenges than high-income countries do; the former need to focus on increasing human development, whereas the latter need to focus on decreasing greenhouse gas emissions.

Chapter 6 complements the normative model developed in chapter 5 by deriving indicators and thresholds for each of the model's key themes. We discuss alternative ways of measuring the essence of such indicators and thresholds and of quantifying the limits of the sustainable development space. The focus of the quantitative analysis is on the level of nations for two main reasons. First, national governments currently offer one of the most powerful levers to push a global sustainable development agenda. Second, national accounting systems and international efforts to harmonize and compare national datasets are major steps towards achieving standardized, high-quality data. In addition to the selection of measures for the sustainable development model, chapter 6 establishes and discusses links to the relevant UN SDGs.

Chapter 7 presents the narratives, using the model in chapter 5 and the numbers in chapter 6. Our final choice of key theme indicators and thresholds is guided by the need to avoid correlation between them to the maximum extent possible. Avoiding correlation between them is a prerequisite for the multidimensional statistical analysis performed in chapter 7. We first locate countries relative to the sustainable development space by judging their performance over time, and then group countries by using cluster analysis. Such a grouping allows us to identify countries with similar societal development patterns, simultaneously accounting for all three imperatives of the sustainable development model. The cluster analysis helps us to derive attention points for a sustainable development, from which we ultimately create a quantitative narrative of change.

Chapter 8 discusses whether and how the global concept of sustainable development can be applied at the local level. Thus local sustainability means translating the global model to municipalities, cities, communities, societal sectors, firms, programmes, products, projects, and individuals. Building on the works of John Rawls and Amartya Sen, this chapter presents two very different routes to sustainable development: the comprehensive route and the comparative route.

Whereas the comprehensive route aims at the perfect, or ideal, definition, the comparative route to sustainable development is much more sensitive to people's actual lives. Thus, whereas the comprehensive route aims at *achieving* sustainable development, the comparative route aims at *advancing* sustainable development. Although the comprehensive route is our first-best option, we realize that sometimes it is insufficient at the local level. Sometimes, comprehensive sustainability is not relevant. Sometimes, the means by which to achieve comprehensive sustainability are not available. We go as far as we reasonably can, taking into account the conditions under which actors actually live and the possibilities they have. The comparative sustainability route reflects the challenge of working with sustainability at the local level.

Chapter 9, the concluding chapter, refers to this introduction to highlight the original thinking behind the book, and its essentially moral and normative starting point, but thinking that is tempered by realism about the priorities for change. The chapter discusses the uncertainties about technological optimism, the need to think about more stringent thresholds, and the balancing of the human dimensions with those of the biosphere, but simultaneously acknowledges that there is no unique solution, only different pathways that can be followed. The chapter also returns to the need for measurement and high-quality data that allow for analysis and an understanding of the different narratives that have been followed. It also looks ahead by identifying four issues that cut across all three imperatives, issues that are also likely to be central to achieving sustainable development. These include population and urbanization, resources (including energy, material resources, and technology), health (including planetary and human health), and governance (including involvement and participation). The final section builds on these four issues, opening a debate on whether the current consumption-based paradigm is sustainable, or whether alternatives must be examined that would result in less consumption by the richer countries.

Looking back over the past quarter century, Jim MacNeill claims that a shift to a more sustainable society has barely begun.[4] In 2008, Barack Obama observed that sustainability required something of a paradigm shift. History shows that paradigm shifts do not happen overnight. If they were to happen at all, they would happen very slowly, resisted all the way by the vested interests of the status quo and by other forms of inertia. The UN SDGs could well challenge the status quo and be the start of a paradigm shift towards sustainable development.

It is, however, crucial to acknowledge that the magnitude of the challenge we are facing requires difficult choices about how humankind is living on this planet. *Transforming Our World* does not acknowledge that we must make difficult, even conflicting choices. Rather, the report excitedly envisages a world in which every country enjoys sustained, inclusive, and sustainable economic growth: 'It is an Agenda of the people, by the people and for the people – and this, we believe, will ensure its success' (UN, 2015, p. 12). *Our Common Future*, on the other hand, was much more concerned about the difficult choices: 'Sustainable global development requires that those who are more affluent adopt life-styles within the planet's ecological means … We do not pretend that the process is easy or straightforward. Painful choices have to be made' (WCED, 1987, p. 9). These choices are central to the thinking behind this book.

Notes

1 The report was officially released on 27 April 1987 in London, and (with minor changes) adopted as resolution 42/187 by the UNGA on 11 December 1987 (Borowy, 2014).
2 Daly and Townsend argued that the term 'sustainable development' was often used as a synonym for 'sustainable growth'. The term 'sustainable growth' when applied to the economy is, they argued, 'a bad oxymoron – self-contradictory as prose, and unevocative as poetry … It must be saved from this perdition' (1992, p. 267).
3 Stafford-Smith (2014) and Stokstad (2015) attack the sustainable development goals adopted by the UNGA in 2015. However, their respective critiques are indirectly an attack on the concept of sustainable development.
4 Jim MacNeill's foreword in Borowy (2014, p. x).

References

Bernstein, S. (2013) Rio+20: Sustainable development in a time of multilateral decline. *Global Environmental Politics*, 13(4), 12–21.
Borowy, I. (2014) *Defining Sustainable Development for Our Common Future. A History of the World Commission on Environment and Development (Brundtland Commission)*. London and New York, Routledge.
Dahl, A. L. (2012) Achievements and gaps in indicators for sustainability. *Ecological Indicators*, 17, 14–19.
Daly, H. E. & Townsend, K. N. (eds) (1992) *Valuing the Earth: Economics, Ecology, Ethics*. 2nd edition. London and Cambridge, MA, MIT Press.
Giddings, B., Hopwood, B., & O'Brien, G. (2002) Environment, economy and society: Fitting them together into sustainable development. *Sustainable Development*, 10(4), 187–196.
Hopwood, B., Mellor, M., & O'Brien, G. (2005) Sustainable development: Mapping different approaches. *Sustainable Development*, 13, 38–52.
Jacobs, M. (1991) *The Green Economy*. London, Pluto.
Lafferty, W. M. & Meadowcroft, J. (2000) *Implementing Sustainable Development: Strategies and Initiatives in High Consumption Societies*. Oxford, Oxford University Press.
O'Riordan, T. (1988) The politics of sustainability. In: Turner, R. K. (ed.) *Sustainable Environmental Management: Principles and Practice*. London, Belhaven Press, pp. 29–50.
Rawls, J. (1999) *A Theory of Justice* (revised edition). Cambridge, MA, Belknap Press.
Sen, A. (2009) *The Idea of Justice*. London, Penguin Books Ltd.
Stafford-Smith, M. (2014) UN sustainability goals need quantified targets. *Nature*, 513(7518), 281.
Steffen, W., Richardson, K., Rockström, J., Cornell, S. E., Fetzer, I., Bennett, E. M., Biggs, R., Carpenter, S. R., de Vries, W., de Wit, C. A., Folke, C., Gerten, D., Heinke, J., Mace, G. M., Persson, L. M., Ramanathan, V., Reyers, B., & Sörlin, S. (2015) Planetary boundaries: Guiding human development on a changing planet. *Science*, 347, 736–746.

Stokstad, E. (2015) Sustainable goals from UN under fire. *Science*, 347(6223), 702–703.

UN (2015) *Transforming Our World: The 2030 Agenda for Sustainable Development*. Resolution adopted by the General Assembly on 25 September 2015, A/RES/70/1. United Nations General Assembly.

WCED (1987) *Our Common Future*. World Commission on Environment and Development. Oxford, Oxford University Press.

1

THE MORAL IMPERATIVES OF SUSTAINABLE DEVELOPMENT

> Two things fill the mind with ever new and increasing admiration and reverence, the more frequently and persistently one's meditation deals with them: *the starry sky above me and the moral law within me.*
>
> Immanuel Kant, *Critique of Practical Reason* (1788)[1]

In 1981, then president of the World Bank, Alden Winship Clausen, delivered the Fairfield Osborn Memorial Lecture in Environmental Science in Washington, DC. The lecture, later published in *The Environmentalist* (Clausen, 1982), was called 'Sustainable Development: The Global Imperative'. The lecture tells us three things. First, it tells us that if our goal is sustainable development, our perspective must be global. Second, it tells us that sustainable development is an 'imperative', something that is, according to *Oxford Dictionary*, essential or urgent. Third, it tells us that the concept 'sustainable development' had been used, admittedly not widely, years before being 'officially' launched by *Our Common Future* (WCED, 1987).[2]

Clausen was not even the first to give lectures about the concept's basic ideas. The concept was probably first coined by the economist Barbara Ward in the 1970s (Borowy, 2014), and sources of 'sustainable thinking' can be traced to the seventeenth and eighteenth centuries (Dresner, 2002; Caradonna, 2014). Thus, although *Our Common Future* did not invent either the concept or the ideas, it nevertheless, according to Jim MacNeill, is primarily responsible for sustainable development now being 'a part of the common everyday lexicon of humankind'.[3]

> Pity the politician, the party programme, the long-term plan or the international agreement which does not pay respect to the idea. The prospect

of a 'nonsustainable society' is on a par with that of a nondemocratic society. It's simply not on.

(Lafferty & Langhelle, 1999, p. 1)

And as the ultimate sign of having established a place in modern society, sustainable development is now on Facebook and Twitter.[4]

This chapter presents a normative definition of sustainable development (which we call the sustainable development space). One may argue that it is better to focus on how to achieve sustainable development than to define sustainable development. In fact, the World Commission on Environment and Development has not been created 'as an academic entity designed to enrich intellectual discourse but as an agent of tangible policy' (Borowy, 2014, p. 4). This is a fair point. Still, that does not make conceptualization (that is, defining sustainable development) unimportant. Indeed, we must know where we are going before we design policies to go there. For a concept to be of tangible use, decision-makers in all sectors and on all levels need 'a normative definition which delineates the direction and range of acceptable policies, laws, investment and private behaviour' (ibid., p. 3). Thus, sustainable development has now *also* become an academic entity designed to enrich intellectual discourse, and rightfully so.

What *is* sustainable development?

A conceptual clarification seems necessary. Some scholars argue that there is a difference between the concepts sustainable development and sustainability, for example, that sustainable development ultimately gives priority to development and that sustainability primarily is about the environment (e.g., O'Riordan, 1988), or that sustainability refers to a goal whereas sustainable development refers to the process that leads us to sustainability (e.g., Shaker, 2015). To us the two concepts entail the same ideas and the same policy implications. Thus, we use them interchangeably.

Sustainable development is a normative value system, on a par with human rights, democracy, and freedom (and it is closely interlinked with all those other normative systems) (Lafferty & Langhelle, 1999). Thus, sustainable development is essentially a strong ethical statement that tells us what we should do (Sen, 2009). *Our Common Future* left no doubt about that: 'We have tried to show how human survival and well-being could depend on success in elevating sustainable development to a global ethic' (WCED, 1987, p. 308). *Transforming Our World* pledges to foster 'an ethic of global citizenship' (UN, 2015, p. 10). Thus, any attempt to conceptualize or operationalize sustainable development must seriously consider these messages. The importance of putting ethical considerations at the heart of sustainable development was almost lost during the 1990s, however. This is now turning. In a lecture hosted by University of Oxford about how to tackle climate change, former Chief Economist at the World Bank, Nicholas Stern referred to 'an ethical turn' as to why we ought to act (Stern, 2015a). This is true for tackling climate change, and it is equally true for achieving sustainable development.

What happens when sustainable development clashes with other interlinked value systems? We have mentioned human rights, democracy, and freedom. One could easily add human security, peace, and happiness to that list. These are all concepts that relate to sustainable development, yet are partially distinct from it. To some extent, there are tension and potential conflicts between these concepts and the concept of sustainable development (Meadowcroft *et al.*, 2012). At some level, however, 'they share a similar agenda which can be framed as focusing the objective of professional efforts on improving people's lives' (Alkire, 2010, p. 28). It is beyond the scope of this book to examine the similarities and differences between sustainable development and related concepts. However, we stress that our approach is one that tries to identify the most important features of sustainable development, or as we have called them, the imperatives and key themes. Thus, some important features of the related concepts are part of our approach, but some fall outside it. This does not mean, however, that important features of related concepts that fall outside our approach to sustainable development are unimportant. Take for example peace. We regard peace as a prerequisite for sustainable development (or indeed any development). We agree that 'there can be no sustainable development without peace and no peace without sustainable development' (UN, 2015, p. 3).

Argument #1: The point of departure for any definition of sustainable development must be an ethical statement.

The economist, philosopher, and Nobel Laureate Amartya Sen (2009) argues that if we understand ethical statements not exclusively as claims enshrined through legislation or common law, two questions immediately arise: first, 'what is its content?' and second, 'what is its viability?' Sen does not pay much attention to sustainable development. Rather, he focuses on another ethical statement: human rights. Regarding the content of human rights, Sen refers to a declaration of human rights, and to what is theorized and practically invoked by those rights. But, Sen asks, where does such a declaration come from? Sen claims that a declaration of an ethical statement may come from persons, from institutions, or from particular groups of people charged to examine these issues (for example the United Nations committee that authored the United Nations Universal Declaration of Human Rights in 1948). In any case, Sen maintains that the content of human rights, articulated or ratified, is an ethical statement.

What is the declaration of sustainable development? Earlier contributions aside, we believe that it is *Our Common Future*. The report has 'declared' the concept and provided global society with the authoritative definition of sustainable development. Thus, the content of sustainable development derives from what is theorized and practically invoked from that declaration. Nothing, in our opinion, has changed the status of *Our Common Future* as the declaration of the ethical statement of sustainable development.

We are not suggesting that *Our Common Future*'s definition (and content) of sustainable development is immune to change though. This brings us to the question of the *viability* of ethical statements, which, according to Sen, is about how we can judge the acceptability of them and, moreover, how we assess the challenges they may face. We take the stance that any society must reflect on its normative foundation, be it human rights or sustainable development. Those who want to defend human rights or sustainable development must be prepared to defend those ethical statements. So how do we do that? Sen's answer is that all ethical propositions must survive open and informed public scrutiny. This means that we must engage in ongoing debate, which allows disputing views of the content. We must be open to information coming from other societies and to arguments coming from afar, too. Thus, a claim that a certain aspect (for example freedom) is important enough to be part of an ethical statement (for example human rights) is also a claim that reasoned scrutiny would sustain that claim.

We believe that *Our Common Future* made very distinct claims, which we will refer to as moral imperatives. We will return to those imperatives shortly, but will first make an important point. *Our Common Future* was very clear about the challenge of achieving sustainable development: 'We do not pretend that the process [of achieving sustainable development] is easy or straightforward. Painful choices have to be made' (WCED, 1987, p. 9). Three decades later, the UN's *Transforming Our World: The 2030 Agenda for Sustainable Development* was much more optimistic: 'It is an Agenda of the people, by the people and for the people – and this, we believe, will ensure its success' (UN, 2015, p. 12). Sustainable development is enthusiastically presented as a 'win–win–win approach' (that is, simultaneously better economic, social, and environmental performance), an approach hardly acknowledged by *Our Common Future*. Thus, one of the central messages of *Our Common Future* – the need to make inconvenient, sometimes conflicting choices a part of global politics as much as of everyday life – has been sidelined (Borowy, 2014). We believe, as the authors of *Our Common Future* did three decades ago, that sustainable development requires those who are affluent to adopt lifestyles within the planet's ecological means. Indeed, that is an inconvenient choice.

> *Argument #2: The central message of* Our Common Future *– the need to make inconvenient choices – has been sidelined; sidelining it reduces the chances of achieving sustainable development.*

We have far to go, though, from an ethical statement to our normative model. The first step is to define the moral imperatives derived from the ethical statement of sustainable development.

The moral imperatives of sustainable development

Ethical statements, according to Sen (2009), demand acknowledgement of imperatives that tell us something must be done. Stern (2015b) too, acknowledges that an examination of the ethics (of tackling climate change) strongly points to a moral imperative for action.[5] Why would we call them moral imperatives and not, say, strategic imperatives? First, because ethical statements obviously require moral imperatives. Second, because achieving sustainable development, according to its declaration, 'is part of our moral obligation to other living beings and future generations' (WCED, 1987, p. 57).

Central to the understanding of moral imperatives is what the American philosopher John Rawls (1999) calls moral powers, of which he presents two: people's capacity for a sense of justice and their capacity for a conception of the good. Thus, we all have some sort of feeling for what is just and unjust. We also have a feeling for the kinds of goods we need. Justice and needs are indeed at the core of sustainable development. Thus, we argue that people have a moral power, which we will call a capacity for a sense of sustainability. Or perhaps we should call it a sense of unsustainability: we sense that poverty is wrong, we sense that it is wrong when injustice is being done, and we sense that destroying the natural environment is wrong. Maybe that is precisely what has made the concept of sustainable development part of the 'everyday lexicon of humankind': we intuitively recognize it!

This might seem a bold suggestion, though, in a world described by many as already being in an unsustainable state, and to make it even worse, continuing on an unsustainable trajectory. Remember, though, that even if there is injustice in the world, we still have a sense of justice. When we see something that is unjust we tend to try to rectify it. Just recall the abolition of slavery in the United States, the elimination of overt apartheid in South Africa, and the emergence of women's liberation. Thus, even if we experience unsustainability in the world, we still have a sense of sustainability. We might have different conceptions of sustainability though, just as we have different conceptions of justice. Nevertheless, to activate and develop that sense of sustainability are prerequisites for achieving sustainable development.

> *Argument #3: People have a sense of sustainability, the activation and development of which are prerequisites for achieving sustainable development.*

A sense of sustainability perhaps does not sound like a very powerful tool. One could argue that instead of waiting for people to come to their senses, we need some sort of Leviathan to steer us. Thomas Hobbes argued that a powerful Leviathan is necessary to overcome a war of all against all (Hobbes, 1998 [1651]). Likewise, one could argue that a powerful Leviathan is necessary to overcome a state of unsustainability (which could in the long run well end up in a war of all against all). Thus, our only choice is to give up our liberty through agreeing a social contract with the Leviathan to stop our lives from being potentially nasty, brutish, and short. Hobbes' Leviathan is the state (as opposed to the state of nature) and we will not deny the importance of having a state. Nevertheless, one could argue that Hobbes has overlooked one thing: morality (Wolff, 2006). People can do the right things without being forced. Contrasting Hobbes, Talcott Parsons believes that members of society share common norms and values (Parsons, 1968 [1937]). Such a normative consensus would ensure integration within societies and they would not collapse into complete unsustainability. Parsons emphasizes that values and norms are crucial to solving problems, to making societies possible, and to ensuring people's lives are not nasty, brutish, and short. Parsons puts his trust in American, or Western, values and norms. *Our Common Future* and *Transforming Our World* go much further. They call for a *global* ethic. This global ethic rests on people's sense of sustainability.

In fact, the Commission early on was well aware of the importance of people's sense of sustainability. At its inaugural meeting in Geneva 1–3 October 1984, the commission members discussed how they could convey their central messages. How could they reach people's hearts and minds? Brundtland summed up the Commission's challenge: 'its attitude must at the same time be sincere, scientific, outspoken, concrete, action-oriented and emotional' (Borowy, 2014, p. 65). She continued by stating that 'the Commission must be willing and able to stir people's imagination, to move their thoughts, feelings and a sense of public responsibility' (ibid.). It is this sense of public responsibility that captures the idea of a global ethic, and leads to what we call a sense of sustainability. Thus, the commissioners always knew that activating people's sense of sustainability is a prerequisite for achieving sustainable development.

People's sense of sustainability leads us back to the moral imperatives. So what are the moral imperatives of sustainable development?

The first moral imperative is to satisfy human needs. This imperative is an explicit part of *Our Common Future*'s definition of sustainable development, which contains within it 'the concept of "needs", in particular the essential needs of the world's poor, to which overriding priority should be given' (WCED, 1987, p. 43). Indeed, *Our Common Future* regards the satisfaction of human needs and aspirations to be so obviously fundamental that it may appear redundant to assert its central role in the concept of sustainable development. *Transforming Our World* is also clear on this matter: 'We recognize that eradicating poverty in all its forms and dimensions, including extreme poverty, is the greatest global challenge and an indispensable requirement for sustainable development' (UN, 2015, p. 1). We acknowledge that satisfying human needs is more than merely satisfying basic needs. Thus, the moral imperative of satisfying human needs must also take into account people's legitimate aspirations to live the life they want to live. To do so, people need capabilities.

According to the latest *Human Development Report*, the world has made major progress in human development. Between 1990 and 2015 income poverty in developing country regions fell by more than two-thirds. The number of extremely poor people worldwide fell from 1.9 billion to 836 million. The child mortality rate fell by more than half, and under-five deaths fell from 12.7 million to 6 million. More than 2.6 billion people gained access to an improved source of drinking water, and 2.1 billion gained access to improved sanitation facilities, even as the world's population rose from 5.3 billion to 7.3 billion (UNDP, 2015).

Yet progress has been uneven among regions, across countries, and within countries. Worldwide 795 million people suffer from chronic hunger, 11 children under the age of five die every minute, and 33 mothers die every hour. About 37 million people live with HIV and 11 million with tuberculosis. More than 660 million people use an unimproved source of drinking water, 2.4 billion people use an unimproved sanitation facility, and nearly a billion people resort to open defecation (ibid.). Thus, there are still millions of poor people in this world, fighting every day to satisfy their most essential needs. This is wrong and indeed violates sustainable development's moral imperatives of satisfying human needs (and our sense of sustainability). The *Human Development Report* concludes that 'considerable challenges remain, from persistent poverty and grinding inequalities to climate change and environmental sustainability in general' (ibid., p. iii). This leads us to the next moral imperative of sustainable development.

The second moral imperative is social justice. *Our Common Future* argues that sustainable development implies a 'concern for social equity between generations, a concern that must logically be extended to equity within each generation' (WCED, 1987, p. 43).[6] (*Our Common Future* commonly refers to equity; we see no major differences in the terms 'equity' and 'justice' and will thus use them interchangeably (Pereira *et al.*, 2017).) Intergenerational justice relates primarily to concern for protecting the global ecosphere for future generations. This concern is about respecting environmental limits, which is our third moral imperative that will be discussed shortly. Intragenerational justice focuses on the North–South issue and the 'overriding priority' already mentioned. *Our Common Future* did not confine intragenerational justice solely to North–South issues, though, but importantly focused on 'social justice within and amongst nations' (WCED, 1987, p. 47). Thus, intragenerational justice, or social justice as we shall call it, is indeed a moral imperative of sustainable development.

Whereas justice, or equity, always was central in *Our Common Future*, Agyeman (2013) claims that there has been an 'equity deficit' in sustainability theory, rhetoric, and practice. Thus, he attempts (rightfully) to reinstate justice in sustainable development by launching the concept of 'just sustainability'. His definition of just sustainability focuses equally on four essential conditions: improving our quality of life and wellbeing; meeting the needs of both present and future generations; justice in terms of procedure and outcome; and living within ecosystem limits. To us, this is identical to our own definition of sustainable development. Thus, 'just sustainability' is redundant in a sense, though we understand why he coins that concept.

There is ample evidence that justice should be imperative to achieving sustainable development. Although not the same, justice is closely related to equality (Sen, 2009). Thus, every normative theory of social justice demands equality in *something*, for example in income and wealth. Alas, the world has become an increasingly unequal place. According to Oxfam, global inequality is surging. Today, 62 people own as much as the poorest half of the world's population does – that is, 3.6 billion people (Hardoon *et al.*, 2016). This number has fallen dramatically. In 2010 it was 388 people. In addition, inequalities within a number of countries have grown too (ibid.; UNDP, 2015). Such inequalities, *Our Common Future* claims, represent great differences not merely in the quality of life of present societies, but also in the capacity of societies to improve their quality of life in the future (WCED, 1987). Two decades later, Wilkinson and Pickett (2009) demonstrated empirically that societies having great inequalities indeed are bad for almost everyone – rich as well as poor. Moreover, a world in which inequity is endemic will always be prone to social (Stiglitz, 2013) and ecological crises (ibid.; UNDP, 2015). This brings us to the third moral imperative.

The third moral imperative is to respect environmental limits. Indeed, environmental limits play a critical role in the vision of sustainable development articulated in *Our Common Future*. The report emphasizes that 'the idea of limitations imposed by the state of technology and social organization on the environment's ability to meet present and future needs' represents one of the key concepts contained within the idea of sustainable development (WCED, 1987, p. 43). Various understandings of limits lie at the heart of contemporary environmental controversy including, for example, recent debates about planetary boundaries, biodiversity loss, carbon budgeting, and the 1.5 degree climate target (Eastin *et al.*, 2011; Biermann, 2012; Meadowcroft, 2013; Morseletto *et al.*, 2016). More generally, reconciling the rapid expansion of human civilization (population growth, the rise in material throughput, and the increasing reach of our technologies) with a bounded biosphere remains a critical problem for the coming century.

Respecting environmental limits is one of the neglected inconvenient messages from *Our Common Future*. Having agonized for years over how best to deal with the reality of nature's ultimate limits, Jim MacNeill was distressed to see that this message was mainly ignored after the 1992 Rio Summit. MacNeill argues that that message is even more urgent today. In 1987, he argued, we had not yet crossed any global limits. Today, scientists tell us that we have crossed several critical planetary boundaries (Steffen *et al.*, 2015).

Why should we respect environmental limits? Just because *Our Common Future* says so is probably not enough to convince everyone. An obvious reason is that we heavily depend on the services a healthy planet provides. We depend on nature for the essentials of life conditions: air, food, material, and water. There are other reasons too. First, we agree with Edith Brown Weiss (1992) that as members of the present generation, we hold Earth in trust for future generations. Hence, not respecting environmental limits most likely prevents future generations from having resources vital to meeting their needs. Second, we agree with Sen (2009) that since we are enormously more powerful than other species, we have responsibility towards them. This responsibility means that we must respect environmental limits.

> *Argument #4: Sustainable development consists of three moral imperatives: satisfying human needs, ensuring social justice, and respecting environmental limits.*

Importantly, the three moral imperatives are interlinked. This is one of the critical insights of *Our Common Future* three decades ago and recently emphasized by *Transforming Our World*. Poverty, injustice, and environmental degradation interact in complex and potent ways. Poverty is a major cause and effect of local and global environmental problems. It is therefore futile to attempt to deal with environmental problems without a broader perspective that encompasses the factors underlying world poverty and international inequality. The inequality between developing and developed countries, *Our Common Future* reminds us, is the planet's main 'environmental' problem; it is also its main 'development' problem. Environmental degradation leads to greater poverty and increases inequalities. The downward spiral of poverty and environmental degradation wastes opportunities and resources. In particular, it wastes human resources. Consequently, these links between poverty, inequality, and environmental degradation formed a major theme in *Our Common Future*'s analysis and recommendations. These links remain strong today.

Figure 1.1 shows the moral imperatives of sustainable development. (Those familiar with the so-called three-pillar model of sustainable development would probably miss the 'economic corner'. We will present the three-pillar model and the 'missing economic corner' in our model shortly.) This figure represents the first step in our normative model that we present fully in chapter 5. We will, however, make two comments at this stage. First, the moral imperatives form a triangular space, which we call the sustainable development space (Holden *et al.*, 2016). Simply speaking, being inside the triangle means that you are sustainable, whereas being outside it means you are unsustainable. Second, the moral imperatives

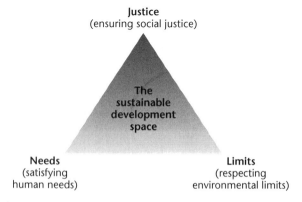

FIGURE 1.1 The moral imperatives of sustainable development and the sustainable development space (modified from Holden *et al.*, 2016).

constitute constraints, specified in our model by thresholds, on development in general and on human behaviour in particular. There are levels of human needs below which we should not go. There are levels of justice below which we should not go; or to phrase it differently: there are levels of injustice that we cannot tolerate. There are environmental limits that we should not cross.

The idea of thinking of a sustainable development space is not new though. More than four decades ago, the so-called Cocoyoc Declaration argued that the task ahead was to guide nations towards a system more capable of 'meeting the "inner limits" of basic human needs for all the world's people and of doing so without violating the "outer limits" of the planet's resources and environment'.[7] Joachim Spangenberg (2002) uses the notion of environmental space[8] to construct a prism of sustainability. The prism forms a space made up of the four dimensions of sustainability in each corner (he adds an institutional dimension to the three dimensions suggested by the three-pillar model). The prism illustrates the interlinkages between the dimensions and, moreover, constitutes a space that defines sustainable development. More recently, Kate Raworth (2012) has picked up the space idea. Between the Cocoyoc Declaration's outer and inner limits, she portrays a 'doughnut' that constitutes an environmentally safe and socially just space in which humanity can thrive. It is fair to say that the idea of a sustainable development space resonates with the main message of *Our Common Future*, whereas it seems to be completely missing in the UN sustainable development goals (UN SDGs).

Argument #5: The moral imperatives of sustainable development constitute a sustainable development space that establishes constraints on human behaviour.

To what extent is there a hierarchy of the moral imperatives and what are we to do if conflicts arise between them? (Our moral imperatives are often, we think wrongfully, referred to as sustainable development's 'main dimensions' in the literature; we will return to our critique shortly.) As several authors do, the Norwegian philosopher Arne Næss interprets the concept of sustainable development in the following way: 'development is not sustainable if it is not ecologically sustainable' (Næss, 1991, p. 37). This interpretation of the concept sustainable development, which also was dominant in the *World Conservation Strategy* (IUCN, 1980), places great emphasis on long-term ecological sustainability, and is often referred to as 'narrow sustainability'. *Our Common Future* identifies a much broader spectrum of issues to be covered by sustainable development, including moral, ethical, aesthetical, political, social, economic, and cultural issues. Thus, sustainability includes more than environmental sustainability, and this interpretation is often called 'broad sustainability'.

As Lafferty and Langhelle (1999) point out, neither of the above interpretations says anything about how possible conflicts between the issues (and the goals assigned to them) should be resolved. Consequently, there is no hierarchy among the issues. In fact, they argue that this is exactly the intention of *Our Common Future*:

> Development is only sustainable when it takes into consideration *both* human needs and long-term ecological sustainability. The point then becomes specifically one of *not* establishing a hierarchy of values between the two dimensions, but one of excluding development paths which do not take both into consideration.
>
> (ibid., p. 13, italics in the original)

This argument is in line with our understanding of the concept of sustainable development: the three imperatives, and the thresholds assigned to them, are not negotiable. They are equally important. None can be trespassed. This approach excludes the possibility of trespassing one threshold because of 'overperformance' in another. Hence, there is no hierarchy among the imperatives.

> *Argument #6: There is no hierarchy between the three moral imperatives of sustainable development; they represent equally important constraints, none of which can be trespassed.*

What is *not* sustainable development?

Having discussed what sustainable development is, we now turn to discussing what sustainable development is not. This discussion could be useful because when the key elements of a concept are difficult to pin down, it helps to ask which elements are not part of that concept. That exercise could help to sharpen the key elements of that concept.

Sustainable development is called many things, including 'a process of human activity' (Sandhu *et al.*, 2014), 'a social movement' (Kates *et al.*, 2005), 'a practice' (Sandhu *et al.*, 2014), 'a discourse' (Dryzek, 2013), and 'a narrative' (Redclift, 2005). *Our Common Future* refers to sustainable development as 'a process of change' (WCED, 1987, p. 9). Not so surprisingly, because 'a global agenda for change' was exactly what the General Assembly of the United Nations asked the Commission to formulate in 1983. And so it did. The Commission also proposed strategies, defined agendas, and considered ways and means by which strategies and agendas should be complied with. But above all, the Commission was mandated to set 'aspirational goals for the world community' (ibid., p. ix). Thus, goals come before strategies, agendas, ways, and means. We simply need to know where we are going before setting sail. A passage from *Alice's Adventures in Wonderland* serves as an illustration:

> 'Would you tell me, please, which way I ought to go from here?'
> 'That depends a good deal on where you want to get to', said the Cat.
> 'I don't much care where', said Alice.
> 'Then it doesn't matter which way you go', said the Cat.
> '–so long as I get SOMEWHERE', Alice added as an explanation.
> 'Oh, you're sure to do that', said the Cat, 'if you only walk long enough'.
>
> (*Alice's Adventures in Wonderland*, Chapter 6)

Well, 'somewhere' is probably not what we are looking for. We need a normative definition of sustainable development to guide us. We need some guidance on which pathways we should avoid, because the risks of irreversible destruction of natural capital are too high or because those pathways lead to unacceptable conditions for people living today. What we need is a map which shows where it is safe to operate. From the current state of unsustainable development each country and region needs to go 'somewhere' within this sustainable development space. The distance to be crossed before a country reaches the border of this space may be loosely defined as the sustainability gap.

A review by Scholz *et al.* (2006) shows that many sustainability case studies across industrial sectors suffered from having an 'ill-defined problem'. That is, while the initial state of unsustainability was clear enough, the future state(s) of sustainability was not, and therefore it was not possible to adequately describe the transition from one state to the other. The problems faced by Scholz's study are shared by many organizations focusing on sustainability as an end-state (Sandhu *et al.*, 2014). They simply do not know where to go.

In addition to knowing where to go, we need to know how to get there. We need clear strategies, feasible policies, efficient policy instruments, well-designed institutions and regulations to get from a situation outside the sustainable development space to a situation within it. However, such a transformation is not the prime focus of our book. Such a focus demands a book by itself, and many such books have already been written (which is a bit strange, because many of them pay little regard to where this transformation leads). More importantly, a key message in our book is that different countries and regions face different challenges, thus they will choose different paths towards sustainability. Moreover, different countries and regions have different preferences and values and these are also changing over time; consequently, there is no single development path that suits all once they are on a sustainable development path. Countries and regions should be free to choose their institutions, policies, and regulations as long as these are guided by the moral imperatives of sustainable development and by the sustainable development space derived from them.

> *Argument #7: The moral imperatives of sustainable development constitute a safe operating space within which societies can pursue any pathway to sustainable development.*

Our first argument claims that sustainable development is an ethical statement that consists of three moral imperatives. To define sustainable development further, we now need to specify the key themes in this definition. Where do these themes come from? Important characteristics of ethical statements are long-term and global thinking. Thus, any attempt at specifying sustainability themes from short-sighted political consensus or stakeholders' parochial preferences is invalid. To understand why, let us again turn to human rights. Proclamations of human rights are strong ethical statements as to what should be done. They are applicable *everywhere* and at *every time* in the sense of being universal. It is not up to a group of stakeholders – for example politicians, communities, or firms – to decide whether they like them. True, they can indeed dislike them and they can even reject them. But that does not change what those rights are. Sustainable development is an ethical statement too, from which the derived moral imperatives are applicable everywhere and at every time. It is not up to a group of stakeholders to decide otherwise. That would make any development sustainable as long as people agree and accept the conditions. Again, they can dislike the imperatives of sustainable development or can outright reject them, but they cannot change what they are.

Indeed, a stakeholder approach will always run the danger of focusing on here (close, at best) and now (tomorrow, at best). Focusing on the here and now is sometimes necessary, but will inevitably rely on what is politically and publicly *feasible* and what is *desirable now*. Neither the feasible nor the desirable is sufficient to acknowledge the long-term, global commitment of achieving sustainable development. We agree with Herman Daly that achieving sustainable development requires that we lean on 'fundamental objective values, not subjective individual preferences' (Daly, 2007, p. 47). We also agree that defining sustainable development should not echo 'what people would like to sustain and how to reach agreement on this, constrained by estimates of what is feasible' (Ehrlich *et al.*, 2012, p. 69).

The stakeholder approach is particularly popular in business. Whereas it is crucial that businesses be involved in sustainable development processes, their point of departure will naturally be on how such processes can benefit their organization. Their input to the discussion will reflect their stakes at risk and more often than not will ignore the ethical point of departure. In a landmark paper, Rob Gray (2010) noted that much of business reporting on sustainability has little, if anything, to do with sustainability as defined in the academic literature. In fact, such reporting more often contains a view of how businesses want sustainability to be perceived, rather than how it is being outlined in that literature. In doing so, Gray argues, 'business is in the process of constructing the dominant discourse around sustainability, but in a way which – at best – ignores discourse in both the development literature and the development community, as well as the growing body of scientific consensus' (Gray, 2010, p. 48). This is an alarming observation, especially because it is confirmed by a range of recent literature reviews (Sandhu *et al.*, 2014).

> *Argument #8: Sustainable development themes can come neither from short-term political consensus nor from parochial stakeholder preferences. Rather, they must come from the moral imperatives of sustainable development and from theories fundamental to understanding those imperatives.*

Does sustainable development require economic growth or is the idea of sustainable growth an incongruity? This question has probably stirred the most heated political and academic debates about defining and achieving sustainable development for three decades (and caused heated controversies in many of the environment and development debates that preceded *Our Common Future*). The answers vary from absolutely yes, we need economic growth to combat poverty and safeguard the environment to definitely not, economic growth is exactly what has caused the problems in the first place. One related question is: Can the development and widespread use of new, 'greener' technology decouple the growth in the value of what we produce (for instance, measured as a country's GDP) from the growth in our use of energy and materials? Another related question is: What part of natural capital must be sustained – all, or only part of it?

Our Common Future was explicit in linking economic growth and sustainable development: 'What is needed now is a new era of economic growth – growth that is forceful and at the same time socially and environmentally sustainable' (WCED, 1987, p. xii). Indeed, the authors saw it as a strategic imperative. Moreover, they saw new technology as a mainspring of economic growth. However, they also saw that while this technology offers the potential for solving environmental problems, it also entails high risks in introducing new ones. Thus, they called for reviving growth by changing the quality of growth. Three decades later, *Transforming Our World* also set forth to create conditions for economic growth. It now became a SDG of its own: Goal 8 urges us to 'Promote sustained, inclusive, and sustainable economic growth' [and, full and productive employment and decent work for all]. We think it is fair to say that the authors of *Transforming Our World* also view new technology as a mainspring of economic growth, though they seem less concerned about the potential downsides and risks of such growth. Meanwhile, the academic community fights fierce battles over the role of economic growth and technology in achieving sustainable development.

The popular three-pillar model of sustainability has social, environmental, and economic pillars (often referred to as dimensions). The economic pillar is usually interpreted as an imperative for economic growth, recently illustrated by the UN SDG no. 8 (see above). Moreover, the economic pillar is often given priority in policies (Giddings *et al.*, 2002). We argue (perhaps controversially) that economic growth should *not* be one of the primary dimensions of sustainable development. True, economic growth may contribute to a more sustainable development by improving social welfare, satisfying human needs, and lifting people out of poverty; but economic growth may also reduce social justice by contributing to income and wealth inequality (Piketty, 2014; Atkinson, 2015). True, economic growth may bring about the technological solutions needed to mitigate greenhouse gases and to adapt to climate change (Stern, 2015b); but economic growth may also contribute to a less sustainable development by increasing greenhouse gas emissions and by overexploiting species and resources for human use. Thus, economic growth is neither inherently sustainable nor inherently unsustainable. It may be part of the solution, it may contribute to the problem, or both; it depends on the policies, the laws and regulations, and the institutions in place. Thus, we present a model that interprets sustainable development as a set of constraints to which economic activities, and all other human activities including the deployment of new technology, must adhere. Human activity is already exceeding environmental limits, income and wealth are unevenly distributed, and extreme poverty exists. These facts show that such constraints are needed.

> *Argument #9: Economic growth is not one of sustainable development's moral imperatives.*

Our final comment in this section regards the three-pillar model of sustainable development, which seeks to balance social, environmental, and economic dimensions (sometimes scholars add cultural, institutional, and/or political dimensions to the model[9]). This model has become immensely popular, and probably is the starting point for most theses, reports, and articles discussing sustainable development. It is now the dominant model for defining sustainable development. Varieties of the model include 'the tripartite model', 'the three-legged stool model', 'the 3P model' (people, planet, profit), and 'triple bottom line'.

We believe this model is inappropriate for two reasons. First, because it merely encourages us to do *something* on each dimension (which probably is the reason for its popularity). It does not tell us what to do, but rather opens up for our being creative about what we consider important for each dimension. Indeed, it opens the door for the short-sighted political consensus and parochial stakeholder preferences we have warned about. Thus, it gives no normative guidance. The only imperative is to do something on all three dimensions rather than focusing on a single dimension.

Second, the three-pillar model encourages us to *balance* the three dimensions.[10] Such an approach allows for trade-offs between the dimensions. We will elaborate in chapter 5 on why we think this balancing is wrong (and particularly dangerous in developing sustainability indicators). For now, an important point: According to the three-legged stool model of sustainable development, which we see as no different than the three-pillar model, sustainable development can figuratively be considered as a stool with three legs (an environmental, a social, and an economic leg). Although we disagree with the naming of the legs (which should rather be named after the three moral imperatives), the stool model seems plausible: a stool simply does not work with one leg. However, a stool needs three equally strong (and long) legs to do what it is supposed to do. It does not make sense to increase the length of one leg because one or two of the other legs are too short. Nor does it make sense to make one leg stronger because one or two of the other legs are too weak. Thus, it is not the legs' *total* length or strength that is important (as sometimes suggested by so-called weak sustainability, see chapter 4). Rather, the legs' length and strength are equally important. More importantly, even if the legs are equally long, the stool's height is not negligible. There are sustainability thresholds we cannot cross. Thus, we need a sufficiently high stool.

Related to this thinking is the concern about the UN SDGs. Although we are encouraged by the fact that 'the Heads of State and Government and High Representatives' finally adopted much-needed SDGs, the UN has not been very successful in specifying those goals. Indeed, by attempting to cover all that is good and desirable in society, the SDGs have ended up as vague, weak, or meaningless (see, for example, Hopwood *et al.*, 2005; Stafford-Smith, 2014; ICSU, ISSC, 2015; Stokstad, 2015). Why?

First, the SDGs are still immature. A report by the International Council for Science (ICSU) and the International Social Science Council (ISSC) finds that of the 169 specific targets of the 17 goals, just 29 per cent are well defined and based on the latest scientific evidence, while 54 per cent need more work and 17 per cent are weak or non-essential (ICSU, ISSC, 2015). Second, they do not distinguish between what we regard as principal and secondary goals. No one will likely question the importance of goals like 'strengthen the prevention and treatment of substance abuse, including narcotic drug abuse and harmful use of alcohol' (goal 3.5); or 'ensure that all youth and a substantial proportion of adults, both men and women, achieve literacy and numeracy' (goal 4.6); or 'ensure that all learners acquire the knowledge and skills needed to promote sustainable development' (goal 4.7). Surely, these goals do not have the same importance as goals like 'eradicate extreme poverty for all people everywhere' (goal 1.1), 'end preventable deaths of newborns and children under 5 years of age' (goal 2.1), and 'achieve universal and equitable access to safe and affordable drinking water for all' (goal 6.1). In not prioritizing its goals, the UN risks being satisfied with achieving secondary goals while simultaneously failing to achieve primary goals. Third, having too many goals (in *Transforming Our World*, the UN announced 17 SDGs, 169 targets, and a preliminary set of 303 indicators (Hák *et al.*, 2016)) amounts to having no goals at all, even more so if prioritization is lacking. Fourth, many SDGs are mere tautologies. Does it really help to have a SDG that will promote 'sustainable' agriculture or make cities 'sustainable'? Fifth, the SDGs are a mixture of goals to be achieved and the means to achieve them. Sixth, whereas the development goals (goals 1–6) are concrete and quantifiable, the environmental goals (goals 12–15) are merely unquantified ambitions to 'protect', 'strengthen', and 'promote'. Thus, the targets rely too much on vague, qualitative language rather than on hard, measurable, time-bound, quantitative targets (ICSU, ISSC, 2015). Clearly, the lack of quantifiable ambitions results from not acknowledging environmental limits. Finally, the SDGs include economic growth as a goal. Moreover, the SDGs are based on the three-pillar model that seeks to balance the three dimensions of sustainable development: the economic, social, and environmental. We have mentioned the weaknesses of doing so. We hasten to add that *having* the SDGs is positive. It shows that the world community has again put sustainable development on the global agenda. Although we criticize the SDGs, we very much acknowledge their importance.

Argument #10: The three-pillar model of sustainable development does not provide an adequate basis for defining sustainable development.

The key sustainability themes and the sustainable development space

So sustainable development is an ethical statement from which we have derived three moral imperatives. We need, however, to go further to develop a model of sustainable development and to quantify the sustainable development space. We now need key themes that give substance to the imperatives. We use two criteria for identifying key themes (details in chapter 5). First, the themes must come from theory. There is a rich supply of theories for each of the moral imperatives, from which the themes can be drawn. These theories draw on philosophical texts about needs and justice, and on new scientific insights about environmental limits. Thus, there is an ethical–theoretical rationale for identifying the themes, not a political–feasibility rationale.

Second, we include only themes that the relevant theories regard as the most important ones. Indeed, some of the vagueness that many scholars have attributed to the concept of sustainable development results from wanting it to cover everything that is good and desirable. Thus, themes must be ranked according to their importance. We call the most important ones key themes and the others secondary themes. Key themes are fundamental in achieving sustainable development, secondary themes are not. Secondary themes are not unimportant; rather, they are merely subordinate to key themes. Thus, unless key themes are addressed, whatever else we do proves insufficient. To use Rawls' terminology, all key sustainability themes have 'lexical priority' over all other sustainability themes. This prioritization requires that we satisfy key themes before we satisfy secondary themes (and secondary themes before tertiary themes, etc.). Themes are not addressed until higher ones are either fully met or do not apply. Thus, a lexical ordering makes balancing themes unnecessary; earlier ones have absolute weight, so to speak, relative to later ones, and hold without exception.

Table 1.1 shows key sustainability themes derived from dominant philosophical and scientific theories (see chapters 2–4 for details). The model's final parts suggest headline indicators and assign thresholds. Chapters 5 and 6 give details on indicators and thresholds and figure 5.5 shows the full sustainable development model.

TABLE 1.1 Key sustainability themes for the three moral imperatives. Table is the work of the authors.

Moral imperative	Satisfying human needs	Ensuring social justice	Respecting environmental limits
Key sustainability themes	• Eradicating extreme poverty • Enhancing human capabilities	• Ensuring rich participation • Ensuring fair distribution	• Mitigating climate change • Safeguarding biosphere integrity

Argument #11: The key sustainability themes must come from dominant theories of the moral imperatives.

Figure 1.1 showed that the moral imperatives of sustainable development form a triangle, which loosely defines the sustainable development space. Having identified key themes, suggested headline indicators, and assigned thresholds, we can define that space quantitatively (see chapter 6 for details). Figure 1.2 shows the sustainable development space.

Entering the sustainable development space is definitely not easy. In fact, chapter 6 shows that no country complies with all thresholds. Thus, no countries have yet achieved sustainable development, a discouraging fact making one ask whether entering the sustainable development space has become too tough, even impossible. Why have goals if no one can achieve them? Is the sustainable development space merely a utopian dream? And would too strict thresholds lead to apathy rather that motivating countries not to exceed them? Perhaps a 'slacker' model with less rigid thresholds would do?

We think not. The moral imperatives are crucial parts of the ethical declaration of sustainable development. The key themes derive from influential contributions in philosophy and science. The headline indicators are valid and robust indicators for the key themes. The thresholds are strict but rest on a strong normative foundation and scientific evidence. They are not unreasonable. Taken one by one, we claim, the thresholds make sense.

Having said that, we have acknowledged that democratic societies must conduct reasoned debate about their normative foundations. The moral imperatives embedded in these foundations change over time though, and they change slowly. Thus, key themes can also change over time. Universal human rights were not on the global agenda a hundred years ago. Today they are. Global sustainable development was not on the global agenda 30 years ago. Now it is. We believe that the moral imperatives derived from sustainable development have become manifest, though we acknowledge that the concept has not been around long and that both the imperatives and the key themes assigned to them can change. Also, the headline indicators and thresholds presented in this book must be changed as new evidence arises in, say, ecology and/or as new and better indicators become available.

Yet ultimately, we believe that our model of sustainable development makes sense. It tells us where we should go. Yes, compliance is difficult; the numbers suggest we are nowhere near where we should be. But being tough does not mean that the model is wrong. If we are way off course, we should change course. Who would, for example, suggest changing the declaration of human rights just because we have not yet achieved them and find achieving them difficult?

Argument #12: The sustainable development space makes possible quantifiable measurement of progress in achieving sustainable development.

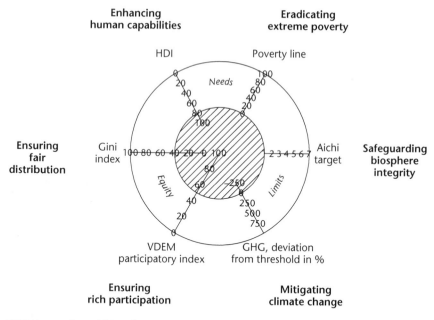

Enhancing
human capabilities

Eradicating
extreme poverty

Ensuring
fair
distribution

Safeguarding
biosphere
integrity

Ensuring
rich participation

Mitigating
climate change

FIGURE 1.2 Quantifying the sustainable development space (hatched area).

Notes: Aichi = biodiversity targets; GHG = greenhouse gas emissions; Gini = measure of inequality; HDI = human development index; VDEM = variety of democracy. See chapter 6 for details. Figure is the work of the authors.

Local sustainability: 'Act locally, think globally'

Any account of sustainable development would be incomplete without some discussion of local sustainability, that is, sustainability at a subnational level. We will discuss local sustainability in detail in chapter 8 but will make a few comments here. *Our Common Future* was well aware of how important it was to include the local level in achieving sustainable development, but did not provide much guidance regarding how to do so. Local Agenda 21 (LA21), chapter 28 in the action plan from the 1992 Rio Summit, aimed at providing such guidance. LA21 cites the special role of local authorities because so many problems in and solutions for achieving sustainable development have their roots in local activities. Therefore, participation and cooperation of local authorities will be determining factors in fulfilling its objectives. For example, local authorities construct, operate, and maintain economic, social, and environmental infrastructure, oversee planning processes, establish local environmental policies and regulations, and assist in implementing national and subnational environmental policies. Thus, as the level of governance closest to the people, they play a vital role in educating, mobilizing, and responding to the public to promote sustainable development.

Therefore, when local authorities work on local sustainability they must always remember the global perspective, thus the slogan 'act locally, think globally'.

Thinking globally about sustainability when acting locally prevents dangerous parochialism (Sen, 2009). Sen thinks we must avoid parochialism because we should identify with others elsewhere in the world and not just with our local community. Many people are truly concerned about acute poverty and loss of biodiversity in distant locations. Showing these concerns by thinking globally is vital to address global sustainability challenges. Moreover, we must avoid parochialism because our (local) actions may affect the lives of others both near *and* far. Although greenhouse gas emissions from private cars do not necessarily pose a threat to the local environment, the accumulated emissions from many cars can seriously threaten people affected by climate change elsewhere in the world. Finally, we must avoid parochialism because it prevents us from being locked-up in under-scrutinized acceptance of strongly manifest values, customs, habits, and presumptions in the local community. Allowing for perspectives from outside the local community can reduce the influence of vested interests that can severely hinder necessary changes needed for achieving global sustainability.

Chapter 8 attempts to translate to local sustainability the normative model of global sustainable development presented in chapter 5. This attempt is not restricted to normative guidance for local authorities, but opens up for guidance at levels other than the global and national levels. Thus, local sustainability means translating the global model to regions, municipalities, cities, communities, societal sectors, firms, programmes, products, projects, and individuals. Specifically, we attempt to develop a normative definition of local sustainability.

We soon realized that this would be an impossible task. Whereas the global model could make sense for municipalities or cities, it is meaningless for firms, products, and projects. Thus, the normative definition of global (and national) sustainable development and the concept of the sustainable development space are not necessarily viable at the local level. Why not abandon the idea of local sustainability altogether? Why not refer to local environmental policy when referring to local environmental problems? Why make it more complicated by calling it local sustainability? Surely, local environmental policy and local sustainability mean the same thing, do they not? We think that it would be a mistake to think they do. Sustainable development bears with it an idea of long-term commitment in time (to future generations) and space (to unprivileged people elsewhere in the world) that we must not take lightly. The term 'sustainability' reminds us so, and it would be a mistake if that reminder were to become lost in local policies and local actions. We must think globally. Thus, we must do better than abandoning the term 'local sustainability'. Our answer is 'comparative sustainability'.

Comparative sustainability builds on Sen's comparative approach to justice (Sen, 2009), which means *advancing* justice rather than *achieving* justice. Correspondingly, comparative sustainability means advancing sustainable development rather than achieving 'perfect' sustainability. (In chapter 8 we contrast comparative sustainability to comprehensive sustainability. The latter means 'perfect' in the sense that we have entered the sustainable development space.) The goal of comparative sustainability would thus be to remove unsustainability whenever we see it rather than waiting for the perfect solution. We go as far as we reasonably can, taking into account the conditions under which local actors actually live and the possibilities they have. The case for allowing for comparative sustainability at the local level, we argue, rests on relevance and availability. In some local cases, all three imperatives of sustainable development, and the respective key themes, are simply not relevant. In some local cases, 'perfect' sustainability is simply not achievable. One must make the best possible choice given available alternatives. Thus, local actors can contribute to the agenda of global sustainability without needing to make an overall assessment of their contribution to that agenda (Sandhu *et al.*, 2014).

> *Argument #13: An assessment of local sustainability makes possible a comparative approach to sustainability.*

Some remarks about the comparative sustainability approach now seem necessary. On the one hand, this approach increases the probability that we actually achieve something rather than just contemplating about the perfect, ideally sustainable world. On the other hand, it would be wrong to see *any* action regarded as relevant as one leading to sustainable development. Accepting that comparative sustainability can sometimes be argued for does not mean that we should lose sight of the overall goal of 'perfect' sustainability. Indeed, sustainability is certainly more than a *carte blanche* for anything that seems like a good idea.

In this chapter we presented arguments that constitute the foundations for our normative sustainable development model. (Chapter 5 presents the model in detail.) Important arguments are that the point of departure for any definition of sustainable development must be an ethical statement (argument 1), that sustainable development consists of three moral imperatives (argument 4), and that key sustainability themes must come from theories that are fundamental to understanding those imperatives (argument 8). The next three chapters present such theories. We start, in chapter 2, with what we believe are the most fundamental theories on satisfying human needs.

Notes

1 Immanuel Kant (2002 [1788]) *Critique of Practical Reason*. Indianapolis/Cambridge, MA, Hackett Publishing Company, Inc., p. 203. Italics in original.
2 It should be noted though that Clausen was a staunch believer in the free market and the imperative of economic growth, and devoted much of his lecture to saying so. After being appointed by Ronald Reagan, Clausen embarked immediately on a major restructuring of the World Bank by purging the institution of employees who had been sympathetic to a social agenda and replacing them with loyal believers in the free market (Borowy, 2014).

3 Jim MacNeill, Secretary of the World Commission on Environment and Development, and chief architect and lead author of *Our Common Future*. Quote from Borowy (2014, p. xi).

4 https://sustainabledevelopment.un.org/, accessed 12 November 2016.

5 *Oxford Dictionary* defines 'ethics' as 'a set of moral principles, especially ones relating to or affirming a specified group, field, or form of conduct' and 'moral' as being 'concerned with the principles of right and wrong behaviour' (https://en.oxforddictionaries.com/, accessed 20 November 2016). One way to see this is that ethics is about 'good or evil' (sustainable development is good and unsustainable development is evil), whereas morality deals with what is 'right or wrong' (eradicating poverty is right, accepting poverty is wrong). We see sustainable development as an ethical statement consisting of several moral principles, or moral imperatives.

6 *Our Common Future* gives no further grounds for this argument. Lafferty and Langhelle (1999) suggest that a possible explanation may be that if the equity considerations oblige us to take further generations into account, it will be inconsistent if equity considerations are not to be found equally binding within our own generation. Indeed, the distribution of costs and benefits within our own generation influences the living conditions of future generations. Viewed as such, there is a 'logical' connection between equity within and between generations.

7 The declaration was the outcome of a symposium organized in 1975 by United Nations Environment Programme (UNEP) and United Nations Conference on Trade and Development (UNCTAD) in Cocoyoc, Mexico under the leadership of Barbara Ward. The declaration was arguably the most radical and moving document of the time (Borowy, 2014, pp. 37–38).

8 The notion of environmental space was coined by Hans Opschoor in the early 1990s (Opschoor and Reinders, 1991), referring to a limitation of various resources available for human consumption. It aimed at calculating the reductions in resource use necessary to guarantee long-term availability of sufficient reserves in order to avoid that resource scarcity might develop into a serious obstacle for economic development in the next century (Spangenberg, 2002).

9 See for example Keitsch *et al.* (2016) for cultural dimension, Spangenberg (2002) for the institutional dimension, and Lafferty and Langhelle (1999) for the political dimension.

10 See for example Cutter *et al.* (n.d.).

References

Agyeman, J. (2013) *Introducing Just Sustainabilities: Policy, Planning, and Practice*. London, Zed Books.

Alkire, S. (2010) *Human Development: Definitions, Critiques, and Related Concepts*. Background paper for the 2010 Human Development Report, OPHI working paper no. 36. Oxford Poverty & Human Development Initiative (OPHI).

Atkinson, A. B. (2015) *Inequality*. Cambridge, MA and London, Harvard University Press.

Biermann, F. (2012) Planetary boundaries and earth system governance. *Ecological Economics*, 81, 4–9.

Borowy, I. (2014) *Defining Sustainable Development for Our Common Future. A History of the World Commission on Environment and Development (Brundtland Commission)*. London and New York, Routledge.

Brown Weiss, E. (1992) Intergenerational equity: A legal framework for global environmental change. In: Brown Weiss, E. (ed.) *Environmental Change and International Law: New Challenges and Dimensions.* Chapter 12. Tokyo, United Nations University Press.

Caradonna, J. L. (2014) *Sustainability: A History.* Oxford, Oxford University Press.

Clausen, A. W. (1982) Sustainable development: The global imperative. *The Environmentalist,* 2, 23–28.

Cutter, A., Osborn, D., Romano, J., Ullah, F. – Stakeholder Forum (n.d.) 'Sustainable development goals and integration: Achieving a better balance between the economic, social and environmental dimensions', a study commissioned by the German Council for Sustainable Development, www.stakeholderforum.org/fileadmin/files/Balancing%20 the%20dimensions%20in%20the%20SDGs%20FINAL.pdf [accessed 12 November 2016].

Daly, H. (2007) *Ecological Economics and Sustainable Development.* Selected Essays of Herman Daly. Cheltenham, UK and Northampton, MA, Edward Elgar.

Dresner, S. (2002) *The Principles of Sustainability.* London, Earthscan.

Dryzek, J. (2013) *The Politics of the Earth: Environmental Discourses.* 3rd edition. Oxford, Oxford University Press.

Eastin, J., Grundmann, R., & Prakash, A. (2011) The two limits debates: 'Limits to growth' and climate change. *Futures,* 43, 16–26.

Ehrlich, P. R., Karevia, P. M., & Daily, G. C. (2012) Securing natural capital and expanding equity to rescale civilization. *Nature,* 486, 68–73.

Giddings, B., Hopwood, B., & O'Brien, G. (2002) Environment, economy and society: Fitting them together into sustainable development. *Sustainable Development,* 10(4), 187–196.

Gray, R. (2010) Is accounting for sustainability actually accounting for sustainability … and how would we know? An exploration of narratives of organisations and the planet. *Accounting, Organizations and Society,* 35, 47–62.

Hák, T., Janouskova, S., & Moldan, B. (2016) Sustainable Development Goals: A need for relevant indicators. *Ecological Indicators,* 60, 565–573.

Hardoon, D., Fuentes-Nieva, R., & Ayele, S. (2016) *An economy for the 1%: How privilege and power in the economy drive extreme inequality and how this can be stopped.* Oxfam. Available from: http://oxf.am/ZniS [accessed 10 November 2016].

Hobbes, T. (1998 [1651]) *Leviathan.* Oxford World's Classic. Oxford, Oxford University Press.

Holden, E., Linnerud, K., & Banister, D. (2016) The imperatives of sustainable development. *Sustainable Development,* DOI: 10.1002/sd.1647.

Hopwood, B., Mellor, M., & O'Brien, G. (2005) Sustainable development: Mapping different approaches. *Sustainable Development,* 13, 38–52.

ICSU, ISSC (2015) *Review of the Sustainable Development Goals: The Science Perspective.* Paris, International Council for Science (ICSU). ISBN: 978-0-930357-97-9.

IUCN (1980) *World Conservation Strategy: Living Resources Conservation for Sustainable development.* Gland, Switzerland, International Union for Conservation of Nature and Natural Resources.

Kates, R. W., Parris, T. M., & Leiserowitz, A. A. (2005) What is sustainable development? Goals, indicators, values, and practice. *Environment: Science and Policy for Sustainable Development,* 47(3), 8–21.

Keitsch, M. M., Kua, H. W., & Skjerven, A. (2016) Special Issue: The Cultural Dimension of Sustainability and Resilience. *Sustainable Development,* 24(5), 273–343.

Lafferty, W. M. & Langhelle, O. (eds) (1999) *Towards Sustainable Development: On the Goals of Development and the Conditions of Sustainability.* Basingstoke, UK, Palgrave Macmillan.

Meadowcroft, J. (2013) Reaching the limits? Developed country engagement with sustainable development in a challenging conjuncture. *Environment and Planning C,* 31(6), 988–1002.

Meadowcroft, J., Langhelle, O., & Ruud, A. (eds) (2012) *Governance, Democracy and Sustainable Development: Moving Beyond the Impasse.* Cheltenham, UK, Edward Elgar.

Morseletto, P., Biermann, F., & Pattberg, P. (2016) Governing by targets: Reductio ad unum and evolution of the two-degree climate target. *International Environmental Agreements,* DOI: 10.1007/s10784-016-9336-7.

Næss, A. (1991) Den dypøkologisk bevegelse: Aktivisme ut fra et helhelssyn (The deep ecology movement: Activism from a holistic view). In: Gjerdåker, S., Gule, L., & Hagtvet, B. (eds) *Den uoverstigelige grense. Tanke og handling i miljøkampen.* Bergen and Oslo, Chr. Michelsens Institutt/JW Cappelens forlag, pp. 21–43.

Opschoor, H. & Reinders, L. (1991) Towards sustainable development indicators. In: Kuik, O. & Verbruggen, H. (eds) *In Search of Indicators of Sustainable Development.* Dordrecht, Kluwer Academic Publishers, pp. 7–27.

O'Riordan, T. (1988) The politics of sustainability. In: Turner, K. (ed.) *Sustainable Environmental Management: Principles and Practice.* London, Belhaven, pp. 29–50.

Parsons, T. (1968 [1937]) *The Structure of Social Action.* 2 vols. New York, Free Press.

Pereira, R. H. M., Schwanen, T., & Banister, D. (2017) Distributive justice and equity in transportation. *Transport Reviews,* 37(2), 170–191.

Piketty, T. (2014) *Capital in the Twenty-First Century.* Cambridge, MA and London, Belknap Press.

Rawls, J. (1999) *A Theory of Justice* (revised edition). Cambridge, MA and London, Belknap Press.

Raworth, K. (2012) A safe and just space for humanity: Can we live within the doughnut. *Oxfam Policy and Practice: Climate Change and Resilience,* 8(1), 1–26.

Redclift, M. (2005) Sustainable development (1987–2005): An oxymoron comes of age. *Sustainable Development,* 13, 212–227.

Sandhu, S., McKenzie, S., & Harris, H. (eds) (2014) *Linking Local and Global Sustainability.* Dordrecht/Heidelberg/New York/London, Springer.

Scholz, R. W., Lang, D. J., Wiek, A., Walter, A. I., & Stauffacher, M. (2006) Transdisciplinary case studies as a means of sustainability learning: Historical framework and theory. *International Journal of Sustainability in Higher Education,* 7(3), 226–251.

Sen, A. (2009) *The Idea of Justice.* London, Penguin.

Shaker, R. R. (2015) The spatial distribution of development in Europe and its underlying sustainability correlations. *Applied Geography,* 63, 304–314.

Spangenberg, J. H. (2002) Environmental space and the prism of sustainability: Frameworks for indicators measuring sustainable development. *Ecological Indicators,* 2, 295–309.

Stafford-Smith, M. (2014) UN sustainability goals need quantified targets. *Nature,* 513(7518), 281.

Steffen, W., Richardson, K., Rockström, J., Cornell, S. E., Fetzer, I., Bennett, E. M., Biggs, R., Carpenter, S. R., de Vries, W., de Wit, C. A., Folke, C., Gerten, D., Heinke, J., Mace, G. M., Persson, L. M., Ramanathan, V., Reyers, B., & Sörlin, S. (2015) Planetary boundaries: Guiding human development on a changing planet. *Science,* 347, 736–746.

Stern, N. (2015a) Why are we waiting? The logic, urgency, and promise of tackling climate change. Lecture hosted by the Oxford Martin School and the Environmental Change Institute, University of Oxford, Oxford, 19 October 2015.

Stern, N. (2015b) *Why Are We Waiting? The Logic, Urgency, and Promise of Tackling Climate Change.* Cambridge, MA and London, MIT Press.

Stiglitz, J. (2013) *The Price of Inequality.* London, Penguin.

Stokstad, E. (2015) Sustainable goals from UN under fire. *Science,* 347(6223), 702–703.

UN (2015) *Transforming Our World: The 2030 Agenda for Sustainable Development.* Resolution adopted by the General Assembly on 25 September 2015, A/RES/70/1. United Nations General Assembly.

UNDP (2015) *Work for Human Development.* Human Development Report 2015. New York, United Nations Development Programme.

WCED (1987) *Our Common Future.* World Commission on Environment and Development. Oxford, Oxford University Press.

Wilkinson, R. & Pickett, K. (2009) *The Spirit Level: Why Equality is Better for Everyone.* London, Penguin.

Wolff, J. (2006) *An Introduction to Political Philosophy* (revised edition). Oxford, Oxford University Press.

2
SATISFYING HUMAN NEEDS

For the world says: 'You have desires and so satisfy them, for you have the same rights as the most rich and powerful. Don't be afraid of satisfying them and even multiply your desires'. That is the modern doctrine of the world. … And what follows from this right of multiplication of desires? In the rich, isolation and spiritual suicide; in the poor, envy and murder …

Fyodor Dostoyevsky, *The Brothers Karamazov* (1880)[1]

In heroically defending the monks' spiritual world against the worldly, material world, Dostoyevsky pointed in *The Brothers Karamazov* to a number of issues concerning the satisfaction of human needs. First, we do not only have needs, we have desires too. Desires that should be satisfied. Indeed, the rich and powerful satisfy their desires, so why should everyone not follow suit? That is what the world tells us. Second, we should never be satisfied with the desires we have, but rather should multiply our desires. And we should by no means be ashamed of doing so. Dostoyevsky, however, bleakly reminds us that there is a price to pay for those who interpret freedom as the multiplication and rapid satisfaction of desires:[2]

Men distort their own nature, for many senseless and foolish desires and habits and ridiculous fancies are fostered in them. They live only for mutual envy, for luxury and ostentation. To have dinner visits, carriages, rank, and slaves to wait on one is looked upon as a necessity, for which life, honour and human feeling are sacrificed, and men even commit suicide if they are unable to satisfy it. We see the same thing among those who are not rich, while the poor drown their unsatisfied need and their envy in drunkenness. But soon they will drink blood instead of wine, they are being led on to it. I ask you is such a man free?

(Dostoyevsky, 1880, p. 646)

The worldly doctrine Dostoyevsky portrayed more than a hundred years ago still seems to apply. We still, as the American rock band the Eagles put it, 'satisfy our endless needs and justify our bloody deeds, in the name of destiny and in the name of God'. Surely Dostoyevsky's monks and the Eagles disagree on God's role here, but the bleak picture they portray is similar.

Or is it? According to the latest *Human Development Report*, the world has made substantial progress in human development between 1990 and 2015 (UNDP, 2015). Alas, progress has been uneven among regions, across countries and within countries. There are still millions of poor people fighting every day to satisfy their most essential needs. This violates the moral imperative of satisfying human needs.

This chapter presents some important positions that constitute the theoretical foundation for the imperative of human needs. But let us first review what *Our Common Future* says about satisfying human needs.

Our Common Future on satisfying human needs

Our Common Future did not use Dostoyevsky's harsh wording. In a more benign wording, however, its message was essentially the same: 'Living standards that go beyond the basic minimum are sustainable only if consumption standards everywhere have regard for long-term sustainability. Yet many of us live beyond the world's ecological means, for instance in our patterns of energy use' (WCED, 1987, p. 44). *Our Common Future* maybe did not agree with Dostoyevsky's assumption that the satisfaction of endless desires would end up in 'nothing but slavery and self-destruction', but nevertheless cautiously warned against living beyond our means.

The concept of 'needs' is central in *Our Common Future*. Particularly important is the imperative of meeting the essential needs of the world's poor 'to which overriding priority should be given' (ibid., p. 43). Thus, the report urged all nations to focus their efforts on eliminating poverty and satisfying essential human needs. Indeed, the report claimed that poverty is not only an evil in itself, but claimed that a world in which poverty is endemic will always be prone to ecological and other catastrophes.

Our Common Future saw, however, the importance of looking beyond the essential needs. Not only does sustainable development require meeting the basic needs of all; sustainable development also requires 'extending to all the opportunity to satisfy their aspirations for a better life' (ibid., p. 44) and that 'beyond their basic needs these people [poor people] have legitimate aspirations for an improved quality of life' (ibid., p. 43). Thus it is clear that *Our Common Future* presented a contingent conception of human needs. On the one hand, there is a minimum level of basic needs that must be met. On the other hand, there seems to be a maximum level beyond which people's aspirations for satisfying additional needs must be constrained. Between the minimum and maximum levels we find sustainable development's level playing field – or what we call the sustainable development space (Holden *et al.*, 2014, 2016).

Theories on basic needs

So what do the theories tells us about the understanding of basic needs? (We return to aspirations later in this chapter.) Now we briefly present three important theoretical contributions to that understanding: Max-Neef's theory of human-scale development, Maslow's hierarchy of needs, and Doyal and Gough's theory of human needs.

Max-Neef and human-scale development

Based on his gloomy first-hand experiences in the 1980s, the Chilean economist Manfred Max-Neef described 'the Latin American situation' as one of crisis and perplexity. Because of the complexity of the symptoms, there was no consensus regarding the proper treatment of the situation. The lack of consensus had led to perplexity that kept Latin America in a 'deadend alley and barred the road to imaginative, novel and bold solutions' (Max-Neef, 1991, p. 1). Max-Neef claimed that intuition suggests that the application of conventional policies will not work. Rather there was a need for radically different approaches that could eventually emancipate Latin America from this state of crisis and perplexity.

His radically different approach was a new praxis that he called human-scale development.[3] Human-scale development aspires to meet human needs and requires a new way to understand the reality of people's lives. The basic postulate of human-scale development is that development is about people and not about objects. Max-Neef argued that accepting this postulate – whether on intuitive, ethical, or rational grounds – leads to the following fundamental questions: How can we determine whether one development process is better than another? What are those fundamental human needs, and/or who decides what they are? To answer these questions, Max-Neef developed a theory of human-scale development.

An important part of the theory is to distinguish between needs and satisfiers. Satisfiers are not the available economic goods. They are related instead to everything which contributes to the satisfaction of human needs. Satisfiers may include, among other things, 'forms of organization, political structures, social practices, subjective conditions, values and norms, spaces, contexts, modes, types of behaviour and attitudes' (ibid., p. 24). There is no one-to-one correspondence between needs and satisfiers; a satisfier may contribute simultaneously to the satisfaction of various needs or, a need may require various satisfiers in order to be met. And these relations may, Max-Neef reminds us, vary according to time, place, and circumstance.

Having established the difference between the concepts of needs and satisfiers, Max-Neef states two additional postulates. First: fundamental human needs are finite, few and classifiable. Second: fundamental human needs are the same in all cultures and in all historical periods. What changes, both over time and through cultures, is the way or the means by which the needs are satisfied (that is, the satisfiers).

Each economic, social, and political system, Max-Neef argues, adopts different methods for satisfying the same fundamental human needs. In every system they are satisfied (or not satisfied) through the generation (or non-generation) of different types of satisfiers. He goes as far as to say that one of the aspects that define a culture is its choice of satisfiers. Whether a person belongs to a consumerist or to an ascetic society, however, his/her fundamental human needs are the same. What changes is his/her choice of the quantity and quality of satisfiers. In short, the satisfiers for those needs are culturally determined, not the fundamental human needs. Cultural change is, among other things, the consequence of dropping traditional satisfiers for the purpose of adopting new or different ones.

Max-Neef goes on to propose a taxonomy which establishes what he believes is a precise difference between needs and satisfiers and, moreover, the relationship between them. He organizes human needs into two categories.[4] On the one hand, there are existential human needs, including the needs of 'being', 'having', 'doing', and 'interacting'. On the other hand, there are axiological[5] human needs, including the needs of 'subsistence', 'protection', 'affection', 'understanding', 'participation', 'idleness',[6] 'creation', 'identity', and 'freedom'. Satisfiers can be found within the grid of a matrix where existential and axiological human needs form the rows and columns, respectively. Furthermore, each cell (i.e., combination of existential and axiological human needs) is open for one or more satisfiers. Max-Neef goes on to categorize satisfiers that can meet these combinations of needs. We will not go into detail about his system of satisfiers (it is indeed complicated). The important thing to remember here is that whereas needs are fundamental and universal, the satisfiers are not. There are indeed many ways to satisfy a given need.

Max-Neef makes an important case about poverty. He argues that his human-scale development allows for a reinterpretation of the concept of poverty. The traditional concept of poverty is limited and restricted, he argues, since it 'refers exclusively to the predicaments of people who may be classified below a certain income threshold' (ibid., p. 18). This concept is strictly economistic. Rather, Max-Neef suggests that we should not speak of poverty but of poverties. In fact, any fundamental human need that is not adequately satisfied reveals a human poverty. He gives some examples of different poverties: poverty of subsistence (due to insufficient income, food, shelter, etc.); poverty of protection (due to bad health systems, violence, arms race, etc.); poverty of affection (due to authoritarianism, oppression, exploitative relations with the natural environment, etc.); poverty of understanding (due to poor quality of education); poverty of participation (due to marginalization and discrimination of women, children, and minorities); and poverty of identity (due to imposition of alien values upon local and regional cultures, forced migration, political exile, etc.). Thus, any person could experience multidimensional poverty (Alkire & Santos, 2010).

Maslow's hierarchy of needs: Needs as drivers

Doyal and Gough (1991) argue that there are two approaches to needs. On the one hand, and this probably is the more common approach, one can refer to needs as drivers to which we must conform. On the other hand, one can refer to needs as goals that we try to achieve. When referring to needs as drivers, one envisages needs as a motivational force caused by a state of disequilibrium or tension existing in an organism because of a particular lack (Thompson, 1987). This way to refer to needs has, according to Doyal and Gough, inspired perhaps the most famous analysis of basic needs, that of the American psychologist Abraham Harold Maslow (1943).

Maslow argues that there are at least five sets of basic needs. First, there are the physiological needs, which are referred to as physiological drivers within motivation theory. Maslow argues that it seems impossible as well as useless to make any list of fundamental physiological needs for they can come to almost any number one might wish, depending on the degree of specificity of description (though he mentions food). Undoubtedly, Maslow claims, these physiological needs are the most dominant of all needs. What this means specifically is, that

> if all the needs are unsatisfied, and the organism is then dominated by the physiological needs, all other needs may become simply non-existent or be pushed into the background. It is then fair to characterize the whole organism by saying simply that it is hungry, for consciousness is almost completely pre-empted by hunger. All capacities are put into the service of hunger-satisfaction, and the organization of these capacities is almost entirely determined by the one purpose of satisfying hunger.
>
> (ibid., p. 373)

Maslow makes another important claim. When a certain need dominates the human organism, the whole philosophy of the future tends also to change. For a chronically and extremely hungry man, Utopia is simply a place where there is plenty of food. He tends to think that, if only he is guaranteed food for the rest of his life, he will be perfectly happy and will never want anything more. Life itself tends to be defined in terms of eating. Anything else is unimportant. Freedom, love, community feeling, respect, morality, may all be waved aside as fripperies which are useless since they fail to fill the stomach. The German poet and playwright Bertolt Brecht summarizes this point nicely: 'Erst kommt das Fressen dann die Moral' (first food, then morals).[7]

But what happens, Maslow asks, to a man's desires when there is plenty of bread and when his belly is always full? His answer is that immediately other (and 'higher') needs emerge and these, rather than physiological needs, dominate the organism. And when these in turn are satisfied, again new (and still 'higher') needs emerge and so on. This is what Maslow means by saying that the basic human needs are organized into 'a hierarchy of relative prepotency' (ibid., p. 375).

Thus, second, there are safety needs. Infants and children, Maslow argues, would feel their safety being threatened by being disturbed or dropped suddenly, by experiencing loud noises or flashing light, by lacking daily routines and rhythms, by being exposed to rough handling, by having general loss of support in their mother's arms, or by being given inadequate support during illness. More generally, people would feel their safety being threatened in states of emergencies, for example, war, disease, natural catastrophes, crime waves, societal disorganization, neurosis, brain injury, a chronically bad situation.

Third, there are love needs.[8] If both the physiological and the safety needs are fairly well gratified, Maslow argues, there will emerge the love and affection and belongingness needs. Now the person will feel keenly, as never before, the absence of friends, or a sweetheart, or a wife, or children. He will hunger for affectionate relations with people in general, namely, for a place in his group, and he will strive with great intensity to achieve this goal. He will want to attain such a place more than anything else in the world and 'may even forget that once, when he was hungry, he sneered at love' (ibid., p. 381).

Fourth, there are esteem needs. All people in society (with a few pathological exceptions) have a need or desire for a stable, firmly based, high evaluation of themselves, for self-respect, or self-esteem, and for the esteem of others. Maslow classifies these needs into two subsidiary sets. These are, first, 'the desire for strength, for achievement, for adequacy, for confidence in the face of the world, and for independence and freedom' (ibid., p. 381). Second, we have what we may call the desire for reputation or prestige (defined as respect or esteem from other people), recognition, attention, importance, or appreciation. Maslow stresses the central importance of the esteem needs. Satisfaction of the self-esteem need leads to feelings of self-confidence, worth, strength, capability, and adequacy of being useful and necessary in the world. But the thwarting of these needs produces feelings of inferiority, of weakness, and of helplessness. These feelings in turn give rise either to basic discouragement or else to compensatory or neurotic trends.

Fifth, there is a need for self-actualization. Even if all four needs mentioned above are satisfied, Maslow argues that we still often (if not always) expect that a new discontent and restlessness will soon develop, unless the individual is doing what he is fitted for. 'A musician must make music, an artist must paint, a poet must write, if he is to be ultimately happy. What a man *can* be, he *must* be' (ibid., p. 382, italics in original). This need he called self-actualization.[9] Maslow refers to self-actualization as the desire for self-fulfilment, namely, as the tendency for a person to become actualized in what he is potentially. This tendency, Maslow suggests, might be phrased as 'the desire to become more and more what one is, to become everything that one is capable of becoming' (ibid., p. 382).

Maslow acknowledges that the ways these needs will be satisfied vary greatly from person to person. Max-Neef, and, as we will see shortly, Doyal and Gough, agree. In one individual it may take the form of 'the desire to be an ideal mother, in another it may be expressed athletically, and in still another it may be expressed in painting pictures or in inventions' (ibid., p. 383). The emergence of the needs of self-actualization rests upon prior satisfaction of the physiological, safety, love, and esteem needs. Maslow calls people who are satisfied in all needs 'basically satisfied people'.

Maslow stresses that there are certain conditions that are immediate prerequisites for the basic-needs satisfactions. Danger to these conditions is reacted to '*almost* as if it were a direct danger to the basic needs themselves' (ibid., p. 383, italics in original). Examples of such preconditions for basic-needs satisfactions are 'freedom to speak, freedom to do what one wishes so long as no harm is done to others (Mill's Liberty Principle), freedom to express one's self, freedom to investigate and seek for information, freedom to defend one's self, justice, fairness, honesty, orderliness in the group' (ibid., p. 383). (Doyal and Gough referred to these as 'societal preconditions'.) These conditions, Maslow argued, are not ends in themselves but they are almost so since they are so closely related to the basic needs. He defended these conditions because without them 'the basic satisfactions are quite impossible, or at least, very severely endangered' (ibid., p. 383).

Doyal and Gough: Needs as universal and objective goals

In *A Theory of Human Needs*, Doyal and Gough (1991) use many of the same concepts as Max-Neef does. Moreover, they share Max-Neef's concern about increasing poverty and inequalities and their conclusions are similar to Max-Neef's. In their book, Doyal and Gough argue that human beings have universal and objective needs and a right to their optimal satisfaction. They develop a system of social indicators to show what such optimization would mean in practice. While the individual's basic needs are universal, they acknowledge that the goods and services required to satisfy these may depend on culture. Indeed, Max-Neef would agree.

Not everyone shares Doyal, Gough, and Max-Neef's view though. Doyal and Gough refer to a number of relativistic positions that argue that satisfying universal and objective needs is impossible (ibid., pp. 9–21). For example, the mainstream economist would argue that needs are the result of interests, preferences, choices, and demand. The New Right regards any notion of objective needs as an excuse for the state to increase undemocratically approved taxes and restrictions on political freedom. Critiques of cultural imperialism[10] strongly reject the idea of objective human needs, because people in positions of power can use the idea to legitimate their existence through arguing that they know what is in the best interests of the powerless. Currents within sociology reject the idea that there are objective and universal needs irrespective of culture; rather, needs should focus on the complex negotiations of meaning which constitute everyday life.

Many of the supporters of relativist positions make valid arguments. Surely, any attempt to exercise power through imposing a preferred notion of need on others is immoral. Surely, any attempt to reduce individuals' right to have a say in constructing their own lives is dubious. Still, Doyal and Gough reject the claims made by the relativists' supporters because such positions denounce universal standards for evaluating needs. We agree with Doyal and Gough because if needs are relativistic, sustainable development is relativistic too. Our model presented in chapter 5 suggests otherwise.

Doyal and Gough do not acknowledge Maslow's motivational approach. Rather, they refer to needs as goals which they believe to be universal. Indeed, they argue that 'there are good reasons why we should divorce the discourse of needs as universal goals from that of motivation or drivers altogether' (ibid., p. 36). There are two reasons for this, they argue:

> First, a strict temporal sequencing of the motivations is simply false. Some people seem far more concerned with their self-actualisation than their safety – mountain climbers, for example. Second, and more important, the motivational approach to understanding needs overestimates the extent to which innate biological, emotional, and cognitive 'grammar' can be said to determine what we should and should not attempt.
>
> (ibid., p. 38)

The difference between the two conflicting approaches, that is Maslow's motivational approach and Doyal and Gough's goal-oriented approach, might seem of purely *academic* interest. Indeed, it is not! Suggesting that people are merely conforming to a disequilibrium in their organisms because of a particular lack does not leave much room for sustainability constraints. Acknowledging instead that people can see needs as goals opens up the possibility for people to align their needs to sustainability constraints.

And of course, the conflicting approaches has everything to do with the difference between needs and wants. The British rock band Coldplay's 'Fix You' touches on the complicated relationship between needs and wants: 'When you get what you want but not what you need'. Indeed, you can want all sorts of things, but are these the things you really need? And who is to tell you what you need as opposed to what you want?

Needs and wants are included in our everyday language, though we tend to use the concepts interchangeably in an inaccurate way. Saying 'I really need a day off now' does not necessarily mean that you need a day off in order to survive. Rather you probably want a day off to rest or do something different from work. Similarly, saying that 'I want some water' could well mean that you really *need* some water or you will die of thirst. Doyal and Gough set forth to establish objective and universal human needs. To do so it is imperative to make a distinction between needs and wants. After all, what is the use of 'a theory of human wants'? (And what could such a theory possibly mean?)

Referring to needs as universal goals raises, however, the question of how we can determine whether a goal is universal. Doyal and Gough's answer is that if some needs are not satisfied by an appropriate 'satisfier', *serious harm* of some specified and objective kind will result. Thus, unsatisfied needs result in serious harm, unsatisfied wants do not. This distinction between needs and wants, however, rests on the belief that there is an agreement about what 'serious harm' is. We argue that individuals face normative constraints of the natural environment and of social equity too. The triangle of constraints, that is, social constraints (human needs), equity constraints, and environmental constraints, constitutes the sustainable development space, in which those three types of constraints should not be trespassed. Crossing any of the thresholds will cause serious harm.

Doyal and Gough argue that physical health and autonomy are the basic needs which humans must satisfy in order to avoid serious harm. They also demonstrate that it is possible in principle to compare levels of basic-needs satisfaction in these terms not only within but also between cultures. Physical health, they argue, is more than mere survival. Indeed, to do well in their everyday lives, people have to do much more than survive. They must possess a minimum of good physical health. To complete a range of practical tasks in daily life requires manual, mental, and emotional abilities with which poor physical health usually interferes. In addition to physical health, one must also sustain and improve individual autonomy. Doyal and Gough argue that three key variables affect levels of individual autonomy:

> the level of understanding a person has about herself, her culture and what is expected of her as an individual within it; the psychological capacity she has to formulate options for herself; and the objective opportunities enabling her to act accordingly.
>
> (ibid., p. 60)

Human needs in practice

After pondering the theoretical foundations of human needs, Doyal and Gough go on to elaborate on the practical implications of their theory. They call all objects, activities, and relationships that satisfy our basic needs 'satisfiers'. Basic needs are always universal, but their satisfiers are often relative (a view that falls nicely in line with Max-Neef's postulates). They identify universal satisfiers, that is, goods, services, activities, and relationships that enhance physical health and human autonomy in all cultures.

They argue that universal satisfiers are most important for basic-needs satisfaction, and refer to them as 'intermediate needs'. The intermediate needs, they argue, 'can provide a secure foundation on which to erect a list of derived or second-order goals which must be achieved if the first-order goals of health and autonomy are to be attained' (ibid., p. 157). True, there is a 'family of lists of needs' (Braybrooke, 1987) provided by international organizations like OECD, national governments, and private individuals. The problem with these lists, however, is, according to Doyal and Gough, their ad hoc character. By contrast, Doyal and Gough argue that they can offer a list where their 'theory dictates which intermediate needs are most important for the satisfaction of basic needs, why this is so and why they are the same for all cultures' (Doyal & Gough, 1991, p. 157).

Doyal and Gough group the intermediate needs as follows: nutrition and clean water, protective housing, a non-hazardous work environment, a non-hazardous physical environment, appropriate healthcare, security in childhood, significant primary relationships, physical security, economic security, appropriate education, and safe birth control and childbearing. The only criterion for inclusion in this list is whether any set of intermediate needs universally and positively contributes to physical health and autonomy. The taxonomy of intermediate needs, Doyal and Gough admit, is in one sense arbitrary. There could be more intermediate needs. Moreover, the wording used is ambiguous. Ultimately, however, the number of intermediate needs and the wording used do not matter. Whatever the taxonomy, their theory requires that the sole condition for selection be the universality of the intermediate needs.

Having defined the intermediate needs, Doyal and Gough set forth to find standards for satisfying them. They seek to determine the level of intermediate-needs satisfaction that yields optimum levels of satisfying basic needs.[11] In the spirit of Rawls, they call this level 'the minimum optimorum'. All intermediate needs should be satisfied up to the minimum optimorum level. There are two reasons why the level of intermediate-needs satisfaction sometimes should be limited. First, at some point, an increase in intermediate-needs satisfaction will not further enhance the satisfaction of basic needs (that is, physical health and autonomy). For example, increasing medication, food supplies, or housing size would at some point cease to improve physical health and autonomy. Thus the crucial task is to 'ascertain *the minimum quantity of intermediate needs-satisfaction required to produce the optimum level of basic need-satisfaction* measured in terms of the physical health and autonomy of individuals' (ibid., p. 162, italics in original).

Second, there could be ecological constraints to universal generalizability of some intermediate needs. For some intermediate needs the level at which provision ceases to enhance the satisfaction of basic needs is so high that 'the minimum optimorum position cannot be universally achieved with available resources' (ibid., p. 164). In this case, a constrained optimum is called for, specifying the highest level of the satisfaction of basic needs generalizable over the relevant population. Doyal and Gough enter here the realm of sustainable development when they alert us to 'the global and inter-temporal constraints on optimising the need satisfaction of the present generation' (ibid., p. 242). Their constraint optimum thus echoes our claim that the moral imperatives of satisfying needs, ensuring equity, and respecting environmental limits represent constraints on present generations' activities, including our efforts to satisfy human needs.

Doyal and Gough believe that there exists a 'moral code that the needs of all people should be satisfied to the optimum extent' (ibid., p. 111). The moral code is valid for the needs of the present generations as well as for the needs of future generations. Satisfying them to the optimum extent entails corresponding duties on individuals to act where appropriate to relieve the suffering of others and to support national and international agencies which can efficiently do so. These are moral responsibilities that we all have.

To act in accordance with the moral code and to fulfil our responsibility there are societal preconditions that must be present. Doyal and Gough identify certain procedural and material preconditions for optimizing need-satisfaction and suggest indicators to chart each precondition.[12] These indicators can then be used to compare countries regarding their procedural and material preconditions for optimizing need-satisfaction and to indicate the direction of improvements and human progress (we do such comparisons in chapter 7). Doyal and Gough link the procedural preconditions to having negative freedom ('being left alone') and link the material preconditions to having positive freedom ('getting access to things we need').

Having *civil and political rights* is a procedural precondition for optimal need-satisfaction because they enable people to engage in open and rational debate and thus to improve decision-making about how to optimize need-satisfaction. Moreover, they enhance 'the capacity of individuals to think about, to advocate and to join in attempts to change the normative authority structure of the form of life within which they live' (ibid., p. 227). To facilitate the enhancement of individual autonomy, the social environment must be open to change and advancement. Here, open debate is crucial, with the maximum possible amount of relevant expertise brought to bear on the problem at hand. Thus, they argue, '*democracy* is an irreplaceable prerequisite for optimising human need-satisfaction' (ibid., p. 228, italics in original).

Moreover, there is a set of material preconditions related to the optimal satisfaction of the basic and intermediate needs. These preconditions relate to four material factors which will determine the level of need-satisfaction of individuals. First, the total quantity, the composition, and the quality of need satisfiers produced (that is, are there enough intermediate needs around to satisfy basic needs). Second, the pattern of distribution of these satisfiers (that is, who gets what). Third, the effectiveness with which these satisfiers are transformed into individual need-satisfaction (that is, the technology used). Fourth, the rate of depletion/accumulation of capital goods, the natural resource base, and human resources (that is, resource and accumulation constraints).

Our Common Future, Max-Neef, Maslow, and Doyal and Gough are all trying to make sense of basic human needs. They all, however, hint at needs that go beyond mere survival; they talk about aspirations, opportunities, freedom, and rights – and this takes us to the capability approach.

More than basic needs: The capability approach

According to the American physician, philosopher, and author Debasish Mridha, 'life begins where needs end'. Thus, there is more to life than merely having the basic needs satisfied. The Indian economist, philosopher, and Nobel Laureate Amartya Sen seems to agree. He argues that seeing people's needs only in terms of basic needs gives a 'rather meagre view of humanity' (Sen, 2009, p. 250). Indeed, *Our Common Future* too acknowledged people's 'legitimate aspirations for an improved quality of life' (WCED, 1987, p. 43) and 'aspirations for a better life' (ibid., p. 44). Surely there must be more to satisfying human needs than various forms of basic-needs approaches? A 'richer' view is called for.

A point of departure for a richer view of human needs is the capability approach. The approach has been pioneered by Amartya Sen[13] and has more recently been further developed by the American philosopher Martha Nussbaum and others. In academia, the approach is now part of the standard curriculum in courses on welfare economics, development studies, and political philosophy, and it is regularly taught as part of courses in education, disability studies, public health, and gender studies, among others (Robeyns, 2006).

The capability approach has had large political effect too. Since 1990, the United Nations Development Programme (UNDP) has annually published the *Human Development Report*, which builds on the capability approach. Most of the academic literature on human development, however, is not focused on the UNDP definition of human development directly but rather on the capability approach (Alkire, 2010). Thus the capability approach is the main philosophical foundation for the concept of human development which inevitably includes the concept of human needs. Alkire claims that there are surprisingly few direct conceptual treatments of human development. Though some authors try to distinguish between human development and the capability approach, there is no consensus as to a conceptually clear distinction between human development and the capability approach. Moreover, Alkire claims that it is not obvious that such a distinction is useful or even required. Thus, we will focus on the capability approach here.

According to Alkire, the capability approach has two strands of interpretation in the literature. The narrow strand focuses on human development issues such as income, education, and health. The broad strand includes attention to principles such as freedom, equity, and sustainability. The narrow strand was for a long time separated from the broad strand (Neumayer, 2013). This seemed to change though, and today interpretation of the capability approach tries to reconcile the two literature strands.

We acknowledge the importance of the broad interpretation, which, in fact, is very close to our model of sustainable development. We argue, however, that each moral imperative in our model should be looked at separately to avoid any concealed trade-offs between them. Thus, the moral imperative of satisfying human needs in our model is in line with the narrow interpretation of the capability approach, while the broad interpretation of the capability approach is captured by other aspects of our model.

The capability approach rests on a number of concepts and core ideas. First, the main concepts used in the capability approach are 'functionings' and 'capabilities'. Functionings are 'beings and doings', that is, various states of human beings, and activities that a person can carry out. Examples of the 'beings' are being well-nourished, being undernourished, being housed in a pleasantly warm but not excessively hot house, being educated, being illiterate, being part of a supportive social network, being part of a criminal network, and being depressed. Examples of the 'doings' are travelling, caring for a child, voting in an election, participating in a debate, taking drugs, killing animals, eating animals, consuming lots of fuel in order to heat one's house, and donating money to charity. Capabilities are a person's real freedoms or opportunities to achieve functionings. Thus, while travelling is a functioning, the real opportunity to travel is the corresponding capability. The distinction between functionings and capabilities is between the actual and the potential, in other words, between achievements, on the one hand, and freedoms or valuable opportunities from which one can choose, on the other (Robeyns, 2011).

Second, an important analytical distinction in the capability approach is that which distinguishes between the means and the ends of wellbeing and development. Only the ends have intrinsic importance, whereas means are instrumental to reach the goals of increased wellbeing, justice, and development. According to the capability approach, the ends of wellbeing, justice, and development should be conceptualized in terms of people's capabilities to function, that is, their effective opportunities to act and do as they please, and to be whom they want to be. The approach stresses that we should always be clear, when valuing something, whether we value it as an end in itself, or as a means to a valuable end. The main reason why the capability approach holds that it is better to focus on the ends rather than the means is that people differ in their ability to convert means into valuable opportunities (capabilities) or outcomes (functionings) (Sen, 1992). Of course, the normative focus on ends does not imply that the capability approach does not at all value means such as material or financial resources. Instead, a capability analysis will typically *also* focus on resources and other means.

Third, the capability approach is people-centred. The capability approach focuses on what people are effectively able to do and to be, that is, on their capabilities. Thus, according to Sen (2009), the capability approach contrasts philosophical normative approaches such as the basic-needs approach (which focuses on necessities), utility-based approaches (which focus on mental states such as individual happiness or pleasure), and resource-based approaches (which focus on income, wealth, or resources). Rather, Sen argues that policies should focus on assessing what people are able to do and be and on removing obstacles in their lives so that they have more freedom to live the kind of life that, upon reflection, they have reason to value. Sen rejects the above-mentioned normative approaches because they, in his view, rely *exclusively* on necessities, utility, or income, and thus exclude non-utility information from our moral judgements.[14]

Fourth, an important idea in the capability approach is the notion of 'conversion factors'. Resources, such as marketable goods and services, but also goods and services emerging from the non-market economy, including household production, have certain characteristics that make them interesting to people. The relation between a good (e.g., a bike) and the achievement of certain beings and doings (e.g., cycling) is captured by the term 'conversion factor': the degree to which a person can transform a resource into a functioning (e.g., being able to cycle). There are three types of conversion factors (Robeyns, 2005). First, personal conversion factors (e.g., metabolism, physical condition, sex, reading skills, intelligence) influence how a person can convert the characteristics of the commodity into a functioning. If a person is disabled, or in a bad physical condition, or has never learned to cycle, then the bicycle will be of limited help to enable the functioning of mobility. Second, social conversion factors (e.g., public policies, social norms, discriminating practices, gender roles, societal hierarchies, power relations) and, third, environmental conversion factors (e.g., climate, geographical location) play a role in the conversion from characteristics of the good to the individual functioning. The three types of conversion factors all stress that it is not sufficient to know the resources a person owns or can use in order to be able to assess the wellbeing that he or she has achieved or could achieve; rather, we need to know much more about the person and the circumstances in which he or she is living.

Fifth, a strong acknowledgement of human diversity is one of the major theoretical driving forces of the capability approach. The capability approach takes account of human diversity in that it focuses on the plurality of functionings and capabilities. By including a wide range of functionings and capabilities, the approach includes issues that may be particularly important for some groups but less so for others. Thus, each individual has a unique profile of conversion factors, some of which are body-related, others of which are shared with all people from her community, and still others of which are shared with people with the same social characteristics (e.g., same gender or class or race characteristics).

Sixth, although Sen seems to regard with disfavour the 'basic needs' concept, he nevertheless uses the concept 'basic capabilities'. In later work, Sen reserved the term 'basic capabilities' to refer to a threshold level for the relevant capabilities. A basic capability is 'the ability to satisfy certain elementary and crucially important functionings up to certain levels' (Sen, 1992, p. 45). The concept of basic capabilities refers to the freedom to do some basic things considered necessary for survival and to avoid or escape poverty or other serious deprivations. The relevance of basic capabilities is not so much in ranking living standards, but in deciding on a threshold for the purpose of assessing poverty and deprivation (Sen, 1986). Nussbaum (2000, p. 84) uses the term 'basic capabilities' to refer to 'the innate equipment of individuals that is necessary for developing the more advanced capabilities', such as the capability of speech and language. Hence, while the notion of capabilities refers to a very broad range of opportunities, the concept of basic capabilities refers to the real opportunity to avoid poverty or to meet or exceed a threshold of wellbeing (Robeyns, 2011). It is important to acknowledge, however, that the capability approach is not restricted to poverty and deprivation analysis but can also serve as a framework for, say, project or policy evaluations or inequality measurement in non-poor communities. Sen's and Nussbaum's extensive writings on the capability approach may mislead us into thinking that the capability approach is about poverty and development issues only, but there is conceptually or normatively no reason to restrict its scope in this way (ibid.).

Three theoretical specifications

The capability approach conceptualizes a metric of functionings and capabilities. However, this conceptualization still leaves open the possibility for a range of very different capability theories to emerge from these metrics. Therefore, one must make some theoretical specifications before one can make a practical application of the capability approach. Four such specifications are widely acknowledged in the capability literature (Robeyns, 2005, 2006, 2011).[15]

The first theoretical specification is whether to focus on capabilities or functionings. The literature gives a number of considerations that are relevant for this choice. The first consideration is normative, and this is the argument Sen and Nussbaum most often offer: by focusing on capabilities rather than functionings, we do not privilege a particular account of good lives but instead aim at a range of possible ways of life from which each person can choose. Thus, it is the liberal nature of the capability approach, or an anti-paternalist consideration, that motivates a principled choice for capabilities rather than functionings (Robeyns, 2011). Obviously, the strength of this argument depends on how bad one takes paternalism to be. There are good reasons to believe that some paternalism is unavoidable, or even desired (Nussbaum, 2000; Sandel, 2009). Moreover, surely there is some paternalism in the selection of capabilities anyway.

A second consideration relates to situations where a capability is available to human beings who are not yet able to choose (infants), who will never be able to choose (severely mentally disabled individuals), or who have lost this ability through advanced dementia or serious brain damage. The same argument applies to future generations and non-human beings who are not able to choose at all. When the ability to choose is restricted, functionings should be the relevant focus. A third consideration relates to the application and measurability that influence the choice of capabilities, functionings, or a combination of the two (Robeyns, 2006). It is, for example, almost always easier to observe and measure functionings than capabilities (Sen, 1992).

The second theoretical specification is the *selection* of capabilities. There is a debate in the capability literature about which capabilities should be selected as relevant and who should decide (or how a decision should be made). At the level of ideal theories of justice, some have argued that every capability is relevant and should count in our moral calculus (Vallentyne, 2005). Others have argued that considerations of justice require that we demarcate morally relevant from morally irrelevant and morally bad capabilities (Pogge, 2002; Nussbaum, 2003).

At one end of this spectrum is Nussbaum's well-known capability list, which contains prescribed capabilities that are grouped together under ten 'central human capabilities': life; bodily health; bodily integrity; senses, imagination, and thought; emotions; practical reason; affiliation; other species; play; and control over one's environment (Nussbaum, 2006, pp. 76–78). Nussbaum justifies this list by arguing that each of these capabilities is needed in order for a human life to be 'not so impoverished that it is not worthy of the dignity of a human being' (Nussbaum,

2000, p. 72). She defends these capabilities as being the moral entitlements of every human being on Earth, entitlements which, she argues, should be enshrined in every country's constitution (Nussbaum, 2000, 2003, 2006). She formulates the list at an abstract level and advocates that the translation to implementation and policies should be done locally, taking into account local differences.[16]

On the other end of the spectrum is Sen. He has been somewhat vague in responding to the question of how to select and weigh capabilities. Yet he draws on his ideal of agency to argue that each group should *itself* select, weigh, trade off, and sequence or otherwise aggregate capabilities as well as prioritize them in relation to other normative considerations, such as agency, efficiency, and stability (Crocker, 2008). Thus, Sen consistently and explicitly refuses to defend 'one pre-determined canonical list of capabilities, chosen by theorists without any general social discussion or public reasoning' (Sen, 2005, p. 158). Of course, groups and theorists might construct lists for various purposes, and lists need not be 'predetermined' or 'canonical', however we might understand these terms. And Sen's refusal to endorse Nussbaum's list has not prevented him from using – for various purposes – particular selections of capabilities in his empirical as well as in his normative work. However, beyond stating in general terms that some democratic process and public reasoning should be involved, Sen has never explained in detail how such a selection could and should be done (Robeyns, 2011).[17]

Several capability scholars have sought to fill the gap between Nussbaum and Sen. Anderson (1999, p. 316) argues that people should be entitled 'to whatever capabilities are necessary to enable them to avoid or escape entanglement in oppressive social relationships' and 'to the capabilities necessary for functioning as an equal citizen in a democratic state'. Alkire (2002) proposes to select capabilities using John Finnis's practical reasoning approach. By iteratively asking 'Why do I do what I do?', one comes to the most basic reasons for acting: life, knowledge, play, aesthetic experience, sociability (friendship), practical reasonableness, and religion. Robeyns (2003) has proposed some pragmatic criteria, mainly relevant for empirical research, for the selection of capabilities for the context of inequality and wellbeing assessments. Crocker (2008) explores the theory and practice of deliberative democracy to bring more specificity to democratic procedures and participatory institutions in the development of an agency-sensitive capability approach.

The third theoretical specification is the *aggregation* of capabilities. If we have a list of relevant capabilities, we would still be left with the question of whether the capabilities should be aggregated and, if so, what their relative weights and the formula to aggregate them would or should be (Robeyns, 2011).[18] A closely related question is how different capabilities should be traded off against one another when they cannot all be realized fully. Some have argued against trade-offs on the basis that the different capabilities are incommensurable or that each capability is an absolute entitlement that never should be overridden by another entitlement or other normative consideration. For example, Nussbaum argues that the ten capabilities on her list, being incommensurable, cannot be traded off against one another (and, hence, have no relative weights), and also that the state should provide each citizen with a minimum level of each capability.

One possible system of weighting or aggregating is to use a democratic or some other social choice procedure (Chakraborty, 1996). The basic idea would be to encourage or prescribe that the relevant group of people decide on the weights. In some contexts, such as small-scale projects or evaluations, such capability weighting (and selection) could be done by participatory techniques. It has also been suggested that we may determine the weights of capabilities as a function of how much they contribute to overall life satisfaction or happiness (Schokkaert, 2007).

Robeyns (2011) thinks it is striking that very few proposals on selecting and weighting or aggregating have been worked out by philosophers using foundational work in ethical theory; instead, most of the proposals on selecting or weighting have been formulated by scholars working in applied ethics or normative political philosophy, or engaged in normative work in the social sciences. She hopes for proposals regarding the selection of dimensions and aggregation that are much more theoretically grounded.

The fourth theoretical specification relates to critical claims that the capability approach: (1) is too individualistic; (2) lacks attention to the influence of groups; and (3) lacks attention to the influence of social structures.

To study the first claim, Robeyns argues that we must distinguish between ethical individualism on the one hand, and methodological and ontological individualism on the other. Ethical individualism makes a claim about who or what should count in our evaluative exercises and decisions. It postulates that individuals, and only individuals, are the units of moral concern. In other words, when evaluating different states of social affairs, we are only interested in the (direct and indirect) effects of those states on individuals. Methodological individualism makes the claim that everything can be *explained* by reference to individuals and their properties only. In contrast, ontological individualism states that only individuals and their properties *exist*, and that all social entities and properties can be identified by reducing them to individuals and their properties. Former UK prime minister Margaret Thatcher probably gave the most precise interpretation of ontological individualism by announcing that 'there is no such thing as society'.[19]

Robeyns finds it difficult to see how the capability approach can be understood to be methodologically or ontologically individualistic, especially since Sen himself has analysed some processes that are profoundly collective:

> The [capability] approach used in this study is much concerned with the opportunities that people have to improve the quality of their lives. It is essentially a 'people-centred' approach, which puts human agency (rather than organizations such as markets or governments) at the centre of the stage. The crucial role of social opportunities is to expand the realm of human agency and freedom, both as an end in itself and as a means of further expansion of freedom. The word 'social' in the expression 'social opportunity'

... is a useful reminder *not to view individuals and their opportunities in isolated terms*. The options that a person has depend greatly on relations with others and on what the state and other institutions do. *We shall be particularly concerned with those opportunities that are strongly influenced by social circumstances and public policy* ...

(Drèze & Sen, 2002, p. 6, our italics)

Thus, Robeyns argues that the capability approach does not rely on ontological or methodological individualism, but that it does embrace ethical individualism. The latter argument makes the capability approach relevant for our understanding of sustainable development as an ethical statement (chapter 1).

The second claim can come in a weaker or a stronger version (Robeyns, 2011). A stronger version of that claim would be that the capability approach *cannot* pay sufficient attention to groups. But that claim is obviously false, because there exists much research that looks at the average capabilities of one group compared with those of another. For example, the UNDP *Human Development Report*s use the capability approach for groups. The weaker version of this claim states that the present state of the literature on the capability approach does not pay *sufficient attention* to groups. While some capability theorists, like Sen, have a great belief in people's abilities to be rational and to resist social and moral pressure stemming from groups, Robeyns argues that there is no reason why the capability approach would not be able to take the normative and constitutive importance of groups fully into account.

The third claim states that the capability approach lacks attention to the influence of social structures. The analysis of this claim follows the same format as that used in the claim that the capability approach lacks sufficient attention to the influence of groups. Robeyns rejects this claim too. The capability approach includes social structures in its conceptual framework, although with the clear recognition that these are the means and not the ends of wellbeing. However, Robeyns admits that there is a potential to use the capability approach more in relation to an analysis of social structures, suggesting that the critique should not be taken lightly.

The capability approach represents a more 'human' take on satisfying human needs than do the basic-needs approaches. Indeed, having opportunities to live the life one values is important to most people. However, people, especially in developed countries, have exploited that opportunity to an unsustainable level. It is therefore an open question whether sustainable development requires that the most affluent have less opportunity. *Our Common Future* argues that it does: 'sustainable global development requires that those who are more affluent adopt life-styles within the planet's ecological means' (WCED, 1987, p. 30). On the other hand, a large part of the global population needs to increase their opportunities.

A theory on satisfying human needs must contain more than merely ways of preventing poverty and deprivation. Indeed, *Our Common Future* argues that in addition to basic needs people have legitimate aspirations for an improved quality of life. Thus, a theory of satisfying human needs must go beyond the basic-needs approach. A richer approach is called for. The capability approach is such an approach, which acknowledges that quality of life should be judged by a person's capability to do things that he or she has reason to value. Providing people with whatever they have reason to value is, however, not without consequences. Indeed, our present unsustainable state of affairs is the bleak result of people having the wrong values, values arising from pure self-interest that have led to grave injustice and escalating environmental problems. Thus, it is important to acknowledge the imperatives of ensuring social justice and respecting environmental limits as constraints when satisfying human needs. Indeed, that was *Our Common Future*'s main message.

Amartya Sen is optimistic though. He consistently argues that we have the capacity as agents to act out of our self-interest to the advantage of justice and the environment. Indeed, those who are unable to acknowledge that capacity would find it hard to welcome the freedom provided by the capability approach. But, Sen concludes, one does not have to be a Gandhi (or a Martin Luther King, or a Nelson Mandela, or an Aung San Suu Kyi) to understand that one's values could stretch well beyond the narrow limits of one's own personal self-interest.

Our Common Future was clear about the link between satisfying human needs and ensuring social justice. It argues that sustainable development requires that it is imperative that 'those poor get their fair share of the resources' and that such justice must be 'aided by political systems that secure effective citizen participation' (ibid., p. 30). With those important requirements in mind, we now turn to theories that are fundamental to understanding the imperative of social justice.

Notes

1 Chapter 3, 'Conversations and Exhortations of Father Zossima', p. 645.
2 Dostoyevsky was mainly concerned about the social consequences of rapid desire satisfaction. Today, we know that there is a high price to pay for the natural environment as well.
3 Max-Neef's work on human-scale development was originally published in a Spanish edition of *Development Dialogue* in 1986, under the title of *Desarrollo a Escala Humana: una opción para el futuro*.
4 Max-Neef admits that there undoubtedly are many ways in which needs may be classified. Hence, any categorization must be regarded as provisional and subject to modification as new evidence arises and calls for changes.
5 Axiological refers to the branch of philosophy dealing with values, such as those of ethics, aesthetics, or religion.
6 Although in Judaeo-Christian culture we have been told that idleness is the mother of all vices, Max-Neef strongly believes that it has many virtues. In fact, idleness and creation seem to be inseparable if the former is understood as 'the state of mind and spirit that is inviting to the muses'. A brilliant argumentation about the subject is found in Bertrand Russell's *In Praise of Idleness*. In any case, idleness is not laziness (Max-Neef, 1991, p. 17).

7 In 'der Ballade über die Frage: Wovon lebt der Mensch?' (1928).

8 Maslow stressed that love is not synonymous with sex. Sex, he argues, may be studied as a purely physiological need. Ordinarily sexual behaviour is multi-determined, that is to say, determined not only by sexual needs but also by other needs, chief among which are the love and affection needs. Also not to be overlooked is the fact that the love needs involve both giving and receiving love (ibid., p. 381).

9 According to Maslow, this term was coined by Kurt Goldstein.

10 The extension of the influence or dominance of one nation's culture over others, now usually through the exportation of cultural commodities such as film, music, etc. (https://en.oxforddictionaries.com/, accessed 28 November 2016).

11 Doyal and Gough suggest a set of indicators for measuring satisfaction of basic needs (ibid., table 9.2, p. 190) and another set of indicators for measuring satisfaction of intermediate needs (ibid., table 10.1, p. 219). They do not, however, suggest the levels of the minimum optimorum.

12 Suggested indicators of societal preconditions for optimization: Doyal and Gough, 1991, table 11.1, p. 245.

13 The writings of Amartya Sen gave rise to the capability approach in 1980 with the publication of a 1979 lecture, 'Equality of What?' (Sen, 1980). His Dewey Lectures 'Well-being, Agency and Freedom' published in 1985 provided a fuller philosophical articulation of the approach (Sen, 1985), while 'The Standard of Living' (Sen, 1986) clarified various linkages to economics and to economic development. In the 1989 article 'Development as capability expansion', the proposition that informed the 1990 *Human Development Report* was clear (Sen, 1989). Sen continued to publish on the capability approach after 1990. In *The Idea of Justice* (Sen, 2009) he re-states the capability approach in the context of a more developed account of justice, relating it to newer philosophical writings and to happiness.

14 The non-utility information that is excluded by utilitarianism, according to Sen, includes a person's additional physical needs, due to being physically disabled for example, but also social or moral principles, such as human rights or the specific principle that men and women should be paid the same wage for the same work. Robeyns (2011) questions whether the attack of Sen and some other capability scholars on utilitarianism is as successful as it may seem to them. One worry is that capability scholars attack the most simplified version of utilitarianism, or that they exaggerate the difference between (some versions of) utilitarianism and the capability approach.

15 Robeyns (2011) mentions a fifth specification: What is needed for a full capability theory of justice to be developed? The next chapter treats this issue.

16 Nussbaum argues that this list can be derived from a Rawlsian overlapping consensus, and stresses that her list remains open-ended and always open for revision (Nussbaum, 2000, p. 77).

17 To be fair to Sen, he was central in developing the human development index (HDI) which is reported yearly in UNDP's *Human Development Report*.

18 Much of the existing literature refers to the issue of 'weighting', but this is only one particular form of the more general 'aggregating', since aggregation may take a different functional form than simply adding up. For example, if you have no food, your other capabilities will be worth very little. Some capabilities may thus be complementary capabilities, implying that their value to a person depends on the presence (or absence) of other capabilities (Robeyns, 2011).

19 Prime Minister Margaret Thatcher, talking to *Woman's Own* magazine, 31 October 1987:

I think we've been through a period where too many people have been given to understand that if they have a problem, it's the government's job to cope with it. 'I have a problem, I'll get a grant.' 'I'm homeless, the government must house me.' They're casting their problem on society. And, you know, there is no such thing as society. There are individual men and women, and there are families. And no government can do anything except through people, and people must look to themselves first. It's our duty to look after ourselves and then, also to look after our neighbour. People have got the entitlements too much in mind, without the obligations. There's no such thing as entitlement, unless someone has first met an obligation.

References

Alkire, S. (2002) *Valuing Freedoms: Sen's Capability Approach and Poverty Reduction.* New York, Oxford University Press.

Alkire, S. (2010) *Human Development: Definitions, Critiques, and Related Concepts.* Background paper for the 2010 Human Development Report, OPHI working paper no. 36. Oxford Poverty & Human Development Initiative (OPHI).

Alkire, S. & Santos, M. E. (2010) *Acute Multidimensional Poverty: A New Index for Developing Countries.* OPHI working paper no. 38. Oxford Poverty & Human Development Initiative (OPHI).

Anderson, E. (1999) What is the point of equality? *Ethics,* 109(2), 287–337.

Braybrook, D. (1987) *Meeting Needs.* Princeton, NJ, Princeton University Press.

Chakraborty, A. (1996) On the possibility of a weighting system for functionings. *Indian Economic Review,* 31, 241–250.

Crocker, D. A. (2008) *Ethics of Global Development: Agency, Capability and Deliberative Democracy.* Cambridge, Cambridge University Press.

Dostoyevsky, F. (1880) *The Brothers Karamazov.* Planet PDF. Available from: www.planetpublish.com/wp-content/uploads/2011/11/The_Brothers_Karamazov_NT.pdf [accessed 5 April 2017]

Doyal, L. & Gough, I. (1991) *A Theory of Human Need.* London, Macmillan.

Drèze, J. & Sen, A. (2002) *India: Development and Participation.* Oxford, Oxford University Press.

Holden, E., Linnerud, K., & Banister, D. (2014) Sustainable development: 'Our Common Future' revisited. *Global Environmental Change,* 26, 130–139.

Holden, E., Linnerud, K., & Banister, D. (2016) The imperatives of sustainable development. *Sustainable Development,* DOI: 10.1002/sd.1647.

Maslow, A. H. (1943) A theory of human motivation. *Psychological Review,* 50, 370–396.

Max-Neef, M. A. (1991) *Human Scale Development: Conceptions, Applications and Further Reflections.* New York and London, The Apex Press.

Neumayer, E. (2013) *Weak versus Strong Sustainability: Exploring the Limits of Two Opposing Paradigms.* 4th edition. Cheltenham, UK and Northampton, MA, Edward Elgar.

Nussbaum, M. (2000) *Women and Human Development: The Capabilities Approach.* Cambridge, Cambridge University Press.

Nussbaum, M. (2003) Capabilities as fundamental entitlements: Sen and social justice. *Feminist Economics,* 9(2/3), 33–59.

Nussbaum, M. (2006) *Frontiers of Justice: Disability, Nationality, Species Membership.* Cambridge, MA, Harvard University Press.

Pogge, T. (2002) Can the capability approach be justified? *Philosophical Topics*, 30(2), 167–228.

Robeyns, I. (2003) Sen's capability approach and gender inequality: Selecting relevant capabilities. *Feminist Economics*, 9(2/3), 61–92.

Robeyns, I. (2005) The capability approach: A theoretical survey. *Journal of Human Development*, 6(1), 93–114.

Robeyns, I. (2006) The capability approach in practice. *Journal of Political Philosophy*, 14 (3), 351–376.

Robeyns, I. (2011) *The capability approach*. The Stanford Encyclopedia of Philosophy. Available from: http://plato.stanford.edu/archives/sum2011/entries/capability-approach/ [accessed 5 April 2017].

Sandel, M. K. (2009) *Justice: What's the Right Thing to Do?* New York, Farrar, Straus and Giroux.

Schokkaert, E. (2007) Capabilities and satisfaction with life. *Journal of Human Development*, 8(3), 415–430.

Sen, A. (1980) Equality of what? In: McMurrin, S. (ed.) *The Tanner Lectures on Human Values*. Salt Lake City, University of Utah Press.

Sen, A. (1985) Well-being, agency and freedom: The Dewey Lectures 1984. *The Journal of Philosophy*, 82(4), 169–221.

Sen, A. (1986) *The Standard of Living*. Cambridge, Cambridge University Press.

Sen, A. (1989) Development as capability expansion. *Journal of Development Planning*, 17, 41–58.

Sen, A. (1992) *Inequality Re-examined*. Oxford, Clarendon Press.

Sen, A. (2005) Human rights and capabilities. *Journal of Human Development*, 6(2), 151–166.

Sen, A. (2009) *The Idea of Justice*. London, Penguin.

Thompson, G. (1987) *Needs*. London and New York, Routledge.

UNDP (2015) *Work for Human Development. Human Development Report 2015.* United Nations Development Programme, New York.

Vallentyne, P. (2005) Debate: Capabilities versus opportunities for wellbeing. *Journal of Political Philosophy*, 13, 359–371.

WCED (1987) *Our Common Future.* World Commission on Environment and Development. Oxford, Oxford University Press.

3

ENSURING SOCIAL JUSTICE

Lyrics in 'The Last Resort' by the American rock band The Eagles asks for the grand design of 'what is yours and what is mine'. Moreover, the lyrics ask who should provide this design. These questions have been troublesome for philosophers since the days of Plato and Aristotle (and probably before that too). How should a group of people divide available resources between them? Should they receive equal shares? Should someone be allowed to get more than others? Who should create the rules that allocate the shares? Should we even allow someone to decide how much each person gets? Who is to decide how we should split the cake? These questions relate to social justice. At the end of the day, social justice boils down to two questions: 'who gets what?' and 'says who?' (Wolff, 2006).

Philosophers are not the only ones who ponder on social justice though. Most people do it all the time, although they are probably more occupied by injustice. Manifest injustice in the social structures that govern our lives are 'as much part of our wiring as our ligaments and arteries' (Sandhu *et al.*, 2014, p. 162). Indeed, injustice, whether experienced personally or by people around us, is something we strongly respond to at a very early age. The orphan Pip, the main character and narrator in the English writer Charles Dickens' *Great Expectations*, reminds us so. Growing up with his abusive older sister, Pip felt injustice at a very early age: 'My sister's bringing up had made me sensitive. In the little world in which children have their existence whosoever brings them up, there's nothing so finely perceived and so finely felt, as injustice.'[1] Those of us who have children of our own would recognize this. Hopefully not growing up under such bleak conditions as Pip, children nevertheless at a surprisingly early age express a sense of injustice. Parents must repeatedly respond to complaints like: 'Why can't I do this or that when my older brother can? It's not fair.'

When we here speak of social justice, we use the word 'should'. Thus, we regard social justice as a normative concept that tells us how we should distribute resources and that tells us who should decide how to distribute them. Indeed, life *is* not necessarily fair. We are surrounded by what most people would regard as injustice. For some, this is not a problem. In *Free to Choose*, the economist Milton Friedman acknowledges that those who grow up in wealthy families and attend elite schools have an unfair advantage over those from less privileged backgrounds. He also concedes that those who, through no doing of their own, inherit talents and gifts have an unfair advantage over others. Friedman insists nevertheless that we should not try to remedy this unfairness: 'Life is not fair. It is tempting to believe that governments can rectify what nature has spawned. But it is also important to recognise how much we benefit from the very unfairness we deplore' (Friedman, 1980, pp. 136–137). The American philosopher John Rawls rejects this view. In an emotive passage, he states a familiar truth that we often forget: the way things are does not determine the way they ought to be. Rawls acknowledges that the natural distribution (in life) is neither just nor unjust, nor is it unjust that people are born into society at some particular position. These are, he says, simply natural facts. However, he stresses, 'What is just and unjust is the way that institutions deal with these facts' (Rawls, 1999, p. 87).

Our Common Future on ensuring social justice

Our Common Future is strong on the importance of ensuring social justice – both across time and space.[2] As a general principle, *Our Common Future* proposes that 'states shall conserve and use the environment and natural resources for the benefit of present and future generations'.[3] They state that our present unsustainable state of affairs is often a product of the relative neglect of economic and social justice within and amongst nations.

Indeed, ensuring social justice within and amongst nations is embedded in *Our Common Future*'s definition of sustainable development:

> A development path that is sustainable in a physical sense could theoretically be pursued even in a rigid social and political setting. But physical sustainability cannot be secured unless development policies pay attention to such considerations as changes in access to resources and in the distribution of costs and benefits. Even the narrow notion of physical sustainability implies a concern for social equity between generations, a concern that must logically be extended to equity within each generation.
>
> (WCED, 1987, p. 43)

Thus, it should be very clear that any notion of sustainable development *must* include the promotion of social justice. Moreover, *Our Common Future* acknowledges that injustice is interlinked to poverty (that is, not having basic needs satisfied) and environmental degradation (that is, not respecting environmental limits). Indeed, a world in which poverty and inequity are endemic will always be prone to ecological and other crises. To make things even worse, as a system approaches ecological limits, poverty increases and inequalities sharpen: 'When a watershed deteriorates, poor farmers suffer more because they cannot afford the same anti-erosion measures as richer farmers. ... Globally, wealthier nations are better placed financially and technologically to cope with the effects of possible climatic change' (ibid., p. 47). Indeed, these concerns are as relevant today as they were three decades ago.

In addition to the interrelated problems of poverty, injustice, and environmental stress, *Our Common Future* states that 'competition [for example due to overpopulation] for non-renewable raw materials, land, or energy can create tension' (ibid., p. 243). In his book of 2005, *Collapse: How Societies Choose to Fail or Succeed*, the American scientist Jared Diamond reminds us that such has been the case repeatedly throughout history (see also chapter 4). Rwanda serves as an especially disturbing example. From April to July 1994, members of the Hutu ethnic majority in the east-central African nation of Rwanda murdered as many as 800,000 people, mostly of the Tutsi minority. Diamond acknowledges that genocide can arise for ultimate reasons; he nevertheless concludes that population pressure and conflict over limited resources were important factors behind the Rwandan genocide. A Tutsi survivor[4] put it this way: 'The people whose children had to walk barefoot to school killed the people who could buy shoes for theirs.'

Finally, *Our Common Future* points out that meeting essential needs requires an assurance that those who are poor get their fair share of the resources. Such justice would be aided by political systems that secure effective citizen participation in decision-making and by greater democracy in decision-making at all levels. Thus, the 'says who' question is indeed an important part of the sustainable development domain.

In *A Theory of Justice*, John Rawls (1999)[5] presents a conception of justice, which he calls 'justice as fairness'. His aim of the book is 'to provide a reasonably systematic alternative to utilitarianism, which in one form or another has long dominated the Anglo-Saxon tradition of political thought' (ibid., p. xi). Rawls simply does not think that utilitarianism can provide a satisfactory account of basic rights and liberties of citizens as free and equal persons, a requirement he regards as 'an absolutely first importance for an account of democratic institutions' (ibid., p. xii). Before presenting Rawls' theory, however, we should say something about the position he so strongly rejects: utilitarianism.

Utilitarianism

Utilitarianism is one of the most powerful and persuasive approaches towards normative ethics in the history of philosophy (Driver, 2014). Though there are many varieties of the view discussed, utilitarianism is generally held to be the view that the morally right action is the action that produces the most good. There are many ways to spell out this general claim. One thing to note is that the theory is a form of consequentialism: the right action is understood entirely in terms of the consequences produced. If a law or an action doesn't *do* any good, then it *isn't* any good (ibid.).

It was the English philosopher Jeremy Bentham who first fully articulated the doctrine of utilitarianism. The doctrine became influential at the time, and it exerts a powerful hold on the thinking of policymakers, economists, business executives, and ordinary citizens to this day (Sandel, 2009). Bentham famously held that humans are ruled by two sovereign masters – pleasure and pain. We seek pleasure and the avoidance of pain; they 'govern us in everything we do and also determine what we ought to do' (ibid., p. 34). Yet, Bentham also declared the principle of utility as the standard of right action on the part of governments as well as individuals. Actions are approved of when they, for example, promote happiness or pleasure, and disapproved of when they have a tendency to cause unhappiness or pain. The main aim of utilitarianism is then, according to Sandel (ibid.), simply stated and intuitively appealing: the highest principle of morality is to maximize happiness, the overall balance of pleasure and pain. According to Bentham, the morally right thing to do is whatever will maximize utility, or as he famously phrased it: to provide the greatest happiness to the greatest number of people.

Two major objections can be raised to Bentham's 'greatest happiness' principle (Sandel, 2009). First, that it does not give adequate weight to human dignity and individual rights. By caring only about the sum of satisfaction, it does not give sufficient attention to individual people. For the utilitarian, individuals matter, but only in the sense that each person's preferences should be counted along with everyone else's. The second objection is that Bentham's principle wrongly reduces everything of moral importance to a single scale of pleasure and pain. Thus, Bentham claims to offer a science of morality, based on measuring, aggregating, and calculating happiness. He recognizes no qualitative distinction amongst pleasures. Simple-minded pleasures, sensual pleasures, are just as good, at least intrinsically, as more sophisticated and complex pleasures. The pleasure of drinking a beer in front of the TV rates as highly as the pleasure one gets solving a complicated maths problem, reading a poem, or listening to Mozart.

John Stuart Mill, a compatriot and follower of Bentham, believed that the two objections could be answered and, by doing so, save utilitarianism by recasting it as a more humane, less calculating doctrine. Mill responds to the first objection in his book *On Liberty* (1859),[6] which is a classic defence of individual freedom in the English-speaking world (Sandel, 2009). Its central principle is that people should be free to do whatever they want, provided they do no harm to others. The government may not interfere with individual liberty in order to protect a person from himself, or to impose the majority's belief about how best to live. The only actions for which a person is accountable to the society, Mill argues, are those that affect others. As long as a person does not harm anyone else, his 'independence is, of right, absolute. Over himself, over his own body and mind, the individual is sovereign' (ibid., p. 49).

Mill responds to the second objection in his book *Utilitarianism* (1861). Unlike Bentham, Mill believes that it is possible to distinguish between higher and lower pleasures – to assess the quality, not just the quantity or intensity,[7] of our desires. Further, he thinks he can make this distinction without relying on any moral ideas other than utility itself. Thus, what Mill calls the intellectual pleasures will score more highly than the sensual ones along several parameters, and this could give us reason to prefer those pleasures – however, it is a quantitative not a qualitative reason, in Bentham's view. For example, when a student decides to study for an exam rather than go to a party, she is making the best decision even though she is sacrificing short-term pleasure. That is because studying for the exam, Bentham could argue, scores higher in terms of the long-term pleasures that doing well in school leads to, as well as the fecundity of the pleasure in leading to yet other pleasures (Driver, 2014). Here too, Sandel (2009) claims that Mill runs into trouble. Mill saves utilitarianism from the charge that it reduces everything to a crude calculation of pleasure and pain, but only by invoking a moral ideal of human dignity and personality independent of utility itself.

In *The Methods of Ethics* (1874), the British philosopher Henry Sidgwick develops his view on utilitarianism out of and in response to those of Bentham and Mill. His *Methods* is one of the most well-known works in utilitarian moral philosophy, and deservedly so according to Driver (2014).[8] It offers a strong defence of utilitarianism. In *The Methods*, Sidgwick is concerned with developing an account of 'the different methods of Ethics that I find implicit in our common moral reasoning'. These methods are egoism, intuition-based morality, and utilitarianism. In Sidgwick's view, utilitarianism is the more basic theory. A simple reliance on intuition, for example, cannot resolve fundamental conflicts between values, or rules, such as truth and justice that may conflict. In Sidgwick's words: 'we require some higher principle to decide the issue'. That will be utilitarianism. Further, the rules that seem to be a fundamental part of common sense morality are often vague and underdescribed, and applying them will actually require appeal to something theoretically more basic – again, utilitarianism. Yet further, absolute interpretations of rules seem highly counter-intuitive, and yet we need some justification for any exceptions – provided, again, by utilitarianism. Sidgwick provides a compelling case for the theoretical primacy of utilitarianism.

John Rawls, however, was not convinced.

John Rawls' theory of justice

Rawls leaves no doubt of the importance of justice:

> Justice is the first virtue of social institutions, as truth is of systems of thought. A theory however elegant and economical must be rejected or revised if it is untrue; likewise laws and institutions no matter how efficient and well-arranged must be reformed or abolished if they are unjust.
>
> (Rawls, 1999, p. 3)

Each person, Rawls claims, possesses an inviolability founded on justice that the welfare of society cannot override. By stating this, it is clear that Rawls discards the utilitarian view that the considerations of the individual can be sacrificed against the increased utility of the society: 'Justice denies that the loss of freedom for some is made right by a greater good shared by others' (ibid., p. 3). Rawls puts the liberties of equal citizenship as an absolute prerequisite in a just society. Thus, the rights secured by justice are not 'subject to political bargaining or to the calculus of social interests' (ibid., p. 3). Injustice is tolerable, Rawls maintains, only when it is necessary to prevent an even greater injustice. Rawls argues that truth and justice are uncompromising, and that these prepositions express our intuitive conviction of 'the primacy of justice'. Pip would probably have agreed with that.

Any society, however, which recognizes certain rules and systems designed to advance the good of those taking part in it, would, according to Rawls, be marked by a conflict as well as by an identity of interest. There is an identity of interest since cooperation makes possible a better life for all than any would have if each were to live only by his own effort. There is conflict of interest since persons care as to how the greater benefits produced by their collaboration are distributed. Thus, 'a set of principles is required for choosing among the various social arrangements which determine this division of advantages and for underwriting an agreement on the proper distributive shares'. Rawls calls the background conditions for such principles the circumstances of justice. First, there are objective circumstances that acknowledge that some sort of cooperation seems necessary in a world where equals live under a condition of moderate scarcity of natural and other resources. Second, there are subjective circumstances that acknowledge that while people have roughly similar needs and interests, they nevertheless have their own plans of life and therefore have conflicting claims on the resources available. Unless these circumstances exist, Rawls argues, 'there would be no occasion for the virtue of justice' (ibid., p. 110).

We can experience justice or injustice on many levels. On the one hand, laws, institutions, and social systems can be just or unjust. On the other hand, particular actions of many kinds, including decisions, judgement, and imputations, can be just or unjust. Sort of in-between, we also call the attitudes and dispositions of people, and people themselves, just or unjust. Rawls has no intention to develop an all-encompassing theory of justice that is valid at all levels. Rather, his topic is that of *social justice*. Thus, his primary subject of justice is the basic structure of society, or more precisely, 'the way in which major social institutions distribute fundamental rights and duties and determine the division of advantages from social cooperation' (ibid., p. 6). Rawls addresses the basic structure as the primary subject of justice because 'its effects are so profound and present from the start' (ibid., p. 7).

Thus, Rawls' scope is limited, in the sense that he presents a theory that regulates a perfect, well-ordered society. Although admittedly not relevant everywhere, Rawls assumes that a deeper understanding of social justice can be gained in no other way; 'the nature and aims of a perfectly just society is the fundamental part of the theory of justice' (ibid., p. 8). Thus, Rawls' theory is not offered as a description of ordinary meanings, but as an account of certain distributive principles for the basic structure of a perfect society. As we will see shortly, Amartya Sen (2009) has a very different view and take on this issue.

The main idea of Rawls' theory of justice

Rawls' guiding idea is that the principles of justice for the basic structure of society are those that free and rational people would accept in an initial position of equality in pursuing their own interests and defining the fundamental terms of their association. These principles are to regulate all further agreements in two ways. First, they specify the kinds of social cooperation that people would enter into. Second, they specify the forms of government that they would establish. This way of regarding the principles of justice Rawls calls justice as fairness: it conveys the idea that the principles of justice are agreed to in an initial situation that is fair.[9]

Rawls' interpretation of the initial situation is one he calls 'the original position'. This original position is not to be thought of as an actual historical state of affairs, much less as a primitive condition of culture (as in the state of nature). Rather, the original position is 'a purely hypothetical situation. Nothing resembling it need ever take place, although we can by deliberately following the constraints it expresses simulate the reflections of the parties' (Rawls, 1999, p. 104). Amongst the essential features of the hypothetical situation of the original position is 'that no one knows his place in society, his class position or social status, nor does anyone know his fortune in the distribution of natural assets and abilities, his intelligence, strength, and the like' (ibid., p. 11). Moreover, the principles of justice are chosen behind a 'veil of ignorance'. Behind the veil of ignorance, no one can take advantage, even unwittingly, of a favourable bargaining position. Some would argue that a hypothetical agreement behind a veil of ignorance is a pale form of an actual contract and therefore a morally weaker thing. This is not so, according to Sandel; a hypothetical agreement is a 'pure form of an actual contract, and so a morally more powerful thing' (Sandel, 2009, p. 151).

The parties in the original position are not completely ignorant though. First, they know that agents in the original position know they want more of what Rawls calls primary goods. These are liberties, opportunities, wealth, income, and social bases of self-respect.[10] What these all have in common, Rawls supposes, is that they are what people should rationally want, whatever else they want. Second, the parties assume that the society is under conditions of moderate scarcity: there is enough to go around, but not enough for everyone to get what they want. This takes the edge off Sen's critique of Rawls' primacy of liberty to the satisfaction of basic needs. Indeed, Rawls acknowledges that in a condition of dire scarcity, his principles would not stand the test. Third, the parties in the original position know general facts about human social life, facts of common sense, and general conclusions of science (including economics and psychology) that are uncontroversial.

Working out a conception of justice as fairness, Rawls states, begins with the choice of the first principles of justice that would be chosen in the original position. Rawls finds it unlikely that the principle of utility would be chosen. A rational man (he would probably use 'person' if he were to write the book today), according to Rawls, would not accept a basic structure of society only because it maximizes the algebraic sum of advantages irrespective of its effects on his own basic rights and interests. Thus, Rawls argues that the principle of utility is incompatible with the conception of social cooperation amongst equals for mutual advantage. Rawls instead maintains that rational men in the initial situation (that is, in the original position) would choose two rather different principles (Rawls, 1999, p. 266):[11]

- First principle: Each person is to have an equal right to the most extensive total system of equal basic liberties compatible with a similar system of liberty for all.
- Second principle: Social and economic inequalities are to be arranged so that they are both: (i) to the greatest benefit of the least advantaged, consistent with the just savings principle,[12] and (ii) attached to offices and positions open to all under conditions of fair equality of opportunity.

The first principle is often referred to as the liberty principle. Part (i) of the second principle is often referred to as the difference principle, and part (ii), the fair opportunity principle. The two principles of justice serve, according to Maffettone (2010), a dual purpose. On one hand, they aim at the best possible set-up of political institutions (the first principle), while on the other, they relate to the socio-economic structure of distributive justice (the second principle). Thus, the first principle of equal basic liberties is to be used to design the political constitution, while the second principle applies primarily to economic institutions (Wenar, 2013).

According to Rawls, the liberty principle has 'lexical priority' over the other two, as does the fair opportunity principle over the difference principle.[13] What this means for Rawls is that, once we have reached a certain level of wellbeing in a well-ordered society, considerations of liberty have absolute priority over matters of economic wellbeing or equality of opportunity. Similarly, once we have reached a certain level of wellbeing, fair equality of opportunity has priority over economic wellbeing.

The first principle refers to a list of liberties: political liberty (the right to vote and to hold public office) and freedom of speech and assembly; liberty of conscience and freedom of thought; freedom of the person, which includes freedom from psychological oppression and physical assault and dismemberment (integrity of the person); [and] the right to hold personal property and freedom from arbitrary arrest and seizure as defined by the concept of the rule of law. These liberties, according to Rawls, 'are to be equal by the first principle' (Rawls, 1999, p. 53).

Two further features make this first principle distinctive (Wenar, 2013). First, as already mentioned, is its priority: the basic rights and liberties must not be traded off against other social goods. The first principle disallows, for instance, a policy that would give draft exemptions to college students on the grounds that educated civilians will increase economic growth. The draft is a drastic infringement on basic liberties, and if a draft is implemented, then all who are able to serve must be equally subject to it.

Second, it requires fair value of the political liberties. The political liberties are a subset of the basic liberties, concerned with the rights to hold public office, the right to affect the outcome of national elections, and so on. Rawls refers to the principle of equal liberty, when applied to the political procedure defined by the constitution, as the principle of (equal) participation (Maffettone, 2010). 'It requires that all citizens are to have an equal right to take part in, and to determine the outcome of, the constitutional process that establishes the laws with which they are to comply' (Rawls, 1999, p. 194). That is, citizens similarly endowed and motivated should have the same opportunities to hold office, to influence elections, and so on, regardless of their social class.

Rawls discusses three points concerning the equal liberty defined by the principle of participation: its meaning, its extent, and its worth (ibid., p. 196). Its meaning reflects the idea that every citizen has more or less the same power in determining the electoral result. Its extent relates to the use of the majority rule that presides over national politics. Thus, the most extensive political liberty is established by a constitution that uses the procedure in which a minority can neither override nor check a majority. Its worth consists in the actual possibility for each citizen – regardless of class, gender, race – to have access to public office and to have an effect on political life. Thus, the constitution must underwrite a fair opportunity to take part in and to influence the political process.

The second principle applies to 'the distribution of income and wealth and to the design of organisations that make use of differences in authority and responsibility' (ibid., p. 53). Thus, while the distribution of wealth and income need not be equal, it must be to everyone's advantage. Moreover, positions of authority and responsibility must be accessible to all. One applies the second principle then 'by holding positions open, and then, subject to this constraint, arranges social and economic inequalities so that everyone benefits' (ibid., p. 53).

The difference principle (the first part of the second principle) requires that social institutions be arranged so that any inequalities of wealth and income work to the advantage of those who will be worst off. The difference principle supports the idea that natural endowments are undeserved. A citizen does not deserve more of the social product simply because she was lucky enough to be born with gifts that are in great demand. Yet, this does not mean that everyone must get the same share. The fact that citizens have different talents and abilities can be used to make everyone better off. In a society governed by the difference principle, citizens regard the distribution of natural endowments as an asset that can benefit all. Those who are better endowed are welcome to use their gifts to make themselves better off, so long as their doing so also contributes towards the wellbeing of those who are less well endowed. The difference principle is, according to Wolff (2006), a broadly egalitarian principle, in the sense that there is a general assumption in favour of an equal distribution of goods amongst all citizens. Thus, although the difference principle does not require an equal distribution of income and wealth, its underlying idea 'expresses a powerful, even inspiring vision of equality' (Sandel, 2009, p. 156).

The fair opportunity principle (the second part of the second principle) requires that citizens with the same talents and willingness to use them have the same educational and economic opportunities regardless of whether they were born rich or poor. In all parts of society, Rawls argues, people should have roughly the same prospects of culture and achievement for those who are similarly motivated and endowed. Therefore, for example, if we assume that natural endowments and willingness are evenly distributed across children born into different social classes, then within any type of occupation (generally specified), we should find that roughly one-quarter of people in that occupation were born into the top 25 per cent of the income distribution; one-quarter were born into the second highest 25 per cent of the income distribution; one-quarter were born into the second lowest 25 per cent; and one-quarter were born into the lowest 25 per cent (Wenar, 2013). Thus, since class of origin is a morally arbitrary fact about citizens, justice does not allow class of origin to turn into unequal real opportunities for education or meaningful work.

The relation between the social primary goods and the two principles of justice is as follows: The primary good of liberty (and rights and freedom) links to the first principle. The primary good of opportunity (that is, having access to offices and positions of responsibility) links to the second part of the second principle. The primary good of income and wealth links to the first part of the second principle (that is the difference principle).

Rawls on justice between generations

Rawls argues that an account of justice as fairness would be incomplete without some discussion of the question of justice between generations. The answer to this discussion depends partly on the level at which the social minimum of primary goods is to be set. Moreover, it depends on how far the present generation is bound to respect the claims of its successors.

Rawls disputes that the right level of social minimum depends upon the average wealth of the country and that, with the other things equal, the minimum should be higher when the average increases. He also disputes that the proper level is determined by customary expectations.

> The first is not precise enough since it does not say how the minimum depends on average wealth and it overlooks other relevant aspects such as distribution; while the second provides no criterion for telling when customary expectations are themselves reasonable. Once the difference principle is accepted, however, it follows that the minimum is to be set at that point which, taking wages into account, maximises the expectations of the least advantaged group.
>
> (Rawls, 1999, p. 251)

In what way to specify the social minimum leads to the problem of justice between generations, and finding a just savings principle is an important aspect of this problem. Rawls argues that the classic principle of utility leads in the wrong direction: 'The utilitarian doctrine may direct us to demand heavy sacrifices of the poor generations for the sake of greater advantages for later ones that are far better off' (ibid., p. 253). Rather, Rawls turns to the contract doctrine and the parties in the original position to adopt an appropriate savings principle.

Rawls points out that some have thought the different fortunes of generations to be unjust. Herzen remarks that human development is a kind of chronological unfairness, since those who live later profit from the labour of their predecessors without paying the same price. Furthermore, Kant thought it disconcerting that earlier generations should carry their burdens only for the sake of the later ones, and that only the last should have the good fortune to dwell in the complete building.[14] Rawls thinks this is a misplaced feeling. It is a natural fact that generations are spread out in time and actual benefits flow only in one direction. This fact, Rawls reminds us, is unalterable; therefore, the question of chronological unfairness does not arise. The recent knowledge about alarming climate change and increased loss of biological diversity tells us that chronological unfairness runs both ways. While the labour of earlier generations could increase living standards for future generations, their labour could also decrease future generations' prospects. Kant's complete building might turn out to be a shack rather than a castle!

When the parties in the original position consider the problem of just savings, they do not know to which generation they belong or the stage of civilization of their society. Rawls argues that 'they have no way of telling whether it is poor or relatively wealthy, largely agricultural or already industrialised, and so on. The veil of ignorance is complete in these respects' (ibid., p. 254). However, since Rawls takes the present time of entry as the interpretation of the original position, the parties know that they are contemporaries. Earlier generations will have either saved or not; there is nothing the parties can do to affect that. Therefore, to achieve a reasonable result, Rawls assumes first that the parties represent family lines, say, who care at least about their more immediate descendants, and second, that the principle adopted must be such that they wish all earlier generations to have followed it. 'These constraints, together with the veil of ignorance, are to insure that any one generation looks out for all' (ibid., p. 255).

In arriving at a just savings principle, Rawls argues that the parties in the original position are to ask themselves how much they would be willing to save on the assumption that all other generations have saved, or will save, in accordance with the same criterion. Rawls thinks it is impossible to be very specific about how much the parties would be willing to save. On the one hand, the parties would avoid imposing very high saving rates in case their society turns out to be poor. On the other hand, they will want all generations to provide some saving, since it is to our advantage if our predecessors have done their share. One might argue that Rawls is too mild on the original position here by focusing on what people are *willing* to save. With escalating climate change and diminishing biodiversity hanging over us, the people in the original position now are to ask themselves how much they *must* save for future generations.

Rawls points out four features of the contract approach and how it applies to the just savings principle (ibid., p. 256). First, while it is evident that a just savings principle cannot literally be adopted democratically (future generations cannot find their way to the ballot box), the conception of the original position achieves the same result because all generations are virtually represented. Second, the contract doctrine puts a just society as the aim for savings between generations. Thus, the just savings principle is an agreement between generations to carry their fair share of the burden of setting up and preserving a just society over time. Third, although all generations must do their part in reaching a just society beyond which no further net saving is required, this just state is not to be thought of as that which gives purpose to the whole process. On the contrary, all generations have their appropriate aims. They are not subordinate to one another anymore than individuals are, and no generation has stronger claims than any other. Fourth, Rawls stresses that the last stage at which saving is called for is not one of great abundance. Justice does not require that early generations save so that later ones are simply wealthier. The present generation saves for the full realization of just institutions and the equal liberties for future generations. Thus, Rawls believes that it is a mistake to believe that a just and good society must wait upon a high material standard of life. Rather,

> what men want is meaningful work in free association with others, these associations regulating their relations to one another within a framework of just basic institutions. To achieve this state of things great wealth is not necessary. In fact, beyond some point it is more likely to be a positive hindrance, a meaningless distraction at best if not a temptation to indulgence and emptiness.
>
> (ibid., pp. 257–258)

The just savings principle has important implications for the difference principle. In any generation, the expectations of the least advantaged are to be maximized subject to the condition of putting aside the savings that would be acknowledged. Thus, the difference principle includes the savings principle as a constraint. According to the main features of the just savings principle then, Rawls argues that

> persons in different generations have duties and obligations to one another just as contemporaries do. The present generation cannot do as it pleases but is bound by the principles that would be chosen in the original position to define justice between persons at different moments of time.
>
> (ibid., p. 258)

Sen's idea of justice

In his book of 2009, *The Idea of Justice* (Sen, 2009), Amartya Sen challenges Rawls' basic approach to justice. Though Sen is keen to stress how influential Rawls has been to his own work, he nevertheless sees several major problems with the Rawlsian approach.

First, Sen thinks that the total priority of liberty in the Rawlsian approach is too extreme. He argues that 'it is indeed possible to accept that liberty must have some kind of priority, but total unrestrained priority is almost certainly an overkill' (ibid., p. 65). Second, in the difference principle, Rawls judges the opportunities that people have through the means they possess, 'without taking into account the wide variations they have in being able to convert primary goods into good living' (ibid., p. 66). There is then, according to Sen, a strong case to move from focusing on primary goods (as Rawls does) to actual assessment of freedoms and capabilities (see chapter 2 for more on the capability approach and 'conversion factors'). Third, Sen argues that Rawls neglects 'the inescapable relevance of actual behaviour' (ibid., p. 67). Though regarding institutions as being important, Sen insists that what really happens to people cannot but be a central concern of a theory of justice. Simply assuming that people would comply with the rules of the institutions is not good enough. Fourth, Sen claims that Rawls' approach lacks relevance for global perspectives. The social contract agreed in the original position 'inescapably limits the involvement of participants in the pursuit of justice to the members of a given polity' [that is, that of a nation-state] (ibid., p. 71). According to Sen, the device of the original position leaves one short of seeking a gigantic global social contract. Indeed, the possibility of setting up just institutions for the global society, that is demanding a world government, is 'deeply problematic' (ibid., p. 71). This leads us to a dilemma, because as the American philosopher Thomas Nagel sees it, 'the idea of global justice without a world government is a chimera' (Nagel, 2005, p. 115).

Sen too stresses the importance of global justice. The world beyond a country's borders, he argues, cannot but come into the assessment of justice in a country. He gives two reasons for this. First, what happens in a country, and how its institutions operate, 'cannot but have effects, sometimes huge consequences, on the rest of the world' (Sen, 2009, p. 71). Second, each country, or each society, 'may have parochial beliefs that call for more global examination and scrutiny' (ibid.). These parochial beliefs, such as the facts and values surrounding women's unequal position, or the acceptability of torture or of capital punishment, are probably better assessed in global rather than local discussions.

Advancing, rather than perfecting global justice

Sen presents a theory of justice in a very broad sense. The theory's aim is to clarify how we can proceed to address questions of enhancing justice and removing injustice, rather than to offer resolutions of questions about the nature of perfect justice. Thus, Sen supports *advancing*, rather than perfecting global justice. Sen regards this to be a clear departure from the pre-eminent theories of justice in contemporary moral and political philosophy.

Sen argues that there are two basic and divergent approaches to theories of justice. On the one hand, there is an approach concentrating on identifying just institutional arrangements for society, which relates to the 'contractarian' mode of thinking that Thomas Hobbes had initiated, and which was further pursued by John Locke, Jean-Jacques Rousseau, Immanuel Kant, and, as we have seen, Rawls. Sen calls this approach 'transcendental institutionalism'. On the other hand, there is a comparative approach that is concerned with social realizations (resulting from actual institutions, actual behaviour, and other influences). Different versions of such comparative thinking can be found in the works of, for example, Adam Smith, Jeremy Bentham, Karl Marx, and John Stuart Mill. Sen argues that they were all, in one way or another, involved in comparisons of societies that already existed or could feasibly emerge, rather than confining their analyses to transcendental searches for a perfectly just society. Sen calls this approach 'realisation-based comparison'. Those focusing on realization-based comparisons are often interested primarily in the removal of manifest injustice from the world that they saw.

Sen strongly supports the latter approach:

> This book is an attempt to investigate realisation-based comparisons that focus on the advancement or retreat of justice. It is, in this respect, not in line with the strong and more philosophically celebrated tradition of transcendental institutionalism ..., but more in the 'other' tradition that also took shape in about the same period or just after.
>
> (ibid., pp. 8–9)

Sen puts the type of question to be answered as the point of departure in formulating his theory of justice. Rather than asking 'what would be perfect just institutions? [as a contractarian would do]', one should be asking 'how would justice be advanced?' This departure has 'the dual effect, first, of taking the comparative rather than the transcendental route, and second, of focusing on actual realisation in societies involved, rather than only on institutions and rules' (ibid., p. 9).

The first problem with choosing the transcendental route (Sen's first point of departure) is that there may be no reasoned agreement at all on the nature of the 'just society'. Sen refers to this as the issue of the *feasibility* of finding an agreed transcendental solution. Even under 'strict conditions of impartiality and open-minded scrutiny' (as in Rawls' original position), there can be many legitimate claims for justice. Sen doubts that a single account of this kind is either possible or necessary. There are many possible theories of justice. To illustrate this point, he tells the engaging story of three children, Ann, Bob, and Carla, who are quarrelling over the fate of a flute (ibid., p. 12). Ann claims the flute on the basis that she is the only one who can play it; Bob claims it because he has no other toys to play with whereas the others do; and Carla's claim is based on the fact that she made the flute in the first place. All of these statements are taken to be true, and Sen's point is that one can produce intuitively plausible reasons for giving the flute to any one of the children. Utilitarians – and for different reasons, Aristotelians – would favour Ann,[15] egalitarians Bob, and libertarians Carla; however, the real point here is that there is no reason to assume, as Rawls and other contractarians do, that we have to decide which of these answers is the right one. Sometimes, there is simply a plurality of 'right' answers.

The second problem with the transcendental route is that in making actual choices, one 'demands a framework for comparison of justice for choosing among the feasible alternatives and not an identification of a possibly unavailable perfect situation that could not be transcended' (ibid., p. 9). Sen refers to this as the issue of the *redundancy* of the search for a transcendental solution. In practice, we measure one possible policy against another possible policy, and not against an ideal. Sen uses another simple analogy to make the point: if asked to say whether a Van Gogh or a Picasso is the better painting, it hardly helps to be told that Da Vinci's Mona Lisa is the best painting of all time. The point Sen is trying to make is clear, namely, that pursuing justice is actually about making comparisons; we ask ourselves whether this policy will make the world a somewhat better place as opposed to that policy, and an ideal world contributes very little, if anything, to this process of comparison.

Sen's second point of departure is 'to wit the need for a theory that is not confined to the choice of institutions, nor to the identification of ideal social arrangements' (ibid., p. 18). He calls for an understanding of justice based on the argument that justice cannot be indifferent to the lives that people can actually live. The importance of human lives, experiences, and realization, Sen underscores, cannot be replaced by information about institutions that exist and the rules that operate. This does not mean that Sen regards institutions and rules unimportant for people's lives. Indeed, Sen acknowledges that institutions and rules cannot but play a significant instrumental role in the pursuit of justice; they are part and parcel of the actual world as well. However, the realized actuality of people's lives goes well beyond institutions and rules, and 'includes the lives that people manage – or do not manage – to live' (ibid., p. 18).

Global imperatives

Sen pays particular attention to human rights. He asks: What exactly are human rights? Are there really such things? As we have mentioned in the introduction of this book, human rights and sustainable development are both normative value systems. Thus, one could correspondingly ask: What exactly is sustainable development? Is there really such a thing? Sen reminds us that the existence of human rights clearly is nothing concrete that we can see and examine (like, he suggests, the Big Ben in the middle of London). Nor are they like the existence of a legislated law in the statute book (though many aspects of human rights have been incorporated in legislation). Rather, human rights are 'really strong ethical pronouncements as to what *should* be done' (ibid., p. 357, italics in original). The same goes for sustainable development, we would argue. Sustainable development is a very strong ethical statement as to what should be done. Such ethical pronouncements, according to Sen, demand acknowledgement of imperatives that tell us that something needs to be done.

If we understand ethical pronouncements not exclusively as claims enshrined through legislation or common law,[16] Sen argues that two questions immediately arise: first, 'what is its content?' and, second, 'what is its viability?'

The question of *content* regards the ethical pronouncement made through the declaration of a human right. Referring to what is theorized and what is practically invoked, Sen argues that the content of human rights is about the importance of certain freedoms (like the freedom from torture, or the freedom to escape starvation) and correspondingly about the social obligations to promote or safeguard these freedoms. However, where does such a declaration come from? Sen claims that a declaration of an ethical pronouncement may come from people or from institutions. It can also be asserted by particular groups of people charged to examine these issues, such as the drafters of the French declaration of 'the rights of man' (1776) and the American Declaration of Independence (1789), or by the United Nations' committee that authored the United Nations of the Universal Declaration of Human Rights in 1948. In any case, what is being articulated or ratified is an ethical pronouncement – not a proposition about what is already legally guaranteed.

What, one could ask, is the declaration of sustainable development? Although sources of 'sustainable thinking' can be traced back to 'early modernity' in the seventeenth and eighteenth centuries (Caradonna, 2014),[17] it is the 1987 UN report *Our Common Future* that has 'declared' the concept and provided the global society with the legitimate content of sustainable development. Thus, the report is the cradle for the ethical pronouncement of sustainable development. Nothing, as we see it, has changed the status of *Our Common Future* as the declaration of the ethical pronouncements of sustainable development (though the practical implication may differ). Still, the UN (2015) declared that they are determined to 'support the needs of the present and future generations', 'protect the planet from degradation', and 'envisage respect for justice'.

The question of the *viability* of an ethical pronouncement is, according to Sen, about how we can judge the acceptability of them and assess the challenges they may face. In other words: How would such a disputation – or a defence – proceed? Sen's answer is (as always!) that all ethical propositions must survive open and informed scrutiny, which

> involves the invoking of an interactive process of critical scrutiny with open impartiality (including being open to information coming inter alia from other societies and to arguments coming from far as well as near), which allows disputations on the content.
>
> (Sen, 2009, p. 385)

Thus, a claim that a certain aspect (for example freedom) is important enough to be a part of an ethical pronouncement (for example human right) is also a claim that reasoned scrutiny would sustain that claim.

In practice, Sen argues, we do not have any actual worldwide undertaking of public scrutiny of ethical pronouncements such as human rights or sustainable development. Poor people, and in the case of sustainable development, nature and future generations, cannot for different reasons take part in public scrutiny. Then, we must act on the general belief that 'if such impartial scrutiny were to occur, the claims made would be sustained' (ibid., p. 386). Thus, the force of a claim for an ethical pronouncement would indeed be seriously undermined if it were possible to show that it is unlikely to survive open public scrutiny. Uncurbed critical scrutiny is, Sen states, essential for dismissal as well as for justification of any ethical pronouncement. We believe Sen underestimates the UN's (and other intergovernmental and international organizations') role when it comes to a worldwide scrutiny of sustainable development. Indeed, the sustainable development goals are an example of such worldwide scrutiny.

Sen recognizes that even with agreement on the content and viability of an ethical pronouncement, there can still be serious debate about the practical implications of this pronouncement. There can also be debate on how the different types of ethical pronouncements (for example, human rights, sustainable development, and democracy) should be weighed against each other and their respective demands integrated together. Thus, the general acceptance of an ethical pronouncement and its practical consequences 'leave room for further discussion, disputation and argument – that is indeed the nature of the discipline' (ibid., p. 386).

Equality, scrutiny, and democracy

What exactly is it that Sen suggests as the cornerstone in a theory of justice? As we saw in chapter 2, Sen is unenthusiastic about suggesting a defined list of capabilities (as Nussbaum does). When it comes to justice, he seems similarly unenthusiastic about suggesting some sort of list, not to mention something like Rawls' principles. Nevertheless, there are some distinct features in his theory that should be mentioned. (The importance of the comparative approach to that seeking perfect just institutions, the plurality of equally justifiable conceptions of justice, and the focus on people's actual lives are already mentioned and will not be repeated here.)

First, although justice is not the same as equality, it is closely related to the concept of equality. Sen is arguing neither for equality of welfare nor for equality of capability to achieve welfare. Still, Sen argues that every normative theory of social justice demands equality of *something* – something that is regarded as particularly important in that theory. The theories can be entirely diverse (focusing on, say, equal liberty or equal income …), and they may be in combat with each other, 'but they still have the common characteristics of wanting equality of *something*' (ibid., p. 291, italics in original).

Second, there is a need for reasoned argument, with oneself and with others, in dealing with justice and injustice. Sen refers to this as reasoned scrutiny. He does not argue that reasoned scrutiny provides some kind of guarantee of reaching the truth about justice and injustice. Indeed, even the most rigorous of searches, in ethics or in any other discipline, could still fail. Thus, Sen believes that the case for reasoned scrutiny lies not in any never-failing way of getting things exactly right (indeed no such way may exist), 'but on being as objective as we reasonably can' (ibid., p. 40).

Sen illustrates the importance of reasoned scrutiny in our neglect of the natural environment. The problem, he claims, does not arise from any desire of people today to hurt those yet to be born, or even to be deliberately unfeeling about the future generations' interests. And yet, 'through lack of reasoned engagement and action, we do still fail to take adequate care of the environment around us and the sustainability of the requirements of good life' (ibid., p. 48). To prevent catastrophes caused by human neglect, we need critical reasoned scrutiny. The fact that we are neglecting the natural environment and future generations leads some to find reliance on reasoning to be deeply problematic. But the difficulty here, Sen argues, comes from *bad* reasoning (for example that some people are easily overconvinced by their own reasoning and ignore counter-arguments), rather than from making use of reason. The remedy for bad reasoning lies in *better* reasoning, and it is indeed the job of reasoned scrutiny to move from the former to the latter.

Third, Sen regards that impartiality in the evaluation of social justice and societal arrangements is central to the understanding of justice. There are, however, two distinct ways of invoking impartiality. One the one hand, there is 'closed impartiality' where impartial judgements invoke only the members of a given society or nation for whom the judgements are being made. On the other hand, there is 'open impartiality'; the procedure of making impartial assessments can (and in some cases, Sen argues, must) invoke judgements, amongst others, from outside the focal group, to avoid parochialism of local perspectives. An example of open impartiality is Adam Smith's concept of the 'impartial spectator'. Here, impartiality requires, as he explains in *The Theory of Moral Sentiments*, the invoking of disinterested judgements of 'any fair and impartial spectator', not necessarily (indeed sometimes ideally not) belonging to the focal group.[18] Impartial views may come from far or from within a community, or a nation, or a culture. Smith argued, and Sen fully agrees, that there is room for – and need for – both.

Fourth, Sen's theory ends with democracy (which, Sen stresses, is indeed not a Western 'invention', but rather an ideal that has long traditions in many non-Western cultures). He sees democracy more generally in terms of 'the capacity to enrich reasoned engagement through enhancing informational availability and the feasibility of interactive discussions' (ibid., p. xiii). Moreover, democracy has to be judged not just by the institutions that formally exist, but also by the extent to which different voices from diverse sections of the people can actually be heard. This way of seeing democracy, Sen argues, can have an impact on the pursuit of it at the global level – not just within a nation-state.

Sen recognizes the central role of democracy for the understanding of justice. As we have seen, public reasoning is at the heart of Sen's idea of justice. New contributions in contemporary political philosophy suggest that public reasoning (that is, political participation, dialogue, and public interaction) is central in the understanding of democracy, as in 'government by discussion'. Thus, if the demands of justice can be assessed only with the help of public reasoning, and if public reasoning is constitutively related to the idea of democracy, then 'there is an intimate connection between justice and democracy, with shared discursive features' (ibid., p. 326).

There is, however, the older (and more formal) view of democracy, which characterizes it mainly in terms of elections and ballots: the Schumpeterian 'government by election'. And yet, Sen maintains, the understanding of democracy is no longer seen just in terms of the demands for public balloting. Sen acknowledges, however, that ballots do play a very important role even in the expression and effectiveness of the process of public reasoning, but they are not the only thing that matters. Indeed, the effectiveness of ballots themselves depends crucially on what goes with balloting, such as free speech, access to information, and freedom of dissent. Thus, balloting can be thoroughly inadequate on its own. Indeed, a great many dictators in the world have achieved gigantic electoral victories even without any overt coercion in the process of voting, mainly through suppressing public discussion and freedom of information, and through generating a climate of apprehension and anxiety. Such conditions would certainly lead to *bad* reasoning.

A conception of what is just or unjust is probably one of people's most fundamental characteristics. Indeed, injustice, whether experienced personally or by people around us, is something we strongly respond to at a very early age. Thus, although people might disagree about what justice is and how it should guide practical life, we all seem to have a capacity for a sense of justice. To ask whether a society is just is to ask how it distributes the things we value – income and wealth, duties and rights, powers and opportunities, offices and honours. A just society distributes these goods in a way we perceive as fair; it gives each person his or her dues. The hard questions begin when we ask what people are due, and why.

We have presented dominant theories of the imperatives of human needs (chapter 2) and social equity (this chapter). As we have seen, these two imperatives are interlinked. Aggravated social injustice fosters endemic poverty and reduces people's capability to satisfy their human needs. Equally important, a world in which social injustice is aggravated and poverty is endemic will always be prone to environmental deterioration. At some point, the deterioration of the environment reaches a state where we trespass environmental limits. Trespassing these limits further aggravates social injustice and poverty. Thus, respecting environmental limits is a prerequisite to satisfy human needs and to ensure social justice. Respecting environmental limits is the third imperative of sustainable development. In the next chapter, we will present theories that are fundamental to understanding the imperative of respecting environmental limits.

Notes

1 We have been inspired by the story of Pip and his felt injustice from Amartya Sen's *The Idea of Justice* (2009).

2 *Our Common Future* uses 'justice' and 'equity' interchangeably with no substantial difference between the two concepts. Neither do we.

3 *Our Common Future*, Annexe 1: Summary of Proposed Legal Principles for Environmental Protection and Sustainable Development Adopted by the WCED Experts Group on Environmental Law.

4 The teacher, interviewed by a French scholar of East Africa, Gerard Prunier, survived only because he happened to be away from his house when the killers arrived and murdered his wife and four of his five children.

5 The book was originally published in 1971. Here we refer to the 1999 revised version. In the revised version, Rawls made several changes to respond to criticism of the original work. He nevertheless still accepts his main outlines and defends the original book's central doctrines. If he were to write *A Theory of Justice* over again, as stated in the foreword of the revised version, he 'would not write a completely different book'.

6 John Stuart Mill, *On Liberty* (1859), ed. Stefan Collini (Cambridge, Cambridge University Press, 1989). Quotes in this section are from Sandel (2009).

7 Bentham notes that there are a variety of parameters along which we quantitatively measure pleasure; intensity is just one of those. His complete list is the following: intensity, duration, certainty or uncertainty, propinquity or remoteness, fecundity, purity, and extent.

8 All the Sidgwick quotes in this paragraph are taken from Driver (2014).

9 In *Justice as Fairness: A Restatement*, Rawls was more explicit than in *A Theory of Justice* as to how justice as fairness is to be understood: namely, 'as a political conception of justice rather than as a part of a comprehensive moral doctrine' (Rawls, 2001, p. xvi).

10 The primary good of self-respect is not directly linked to Rawls' two principles of justice. Rather it reflects justice as fairness at a more fundamental level. Rawls argues in fact that perhaps the most important primary good is that of self-respect (ibid., p. 386).

11 In his later works, for example *Political Liberalism* (Rawls, 1993) and *Justice as Fairness: A Restatement* (2001), Rawls changed the order of the two parts of the second principle, which, referring to their lexical ordering, is more appropriate.

12 Rawls argues that the main duty owed to future generations is the saving of sufficient material capital to maintain just institutions over time. Rawls calls this duty the 'just savings principle'.

13 Rawls put his principles in what he calls a serial or lexical order. This is an order that 'requires us to satisfy the first principle in the ordering before we can move on to the second, the second before we consider the third, and so on' (ibid., p. 38). Thus, a principle does not come into play until those previous to it are either fully met or do not apply. A serial ordering 'avoids, then, having to balance principles at all; those earlier in the ordering have an absolute weight, so to speak, with respect to later ones, and hold without exception' (ibid., p. 38).

14 The remark of Alexander Herzen is from Isaiah Berlin's introduction to Franco Venturi, *Roots of Revolution* (New York, Alfred Knopf, 1960), p. xx. For Kant, see 'Idea for a Universal History with a Cosmopolitan Purpose', in *Political Writings*, ed. Hans Reiss and trans. H. B. Nisbet (Cambridge, Cambridge University Press, 1970), p. 44. Quoted from ibid., footnote 21, p. 254.

15 A utilitarian would argue that the greatest happiness would come from listening to the flute in the hands of an expert, while an Aristotelian would argue that it was the *telos* of the flute, its purpose to be played as expertly as possible (Brown, 2010).

16 Sen has some important remarks on the legislative status of ethical pronouncements. Though he acknowledges the importance of the 'legislative route', he nevertheless asks whether that is all there is to human rights. Surely, he believes that the idea of human rights also can be – and indeed is – used in several other ways as well. Organizations such as Human Rights Watch, Amnesty International, and the Red Cross have enormous influence on promoting human rights. In such cases, legislation may not be involved at all. Thus, he argues that public monitoring and pressure can make a considerable difference. Therefore, he states that 'it is important to give the general ethical status of human rights its due, rather than locking up the concept of human rights prematurely within the narrow box of legislation – real or ideal' (ibid., p. 366).

17 Caradonna (2014) argues that 'sustainable thinking' could start in the Middle Ages, with the hunting reserves and protected forests established by European rulers in Venice and elsewhere. It could start with an analysis of indigenous societies, from Easter Island to the Maya, having failed to live sustainably and eventually collapsing (see chapter 4 in this book). It could even begin in antiquity, with Pliny the Elder and his encyclopaedic *Natural History*. But it is, Caradonna argues, in the early modernity that we find the clear linkages to the modern sustainability movement.

18 Adam Smith, *The Theory of Moral Sentiments* (1759; revised edn, 1790; republished, Oxford: Clarendon Press, 1976).

References

Brown, C. (2010) On Amartya Sen and the idea of justice. *Ethics & International Affairs*, 24(3), 309–318.

Caradonna, J. L. (2014) *Sustainability: A History*. Oxford, Oxford University Press.

Diamond, J. (2005) *Collapse: How Societies Choose to Fail or Survive*. London, Penguin Books.

Driver, J. (2014) The history of utilitarianism. *The Stanford Encyclopedia of Philosophy*. Available from: http://plato.stanford.edu/entries/utilitarianism-history/ [accessed 5 April 2017].

Friedman, M. (1980) *Free to Choose*. New York, Houghton Mifflin Harcourt.

Maffettone, S. (2010) *Rawls: An Introduction*. Cambridge, UK and Malden, US, Polity Press.

Nagel, T. (2005) The problem of global justice. *Philosophy and Public Affairs*, 33, 113–147.

Rawls, J. (1993) *Political Liberalism*. New York, Columbia University Press.

Rawls, J. (1999) *A Theory of Justice* (revised edition). Cambridge, MA, Belknap Press.

Rawls, J. (2001) *Justice as Fairness: A Restatement*. Kelly, E. (ed.). Cambridge, MA, Harvard University Press.

Sandel, M. K. (2009) *Justice. What's the Right Thing to Do?* New York, Farrar, Straus and Giroux.

Sandhu, S., McKenzie, S., & Harris, H. (eds) (2014) *Linking Local and Global Sustainability*. New York and London, Springer.

Sen, A. (2009) *The Idea of Justice*. London, Penguin.

UN (2015) *Transforming our World: The 2030 Agenda for Sustainable Development*. Resolution adopted by the General Assembly on 25 September 2015, A/RES/70/1. United Nations General Assembly.

WCED (1987) *Our Common Future*. World Commission on Environment and Development. Oxford, Oxford University Press.

Wenar, L. (2013) John Rawls. *The Stanford Encyclopedia of Philosophy*. Available from: http://plato.stanford.edu/archives/win2013/entries/rawls/ [accessed 5 April 2017].

Wolff, J. (2006) *An Introduction to Political Philosophy* (revised edition). Oxford, Oxford University Press.

4

RESPECTING ENVIRONMENTAL LIMITS

Lyrics in 'The Last Resort' by the American rock band The Eagles pinpoint the essence of environmental limits. They sing that there are no more new frontiers and that 'we have got to make it here'. Thus, at some point, there simply are no more environmental resources to extract and use, and there is no more environment in which to deposit our waste. At this point, the world will be simultaneously empty of resources and full of waste.

The Eagles were perhaps inspired by a famous photo of Earth when they wrote the song. 'The Blue Marble' was taken on 7 December 1972, by the crew of the Apollo 17 spacecraft. It is one of the most iconic and among the most widely distributed images in human history.[1] A large part of its lasting appeal surely has something to do with the fact that the photo of an almost perfectly round Earth, seen from a distance of about 28,000 miles, is so familiar. Whereas the Eagles' migrants were facing the frontier of the western US more than a century ago, 'The Blue Marble' dramatically showed that the global frontier is finite. Earth is what we have, and we have got to make it here.

To make it here, we need to understand the current state of the planet, and for that, we need facts. We also need to know how these facts can be translated into action and decisions. The timing of these decisions must reflect the complexity of the biosphere, our incomplete knowledge of the system, and the irreversible consequences of inaction.

This chapter gives an account of the status of global natural capital, how humans interact with and depend on these resources, and how we can define thresholds for critical natural capital to sustain the services of nature. An important message in this chapter is that there are planetary boundaries that we must respect to ensure a safe operating space for humans over time, and the most important boundaries are those related to climate change and biosphere integrity. This leads to a discussion of what parts of natural capital should be sustained for the future and the notions of weak and strong sustainability. We conclude the chapter by presenting some related views from the field of economics and discussing how they can help us understand, measure, and deal with environmental limits.

First, we recapture what *Our Common Future* (WCED, 1987) had to say about environmental limits.

Our Common Future on respecting environmental limits

Environmental limits play a critical role in the vision of sustainable development articulated in *Our Common Future*. The report emphasizes that 'the idea of limitations imposed by the state of technology and social organization on the environment's ability to meet present and future needs' represents one of the "key concepts" contained within the idea of sustainable development' (WCED, 1987, p. 42). At the core of this idea lies the requirement that 'at a minimum, sustainable development must not endanger the natural systems that support life on Earth: the atmosphere, the waters, the soils, and the living beings' (ibid., p. 44).

Our Common Future raises particular concern about limits at the global level. The authors argue that at this level, there are ultimate limits determined by the availability of energy resources and by the biosphere's capacity to absorb the by-products of energy use. Indeed, these energy limits may be approached far sooner than limits imposed by other material resources. The report refers to well-known issues such as the depletion of oil reserves, the high cost and environmental impact of coal mining, the hazards of nuclear technology, and the increased level of acid pollution and carbon dioxide emissions to support this view.

Our Common Future does not, however, set concrete limits in terms of resource use (or population) beyond which lies ecological disaster. The authors acknowledge that different limits hold for the use of energy, materials, water, and land. Optimistically, they think that many of these limits will manifest themselves in the form of rising costs and diminishing returns, rather than in the form of any sudden loss of a resource base. Moreover, and equally hopefully, they believe that the accumulation of knowledge and the development of technology can enhance the carrying capacity of the resource base. But, the report stresses, '*ultimate limits there are, and sustainability requires that long before these are reached*, the world must ensure equitable access to the constrained resource and reorient technological efforts to relieve the pressure' (ibid., p. 45, our italics).

Why was *Our Common Future* so concerned with environmental limits? The report's answer is that respecting environmental limits is a prerequisite for meeting basic needs for present and future generations. The report states that if basic human needs are to be met on a sustainable basis, Earth's natural base must be conserved. Unfortunately, human development tends to damage ecosystems, which reduces the number of species. Thus, the loss of plant and animal species can greatly limit the options of future generations. Therefore, the report argues that 'sustainable development requires the conservation of plant and animal species' (ibid., p. 46).

Interestingly, the outcome document from the 2012 UN Conference on Sustainable Development (UN, 2012) has almost no mention of environmental limits,[2] nor does the 2030 UN Agenda for Sustainable Development (UN, 2015). *Our Common Future*, on the other hand, incorporated the idea of limits in its proposed legal principles: 'States shall maintain ecosystems and ecological processes essential for the functioning of the biosphere, shall preserve biological diversity, and shall observe the principle of optimum sustainable yield in the use of living natural resources and ecosystems'.[3] Indeed, maintaining ecosystems and preserving biological diversity reflect the idea of limitations.

Two other messages from *Our Common Future* seem to have vanished over time. The first contains the idea that people in rich countries should reconsider their high living standard. Boldly, the report acknowledges that 'sustainable global development requires that those who are more affluent adopt life-styles within the planet's ecological means – in their use of energy, for example' (WCED, 1987, p. 9). The second message contains the moral responsibility that the present generation has both to future generations and to other species. Boldly, the report acknowledges that 'the case for the conservation of nature should not rest only with the development goals. It is part of our moral obligation to other living beings and future generations' (ibid., p. 57). Thus, notwithstanding the importance of preserving ecosystems to safeguard our needs, the report acknowledges that there are many other reasons why we should do so: 'But utility aside, there are also moral, ethical, cultural, aesthetic, and purely scientific reasons for conserving wild beings' (ibid., p. 13).

Though *Our Common Future*'s tone is somewhat gloomy, the report is not without hope. There is, the report argues, still time to save species and their ecosystems. Indeed, humanity 'has the ability to make development sustainable to ensure that it meets the needs of the present without compromising the ability of future generations to meet their own needs' (ibid., p. 8). The report leaves, however, no doubt about the utter importance of the work: 'Our failure to do so [that is, achieving sustainable development] will not be forgiven by future generations' (ibid., p. 166).

Planetary boundaries

Presently, the most promising take on stressing the importance of environmental limits and, moreover, on attempting to quantify these limits is the 'planetary boundary approach'. This approach originated in 2008 from a group of researchers at Stockholm Resilience Centre, Stockholm Environment Institute, and the Tällberg Foundation. Since then, the group has grown to include researchers from many institutes around the world, and the group's work has frequently been reported in high-ranking journals (e.g., Rockström *et al.*, 2009; Steffen *et al.*, 2015).

The planetary boundary research group made a preliminary effort to identify planetary boundaries in 2009 (Rockström *et al.*, 2009). They defined planetary boundaries as the safe operating space for humanity with respect to Earth's systems. They attempted to quantify the boundary level that should not be transgressed for each process to avoid unacceptable global environmental change. The researchers then defined unacceptable change in relation to the risks humanity faces in the planet's transition from the Holocene to the Anthropocene.

Nine planetary boundaries were proposed: climate change, ocean acidification, stratospheric ozone depletion, interference with the global phosphorus and nitrogen cycles, rate of biodiversity loss, global freshwater use, land-system change, aerosol loading, and chemical pollution. The researchers assessed that there was enough scientific evidence to make a preliminary attempt at quantifying control variables for seven of the boundaries. They thought the remaining two (aerosol loading and chemical pollution) should be included among the planetary boundaries, but they were unable to suggest quantitative boundary levels at that time.

In a more recent study, the group presents an updated list of planetary boundaries (Steffen *et al.*, 2015), in which the basic framework remains to define a safe operating space for humanity. Although the framework keeps the same boundaries, two of them have been given new names to better reflect what they represent. 'Loss of biodiversity' is now called 'Loss of biosphere integrity (biodiversity loss and extinctions)', and 'Chemical pollution' is 'Chemical pollution and the release of novel entities'. A brief description of each updated boundary and how we are doing in 2015 follows.[4]

Climate change: Atmospheric concentration of carbon dioxide should not exceed 350 ppmv (i.e., parts per million by volume). However, the levels are at 400 ppmv and climbing. We have almost certainly reached irreversible tipping points with respect to loss of summer polar sea-ice and destruction of the world's rainforests.

Loss of biosphere integrity (biodiversity loss and extinctions): We should maintain 90 per cent of biodiversity. However, biodiversity has dropped to 84 per cent in parts of the world such as Africa. The 2005 Millennium Ecosystem Assessment (MEA) concluded that changes to ecosystems due to human activities were more rapid in the past 50 years than at any other time in human history, increasing the risks of abrupt and irreversible changes.

Nitrogen and phosphorus flows to the biosphere and oceans: The worldwide use per year should not exceed 11 teragrams of phosphorus and 62 teragrams of nitrogen. The current uses exceed these limits. The biogeochemical cycles of nitrogen and phosphorus have been radically changed by humans as a result of many industrial and agricultural processes. Nitrogen and phosphorus are both essential elements for plant growth, so fertilizer production and application is of primary concern.

Land-system change: 75 per cent of the planet's original forests should be maintained. The current status is 62 per cent. Land is converted to human use all over the planet. Forests, grasslands, wetlands, and other vegetation types have been converted to agricultural land. This land-use change is a driving force behind serious reductions in biodiversity and has impacts on water flows and on the biogeochemical cycling of carbon, nitrogen, phosphorus, and other important elements.

Atmospheric aerosol loading: Emissions of aerosol (microscopic particles) into the atmosphere affect climate and living organisms. No global boundary has been set, but regional effects (such as on the South Asian Monsoon) occur when the Aerosol Optical Depth (AOD) is more than 0.25. AOD of more than 0.30 has been estimated for South Asia, but the levels are probably well below the boundary for other parts of the world.

Stratospheric ozone depletion: The boundary is set at 5 per cent below 290 Dobson Units. The levels are currently safely above this level, except over Antarctica during spring, when levels drop to 200 Dobson Units. The stratospheric ozone layer in the atmosphere filters out ultraviolet radiation from the sun. If this layer decreases, increasing amounts of ultraviolet radiation will reach ground level. This can cause a higher incidence of skin cancer in humans as well as damage to terrestrial and marine biological systems.

Ocean acidification: The boundary is defined as the point when the oceans become acid enough that the minerals sea creatures need to make shells begin to dissolve. Earth is within this limit. Around a quarter of the carbon dioxide that humans emit into the atmosphere is ultimately dissolved in the oceans where it forms carbonic acid, thereby altering ocean chemistry and decreasing the pH of surface water.

Global freshwater use and the global hydrological cycle: The boundary on use is set to 4000 cubic kilometres, and Earth is still within this boundary. The freshwater cycle is strongly affected by climate change and its boundary is closely linked to the climate boundary, but human pressure is now the dominant driving force determining the functioning and distribution of global freshwater systems.

Chemical pollution and the release of novel entities: The boundaries are unknown. Emissions of toxic and long-lived substances such as synthetic organic pollutants, heavy metal compounds, and radioactive materials represent some of the key human-driven changes to the planetary environment. These compounds can have potentially irreversible effects on living organisms and on the physical environment (by affecting atmospheric processes and climate).

According to Steffen *et al.* (2015), the first four of these boundaries have already been crossed. Crossing a boundary could well, according to the authors, drive the Earth system into a much less hospitable state, limit efforts to reduce poverty, and deteriorate human wellbeing in many parts of the world, including in wealthy countries.

Two of these, climate change and biosphere integrity, are what the researchers call 'core boundaries'. Each of the two core boundaries has 'the potential on its own to drive the Earth system into a new state should they [*sic*] be substantially and persistently transgressed' (Steffen *et al.*, 2015, p. 1). The crossing of one or more of the other seven boundaries is also problematic, but does not by itself lead to a new Earth system state.

Keep in mind that keeping within the limits of all of the planetary boundaries by no means implies that all socio-economic deficits or ecological damages can be averted. Indeed, these global boundaries cannot under any circumstances take account of all of the widely differing regional and sectoral impacts of global change. Furthermore, knowledge about global environmental change is still limited and potential for misjudgements exists. Thus, observance of the boundaries is a necessary, but not sufficient, premise for the sustainability of future development.

The environment and the economy

Humans interact with and depend on the environment. The environment provides ecosystem services necessary for human wealth, health, and general welfare as well as ecosystem services crucial for the survival of ecosystems and human beings. Below we present three ways of presenting these relations. We pay special attention to the role of the human economy, that is, how we use natural capital to produce products and services and the resulting wastes that must be absorbed by the environment. Although the concepts used and the perspectives chosen (anthropocentric versus biocentric) differ, there is no disagreement on how the ecosystems function in the three approaches. There is, however, disagreement on the ability of the human economy to adjust so that ecosystems can be sustained while maintaining economic growth.

The Millennium Assessment Reports *and ecosystem services*

During the last decade, the concept of 'ecosystem services' has been developed about the relationship between ecosystems and people. Although the concept has older roots,[5] the ecosystem services age starts with the 2005 *Millennium Assessment Reports* (MEA, 2005), which were created as an answer to UN Secretary-General Kofi Annan's call for the MEA.[6] The objective of the reports was to 'assess the consequences of ecosystem change for human well-being and to establish the scientific basis for actions needed to enhance the conservation and sustainable use of ecosystems and their contributions to human well-being' (ibid., p. ii). The *Millennium Assessment Reports* put ecosystem services firmly on the policy agenda, and since their release the literature on ecosystem services has grown exponentially (Gómez-Baggethun *et al.*, 2010).[7]

The *Millennium Assessment Reports* focused on three key concepts and the linkages between them: 'ecosystems', 'human well-being', and 'ecosystem services' (MEA, 2005). An ecosystem is a dynamic complex of plant, animal, and microorganism communities and the non-living environment interacting as a functional unit. Human wellbeing, according to the reports, has five main elements, including security, basic material for a good life, health, good social relations, and freedom of choice and action. Finally, ecosystem services are the benefits people obtain from ecosystems, which include the following types of services: provisioning services (such as food, water, timber, and fibre), regulating services (which affect climate, floods, disease, wastes, and water quality), cultural services (which provide recreational, aesthetic, and spiritual benefits), and supporting services (such as soil formation, photosynthesis, and nutrient cycling).

Environmental economics and the natural capital approach

Environmental economics takes an anthropocentric perspective on the relations between the environment and the economy and perceives the natural environment as a form of capital asset, or natural capital (see, for example, Atkinson *et al.*, 2012; Barbier, 2014; Ekins, 2014; Helm, 2015). Paul Ekins shows how the concept of sustainable development can be related to ecosystem services, saying that 'what needs to be sustained from the environment conceived as natural capital is the flow of benefits that humans derive from it' (Ekins, 2014, p. 56). The natural capital provides a range of benefits to the human economy and to human welfare through the operations of a wide range of 'environmental functions', or ecosystem services as the authors of the *Millennium Assessment Reports* prefer to call them.[8] Ekins distinguishes between four kinds of environmental functions or ecosystem services: the provisions of resources, the absorption and neutralization of wastes by nature's sinks (e.g., the atmosphere, oceans, and land), the generation of human welfare services (e.g., health, security, and recreational services), and the generation of life-support services, relating to ecosystem health and function such as the maintenance of a stable climate. Another useful distinction is between environmental 'functions for' humans and 'functions of' the environment. Whereas the first contributes to human economy and welfare, the second contributes to maintenance of the biosphere. Obviously, the functions for that directly benefit humans are more easily understood and valued than are the functions of. One simple reason for this is that scientific knowledge about the functions of the environment is uncertain and incomplete and provided to us for free.

To sustain the flow of benefits that humans derive from natural capital, we must maintain the environmental functions (i.e., the ecosystem services) at such levels that they will be able to both sustain their contributions to human benefits and maintain the biosphere. Maintaining renewable natural resources and ecosystems above critical thresholds requires capital maintenance, a monetary cost to keep physical units of the most critical natural resources intact. Obviously, our decisions of what to maintain and at what level are made under conditions of uncertainty, and failure to make the right decisions can entail irreversible consequences for the biosphere. We need to combine environmental science and social science to make the right decisions. The standards we set for maintenance will reflect to what extent we assume that different forms of natural capital are substitutable for each other.

Ecological economics and the finite biosphere

Ecological economics takes a biocentric perspective on the relations between the environment and the economy, and emphasizes that the biosphere is finite (see, for example, Daly, 2007). Growth in our use of natural resources is a product of growth in population and growth in per-capita resource use. This total resource use represents a flow from nature's sources through transformations of production and consumption within the economy and then back to nature as wastes in its sinks. Similarly, animals and humans consume food and return wastes to the environment. Most human wastes are recycled by biogeochemical processes powered by the sun. However, if the number of humans and the amount of their waste products 'are so large that the throughput necessary to maintain them requires inputs from nature's sources and output to nature's sinks at rates beyond nature's replenishing and absorptive capacities, then the throughput flow becomes ecologically unsustainable' (ibid., p. 9). Moreover, 'The economy is a subsystem of the larger ecosystem, and the latter is finite, non-growing, and materially closed' (ibid., p. 9).

There are clear similarities between how ecological economics, environmental economics, and the *Millennium Assessment Reports* portray the interaction between the environment and the economy. Still, their focuses differ, as do their advices on how to sustain the services from and of the environment (i.e., eco-services). We will return to these two strands of economics, but first we examine how social science answers a crucial question: How much nature should we sustain – all of it or just a part?

Substitution and sustainability

The human economy uses different forms of capital to produce goods and services. In mainstream economics (often referred to as neoclassical economics), this process is described by a production function in which the different forms of capital may be combined in different proportions; that is, they are substitutable for each other. In standard economic terms, the marginal rate of technical substitution of one form of capital for another is often assumed to be falling (i.e., substitutes are imperfect), but none is considered to be independently essential (i.e., complete complements) in the production of human welfare.[9] Consequently, the mainstream economics production function suggests that we can substitute natural capital with other forms of human-made capital, although it will become increasingly expensive.

Obviously, this model of capital, production, and welfare has its limitations as it applies to natural capital. As discussed above, there are essential goods and services for human welfare and survival that no combination of human-made, social, and organizational capital can deliver. Therefore, no scientists (including economists) believe in the full substitutability of natural capital. On the other hand, no scientists believe in the complete lack of substitutability of natural capital either. Rather, they take positions between these two extremes. Consequently, they reach different conclusions with respect to why, how, and to what extent natural capital should be preserved.

The concepts of strong and weak sustainability reflect the degree of substitutability between natural capital and other forms for capital (Pearce et al., 1990; Turner, 1993; Neumayer, 2013). In the book *Weak versus Strong Sustainability*, Eric Neumayer (2013) gives an overview of the literature on this topic and presents what he regards as two opposing paradigms of sustainability: 'weak sustainability' and 'strong sustainability'. Neumayer argues that weak sustainability can be interpreted as an extension to neoclassical welfare economics, particularly the theories developed by the economists Robert Solow and John Hartwick (see the subsection *Neoclassical economics and the environment* for more details on the contributions of Solow and Hartwick). These theories are based on the belief that what matters for future generations is the utility created by the aggregate stock of human-made, human, and natural capital (i.e., weak sustainability). The essence of strong sustainability, conversely, is that natural capital is regarded to be non-substitutable in the production of consumption goods (the 'source' side of the economy), in its capacity to absorb pollution (the 'sink' side of the economy), and as a direct provider of utility in the form of environmental amenities.

In *Sustainability: Principles and Practice*, Kerry R. Turner (1993, pp. 9–15) argues that there is a spectrum of interpretations ranging from 'very weak sustainability' (which assumes complete substitutability between natural capital and other capital types) to 'very strong sustainability' (which assumes no substitutability so that all natural capital must be conserved). Turner traces these two opposing positions to the techno-optimists and their anthropocentric perspective, and the deep ecologists and their biocentric perspective, respectively. Very strong sustainability means a constant or increasing stock of natural capital and the maintenance of all of the environmental functions to which it gives rise. As noted above, few would contend that all natural capital is non-substitutable, so that very strong sustainability has been called 'absurdly strong sustainability' (Daly, 1995, p. 49). Very weak sustainability means the overall stock of capital assets should remain constant over time, but it allows for the reduction of one asset as long as another capital asset (or assets) is increased to compensate for the reduction. Thus, every reduction of natural capital must be offset by an increase in some other form or forms of natural or human-made capital. This rule, which was originally developed for non-renewable natural capital by Hartwick (1977), is absurd when applied to renewable natural capital.

Most scientists take an intermediate position, in which some, but not all, natural capital should be sustained. However, there are theoretical reasons for not choosing a position close to very weak sustainability (Victor, 1991; Turner & Pearce, 1992; Dietz & Neumayer, 2007; Ekins, 2014). In essence, natural capital is fundamentally different from manufactured capital. First, manufactured capital is rarely irreversible;

that is, human capital or knowledge rarely is lost. However, species extinction, climate change, and combustion of fossil fuels are all examples of irreversible processes in nature. Second, manufactured capital often requires natural capital for its production but not vice versa; thus, manufactured capital cannot be a complete substitute for natural capital. Most importantly, some forms of natural capital provide basic life-support functions. Finally, we are largely uncertain or ignorant about the detrimental consequences and the lost opportunities of depleting natural capital. Consequently, we are highly averse to losses in natural capital.

We agree with Paul Ekins (2014, p. 60) that resolving this dispute of whether strong or weak sustainability is the right assumption should be an empirical rather than a theoretical or ideological matter. But, as Ekins emphasizes, strong sustainability is greatly preferred as the a priori position from a scientific methodology point of view. Under the assumption of weak sustainability, there is no difference between different forms of capital and the welfare they generate; therefore, they can all be expressed in the same monetary unit. Under the assumption of strong sustainability, the different types of capital must be kept distinct from each other to examine each type's particular contribution to welfare. Therefore, they cannot be measured in the same unit. In some cases, the welfare derived from one type of natural capital is fully commensurable with the welfare derived from another type of capital. Sustaining the aggregate capital stock is then sufficient to sustain welfare. In other cases, such substitution is not possible, and we must protect stocks of specific forms of natural capital to sustain welfare. The point made by Ekins, which we share, is that when starting with a strong sustainability perspective, it is possible to shift to the weak sustainability position where it is shown to be appropriate. It is not, however, possible to move in the other direction, that is, from weak to strong.

Neumayer (2013) argues that there are two different interpretations of strong sustainability in the literature. The first interpretation requires keeping the aggregate *value* of the total natural stock constant (see, for example, Barbier *et al.*, 1990; Hohmeyer, 1994). According to Neumayer, this interpretation is clearly at odds with the spirit of strong sustainability because it does not constrain substitutability within natural capital. He uses the following example to illustrate his point: 'It would be strange to assume that more man-made capital cannot substitute for a bigger hole in the ozone layer, but an increased number of whales can' (Neumayer, 2013, p. 26). In the second interpretation, strong sustainability is not defined in value terms, but instead calls for the preservation of the *physical stock* of those forms of natural capital that are regarded as non-substitutable, so-called critical natural capital (see, for example, Ekins, 2003a, 2003b, 2014). Although the second interpretation does not allow for any substitutability among different forms of critical natural capital, it does not imply keeping nature as it is. Rather, it calls for maintaining nature's environmental functions (Goodland, 1995; Hueting & Reijnders, 1998). We agree with the second interpretation of strong sustainability, and this position influences our discussion on the choice of indicators and corresponding thresholds for 'mitigating climate change' and 'safeguarding biosphere integrity' in chapters 5 and 6.

Environmental indicators expressed in monetary form assume weak sustainability. One example is the Index of Sustainable Economic Welfare (ISEW), first proposed by Daly and Cobb (1989), which seeks to improve on gross domestic product (GDP) as an indicator by adding various social and environmental benefits and costs. Another example is the World Bank's genuine saving indicator (World Bank, 2000, 2006), which seeks to express the change in total capital, including natural capital growth and destruction, in monetary terms. A strong sustainability assumption, on the other hand, requires a range of indicators that covers the main concerns related to selected critical natural capital. Although we appreciate this last line of reasoning (see chapter 6), we understand that translating environmental benefits, costs, and assets into monetary terms may send a strong message to politicians and other decision-makers. An approach that combines these two features – the strong sustainability assumption and the use of both monetary and physical units – is known as the capital approach. We discuss this approach below, but first we elaborate on the strengths and weaknesses of mainstream neoclassical economics.

Neoclassical economics and the environment

Neoclassical economics is designed to examine how scarcity of resources should affect human decisions. Lionel Robbins (1932, p. 15) provided perhaps the most commonly accepted current definition of economics: 'a science which studies human behaviour as a relationship between ends and scarce means which have alternative uses' (Backhouse & Medema, 2009). For example, a waterfall can be used to generate renewable electricity or it may alternatively be protected against such uses to yield direct benefits to observers and to preserve related ecosystems. According to economics, the social benefits and costs of each alternative must be compared to reach an optimal decision.

A central insight in neoclassical or mainstream economics is that there are mutual gains from transactions. Buying and selling products in a market benefits both buyers and sellers. Buyers pay a price that is less than what the product is worth to them; sellers receive a price which is above what it costs to produce the product. On the margin, the willingness to pay equals the cost to produce. Hence, in a perfect market, these transactions will maximize the total gains to producers and consumers, and the allocation of resources will be 'Pareto efficient', meaning that nobody can become better off without making someone else worse off.[10] Of course, there is no reason to assume that free markets will deliver an outcome that we consider just, but the logic of neoclassical economics says that we should let markets do their job, making efficient use of scarce resources, then use taxes and transfers to achieve equity.

Mitigating climate change

What if a transaction imposes costs on people who are not part of the exchange, for example, emitting carbon dioxide into the air? Arthur Cecil Pigou, whose book *The Economics of Welfare* is generally regarded as the origin of environmental economics, provided an elegant answer to that question (Pigou, 1932). People who generate such 'negative externalities' should pay a fee – what has come to be known as a 'Pigovian tax' – reflecting the costs they impose on others. The level of the tax should be set so that, for society, the marginal cost of reducing the emissions by one unit is equal to the marginal benefit, resulting in the socially desirable level of emissions.

A variant to taxes is a system of tradable emissions permits, or so-called cap-and-trade. In this model, a central authority (usually a governmental body) issues a limited number of permits to emit a specified pollutant, such as carbon dioxide. Polluters are required to hold permits in amounts equal to their emissions. Polluters that want to increase their emissions must buy permits from those who are willing to sell them.

Environmental economists agree that setting a price on carbon dioxide emissions – either through a tax or a cap-and-trade system – is the most efficient way of reducing emissions (see, for example, Stern, 2015). We agree that the very scale and complexity of carbon dioxide emissions requires a market-based approach. After all, almost any product or service provided by the market entails the consumption of some amount of carbon; consequently, mitigating these emissions solely by standards, regulations, prohibitions, public investments, or informational means seems to be an impossible task. Although environmental economists generally agree on how to mitigate carbon dioxide emissions, they very much disagree on how quickly these emissions should be reduced (Dietz & Stern, 2008; Nordhaus, 2008), a discussion we return to at the end of this chapter.

However, sometimes, imposing a price is not sufficient. Certain greenhouse gas emissions should be forbidden entirely. And, innovation in climate-friendly technologies may need active public ownership or centralized planning of city infrastructures. Thus, we acknowledge the need for using both the command-and-control policies (e.g., prohibitions, standards, regulations, and public investments) suggested by ecological economics and the market instruments (e.g., taxes, subsidies, auctions, and quotas) suggested by environmental economists.

Finally, mitigating climate change is not just about mitigating greenhouse gas emissions. Nature's ability to absorb emissions depends on how we safeguard biosphere integrity, a topic we turn to next.

Safeguarding biosphere integrity

Neoclassical economics may be less suited to deal with complex interactions in the biosphere. As mentioned above, the neoclassical economics production function suggests that natural capital and other forms of capital are substitutable and can therefore be expressed in a single monetary unit. The assumption of weak sustainability underlies the standard neoclassical economic approach to decision-making. To maximize utility, or social welfare, the various forms of capital should be allocated so that marginal costs of production equal marginal benefits from the goods and services consumed.

This kind of marginal approach may be less suited to address complex ecosystems where marginal changes may result in non-marginal and irreversible damage to environmental functions caused by the loss of ecosystems, habitats, and other critical components of natural capital. In these instances, the result of the damage is uncertain and possibly irreversible, long-term, and even catastrophic. Ecosystems are complex and a better understanding of how the economy and the ecosystems are interrelated is required. Because changes are often non-marginal and irreversible, marginal cost–benefit analysis does not apply (Victor, 1991). In addition, uncertainty may not be well described by probability distributions because we lack knowledge of what probabilities or even possible outcomes to apply. Moreover, there is also a lack of agreement about the appropriate discount rate to apply for intergenerational problems (Dietz & Stern, 2008; Nordhaus, 2008) and about the monetary values of human life, health, and various forms of natural capital (Foster, 1997; Kumar, 2010). Consequently, many of the inputs into social welfare maximization problems applied in standard economics are disputed, which undermines the approach's value as a decision support tool. One approach that deals with these critiques but that is still in line with basic economic reasoning is the natural capital asset approach, which we discuss next.

Natural capital asset approach

An alternative to the utility-based neoclassical economics framework is an asset-based approach to natural capital (see, for example, Ekins, 2014; Helm, 2015). Whereas the standard neoclassical economic approach would be to sustain the 'utility' from consuming products and services, the natural capital approach is to sustain the 'capital' that can generate future products and services. That is, to sustain the human welfare from consuming goods and services, *the stock of capital* that produces them must be sustained. In doing so, some natural capital can be destroyed or reduced as long as critical ecosystems, habitats, and species are sustained and the overall size of renewable natural capital is not reduced. Paul Ekins defines environmental sustainability so as to require 'the maintenance of important environmental functions and the natural capital which generates them' (Ekins, 2014, p. 57). This asset transfer will then enable the next generation to make the best use of their lives.

The natural capital approach resonates well with the Brundtland definition of sustainable development, which requires us to pass on a set of assets at least as good as the one we inherited. However, the Brundtland definition gives no guidance as to which assets should be bequeathed to the next generation to meet the criterion of being at least as good as the ones we inherited, but the literature on the natural capital approach does provide some answers.

Non-renewables

Depletion of *non-renewable* natural resources may be viewed as a pure intergenerational equity problem, at least if it is done without causing damaging pollution or changes in climate. As Dieter Helm (2015, p. 146) puts it: 'One generation uses the resources, and therefore another cannot. The question is how to compensate the future generations for the fact that the asset will no longer be there for them to use.' The 'Hartwick–Solow rule' refers to the depletion primarily of non-renewable natural capital and requires reinvestment of the economic rents from such a depletion. It defines the amount of investment in human-made capital (buildings, roads, knowledge stocks, etc.) that is needed to offset declining stocks of non-renewable resources (Solow, 1974; Hartwick, 1977). This investment is undertaken so that the standard of living does not fall as society moves into the indefinite future.

Norway, for example, applies Hartwick's rule when it sets aside part of its revenues from North Sea oil and natural gas operations in a sovereign wealth fund. Following Norway's example, the benefits from depleting non-renewable natural resources could be spread over many generations to come, but there are few such examples. Rather, resource-rich countries tend to spend their entire income from resource depletion and then get into serious problems when the resources are depleted (Helm, 2015).

Alternatively, revenues from depleting non-renewable resources could be invested in assets necessary to deliver social primary goods such as health, housing, education, energy, security, and democratic rights. Such investment may provide future generations with the 'institutions' and 'primary goods' to cover human needs, as emphasized by John Rawls (see chapter 3), as well as the 'capabilities' that enable them to lead the life they want, as emphasized by Amartya Sen (see chapter 2). Even so, the aggregate natural capital will be reduced.

A more radical version of Hartwick's rule is discussed by Dieter Helm in *Natural Capital: Valuing the Planet* (Helm, 2015). This rule says that the depletion of non-renewable natural capital should be compensated for by increasing renewable natural capital. For example, rents from oil and gas extraction could be invested in protecting the rainforest, investing in national parks, or maintaining specific species. Such a rule would keep the aggregate natural capital intact.

Reinvesting rents from depletion of non-renewable resources in human-made capital may be expressed in monetary terms. One method that captures the difference between total investment in some kinds of capital and total disinvestment in other types of capital has been labelled 'genuine savings'. These savings have been estimated for many countries by the World Bank and others (Hamilton & Atkinson, 2006). A positive value for a nation's genuine savings has been linked to the possibility of long-term economic sustainability (Asheim *et al.*, 2007).

We believe the above suggestions on how to manage non-renewable natural resources should be followed, that depletion of non-renewable resources is mainly an intergenerational equity problem, and that changes in total assets resulting from such depletion should be measured in monetary terms. However, we think a word of caution is warranted with respect to how fast we use non-renewable resources, especially with regard to our extraction of coal, oil, and natural gas. The following three precepts for environmental sustainability by the ecological economist Herman E. Daly (2007, p. 14) nicely sums up our thinking in this respect:

1   Limit use of all resources to rates that ultimately result in levels of waste that can be absorbed by the ecosystem.
2   Exploit renewable resources at rates that do not exceed the ability of the ecosystem to regenerate the resources.
3   Deplete non-renewable resources at rates that, as far as possible, do not exceed the rate of development of renewable substitutes.

Renewables

Managing *renewable* natural resources is far more challenging. These resources provide ecosystem services in perpetuity and for free, provided the stocks are not driven so low that they are no longer capable of reproducing themselves. Also, many of the ecosystem services are 'functions of' the environment rather than 'functions for' human economies, as discussed above. Thus, it is easy to take them for granted and to undervalue them. Furthermore, renewable natural resources may be part of complex ecosystems, where damage to one part of the system may have irreversible, permanent, and large consequences. Moreover, we are almost always ignorant about both the cost and the value of these ecosystems.

Paul Ekins (2014) says that we should sustain important environmental functions and the natural capital that generates them. However, not all natural capital is equally important. Ekins draws attention to *critical natural capital* that generates environmental functions crucial for the maintenance of health and the avoidance of substantial threats, such as climate stability, and whose destruction would be permanent and irreversible (Ekins, 2003b). Similarly, Helm (2015) emphasizes that special attention should be paid to protecting critical ecosystems and renewable natural capital that is approaching critical thresholds. Consequently, these economists use the second interpretation of strong sustainability where the focus is on the preservation of the *physical stock* of those forms of natural capital that are regarded as non-substitutable. In doing so, they do not delimit their attention to particular elements of natural capital, but acknowledge the interaction between these elements in ecosystems necessary to generate critical environmental functions.

The first challenge is to determine which environmental functions are 'critical'. Instead of assigning a cost and a benefit to the maintenance of environmental functions and conducting a traditional cost–benefit analysis, economists using the natural capital approach suggest that we focus on the fundamental importance of selected environmental functions, such as maintaining human health, avoiding threats entailing unpredictable large costs and irreversible consequences, and maintaining ecological resilience (De Groot *et al.*, 2003; Brand, 2009; Ekins, 2014; Helm, 2015).

The second challenge is to measure how exposed each of these functions is to destruction and what it will cost to maintain them. Ekins (2014) suggests that we first find indicators that measure the status of critical natural capital in physical terms and then define standards which the indicator values must satisfy to maintain the selected environmental functions. The difference between the current status and the standard can be measured in physical terms as a *physical sustainability gap*. Assuming that this gap does not represent an irreversible effect, it will be possible to reduce the gap through abatement or avoidance activities for environmental pressures (e.g., mitigating carbon dioxide emissions and regulating hunting and harvesting activities) or restoration activities for environmental states (e.g., planting trees to fight desertification). These activities may have a cost, and hence a physical sustainability gap for a specific environmental function may be related to a *monetary sustainability gap*, which can be aggregated to a national gross measure.[11, 12]

Paul Ekins' focus on identifying standards is equivalent to Dieter Helm's (Helm, 2015) focus on identifying thresholds. Helm admits that such thresholds do not represent optimal values. However, he takes a pragmatic stance and argues (ibid, p. 73): 'the aggregate natural capital rule is so far from being met that it is this constraint that should be applied now. If it turns out to be possible to go beyond it … this would be a bonus.' Thus, his line of reasoning is not that far from that of Rockström *et al.* (2009), who seek to define the 'safe operating space for humanity' or our argument for defining a 'sustainable development space'. Moreover, these natural capital approaches provide for the use of both physical and monetary measures, where the latter are useful in a political context and the former satisfies Neumayer's (2013) strong sustainability requirement. Also, as Ekins (2014) notes, this approach avoids many of the limitations of aggregate indicators identified by Pillarisetti and van den Bergh (2010) in their analysis of the World Bank's genuine saving indicator (World Bank, 2000, 2006), the ecological footprint (see, for example, WWF, 2016) and the environmental sustainability index.[13] It does not assume substitutability (the genuine saving indicator does), it depends on the carrying capacity of Earth (the Ecological Sustainability Index doesn't), and it avoids the methodological problems of ecological footprints.

Irreversibility, risk, and uncertainty

Environmental decisions may have uncertain and irreversible consequences. Thus, analyses based upon the simplifying assumption that we have perfect knowledge about the future and that we can reverse the impact of decisions made today will result in flawed policy advice. Below we present theories and related concepts that show how recognition of irreversibility, risk, and uncertainty should influence policy decisions that affect the climate and biosphere integrity.

Knight (1921) makes a useful distinction between the concepts of risk and uncertainty. According to him, situations involving risk are those where the possible consequences of a decision can be completely enumerated and probabilities can be assigned to each possibility. If this is not possible, we are dealing with uncertainty.

Decision-making in the face of risk is covered in standard microeconomic textbooks like Mankiw (2015) and in environmental economic textbooks like Tietenberg (2006) and Perman *et al.* (2011). Individuals are assumed to be risk averse, which means that a sure amount will always be preferred over a risky gamble having the same expected value. People make decisions by maximizing expected utility and risk aversion is captured by assuming that the utility function exhibits diminishing marginal utility. Thus, the utility gain from consuming one unit more is less in magnitude than the utility loss from consuming one unit less, and this asymmetry reflects humans' risk aversion. The cost of risk bearing can be measured as the difference between the expected value of the risky gamble minus the sure amount that you would accept as equivalent to take part in the gamble (i.e., the certainty equivalent). Applied to policy decisions with risky environmental consequences, it follows that society has to be compensated for the cost of bearing risk. Simply making decisions where expected benefits equal expected costs, such as standard cost–benefit analysis suggests, will not suffice.

Options theory yields further insights into environmental decision-making in the face of risk and irreversibility. Weisbrod (1964) examined the decision to close down a national park, a decision that would drive the value of the wilderness amenity services down to zero. He argued that the value of keeping the park open would be understated by a measure of the known benefit to current visitors, and that an additional measure capturing the uncertainty of the benefits to potential future visitors, which he coined the 'option value', should be added. Cichetti and Freeman (1971) demonstrated that Weisbrod's insights were correct, that an option value exists separately from consumer surplus, when the decision to close down a park is irreversible, future demand for (or supply of) national park services are uncertain, and individuals are risk averse. Consequently, the park should be closed only if the benefit of land development exceeds the consumer surplus of current visitors plus an option value reflecting the cost of risk bearing.

Even when individuals are risk neutral, an option value may exist in Weisbrod's example of land preservation. Assuming future generations will value wilderness amenity services relatively more than inputs to and outputs from development, and a closure of the park will have irreversible consequences, the park should be closed only if the benefit of land development exceeds the consumer surplus of current visitors and an option value reflecting the (expected) growth in future preservation benefits. Krutilla and Fisher (1975) introduced important and persuasive arguments for the relative value of wilderness amenity services. And, as argued in Perman *et al.* (2011, p. 462),

> At least on a timescale relevant to human decision making, the assumption that once lost, the benefits of wilderness preservation are lost for ever appears to be a reasonable approximation to the relevant stylised facts of wilderness development. A decision in favour of preservation, on the other hand, is clearly reversible.

The ability to acquire knowledge and information over time, may also add to the option value of preserving the wilderness even if individuals are risk-neutral. Arrow and Fisher (1974) argued that, with the prospect of improved information, 'the expected benefits of an irreversible decision should be adjusted to reflect the loss of options it entails' (p. 319).

By incorporating risk and irreversibility, options theory provides a more nuanced analysis of biodiversity value and species preservation than does traditional neoclassical economic analysis. For instance, Kassar and Laserre (2003) investigate species preservation in a two-species model where the resources are substitutable, their future values are uncertain, and a biodiversity loss is irreversible. They find that increased uncertainty about the future uses of a species raises its biodiversity value (i.e., option value) and hence the argument for its preservation. A negative correlation between the value of a species and the value of other species raises its biodiversity value further because of its higher probability to be available for substitution if the value of the species in use diminishes.[14]

Pindyck (2007) points to three characteristics of environmental policy issues that make them different from other private and public policy decisions. First, environmental cost and benefit functions tend to be highly non-linear; that is, damage caused by greenhouse gas emissions or reductions of ecosystems may become severe or catastrophic once some (uncertain) threshold is reached. Second, environmental policies often involve important irreversibilities (i.e., sunk costs or benefits). On one hand, environmental policies impose sunk costs on society, such as installing scrubbers in a coal-burning utility or paying carbon taxes. On the other, environmental policies impose sunk benefits on society by preventing environmental damage that is partly or totally irreversible. By ignoring sunk policy costs/benefits, standard cost–benefit analyses will bias decisions in favour of too early/late policy intervention. The net effect depends on the nature and extent of the uncertainties over costs and benefits, and how these uncertainties are likely to be resolved over time. Environmental policies also often involve very long time horizons, making uncertainty over costs, benefits, and discount rates even more important. Pindyck demonstrates how the characteristics discussed above make conventional cost–benefit analysis based on expected values less suitable for environmental policy issues and concludes that using an option analysis approach will result in an environmental policy that is often more 'precautionary' in the sense of favouring earlier and more intense intervention.

Many environmental decision-making problems, such as mitigating climate change and safeguarding biosphere integrity, are characterized by uncertainty and not risk. That is, it may be impossible to assign probabilities for different outcomes of a decision based on prior knowledge. Without a probability distribution to define risk, we cannot derive an optimal decision rule. Inspired by game theory, a number of other rules have been suggested. These can be illustrated with reference to a 'pay-off matrix', which presents the pay-offs associated with each combination of policy and state of nature. The 'maximax' rule focuses on the best pay-offs under each policy and chooses the policy that yields the maximum pay-off. The 'maxmin' rule focuses on the worst pay-off under each policy and chooses the policy that yields the maximum minimum value. The 'minimax regret' rule focuses on the biggest difference in pay-offs under each state and chooses the strategy that yields the minimum of these regrets. Obviously, each of these rules suffers from weaknesses because they focus on only one part of the information provided in the pay-off matrix.

However, assuming risk aversion exists, a rule that reduces the chances of loss may often be preferable to one that increases the chances of gain. Interestingly, this is precisely the argument used by John Rawls for applying the 'maxmin' rule in *A Theory of Justice* (Rawls, 1999, pp. 130–139). Referring to the 'original position', where the parties have no basis for determining the probable nature of their society, or their place in it, and assuming the parties are risk averse, Rawls argues that a 'maxmin' rule should be used (see chapter 3 for a presentation of Rawls' theory of justice).

A more radical kind of uncertainty may exist where the decision-maker is not even able to list all of the possible outcomes of a decision. Emissions of greenhouse gases to levels with which we have no prior experience and depletion of important ecosystems such as rainforests are examples of such decisions. As argued by Bishop (1978), species extinction involves an irreversible reduction in the stock of potentially useful resources. We are socially ignorant about future preferences, needs, and technologies in this instance, and we are scientifically ignorant about how existing species can relate to future social possibilities and needs. As pointed out by Perman *et al.* (2011, p. 473), 'the species that may become extinct may turn out to be one for which there is no substitute'. Thus, radical uncertainty strengthens the case for preservation. As Martin Weitzman has argued in several influential papers on environmental risk, using climate change as the prototype example (see, for example, Weitzman, 2009), if there is a significant chance of utter catastrophe, that chance – rather than what is most likely to happen – makes the most powerful case for strong climate and environmental policies.

One way to proceed is to apply the 'safe minimum standard of conservation' (SMS) according to which all projects and decisions that could entail species extinction should be rejected. This is a very conservative rule, in line with the very strong sustainability position discussed above. It means we should maintain nature exactly as it is without considering any foregone gains, however large, from alternative uses of the natural resources.

A modified SMS has been proposed in which the strategy ensures the survival of a species, unless it entails unacceptably large costs. One may view the modified SMS as a constraint on standard cost–benefit analyses: environmental policy decisions should in general be determined using an efficiency criterion (i.e., a social cost–benefit analysis) but subject to the overriding constraints that a modified SMS provides. Closely related to the SMS is 'the precautionary principle' as referred to in the 1992 Rio Declaration: 'Where there are threats of serious or irreversible damage, lack of full scientific certainty shall not be used as a reason for postponing cost-effective measures to prevent environmental degradation.'[15] Unfortunately, there is no reference to the precautionary principle in the current UN Sustainble Development Goals (UN, 2015), and the issues of risk, uncertainty, and irreversibility are hardly mentioned.[16]

Sustainability and the role of economic growth

In the foreword to *Our Common Future*, Gro Harlem Brundtland says: 'What is needed now is a new era of economic growth – growth that is forceful and at the same time socially and environmentally sustainable.' The authors of the report suggest 'reviving growth' in developing countries to avoid the downward spiral of poverty, inequality, and environmental degradation; they also suggest 'changing the quality of growth' to make it less material- and energy-intensive and more equitable. They conclude that economic growth can be an important means to achieve sustainability.[17]

In 1992, the international community gathered in Rio de Janeiro, Brazil, to operationalize the concept of sustainable development. The Rio Declaration on Environment and Development (UN, 1992a) and Agenda 21 (UN, 1992b) did, by explicitly referring to the economic, social, and environmental dimensions of sustainable development, pave the way for the popular three-pillar model: consisting of three pillars, sustainable development seeks to achieve, in a balanced manner, economic development, social development, and environmental development.[18] This operationalization had two implications. First, economic growth is presented not as a means for achieving sustainable development, but as a part of the sustainability concept (or goal) itself, on a par with the social and environmental dimensions. Second, by balancing the three dimensions, it is accepted that environmental and social values may be traded off against economic values. Thus, there is no focus on absolute limits or thresholds beyond which we shall not go. The three-pillar model has become the most powerful and influential interpretation of sustainable development, and its logic is reflected in the 'triple bottom line' accounting framework for businesses developed by John Elkington in 1994 (Elkington, 1997, 2004) and in the UN Sustainable Development Goals for 2030.[19]

Treating economic growth as part of the sustainable development goal is in conflict with *Our Common Future*, which states:

> Sustainable development clearly requires economic growth in places where such [human] needs are not being met. Elsewhere, it can be consistent with economic growth, provided the content of growth reflects the broad principles of sustainability and non-exploitation of others. But growth by itself is not enough.
>
> (WCED 1987, p. 44)

In this context, economic growth must be considered as having a *contingent* relationship to sustainable development.

We argue that economic growth should not be a part of the three-pillar model of sustainable development. It is true that economic growth may contribute to more sustainable development by improving social welfare, satisfying human needs, and lifting people out of poverty, but economic growth may also reduce social equity by contributing to income and wealth inequality (Piketty, 2014; Atkinson, 2015). It is true that economic growth may bring about the technological solutions needed to mitigate greenhouse gases and adapt to climate change (Stern, 2015), but economic growth may also contribute to less sustainable development by increasing greenhouse gas emissions and by overexploiting species and resources for human use. Thus, economic growth is neither inherently sustainable nor inherently unsustainable. Economic growth may be part of the solution or it may contribute to the problem, or both. It depends on the policies, laws, regulations, and institutions in place; it depends on our creativity in developing new technologies and new behavioural patterns that meet the requirements of sustainable development; and it depends on our willingness to adjust.

We argue that sustainability should be interpreted as a set of constraints on human behaviour, including economic activities. That is, we have to act in a way that satisfies human needs, ensures social justice, and respects environmental limits. We already exceed environmental limits, income and wealth are unevenly distributed, and extreme poverty exists so such constraints are needed. A well-designed tax and subsidy policy, including policy instruments such as auctions and tradable quotas, can help an economy stay within sustainability constraints. However, market-based policies must be complemented with command-and-control policies where authorities regulate human activities and/or provide the necessary institutions and infrastructure for the economy to work as intended. For example, for many environmental resources and services, markets do not (and should not) exist, and many of the social sustainability goals cannot be met solely through the use of markets. Imposing constraints on an economy will make it grow at a slower rate in the short run, but in the long run, such constraints will ensure a better use of human and natural resources, thus sustaining long-term economic growth at a higher level.

We take a neutral stance on whether economic growth is consistent with sustainable development. Economic growth may or may not be part of a sustainable development path. It depends on how successful we are in inventing radically new technologies, changing our behaviours, controlling population growth, and using economic growth to eradicate poverty and ensure social justice. Time will show. In the meantime, the sustainable development literature should focus more on defining what sustainable development is and how to meet its requirements and less on guessing how much the economy can grow and still be deemed sustainable.

In this chapter, we have presented the current status of knowledge about global natural capital, how humans interact with and depend on these resources, and how to make policy decisions when the environmental problems to be solved are complex and decisions (including decisions to do nothing) have uncertain and possibly irreversible consequences. We conclude that the most important environmental challenges are related to climate change and biosphere integrity and suggest that related thresholds must be set that reflect the 'precautionary principle' in the sense of favouring earlier and more intense intervention rather than conventional cost–benefit analysis.

Having presented the dominant theories of the imperatives of human needs (chapter 2), social justice (chapter 3), and environmental limits (chapter 4), the next step is to develop a normative model of sustainable development that links imperatives and theories to indicators and thresholds, that is, describes a sustainable development space within which humans can safely operate. The structure of this model is described in chapter 5, and its individual components are discussed in chapter 6.

Notes

1　The first photographs of Earth from space were taken on 24 October 1946. The black-and-white photos were taken at an altitude of 65 miles by a 35-millimetre motion picture camera riding on a V-2 missile launched from the White Sands Missile Range. The V-2 photos showed for the first time 'how our Earth would look to visitors from another planet coming in on a space ship' (www.airspacemag.com/space/the-first-photo-from-space-13721411/?no-ist, accessed 21 January 2016).

2　There is one reference to limits in the outcome document referring to the *local* capacity to deal with hazardous waste.

3　*Our Common Future*, Annexe 1: Summary of Proposed Legal Principles for Environmental Protection and Sustainable Development Adopted by the WCED Experts Group on Environmental Law. General Principles, Rights, and Responsibilities; Conservation and Sustainable Use (WCED, 1987, p. 347).

4　www.stockholmresilience.org/research/planetary-boundaries/planetary-boundaries/about-the-research/the-nine-planetary-boundaries.html, accessed 11 February 2017. See also http://ideas.ted.com/the-9-limits-of-our-planet-and-how-weve-raced-past-4-of-them/, accessed 11 February 2017.

5　The origins of the modern history of ecosystem services are found in the late 1970s (Gómez-Baggethun *et al.* 2010). It starts with the utilitarian framing of beneficial ecosystem functions as services to increase public interest in biodiversity conservation. It then continues in the 1990s with the mainstreaming of ecosystem services in the literature and with increased interest on methods to estimate their economic value (see, for example, Costanza *et al.*, 1997).

6　The MEA was initiated in 2001 and was conducted under the auspices of the United Nations. The MEA was carried out between 2001 and 2005.

7　Ecosystem services are reported in *Global Biodiversity Outlook*, which is the flagship publication of the Convention on Biological Diversity. Action 5 of the EU Biodiversity Strategy to 2020 calls for Member States to map and assess the state of ecosystems and their services in their national territory with the assistance of the European Commission. The Economics of Ecosystems and Biodiversity's principal objective is to mainstream the values of biodiversity and ecosystem services into decision-making at all levels. The establishment of the Intergovernmental Platform on Biodiversity and Ecosystem Services

(IPBES) was another breakthrough for the ecosystem services concept. IPBES was established in April 2012, as an independent intergovernmental body open to all member countries of the United Nations. The members are committed to building IPBES as the leading intergovernmental body for assessing the state of the planet's biodiversity, its ecosystems, and the essential services they provide to society. The Ecosystem Services Partnership (ESP), launched in 2008, is a worldwide network to enhance the science and practical application of ecosystem services. ESP is (since 2012) associated with *Ecosystem Services*, an international, interdisciplinary journal that deals with the science, policy, and practice of ecosystem services.

8 Heuting (1980) was first to use this concept in economic analysis. He defined environmental functions as 'possible uses' of the environment (p. 95).

9 The production functions can be modelled in various ways. Perhaps the most popular version is the Cobb-Douglas production function in which the two forms of capital are imperfect substitutes, $F = AK^a L^\beta$, and the marginal rate of technical substitution (MRTS) is given by $MRTS = \dfrac{\partial F/\partial K}{\partial F/\partial L} = \dfrac{\alpha}{\beta}\dfrac{L}{K}$. Consequently, when capital K approaches 0, MRTS approaches infinity, and vice versa. Its popularity stems from its attractive mathematical characteristics, such as diminishing marginal returns to each factor of production. However, it has been criticized for its lack of a theoretical micro foundation.

10 The Pareto principle states that a change should be made if it leaves at least one person better off and no one worse off in utility terms. The first fundamental theorem of welfare economics connects this with a perfectly competitive general equilibrium.

11 This monetary sustainability gap can be measured by compiling an ascending marginal abatement cost curve for the technologies needed to reach the sustainability standard (see Enkvist *et al.* (2007) for an application to carbon dioxide mitigation, global and national). Consequently, the monetary sustainability gaps can be aggregated to a national gross measure and divided by national GDP to get a ratio that indicates the intensity of environmental monetary unsustainability.

12 Ekins (2014) argues that it is possible to identify indicators and set standards for most source and sink functions and sometimes for the life-support and human health and welfare functions. Some may be related to local impacts (e.g., critical loads for a particular ecosystem), some to national impacts (e.g., air quality standards for human health), and other to global impacts (e.g., greenhouse gas emissions consistent with climate stability). These standards may be expressed in terms of state or pressure indicators, where the former shows the minimum threshold of the natural capital stock that is necessary for the function to be maintained, and the latter shows the maximum pressure that the natural capital stock can withstand, while maintaining the function.

13 Available from: http://sedac.ciesin.columbia.edu/data/collection/esi/, accessed 13 February 2017. The environmental sustainability index (ESI) was published between 1999 and 2005 by Yale University's Center for Environmental Law and Policy in collaboration with Columbia University's Center for International Earth Science Information Network (CIESIN), and the World Economic Forum. Due to a shift in focus by the teams developing the ESI, a new index was developed in 2006, the Environmental Performance Index (EPI).

14 For an interesting discussion of the uncertain benefits of current species, see the presentation by Cary Fowler at Ted Talk: www.ted.com/talks/cary_fowler_one_seed_at_a_time_protecting_the_future_of_food.

15 The Rio Declaration (UN, 1992a) is a set of 28 short, non-binding, statements of principle unanimously adopted at the United Nations Conference on Environment and Development that took place in Rio de Janeiro in June 1992.

16 A search in the document (UN, 2015) shows among the 17 goals and their corresponding 169 targets, the concepts 'uncertainty' and 'irreversibility' were never mentioned while the concept 'risk' was mentioned only twice, relating to health (goals 3.8 and 3d) and disaster management in cities (goal 11b).

17 The report suggests 'reviving growth' and 'change the quality of growth' as two of seven imperatives leading to sustainable development paths. See part III 'Strategic imperatives' in *Our Common Future*.

18 The Rio Declaration does not explicitly mention the three-pillar model, but it presents the pillars using the concept 'dimensions'. The definition of the three-pillar model presented here is a quote from the official webpage for the General Assembly for the United Nations. Available from: www.un.org/en/ga/president/65/issues/sustdev. shtml, accessed 31 January 2017.

19 One of the 17 UN goals is devoted to economic growth, stating: 'Promote inclusive and sustainable economic growth, employment and decent work for all.'

References

Arrow, K. & Fisher, A. C. (1974) Environmental preservation, uncertainty and irreversibility. *Quarterly Journal of Economics*, 88, 313–319.

Asheim, G. B., Buchholtz, W., Hartwick, J. M., Mitra, T., & Withagen, C. (2007) Constant saving rates and quasi-arithmetic population growth under exhaustible resource constraints. *Journal of Environmental Economics and Management*, 53(2), 213–229.

Atkinson, A. B. (2015) *Inequality*. Cambridge, MA, Harvard University Press.

Atkinson, G., Bateman, I., & Mourato, S. (2012) Recent advances in the valuation of ecosystem services and biodiversity. *Oxford Review of Economic Policy*, 28, 22–47.

Backhouse, R. E. & Medema, S. G. (2009) Retrospectives: On the definition of economics. *Journal of Economic Perspectives*, 23(1), 221–233.

Barbier, E. (2014) Ecosystems as assets. In: Atkinson, G., Dietz, S., Neumayer, E., & Agarwala, M. (eds) *Handbook of Sustainable Development*. Cheltenham, UK and Northampton, MA, Edward Elgar, pp. 72–89.

Barbier, E., Pearce, D. W., & Markandya, A. (1990) Environmental sustainability and cost-benefit analysis. *Environment and Planning A*, 22(9), 1259–1266.

Bishop, R. C. (1978) Endangered species and uncertainty: The economics of a safe minimum standard. *American Journal of Agricultural Economics*, 60, 10–18.

Brand, F. (2009) Critical natural capital revisited: Ecological resilience and sustainable development. *Ecological Economics*, 68(3), 605–612.

Cichetti, C. J. & Freeman, A. M. (1971) Option demand and consumer surplus: Further comment. *The Quarterly Journal of Economics*, 85(3), 528–539.

Costanza, R., d'Arge, R., de Groot, R., Farber, S., Grasso, M., Hannon, B., Limburg, K., Naeem, S., O'Neill, R. V., Paruelo, J., Raskin, G. R., Sutton, P., & van der Belt, M. (1997) The value of the world's ecosystem services and natural capital. *Nature*, 387, 253–260.

Daly, H. E. (1995) On Wilfred Beckerman's critique of sustainable development. *Environmental Values*, 4, 49–55.

Daly, H. E. (2007) *Ecological Economics and Sustainable Development*. Selected Essays of Herman Daly. Cheltenham, UK and Northampton, MA, Edward Elgar.

Daly, H. E. & Cobb, J. (1989) *For the Common Good: Redirecting the Economy Towards Community, the Environment and a Sustainable Future*. Boston, Beacon Press (UK edition 1990, London, Green Print, Merlin Press).

De Groot, R., Van der Perk, J., Chiesura, A., & Van Vliet, A. (2003) Importance and threat as determining factors for criticality of natural capital. In: Ekins. P., de Groot, R., & Folke, C. (eds) *Identifying Critical Natural Capital*, special issue of *Ecological Economics*, 44(2–3), 187–204.

Dietz, S. & Neumayer, E. (2007) Weak and strong sustainability in the SEEA: Concepts and measurement. *Ecological Economics*, 61, 617–626.

Dietz, S. & Stern, N. (2008) Why economic analysis supports strong actions on climate change: A response to the Stern Review's critiques. *Review of Environmental Economics and Policy*, 2(1), 94–113.

Ekins, P. (2003a) Identifying critical natural capital: Conclusions about critical natural capital. *Ecological Economics*, 44(2–3), 277–292.

Ekins, P. (2003b). Sustainable development. In: Proops, J. & Page, E. (eds) *Environmental Thought*. Cheltenham, UK and Northampton, MA, Edward Elgar, pp. 144–172.

Ekins, P. (2014) Strong sustainability and critical natural capital. In: Atkinson, G., Dietz, S., Neumayer, E., & Agarwala, M. (eds) *Handbook of Sustainable Development*. Cheltenham, UK and Northampton, MA, Edward Elgar, pp. 55–71.

Elkington, J. (1997) *Cannibals with Forks: The Triple Bottom Line for 21st Century Business*. Oxford, Capstone.

Elkington, J. (2004) Enter the triple bottom line. In: Henriques, A. and Richardson, J. (eds) *The Triple Bottom Line: Does it All Add Up?* London, Earthscan, pp. 1–16.

Enkvist, P., Nauclér, T., & Rosander, J. (2007) A cost curve for greenhouse gas reduction. *McKinsey Quarterly*, 1, 34.

Foster, J. (ed.) (1997) *Valuing Nature? Ethics, Economics and the Environment*. London, Routledge.

Gómez-Baggethun, E., de Groot, R., Lomas, P. L., & Montes, C. (2010) The history of ecosystem services in economic theory and practice: From early notions to markets and payment schemes. *Ecological Economics*, 69, 1209–1218.

Goodland, R. (1995) The concept of environmental sustainability. *Annual Review of Ecological Systems*, 26(1), 1–24.

Hamilton, K. & Atkinson, G. (2006) *Wealth, Welfare and Sustainability: Advances in Measuring Sustainable Development*. Northampton, MA, Edward Elgar.

Hartwick, J. (1977) Intergenerational equity and the investing of rents from exhaustible resources. *American Economic Review*, 67(5), 972–974.

Helm, D. (2015) *Natural Capital: Valuing the Planet*. New Haven, CT and London, Yale University Press.

Heuting, R. (1980) *New Scarcity and Economic Growth*. Amsterdam, North-Holland.

Hohmeyer, O. (1994) Beyond external costs: A simple way to achieve a sustainable energy future, international and intergenerational equity by a straightforward reinvestment surcharge regime. In: Hohmeyer, O. and Ottinger, R. L. (eds) *Social Costs of Energy: Present Status and Future Trends*. Berlin and Heidelberg, Springer, pp. 405–425.

Hueting, R. & Reijnders, L. (1998) Sustainability is an objective concept. *Ecological Economics*, 27(2), 139–147.

Kassar, I. & Lasserre, P. (2003) Species preservation and biodiversity value: A real options approach. *Journal of Environmental Economics and Management*, 48(2), 857–879.

Knight, F. H. (1921) *Risk, Uncertainty and Profit.* New York, Houghton Mifflin.

Krutilla, J. V. & Fisher, A. C. (1975) *The Economics of Natural Environments: Studies in the Valuation of Commodity and Amenity Resources.* Baltimore, MD, The John Hopkins University Press.

Kumar, P. (2010) *The Economics of Ecosystems and Biodiversity: Ecological and Economic Foundations.* London and Washington, DC, Earthscan/UNEP.

Mankiw, N. G. (2015) *Principles of Microeconomics.* 7th edition. Stanford, CA, Cengage Learning.

MEA (2005) *Ecosystems and Human Well-being: Synthesis.* Millennium Ecosystem Assessment. Washington, DC, Island Press.

Neumayer, E. (2013) *Weak and Strong Sustainability: Exploring the Limits of Two Opposing Paradigms.* 4th edition. Cheltenham, UK and Northampton, MA, Edward Elgar.

Nordhaus, W. D. (2008) *A Question of Balance: Weighing the Options on Global Warming Policies.* New Haven, CT, Yale University Press.

Pearce, D., Barbier, E., & Markandya, A. (1990) *Sustainable Development: Economics and Environment in the Third World.* Cheltenham, UK and Northampton, MA, Edward Elgar.

Perman, R., Ma, Y., Common, M., Maddison, D., & McGilvray, J. (2011) *Natural Resource and Environmental Economics.* 4th edition. Essex, UK, Pearson Education Limited.

Pigou, A. C. (1932) *The Economics of Welfare*, 4th edition (1st edn 1920). London, Macmillan.

Piketty, T. (2014) *Capital in the Twenty-First Century.* Cambridge, MA, Belknap.

Pillarisetti, R. and van den Bergh, J. C. J. M. (2010) Sustainable nations: What do aggregate indexes tell us? *Environment, Development, and Sustainability*, 12(1), 49–62.

Pindyck, R. S. (2007) Uncertainty in environmental economics. *Review of Environmental Economics and Policy*, 1(1), 45–65.

Rawls, J. (1999) *A Theory of Justice.* Revised edition of 1971 edition by Harvard University Press, Cambridge, MA and London, Harvard University Press.

Robbins, L. (1932) *An Essay on the Nature and Significance of Economic Science.* London, Macmillan (1932). Auburn, Australia, Mises Institute (reprint, 2007).

Rockström, J., Steffen, W., Noone, K., Persson, Å., Chapin, F. S. III, Lambin, E. F., Lenton, T. M., Scheffer, M., Folke, C., Schellnhuber, H. J., Nykvist, B., de Wit, C. A., Hughes, T., van der Leeuw, S., Rodhe, H., Sörlin, S., Snyder, P. K., Costanza, R., Svedin, U., Falkenmark, M., Karlberg, L., Corell, R. W., Fabry, V. J., Hansen, J., Walker, B., Liverman, D., Richardson, K., Crutzen, P., & Foley, J. A. (2009) A safe operating space for humanity. *Nature*, 461(24), 472–475.

Solow, R. M. (1974) Intergenerational equity and exhaustible resources. *Review of Economic Studies*, 41, 29–46.

Steffen, W., Richardson, K., Rockström, J., Cornell, S. E., Fetzer, I., Bennett, E. M., Biggs, R., Carpenter, S. R., de Vries, W., de Wit, C. A., Folke, C., Gerten, D., Heinke, J., Mace, G. M., Persson, L. M., Ramanathan, V., Reyers, B., & Sörlin, S. (2015). Planetary boundaries: Guiding human development on a changing planet. *Science* 347, 736–746.

Stern, N. (2015) *Why Are We Waiting? The Logic, Urgency, and Promise of Tackling Climate Change.* Cambridge, MA and London, MIT Press.

Tietenberg, T. (2006) *Environmental and Natural Resource Economics.* 7th edition. Boston, MA, Addison Wesley.

Turner, R. K. (1993) Sustainability: Principles and practise. In: Turner, R. K. (ed.) *Sustainable Environmental Economics and Management: Principles and Practise*, New York and London, Belhaven Press, pp. 3–36.

Turner, R. K. and Pearce, D. W. (1992) Sustainable development: Ethics and economics. In: Barbier, E. B. (ed.) *Economics and Ecology: New Frontiers and Sustainable Development.* Dordrecht, Netherlands, Springer, pp. 177–194.

UN (1992a) *The Rio Declaration on Environment and Development.* The United Nations Conference on Environment & Development. Rio de Janeiro, Brazil, 3–14 June 1992. Available from: www.unesco.org/education/nfsunesco/pdf/RIO_E.PDF.

UN (1992b) *Agenda 21.* United Nations Conference on Environment & Development. Rio de Janeiro, Brazil, 3–14 June 1992. Available from: https://sustainabledevelopment. un.org/content/documents/Agenda21.pdf.

UN (2012) *The Future We Want.* Resolution adopted by the General Assembly on 27 July 2012. A/RES/66/288. United Nations General Assembly.

UN (2015) *Transforming Our World: The 2030 Agenda for Sustainable Development.* Resolution adopted by the General Assembly on 25 September 2015, A/RES/70/1. United Nations General Assembly.

Victor, P. A. (1991) Indicators of sustainable development: Some lessons from capital theory. *Ecological Economics,* 4, 191–213.

WCED (1987) *Our Common Future.* World Commission on Environment and Development. Oxford, Oxford University Press.

Weisbrod, B. A. (1964) Collective consumption services of individual consumption goods. *Quarterly Journal of Economics,* 78(3), 471–477.

Weitzman, M. (2009) On modelling and interpreting the economics of catastrophic climate change. *The Review of Economics and Statistics,* 91(1), 1–19.

World Bank (2000) *Genuine Saving as a Sustainability Indicator,* by Kirk Hamilton, Paper No. 77, Environmental Economics Series, World Bank, Washington, DC. Available at: http://documents.worldbank.org/curated/en/908161468740713285/ Genuine-saving-as-a-sustainability-indicator.

World Bank (2006) *Where is the Wealth of Nations?* World Bank, Washington, DC. Available at: http://siteresources.worldbank.org/INTEEI/214578-1110886258964/20748034/ All.pdf.

WWF (2016) *Living Planet Report 2016.* Gland, Switzerland, World Wide Fund for Nature.

5

A NORMATIVE MODEL OF SUSTAINABLE DEVELOPMENT

If a thing is worth doing, it is worth doing badly.

G. K. Chesterton, *What's Wrong with the World* (1910)

In this chapter we transform sustainable development's imperatives into a concrete normative model. In doing so, we think Chesterton's statement provides some valuable insights. Indeed, modelling sustainable development is worth doing. There is no question about that. But should we model it badly? Well, no, at least not in the ordinary sense of the word. Rather, urging for something to be done 'badly' is a response to those who seek the perfect solution. While we wait for the perfect model, we might end up doing nothing. In this sense, it might well turn out that 'badly' is good enough. Several philosophers have made this point. Voltaire phrased it 'the best is the enemy of the good'. Confucius claimed that 'better a diamond with a flaw than a pebble without'. Shakespeare insightfully wrote 'striving to better, oft we mar what's well'. Indeed, the pursuit of perfection is noble, but unless we are willing to settle for 'badly', we may have to settle for nothing at all. We hasten to add (and Chesterton would most certainly agree) that doing a thing 'badly' is not an excuse for poor effort.[1]

There is another, more subtle, insight that Chesterton's statement provides though. Chesterton persistently defended the amateur against the professional, or the generalist's lay knowledge against the specialist's expert knowledge. Our model does not start with the specialist's expert knowledge. Rather, our model starts with an ethical statement developed by lay people over a long time. This ethical statement, which is the result of people's sense of sustainability, tells us what we *should* do. As ethical statements survive reasoned public scrutiny over time, they can enter legislation or common law (more on this in chapter 3).

Let us give an example to illustrate the difference between a model that rests on a specialist's expert knowledge (typically a scientist's) and a model that rests on an ethical statement. Scientists repeatedly tell us that we are crossing environmental limits. They also tell us that inequalities increase in many countries and that many people suffer under extreme poverty. These facts do not, however, mean that we *must* do something about such problems. We can choose to do nothing. Our sense of sustainability tells us, however, that we *should* do something about such problems. Our model starts with that sense.

This chapter presents a five-step model of sustainable development.[2] The first step acknowledges that sustainable development is an ethical statement, which consists of three moral imperatives. The second step presents relevant theories that give importance to those imperatives. The third step derives key themes from those theories. The fourth step suggests headline indicators for each key theme. The fifth step assigns thresholds to those indicators. The subsequent sections present each step. The final section presents the sustainable development space. Before we present the model and the sustainable development space, however, we will briefly present the history of, discuss some of the difficulties with, and offer some critique of earlier attempts to develop sustainable development models.

The quest for sustainability indicators

Some would argue that trying to model sustainable development is a hopeless task. The reason is that sustainable development is what philosophers have called 'an essentially contested concept', one of those terms we can never all agree to define (or model) in the same way because every definition carries a different social, moral, or political agenda (Crick, 2002). And indeed, since the concept of 'sustainable development' entered the international political and academic agenda in 1987, it has been knocked around regularly. Academics have criticized the concept for being an oxymoron; shamefully anthropocentric; too development oriented; too environment oriented; blatantly social democratic; dogmatic; socialism in disguise; fuzzy about needs, wants, and desires; hopelessly naïve in its orientation (that is, you can have your cake and eat it too); vague about what is needed to achieve sustainable development; and more (Langhelle, 2016). It gets even worse if one tries to *measure* sustainable development by assigning indicators and thresholds to it, that is, making a model. In a book about sustainability indicators, the subtitle is telling: *Sustainability Indicators: Measuring the Immeasurable?* (Bell & Morse, 2008). Many academics would certainly want to underscore that question mark!

Nevertheless, measuring sustainable development is precisely what policymakers and researchers are encouraged – even instructed – to do. Agenda 21 (UN, 1992b), the action plan from the 1992 Rio Summit (more on this in chapter 8), was clear about that:

> The organs and organizations of the United Nations system, in coordination with other relevant international organizations, could provide

recommendations for harmonized development of indicators at the national, regional and global levels, and for incorporation of a suitable set of these indicators in common, regularly updated, and widely accessible reports and databases, for use at the international level, subject to national sovereignty considerations.

(Agenda 21, chapter 40.7)

Twenty-five years later the quest for measuring sustainable development continues. At a Development Committee ministerial lunch in Peru on 10 October 2015, the United Nations' Secretary-General Ban Ki-moon (2015) echoed Agenda 21 in his 'investing in evidence' remark:

> The 2030 Agenda for Sustainable Development is explicit about the need for quality, accessible and timely data. Data are the basis for sound decision-making. They are fundamental to the implementation and success of the Agenda. … Let us together commit to measure what we treasure.

The 25 years between Agenda 21's recommendations and Ban Ki-moon's commitment have been busy. A number of intergovernmental organizations, national governments, regional authorities, local communities, business organizations and other economic actors, academic institutions, and civil society organizations of many kinds have been, and still are, developing and using sets of indicators to measure sustainable development. The number of indicator sets and individual metrics is now massive. Although no exhaustive accounts of indicators exist (and would probably be too time consuming to make), there are some notable milestones on the international indicator agenda.

A first milestone is the founding of the UN Commission on Sustainable Development (UNCSD) with the goal to assist countries in developing and using sustainable development indicators. UNCSD presented its first indicator set in 1995 (UNESC, 1995). A second milestone is the development of indicators by the Organisation for Economic Co-operation and Development (e.g., OECD, 2002, 2010). A third milestone is the UN Environmental Programme, which regularly publishes a set of sustainability indicators in its Global Environmental Outlook (e.g., UNEP, 2007). A fourth milestone is the establishing of a 2001 Working Group within the statistical body of the European Union – Eurostat – to respond to the demand for measuring progress towards sustainability with a set of agreed indicators (e.g., Eurostat, 2009). A fifth milestone is the joint effort by the UN, the OECD, and the EU to develop a unified set of indicators (UNECE, OECD, Eurostat, 2008). A sixth milestone is the UN set of 17 sustainable development goals (SDGs) launched in 2015 (UN, 2015). It is probably fair to say that this work had already started in 2000 with the launching of the millennium development goals (MDGs). The first six SDGs build on the core agenda of the MDGs, while the remaining 11 goals break new ground. Currently, most attempts to develop sustainable indicators are responses to the SDGs and Ban Ki-moon's remark.

Notwithstanding the many attempts, there has not been consensus on how to measure sustainability (Stiglitz *et al.*, 2010).

At this point, we would like to make two comments.

First, we present a normative model, that is, a model suggesting where we *should* go (we return to how countries actually comply in chapter 7 and to ways to comply in chapters 8 and 9). We need a goal to know where we should go. That goal is sustainable development. We believe that goal must be quantifiable. Thus, we need to know if we are heading in the right direction and we need to know when we have reached the goal. However, rather than defining sustainable development as a fixed end-state, we define sustainable development as a space. This space, which we call the sustainable development space, contains many potential end-states. The space is, however, constrained by thresholds that cannot be overstepped. Achieving sustainable development means that we are entering that space.

Some would disagree. Rather than acknowledging that sustainable development is a substantive goal, they would argue that sustainable development is a process. *Our Common Future* could have contributed to that argument by writing 'yet in the end, sustainable development is not a fixed state of harmony, but rather a process of change ...' (WCED, 1987, p. 9). Thus, one could argue that sustainable development is not about achieving a fixed state (or space) but rather a process that takes us away from an unsustainable state. But a process of change to what? How could one possibly know where to turn if one does not have a goal in sight? If one reduces sustainable development to a process of change, it could indeed mean anything. One needs to say something about *how much* that process will change the present state. Our view is that sustainable development is a goal and that actions taken towards that goal are necessary steps – or processes – to achieve that goal. Indeed, reaching the 5-kilometre sign in a full marathon is a necessary part of running. But you need to run (or go) the full 42 kilometres to get the medal.

Part of the disagreement comes from different ways to define *goal* and *process*. Our goal is the sustainable development space. We acknowledge, however, that this space can change as new evidence arises in, for example, ecology and/or new and better indicators become available. Indeed, the world changes and our knowledge of it changes too. In that sense, the space is 'not a fixed state of harmony' and defining it is 'a process of change'. Nevertheless, our goal is the sustainable development space.

A process, on the other hand, can be understood in at least three ways. First, a process can refer to doing 'something' without having a defined goal in sight. Understood in this way, sustainable development can be anything. Second, a process can refer to the means, the measures, the policies, the institutions, or the enabling mechanisms one needs to make changes. So understood, sustainable development is about finding out what to do. Third, a process can refer to the pathways that lead to the goal. So understood, sustainable development is about being on the right track. Our normative sustainable development model – that is, the model that defines the sustainable development space – has nothing to do with a process in these three understandings. (We will, however, say something about sustainable development pathways in chapter 7 and discuss means and measures in chapter 9.)

The second comment we want to make at this point is that there are two competing approaches to indicator development: the 'top-down' and the 'bottom-up' approaches.[3] The tension between the two approaches runs deep in the sustainable development indicator literature, with scholars supporting one or the other approach. A top-down approach implies that indicators are dictated from the top, for example from a national government or a group of scientific experts. A bottom-up approach implies that indicators are suggested from the bottom, for example from a local community or a firm. As such, a top-down approach is typically portrayed as being more authoritarian (and even totalitarian), whereas a bottom-up approach is portrayed as being more democratic. The distinction is particularly present in discussing local sustainability (see also chapter 8).

We believe that this distinction is unfruitful in developing our normative model. Remember first that our model represents a goal, not a process. A bottom-up approach is *always* preferable when finding ways to achieve sustainable development. A bottom-up approach is, however, not necessarily appropriate for setting the goals. To understand why, we must remember two of sustainable development's main features: long-term commitment and global thinking. A bottom-up approach will always run the danger of focusing on here (close, at best) and now (tomorrow, at best). Indeed, focusing on the here and now is sometimes necessary, but it will inevitably rely on what is *possible* and what is *desirable*. Neither is sufficient to acknowledge the long-term, global commitment of achieving sustainable development. A top-down approach has its problems too. At worst, it can thwart democratic debate and dialogue, and can thus impede necessary reflection about the normative foundations of society.

Thus, SDGs can grow neither from parochial, bottom-up suggestions nor from undemocratic, top-down dictates. Rather, they must grow out of ethical statements. These statements, Amartya Sen reminds us, must survive open and informed scrutiny, which 'involves the invoking of an interactive process of critical scrutiny with open impartiality' (Sen, 2009, p. 385). Thus, a claim that a certain aspect (for example, the imperative of ensuring social justice) is important enough to be part of an ethical statement (for example, sustainable development) is also a claim that reasoned scrutiny would sustain that claim. We believe that the three imperatives of satisfying human needs, ensuring social justice, and respecting environmental limits would indeed survive such scrutiny. Our claim rests on all citizens' deep-rooted sense of sustainability. Thus, defining SDGs is not about choosing a top-down or a bottom-up approach. Rather, it is about constantly alternating between the two.

A critique of sustainability indicator development

There is no shortage of responses to Agenda 21's call for sustainability indicators and to Ban Ki-moon's recent call for finding ways to measure what we treasure.

Indeed, the academic community has responded firmly to these calls. Responses include attempts like 'indicator development' (Bell & Morse, 2008; Rametsteiner et al., 2011; Morse, 2015); 'conceptual framework' (Hak et al., 2012, 2016); 'formal framework' (Christen & Schmidt, 2012); 'conceptual model' (Aslaksen et al., 2010); 'data envelope analysis' (Chansarn, 2014); 'sustainable progress welfare vector' (Momete, 2016); 'prism of sustainability' (Spangenberg, 2002); 'indicator definition' (Heink & Kowarik, 2010); 'sustainability assessment methodologies' (Sing et al., 2012); 'design of sustainability indicators' (Dahl, 2012); and 'measuring sustainable development performance' (Gasparatos et al., 2008).

We see, however, three major problems with the attempts above. The first problem is that the ethical foundation is not given sufficient attention in indicator development. Many studies start by acknowledging sustainable development's normative basis, for example: 'the concept of sustainability is grounded on a normative foundation' (Christen & Schmidt, 2012, p. 404); 'the essentially normative dimension of the concept of sustainability' (Rametsteiner et al., 2011, p. 61); and 'the concept of sustainability has always had an ethical dimension of justice for all the planet's inhabitants and for future generations' (Dahl, 2012, p. 18). This praise of normativity and this call for ethical pronouncements are, however, not sufficiently elaborated on or sufficiently reflected in sustainability indicators (Rametsteiner et al., 2011). Rather, the technicalities of sustainability indicator development have dominated the sustainability literature (Morse, 2015). Thus, Morse argues, the focus is on objectivity and science much more than on norms. One probably has to go back to the period from 1987 to the early 1990s to find studies that truly acknowledge the ethical foundation of sustainable development (see, for example, Lafferty & Langhelle, 1999).[4] There are, however, signs that the tide is turning and that ethics is once again at the forefront of the sustainable development debate (including indicator development). This book is part of that tide.

The second problem is that many attempts do not clearly distinguish between 'what to treasure' and 'how to measure'. When working on indicator development, it is necessary to make a distinction between the phenomena of interest (the indicandum; plural indicanda) and the indicator (Heink & Kowarik, 2010). The indicator is a measure from which conclusion of the phenomena can be inferred, or a measure that makes a problem visible (Dahl, 2012). Thus, indicanda tell us what we treasure, whereas indicators tell us how we measure what we treasure. Heink and Kowarik refer to sustainable development as a multidimensional indicandum that needs to be clarified before one starts to suggest indicators:

> If the indicandum itself is an unclear concept, further problems will result. [Studies] describe 'sustainability' as a 'presently undefined balance among economic, ecological, and sociological goals' but they nevertheless use sustainability as an indicandum. This is an example where the operationalization of a term precedes its conceptualization ... But how can one judge if adequate indicators have been chosen, if it is not really clear

what should be indicated? *In cases where the indicandum is unclear, the selection of indicators will necessarily be somewhat arbitrary. Therefore a clarification of the indicandum is mandatory.*

(Heink & Kowarik, 2010, p. 591, italics added)

Studies often mix conceptualization (the realm of stating *indicanda*) with operationalization (the realm of suggesting indicators). For example, the Czech Republic's sustainable development strategy (Hak *et al.*, 2012) mixes *indicanda* and indicators. Nine of the suggested sustainability themes – for example 'public transport' (theme 1), 'waste treatment' (theme 5), and 'agriculture' (theme 6) – are clearly closer to operationalization than to conceptualization.

The third problem in indicator development relates to the question of what should be accepted as primary *indicanda* as opposed to secondary *indicanda* (we will elaborate on that problem shortly).

We are very clear in this book that the *indicandum* of sustainable development is an ethical statement that entails three moral imperatives. The starting point for sustainability indicator development should thus be ethics. Indicators must reflect that fact. With that fact in mind, we now turn to our model of sustainable development.

Step 1: The moral imperatives of sustainable development

The first step is to acknowledge that sustainable development is an ethical statement from which three moral imperatives can be derived (figure 5.1). We have elaborated the relationship between the ethical statement and its moral imperatives in chapter 1, and will not repeat this relationship here.

A five-step model could easily suggest that defining sustainable development is a smooth, linear process that runs from an ethical statement to a series of thresholds. Such an understanding makes our model a rational one. In 'Ends and means in planning', the American political scientist Edward Banfield (1973) describes such a process as rational (synoptic), unfolding in neatly, sequential stages. This rational

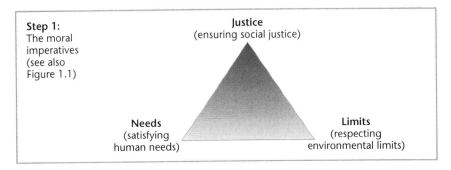

FIGURE 5.1 A normative model for sustainable development. Step 1: The moral imperatives of sustainable development (modified from Holden *et al.*, 2016).

process, and its stages, has later been generally accepted as a recipe for how rational planning processes should be carried out. A clearly defined goal, or end-state, is paramount in such processes. It is a kind of rational planning process that engineers probably love, but one that most social scientists argue is far from how things work in real life. Rather than smooth rationality, social scientists would argue, we face what the American political scientist Charles Lindblom (1973) describes as a process of 'muddling through'. Lindblom does not need a goal. Rather, he suggests doing whatever is possible considering the alternatives at hand (Amartya Sen would probably support that view). No one will question the reality of Lindblom's description. Some would even suggest that his descriptive model is a normative ideal. We have sympathy with that view. We nevertheless find it difficult to support a view that sets SDGs according to whatever is possible to achieve. Surely, sustainable development must be more than what is possible.

Our model is one that attempts to define sustainable development as a goal that we call a sustainable development space. We must know where we should navigate or at least know what waters we should avoid. Thus, our model leans on Banfield's normative rationality rather than on Lindblom's descriptive, incremental approach. Moreover, we think that sustainable development presently needs much more than the possible, incremental changes suggested by Lindblom's approach.

Step 2: The theories

So far we have established that sustainable development is an ethical statement from which we have derived three moral imperatives. We need, however, to go further to develop a sustainable development model and to quantify the sustainable development space. What we need now is to find the sustainability themes that make it possible to operationalize the moral imperatives. How do we find those themes? Where should we go to seek them? What is the legitimate source of those themes? Here we make an important claim: The themes must come from theory. There is a rich supply of theories within each of the moral imperatives from which the themes can be drawn. These theories include philosophical texts on needs and justice, and new scientific insights on environmental limits. Consequently, key sustainability themes derive from theories on long-term ethical imperatives rather than from political consensus or stakeholders' preferences. Thus, there is an ethical–theoretical rationale for identifying the themes, and not a political–feasible rationale.

What is the theoretical foundation of sustainable development's imperatives? Numerous scholars have over the years developed significant contributions to that foundation. Selecting which theories are fundamental will always be somewhat arbitrary and subject to one's preferences. Nevertheless, we need to make a selection (while we acknowledge that other scholars have selected other theories). We have presented the theories in chapters 2–4. Figure 5.2 shows our model, including some of the fundamental theories. Having established the theories that are fundamental to understanding sustainable development's imperatives, we can now identify the key sustainability themes.

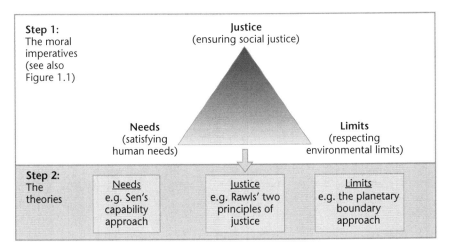

FIGURE 5.2 A normative model for sustainable development. Step 2: The theories fundamental to understanding sustainable development's moral imperatives (modified from Holden *et al.*, 2016).

Step 3: The key sustainability themes

The fact that sustainable development rests on an ethical statement, moral imperatives, and theories does not bring us much further though. Although that fact is an important first step towards finding what we treasure – or, as Daly (2007) puts is, what is to be sustained – we must be more specific about what we want to treasure. Thus, we must turn to the problem of defining sustainable development's *indicanda*. However, rather than using the term *indicanda*, we will from now on use the term 'themes', because it resonates more nicely with everyday vocabulary and is more frequently used in the academic literature.

Regarding sustainability themes, it is important to distinguish between 'key sustainability themes' and 'any other sustainability themes'. Thus, we include only themes that theories from chapters 2–4 regard as the most important ones. We call those the key themes. Indeed, some of the vagueness that many scholars have attributed to the concept of sustainable development is a result of wanting it to cover everything that is good and desirable, and thus they have not made a necessary prioritization among the themes. Thus, themes must be ranked according to importance: the most important ones, which we call key, and other themes, which we call secondary. The difference between a key theme and a secondary theme is that whereas the former is fundamental in achieving sustainable development, the latter is not. This is not to say the secondary themes are unimportant, rather that they are subordinated to the key themes. Thus, unless key themes are addressed, whatever else we do proves insufficient. To use Rawls' terminology, all key sustainability themes have 'lexical priority' over all other sustainability themes. This is an order that requires that we satisfy the key themes in the ordering before we satisfy the secondary themes (and the secondary before we consider the tertiary, etc.). A theme does not come into play until higher ones are either fully met or do not apply. A lexical ordering avoids, then, having to balance themes at all; those earlier in the ordering have an absolute weight, so to speak, with respect to later ones, and hold without exception.

To illustrate our claim, we go back four decades to a rather heated debate in planning research. In 1973 an article entitled 'If planning is everything, maybe it's nothing' appeared in the journal *Policy Sciences*. The article, by Aaron Wildavsky (1973), provided provocative reading for planners of that period. Wildavsky argued that the planner had become the victim of planning; his own creation had overwhelmed him because planning had become so large and complex that planners could no longer control its dimensions. Moreover, planning extended in so many directions that the planner could no longer shape it: 'He [the planner] may be economist, political scientist, sociologist, architect or scientist. Yet the essence of his calling – planning – escapes him. He finds it everywhere in general and nowhere in particular. Why is planning so elusive?' (ibid., p. 127).

About a decade later, Wildavsky got a fierce reply from Ernest Alexander in *Town Planning Review* (Alexander, 1981): 'If planning isn't everything, maybe it's something'. He took up the cudgels for planners and others associated with planning. Alexander felt that for too long he and his colleagues had failed to articulate a reasoned response to Wildavsky, because the article's provocative title and deliberately polemic style made its unpleasant conclusions easy to dismiss: 'This last audience, of planners and people involved in planning, is the most important one for Wildavsky's argument. Unfortunately, in dismissing it, either through ignorance or through apathy, we may have thrown the baby out with the bathwater' (ibid., p. 131).

The link between the contemporary debate about the content and policy implications of sustainable development on the one hand and the planning controversy four decades ago on the other is relevant. There is every reason to believe that sustainable development is about to become, like planning did, everything (remember the all-inclusive UN SDGs). Thus, sustainable development has increasingly been presented as a pathway to all that is good and desirable in society. Thus, the parallel to Wildavsky's concern is all too relevant. The concept of sustainable development has become so large and complex that decision-makers can no longer control its dimensions (though we must give the UN credit for trying). Moreover, the concept extends in so many directions that decision-makers can no longer shape it. Not surprisingly therefore, as we mentioned in the introduction of this book, a number of scholars argue that the concept of sustainable development is about to become, if it has not already become, a useless concept. However, as Alexander stressed in his heroic defence of his profession, it is unquestionable that sustainable development is *something*. We use the term 'key themes' to separate the important 'somethings' of sustainable development from the 'everythings'. So what do the theories from chapters 2–4 tell us about sustainable development's somethings?

Satisfying human needs

Using different concepts, most theories on satisfying human needs start by laying out conditions for preventing poverty and deprivation. Maslow (1943) puts *physiological* needs, that is, physical requirements for human survival, at the bottom of his well-known pyramid. Max-Neef (1991) develops a theory of human needs in which he identifies *fundamental* human needs. Doyal and Gough (1991) argue that physical health and autonomy are the *basic* needs which humans must satisfy to avoid serious harm. Rawls (1999) suggests that there are *primary goods* that people should rationally want, whatever else they want. We always want liberty, opportunity, and money (the primary goods), supposes Rawls, as all-purpose means to our personal ends in life. *Our Common Future* (WCED, 1987) urges all nations to focus their efforts on eliminating poverty and satisfying *essential* needs. And UN SDG 1.1 aims to eradicate extreme poverty for all people everywhere by 2030.

A theory on satisfying human needs contains, however, more than merely ways of preventing poverty and deprivation. Indeed, *Our Common Future* argues that in addition to basic needs people have legitimate aspirations for an improved quality of life. Doyal and Gough acknowledge that even their basic-needs approach is about more than mere survival. To do well in their everyday lives, they argue, people must do much more than survive. Amartya Sen (2009) seems to agree. He argues that seeing people's needs only as basic needs gives a rather meagre view of humanity. In *Monitoring Global Poverty*, the World Bank (2017) suggests a twin goal of ending extreme poverty and promoting shared prosperity.[5] Thus, a theory of satisfying human needs must go beyond the basic-needs approach. A richer approach is called for. Indeed, one can argue that a meaningful life begins where basic needs end.

We acknowledge that a theory of human needs must be richer than one solely focusing on survival and preventing poverty and deprivation, and this introduces us to theories on human development. This makes sense. After all, we are talking about sustainable *development*. Alkire (2010) argues that most of the academic literature on human development now focuses on the capability approach. Thus, the capability approach is the main philosophical and theoretical foundation for the concept of human development, which inevitably includes the concept of human needs. The capability approach has been pioneered by Amartya Sen and others and has more recently been further developed by the American philosopher Martha Nussbaum and others. Sen (2009) contrasts the capability approach to the utility-based or resource-based lines of thinking. The capability approach acknowledges that quality of life should be judged by a person's capability to do things that he or she has reason to value.

The capability approach acknowledges though that some capabilities are more critical than others. Sen (1987) refers to basic capabilities, which are the basics considered necessary for survival and to avoid or escape poverty or other serious deprivations. Nussbaum (2000) argues that basic capabilities are necessary for developing the more advanced capabilities. Hence, while the notion of capabilities refers to a very broad range of opportunities, the concept of basic capabilities refers to the real opportunity to avoid poverty or to meet or exceed a threshold of wellbeing (Robeyns, 2011). Thus, a theory of human needs can be seen as a two-stage process. First, persons must be provided with the means and opportunities to prevent poverty and deprivations. Second, persons must be provided with an enhanced set of capabilities to do things they have reason to value.

Thus, the key sustainability themes for the imperative of satisfying human needs are:

- eradicating extreme poverty
- enhancing human capabilities.

Ensuring social justice

Injustice, whether experienced personally or by people around us, is something we strongly respond to at a very early age (Sen, 2009). Thus, although people might disagree about what justice is and how it should guide practical life, we all seem to have a capacity for a sense of justice. Rawls refers to this capacity as one of our moral powers. To ask whether a society is just is to ask how it distributes the things we prize – income and wealth, duties and rights, powers and opportunities, offices and honours. A just society distributes these goods in the right way; it gives each person his or her due. The hard questions begin when we ask what people are due, and why.

Starting with social contract theory, Rawls develops a theory of justice that he calls 'justice as fairness' (Rawls, 1999). In a purely hypothetical situation he places people in an original position behind a 'veil of ignorance' to agree upon principles of justice which are those free and rational men would accept. He argues that people in the original position would choose two principles of justice.[6] The first principle is often referred to as the liberty principle. Part (a) of the second principle is often referred to as the difference principle, and part (b) the fair opportunity principle.

Maffettone (2010) argues that the liberty principle is particularly important in social justice, and that participation is a particular feature of this liberty. Correspondingly, we argue that the liberty principle is particularly important in sustainable development. Maffettone further argues that the first principle implies a principle of equal participation. Participation, he says, 'takes place in the traditional constitutional context through the democratic election of a representative body with extensive legislative powers' (ibid., p. 63).[7]

The right to vote is an important part of participation. However, we need an understanding of participation that in two senses is 'richer' than 'seen in terms just of ballots and elections' (Sen, 2009, p. 326). First, though ballots have an important role, they can be seen as just one part of the participation process. The effectiveness of ballots themselves 'depends crucially on what goes with balloting' (ibid., p. 327).

Indeed, balloting can be thoroughly inadequate on its own, as is amply illustrated by the astonishing electoral victories of ruling tyrannies. This understanding of participation was acknowledged in *Our Common Future*: 'participation requires a political system that secures effective citizen participation in decision making' (WCED, 1987, p. 65). Thus, participation in itself is not enough, but must be embedded in a system that makes it possible to transfer individual voices into action. In this sense, participation is a central part of governance, which in its broadest sense refers to 'the intersection of power, politics and institutions' (Leach *et al.*, 2010, p. 65). Second, participation of the 'low voices' should be given particular attention. Such voices include poor people, nature, and future generations. Whereas poor people have a low voice, nature and future generations have no voice at all; they are what Meadowcroft (2012) refers to as 'absent constituents'.

There are three additional reasons to include rich participation in our definition of social justice. First, rich participation acts as a safety valve against political neglect in following up the imperative of ensuring social justice (Sen, 2009). Second, rich participation enables collective processes of monitoring, reflection, debate, and decision that establish the goals to be pursued (Meadowcroft *et al.*, 2005). Thus, rich participation can influence norms and values, and can make acceptable any necessary changes in unsustainable policies and practices. Third, we acknowledge the 'pervasive demands for participatory living' around the world (Sen, 2009, p. 322).

Sen and Rawls both underscore the link between justice, participation, and democracy. Rawls sees the central ideas and aims of his justice-as-fairness conception as those of a conception for a constitutional democracy. Sen argues that there is an intimate connection between justice and democracy.

Notwithstanding the importance of the liberty and opportunity principles, justice relates closely to how we distribute wealth and income in society, making Rawls' difference principle, which regulates the primary goods of income and wealth, particularly relevant. Sen argues that although justice is not the same as equality, justice is closely related to the concept of equality. Sen is arguing neither for equality of welfare nor for equality of capability to achieve welfare. Still, Sen argues that every normative theory of social justice demands equality of *something* – something that is regarded as particularly important in that theory. Rawls too regards equality as a central part of social justice. Although his difference principle does not require an equal distribution of income and wealth, its underlying idea expresses a powerful, even inspiring vision of equality (Sandel, 2009).

Ultimately, conceptions of social justice concern two questions: Who gets what? and Says who? Ideas of democratic, 'rich' participation and of equal (or fair) distribution of primary goods come close to answering those questions.[8]

Thus, the key sustainability themes for the imperative of ensuring social justice are:

• ensuring rich participation
• ensuring fair distribution.

Respecting environmental limits

To respect environmental limits, we need to know the current status of global natural capital, how humans interact with and depend on these resources, and how to make policy decisions when the environmental problems to be solved are complex and decisions (including to do nothing) have uncertain and possibly irreversible consequences.

Presently, the most promising take on identifying and quantifying environmental limits is the 'planetary boundary approach', an approach that originated from a group of researchers at the Stockholm Resilience Centre, Stockholm Environment Institute, and the Tällberg Foundation (Rockström *et al.*, 2009; Steffen *et al.*, 2015). These researchers have identified nine planetary boundaries that define a safe operating space for humanity with respect to Earth's systems. Two of these boundaries, climate change and biosphere integrity, are what the researchers call 'core boundaries'. Each of the two core boundaries has 'the potential on its own to drive the Earth system into a new state should they be substantially and persistently transgressed' (Steffen *et al.*, 2015, p. 1).

Neoclassical economics is designed to examine how scarcity of resources should affect human decisions (Backhouse & Medema, 2009). A central insight is that there are mutual gains from transactions, and that, in a perfect market, the allocation of resources will be 'Pareto efficient', meaning that nobody can become better off without making someone else worse off. If, however, a transaction imposes costs on people who are not part of the exchange, such as the emission of carbon dioxide into the air, the people who generate such 'negative externalities' should pay a fee reflecting the costs they impose on others. This type of fee is known as a Pigovian tax (Pigou, 1932).

However, traditional neoclassical economics may not adequately deal with complex interactions in the biosphere. The theory is based on the assumption that natural capital and other forms of capital are substitutable and can therefore be expressed in one unit, either utility or monetary. To maximize utility, the various forms of capital should be allocated so that the marginal costs of production equal the marginal benefits from the goods and services consumed. This kind of marginal approach may be less suited to address complex ecosystems where marginal changes may result in non-marginal and irreversible damage to ecosystems, habitats, and other critical components of natural capital.

A promising alternative to the utility-based neoclassical economics framework is the asset-based approach to natural capital (see, for example, Ekins, 2014; Helm, 2015). Whereas the standard economic approach is to sustain 'utility' from consuming products and services, the natural capital approach is to sustain the 'capital' that can generate future products and services. This approach leads to a discussion of what part of how much natural capital should be sustained for the future – all of it or part – and results in the notions of strong and weak sustainability (Pearce *et al.*, 1990; Turner, 1993; Neumayer, 2013). Environmental economists, using the natural capital approach, argue that on aggregate, renewable natural capital should not decline over time, and that special attention should be paid to maintain the 'critical natural capital' necessary for essential ecosystem services (Ekins, 2014; Helm, 2015). Ecological economists argue that because the biosphere is finite, the growth of physical throughput cannot be sustained indefinitely, and that economic growth must be reduced (Daly, 2007).

Environmental policy decisions may have uncertain, irreversible, non-linear, and long-term consequences. Pindyck (2007) demonstrated how these characteristics make conventional cost–benefit analysis based on expected values less suitable for environmental policy issues, and concluded that using an option analysis approach, which incorporates these characteristics, will result in an environmental policy that is often more 'precautionary' in the sense of favouring earlier and more intense intervention.

Many environmental decision-making problems, such as mitigating climate change and safeguarding biosphere integrity, are characterized by radical uncertainty where decision-makers are not able to know all of the possible outcomes of a decision. Emissions of greenhouse gases to levels with which we have no prior experience and depletion of important ecosystems like the rainforests are examples of such decisions. In these cases, we cannot derive optimal decision rules based on probability distributions of outcomes and options theory. One way to proceed is to apply the 'safe minimum standard of conservation', according to which all projects and decisions that could entail species extinction should be rejected. Closely related to this standard is 'the precautionary principle' as referred to in the 1992 Rio Declaration: 'Where there are threats of serious or irreversible damage, lack of full scientific certainty shall not be used as a reason for postponing cost-effective measures to prevent environmental degradation.'[9] As Martin Weitzman has argued in several influential papers on environmental risk (e.g., Weitzman, 2009), if there is a significant chance of utter catastrophe, that chance – rather than what is most likely to happen – makes the most powerful case for strong climate and environmental policies.

Keeping these concepts and approaches in mind, the key sustainability themes for the imperative of respecting environmental limits are:

*   mitigating climate change
*   safeguarding biosphere integrity.

Having finished step 3 by deriving six key sustainability themes from theories laid out in philosophical texts on needs and justice, and from recent scientific insights on environmental limits, our model for sustainable development now looks like figure 5.3.

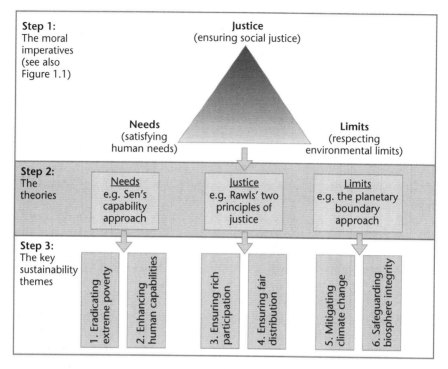

FIGURE 5.3 A normative model for sustainable development. Step 3: Identifying key sustainability themes (modified from Holden *et al.*, 2016).

Step 4: Headline indicators

There seems to be broad consensus that five criteria apply to the choice of indicators (see for example, Bell & Morse, 2008; Hein & Kowarik, 2010; Dahl, 2012; Hak *et al.*, 2016). First, indicators must be relevant in the sense that they say something about the theme they measure. For example, if one wants to develop indicators for height and weight, metre and kilo are obvious choices. Second, indicators must be easy to understand and communicate. For example, if one wants to develop indicators for height, 'the length of the path travelled by light in vacuum during a time interval of 1/299792458 of a second' (The International System of Units' definition of a metre) would surely be hard to communicate. Third, indicators must be reliable in the sense that one can trust the information they provide. To develop reliable indicators, one needs a sound methodology. For example, if one wants to measure length, one needs some sort of an authorized measuring tape, not a stick that is supposed to be approximately one metre long. Fourth, data must either be readily available or be made available within a reasonable time and at a reasonable cost. If, for example, one wants to know more about the Maya people's attitudes towards homosexuality, it might be hard to find the necessary data (though not impossible). Fifth, there seems to be a common understanding in the indicator literature that the indicator set should be of a 'manageable size'. A manageable set must balance between the dangers of being too complex or too simplified (Spangenberg, 2002). Summarizing the criteria above into everyday language, we suggest that indicators must be fruitful and trustworthy. They simply must make sense.

Although the SDGs agenda does not yet specify the scope of indicators, the high number of goals (17) and targets (169) suggests that we are looking at hundreds of indicators. Such a number is hardly manageable. Hak *et al.* (2016) claim that the standard solution to an unmanageable number of indicators suggests itself, namely a larger set of indicators and a small set of headline indicators. Dahl (2012) suggests that, whereas managers and policymakers may find a wide set of indicators useful, decision-makers and the public prefer a narrow set of 10–15 indicators. The World Bank (2017) recommends that the number of such indicators should be sufficiently small so they can receive prominence in public debate and in policymaking. We suggest a set of six headline indicators, which we will present shortly.

Main approaches to sustainability indicators in the literature

Reviewing the literature on sustainability indicators, we suggest that indicators broadly fall into four categories: three-pillar-model indicators, sustainability-theme indexes, extended-sustainability-theme indexes, and composite-sustainability indexes. Here we define indexes and composite indexes as follows: An index is a number derived from a series of individual indicators. A composite index is a number derived from several indexes.

Three-pillar-model indicators: The first category starts with the three-pillar model (see chapter 1) and develops indicators for each dimension (the dimensions correspond to themes in our model). Examples of indicators for the economic dimension are gross domestic product (GDP) per capita, debt-to-GNI ratio, and employment–population ratio. Examples of indicators for the environmental dimension are carbon dioxide emissions, proportion of total water resources used, and proportion of terrestrial area protected. Examples of indicators for the social dimension are proportion of population living below national poverty line, share of households without electricity or other modern energy services, and life expectancy at birth. The indicators above are examples from the UN Commission of Sustainable Development's report *Indicators of Sustainable Development: Guidelines and Methodologies* (UN, 2007). Though the report does not explicitly refer to the three-pillar model, its 14 themes and several subthemes fall nicely into that model. The UN SDGs are, however, explicit about the three-pillar model: 'They [the SDGs] are integrated and indivisible and balance the three dimensions of sustainable development: the economic, social and environmental.' Future indicators will certainly fit into the three-pillar model.

Of course, one usually ends up with a large number of indicators in this indicator category. Although the UN (2007) has introduced a set of core indicators to keep the larger set of 96 indicators of sustainable development manageable, the core set still consists of 50 indicators. As mentioned, Hak *et al.* (2016) suggest there will eventually be hundreds of indicators to follow up on the SDGs. Several approaches try to solve this unmanageable number of indicators. A common solution is to introduce so-called composite indexes.

Sustainability-theme indexes: The second category presents indexes for each sustainability theme (or dimension). Examples of sustainability-theme indexes are carbon footprint (Wright *et al.*, 2011; theme: climate change) and multidimensional poverty index (Alkire & Robles, 2015; theme: poverty). Examples of sustainability-dimension indexes are ecological footprint (Wackernagel & Rees, 1994; the environmental dimension), gross domestic product (the economic dimension), and human development index (UNDP, 2015; the social dimension). The sustainability-theme indicators do not measure overall sustainability because they confine themselves to one particular sustainable development theme (or dimension). Typically, these indexes correspond to concepts like 'environmental' (e.g., MEA, 2005), 'economic' (e.g., Common & Perrings, 1992), 'social' (e.g., Dempsey *et al.*, 2011), or 'just' sustainability (e.g., Agyeman, 2013). However, these concepts are redundant in a sense because the concept of sustainability *per definition* contains environmental, social, (sometimes) economic, *and* justice themes. Thus a concept like 'just sustainability' is wrong for two reasons. First, justice is already an integral part of sustainability, so there is no reason to repeat it. Second, it gives the impression that sustainability is *not* about justice and one therefore must add it. Again, there is no reason to do that, because sustainability already contains (among other things) an idea of justice.

There are reasons why some still would like to use a concept like 'just sustainability'. On the one hand, some think that justice is the most important part of sustainability and like to make that point by adding 'just' to sustainability. We argue that this is wrong; all key sustainability themes are equally important. On the other hand, some want to make the point that justice is not given sufficient weight in the sustainability concept and thus add justice to make sure that it is not forgotten. Though we sympathize with that view, we argue that adding justice to sustainability is superfluous.

Extended-sustainability-theme indexes: The third category comprises indexes that include more than one theme (or dimension). An index might be criticized for being too development oriented, and attempts are thus made to remedy that critique by adding another theme (or dimension) into the index. Examples are the inequality-adjusted human development index (UNDP, 2015) that combines the themes capability and justice, and the genuine-savings index (Hanley *et al.*, 2014) that combines the economic and environmental dimensions. Though better than the sustainability-theme indexes, they nevertheless leave out important sustainability themes.

Composite-sustainability indexes: The fourth category comprises indexes that, according to their advocates, measure overall sustainability. The indexes are intended to capture in a single snapshot whether sustainable development has been achieved. Examples are the composite-sustainability-performance index (Singh *et al.*, 2007) and the sustainable development goal index (Sachs *et al.*, 2016). Both these composite indexes use the three-pillar model of sustainable development. The latter index is supplemented with a 'SDG dashboard' for each country using a colour-coded schema. The SDGs are highlighted in green, yellow, or red, with the latter emphasizing a country's most acute challenges. Green signifies that a country is on a good path towards reaching an SDG and its targets, or that a country has already achieved the threshold consistent with SDG achievement. To construct the SDG dashboards and to give a colour rating for each underlying indicator, it determines four quantitative thresholds ranging from best to worst scores (ibid.). A similar approach uses a dashboard and colours to assess the likelihood of meeting the 17 SDGs in five world regions (DNV GL, 2016).[10] Rather alarmingly, the report concludes that none of the 17 SDGs will be achieved in all regions by 2030.

All four categories have their weaknesses. Three-pillar-model indicators do not sufficiently acknowledge the ethical foundation of sustainable development. Rather, indicators are developed from the model's three dimensions without much regard to the normative imperative of sustainable development. Thus, indicators are mostly consensus based and reflect what is possible and feasible, which opens up for developing indicators on the basis of short-sighted political consensus and parochial stakeholder preferences (which we have warned against doing).

Sustainability-theme indexes do not, as indicated, measure overall sustainability. Rather, they are part of a set of indexes that collectively measure sustainable development. Thus, in practice there is not much difference between sustainability-theme indexes and, say, environmental indexes. To illustrate where sustainability-theme indicators go wrong, we can use the 'three-legged stool model of sustainable development'. According to this model, sustainable development can be considered as a stool that rests on three legs (an environmental, a social, and an economic leg). Although we disagree with the naming of the legs (which should rather be the three moral imperatives), the stool model tells us two things. First, a stool simply does not work with one leg. Thus, focusing on a single sustainability theme is incompatible with the idea of a stool (and sustainable development too). Second, a stool needs three equally strong (and long) legs to do what it is supposed to do. It does not make sense to increase the length of one leg because one or two of the other legs are too short. Nor does it make sense to make one leg stronger because one or two of the other legs are too weak (which is what the notion of 'weak sustainability' suggests). Thus, it is not the legs' *total* length or strength that is important. Rather, the legs' length and strength are equally important.

The stool analogy tells us why the extended-sustainability-theme indexes are not much better. Two legs instead of one would probably be better if one has good balance. Three legs would certainly make more sense. One still needs that final leg to sit comfortably.

The composite-sustainability indexes are probably the most dangerous of all. By focusing on *overall* performance, the indexes can conceal all sorts of deficiencies. Consider the sustainable development goal index. The Scandinavian countries are at the top of the list, which would suggest that these countries are 'closest now to achieving the SDG endpoints envisaged for 2030' (Sachs *et al.*, 2016, p. 14). The authors are aware of the problems with measuring sustainability by a single indicator though, and therefore introduce a dashboard to show that even the Scandinavian countries must improve their performance:

> Even these relative top performers have their work cut out, as demonstrated further by the OECD Dashboards. For example, these countries need to shift their energy systems from high-carbon to low-carbon primary energy in order to fulfill (*sic*) SDGs 7 and 13. In general, the SDG Index and the SDG Dashboards show that even many high-income countries fall far short of achieving the SDGs.
>
> (ibid.)

Nevertheless, all the tables in the report place the Scandinavian countries firmly atop the list. Why is it more sustainable to trespass environmental limits (which all the Scandinavian countries definitely do) than to perform poorly on social justice? For all the warnings in the text and footnotes, composite-sustainability indexes make it possible to compensate poor performance on one theme with excellent performance on other themes.

Our approach to sustainability indicators

We suggest one headline indicator for each key theme. True, the number of headline indicators is somewhat arbitrary. There could be more and there could be fewer. The important point is that the number of headline indicators is small (that is, manageable) and that a priority is allocated to them. Thus, 'headline' tells us that this is the most important indicator for each theme. In practical policy terms, the headline indicators must be supplemented by more indicators; these supplementary indicators must, however, relate to the key themes.

Ideally, we would like to suggest a single, independent, one-issue indicator for each theme. Although we have warned against using composite indexes that make trade-offs *across* themes, we open up the possibility for using composite indexes *within* themes. There are three reasons for this. First, because a theme might not be directly measurable (e.g., biosphere integrity). Second, because available composite indexes (e.g., the human development index) better capture the multidimensional nature of the themes (e.g., a set of capabilities). Third, because we believe that the advantage of allowing for composite indexes which build on an implicit trade-off between sub-indicators within a theme is greater than the disadvantage of allowing for such trade-offs. Thus, our headline indicators are mostly headline indexes for each theme. However, we acknowledge that striving for more or less independent, one-issue indicators for each theme would be preferable.

Whereas the key sustainability themes come from theory, the headline indicators inevitably must open up for practical considerations. There is always a question of data availability and possible correlation between individual indicators across

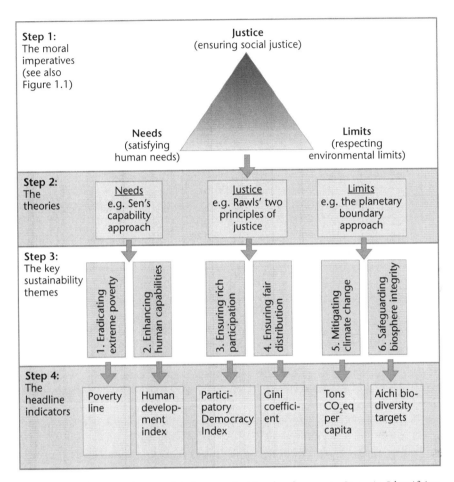

FIGURE 5.4 A normative model for sustainable development. Step 4: Identifying headline indicators (modified from Holden *et al.*, 2016).

themes. Chapter 6 goes into detail on these issues and we will not repeat those considerations here. Figure 5.4 shows the suggested headline indicators.

Step 5: Thresholds

The final step of our model is to assign thresholds to the headline indicators. This step brings us back to the discussion about whether sustainable development is 'a process of change' or about achieving a fixed end-state. Sandhu *et al.* (2014) support the former view. They deliberately do not attempt to define global sustainability as an end-state. They argue that it is almost impossible to make a full and properly scientific assessment of individual activities in relation to global sustainability. And even where it may be possible, they argue, it would be well beyond the capability of actors at the local level to do so. Rather, they see sustainable development as:

A collective, progressive and self-reflective *activity*, undertaken within communities, designed to develop more sustainable relationships with the natural environment, including its own members and members of other communities.

(ibid., p. 225, our italics)

We agree that a full assessment of global sustainability at a local level is difficult (though not impossible), and we will return to that question in chapter 8. Nevertheless, we agree with Sutton, for whom the move to define sustainability as a process can be symptomatic of denial:

As the scale of the task of achieving a sustainable environment and society has become apparent many people have tried to insulate themselves from the enormity of the challenge by retreating into small incremental changes. So some people have started to say that sustainability is a process of change and not an end state, and that it's the journey that counts, not the destination.

(Sutton, 2004, p. 2)

Though Sutton acknowledges that 'the "destination" of sustainability is not a fixed place in the normal sense that we understand destination', he nevertheless acknowledges that 'achieving the "destination" is the purpose of the journey' (ibid., p. 5). On the face of it, one could argue that *Our Common Future* too rejects the idea that sustainable development is a fixed end-state:

Yet in the end, sustainable development is not a fixed state of harmony, but rather a process of change in which the exploitation of resources, the direction of investments, the orientation of technological development, and institutional change are made consistent with future as well as present needs.

(WCED, 1987, p. 9)

Still it is difficult to argue that *Our Common Future* does not see sustainable development as a distinct goal to be achieved. Indeed, the *processes* of, say, eradicating poverty and preventing climate change are not good enough. Rather, the *goals* of eradicating poverty and preventing climate change are at the heart of sustainable development. Thus, we agree with Lancker and Nijkamp (2000) that each indicator requires a normative reference value, which they call a critical threshold value. Thus, 'a given indicator doesn't say anything about sustainability, unless a reference value such as thresholds is given to it' (ibid., p. 114). Indeed, there can be no assessing of sustainability without thresholds!

Having said that, we acknowledge that sustainable development is not a fixed destination in the sense that its goals cannot be changed. Indeed, a democracy should always allow for open debate and reasoned scrutiny about its normative foundation. Moreover, the key themes, headline indicators, and thresholds presented in this book must be changed as new evidence arises in, say, ecology and/or new and better indicators become available. Thus, the meaning of sustainable development is always open for debate and new knowledge. In that sense *defining* sustainable development is a process. Sustainable development is not, however, the process of getting there. Simply trying is not good enough.

Assigning the threshold values is closely interlinked to suggesting the headline indicators. Thus, please see chapter 6 for details about thresholds. Figure 5.5 shows the complete sustainable development model. This is a demanding model in the

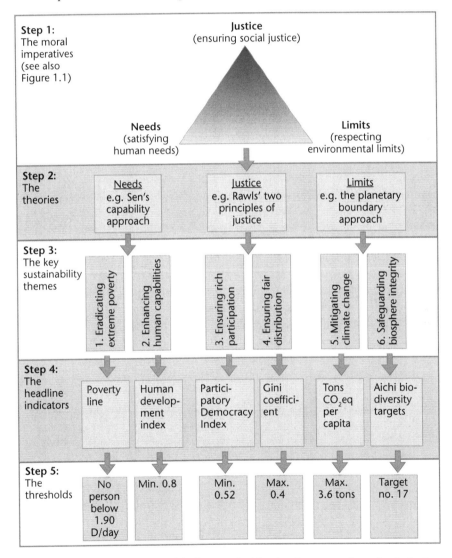

FIGURE 5.5 A normative model for sustainable development. Step 5: Assigning thresholds. See chapter 6 (e.g. table 6.1, p. 165) for details on headline indicators and thresholds (modified from Holden *et al.*, 2016).

sense that it is difficult for countries to comply with the thresholds (chapter 7 shows that no countries currently manage to do so). Thus, achieving sustainable development is indeed a challenging task. But let us hope that it is possible to achieve it voluntarily and that Daly (2007) is wrong when he says that 'we may have to suffer a bit' before we do so.

Some might object that this is a Western model, one developed by and for the dominant Western societies' values. And indeed, sustainability indicators typically place Western liberal democracies atop the list; Western nations typically occupy all but a few of the top 20 places (Eckersley, 2016). Though we do not take this objection lightly, we think that our model does not exclusively favour Western democratic countries. The model stresses the need to eradicate poverty and enhance human capabilities. There is nothing inherently Western about that. The model stresses the need for democratic participation and fair distribution. Sen argues that seeing social justice as an exclusively Western phenomenon is limited and to some extent parochial. The model stresses the need to respect environmental limits. Indeed, the consequences of not doing so would hit non-Western countries hardest.

The sustainable development space

The triangle at the top of figure 5.5 suggests that our model presents sustainable development as a space. Thus, sustainable development is not a fixed end-state (you're welcome, Sandhu *et al.*!) which should be reached, but rather a space within which we should be. According to the *Merriam-Webster Dictionary*, a space is 'the amount of an area, room, surface, etc., that is empty or available for use'. Alas, regarding sustainability, that space is currently empty: chapter 7 shows that currently no countries are inside the sustainable development space. Yet the space is definitely 'available for use'; our sense of sustainability tells us so. The triangle does not provide much help for policymakers though. We need to specify sustainable development in more detail. Having identified the key sustainability themes, suggested headline indicators, and assigned thresholds, we are now able to define the space quantitatively. Figure 5.6 (see also Figure 1.2) shows the sustainable development space.

Acknowledging that sustainable development is a space rather than a fixed end-state has three important consequences. First, it clearly demonstrates that sustainable development contains the idea that there are many constraints to which human activities must adhere. These constraints, which are manifest by the thresholds on key themes, make up the boundaries that surround the space. Presently, most countries are outside those boundaries, so we should start acting to get inside them.

Second, it opens up for a variety of states of sustainable living and a variety of ways to get into the space. Thus, finding oneself inside the sustainable development space, there should still be room for different positions *within* that space. Although the constraints apply globally and cannot be trespassed, the space somewhat opens up for national and local adaptations. This book's first part (chapters 1–5) shows

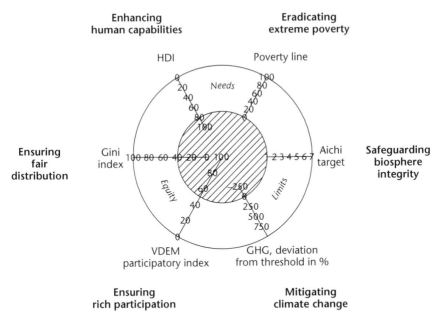

FIGURE 5.6 Quantifying the sustainable development space (hatched area).

Notes: Aichi = biodiversity targets; GHG = greenhouse gas emissions; Gini = measure of inequality; HDI = human development index; VDEM = variety of democracy. See chapter 6 (e.g. table 6.1, p. 165) for details. Figure is the work of the authors.

how to define the sustainable development space. We have not said much about how to get there; we will return to that in chapters 7–9. Indeed, there are many ways, including increasing the use of greener technology, applying green taxes, promoting behavioural changes, and more. Different countries and local actors must find their own ways.

Third, a country's position in the sustainable development space shows how it complies on all key themes. Thus, there is no way to hide poor performance on one theme by excellent performance on others. The sustainable development space tells countries which key themes are most in need of assistance, thus symbolizing the priorities set. Once the thresholds are set, the space is specifically suited to its purpose as it demonstrates a sphere of sustainability *inside* and the domain of unsustainability *outside* the space (Spangenberg, 2002).

Finally, we would like to add that the thresholds can (and probably should) be changed over time. For example, the poverty level can be raised to $2.50 or more in 2020 and $4.00 in 2030, or the per-capita CO_2eq level may have to be reduced to 3 tons (from 3.6 in the present model) or even less, as population increases and as impacts become better understood.

We are now at the end of the book's first part. Chapter 1 claims that the concept of sustainable development is an ethical statement, from which we can derive three equally important moral imperatives. Chapters 2–4 present the theories that are fundamental to those imperatives. Chapter 5 presents a normative model of sustainable development, which defines the sustainable development space. The model is a reflection of what we treasure. The space is where we should be or, if we are far off, where we should be going.

Chapter 7 shows how different countries comply with the normative model and, moreover, shows different pathways towards the sustainable development space. First, however, we must find out how to measure what we treasure. We must find trustworthy, robust, and scientifically sound headline indicators and thresholds. In doing so, we must inevitably account for a number of practical considerations, such as the choice between competing headline indicators, the correlation between headline indicators, the correlation and overlap between sub-indicators for each headline indictor, data availability, and data quality. These practical considerations are topics for the next chapter.

Notes

1 We must make one important point here. Although it is difficult, we argue that it is worth making a (perfect) sustainable development *model* based on the best available knowledge. Just because it is difficult to make such a model is no excuse for not doing it. On the other hand, there are cases where we cannot *achieve* (perfect) sustainable development; we are not in the position of doing what the model tells us to do. In these cases, we might have to settle with the best we can achieve given the circumstances. We will return to these cases and these circumstances in chapter 8.

2 The first version of the model was published in Holden and Linnerud (2007). The model was later upgraded and published in different versions in Holden (2007), Holden *et al.* (2013, 2014), and Linnerud and Holden (2016). The model presented in this book is a minor modification of the latest version of the model published in Holden *et al.* (2016).

3 These approaches are sometimes referred to as macro-level and micro-level approaches, respectively (Sandhu *et al.*, 2014). There is also a meso-level approach, sometimes also called the 'middling out' approach, that is sensitive to both the macro and micro levels.

4 Originally published in Norwegian in 1995.

5 The indicator for the shared prosperity goal should be unambiguously stated as raising the living standards of the bottom 40 per cent in each country (not confounded with their relative share), and extended to include an indicator identifying the growth of per-capita real consumption of the bottom 40 per cent of the world distribution of consumption (World Bank, 2017).

6 In later works, Rawls has changed the formulation and content of the two principles. Their main ideas remain, however.

7 Rawls refers to the principle of equal liberty, when applied to the political procedure defined by the constitution, as the principle of (equal) participation. It requires that all citizens are to have an equal right to take part in, and to determine the outcome of, the constitutional process that establishes the laws with which they are to comply (Rawls, 1999, p. 194).

8 Rawls argues that fulfilment of the first principle takes priority over fulfilment of the second principle, and within the second principle fair equality of opportunity takes priority over the difference principle. We argue that the two are equally important in accordance with argument no. 6 (see chapter 1 in this book).

9 The Rio Declaration (UN, 1992a) is a set of 28 short, non-binding, statements of principle unanimously adopted at the United Nations Conference on Environment and Development that took place in Rio de Janeiro in June 1992.

10 The five world regions are: USA, OECD (excl. USA), CHINA, BRISE (Brazil, Russia, India, South Africa and ten other Emerging economies), and ROW (Rest of the World).

References

Agyeman, J. (2013) *Introducing Just Sustainabilities: Policy, Planning, and Practice*. London, Zed Books.

Alexander, E. (1981) If planning isn't everything, maybe it's something. *Town Planning Review*, 52(4), 131–142.

Alkire, S. (2010) *Human development: Definitions, critiques, and related concepts*. Background paper for the 2010 Human Development Report, OPHI working paper no. 36. Oxford Poverty & Human Development Initiative (OPHI), Oxford.

Alkire, S. & Robles, G. (2015) *Multidimensional Poverty Index – 2015: Brief methodological note and results*. Oxford Poverty & Human Development Initiative (OPHI).

Aslaksen, I., Ericson, T., Funtowicz, S., Garnåsjordet, P. A., & Giampietro, M. (2010) *A general model for selection and specification of national sustainable development indicators (SDI) in a precautionary context*. Paper presented to the International Society for Ecological Economics. ISSE, 22–25 August 2010, Oldenburg, Germany.

Backhouse, R. E. & Medema, S. G. (2009) Retrospectives: On the definition of economics. *Journal of Economic Perspectives*, 23(1), 221–233.

Banfield, E. (1973) Ends and means in planning. In: Faludi, A. (ed.) *A Reader in Planning Theory*. Oxford, Pergamon Press.

Ban Ki-moon (2015) Available from: https://www.un.org/sg/en/content/sg/speeches/2015-10-10/remarks-development-committee-ministerial-lunch-%E2%80%9Cinvesting-evidence%E2%80%9D#.V49Iou3h77A].

Bell, S. & Morse, S. (2008) *Sustainability Indicators: Measuring the Immeasurable?* 2nd edition. London, Routledge.

Chansarn, S. (2014) The evaluation of the sustainable human development: A cross-country analysis employing slack-bases DEA. *Procedia Environmental Science*, 20, 3–11.

Christen, M. & Schmidt, S. (2012) A formal framework for conceptions of sustainability: A theoretical contribution to the discourse in sustainable development. *Sustainable Development*, 20(6), 400–410.

Common, M. & Perrings, C. (1992) Towards an ecological economics of sustainability. *Ecological Economics*, 6, 7–34.

Crick, B. (2002) *Democracy: A Very Short Introduction*. New York, Oxford University Press.

Dahl, A. L. (2012) Achievements and gaps in indicators for sustainability. *Ecological Indicators*, 17, 14–19.

Daly, H. (2007) *Ecological Economics and Sustainable Development: Selected Essays of Herman Daly*. Cheltenham, UK and Northampton, MA, Edward Elgar.

Dempsey, N., Bramley, G., Power, S., & Brown, C. (2011). The social dimension of sustainable development: Defining urban social sustainability. *Sustainable Development*, 19, 289–300.

DNV GL. (2016) *Future of Spaceship Earth*. Høvik, Norway, DNV GL AS.

Doyal, L. & Gough, I. (1991) *A Theory of Human Need*. London, Macmillan.

Eckersley, R. M. (2016) *Is the West Really the Best? Modernisation and the Psychosocial Dynamics of Human Progress and Development*. Oxford, Oxford Development Studies.

Ekins, P. (2014) Strong sustainability and critical natural capital. In: Atkinson, G., Dietz, S., Neumayer, E., & Agarwala, M. (eds) *Handbook of Sustainable Development*. Cheltenham, UK and Northampton, MA, Edward Elgar, pp. 55–71.

Eurostat (2009) *Sustainable Development in the European Union – 2009 Monitoring Report on the EU Sustainable Development Strategy*. Eurostat, Luxembourg.

Gasparatos, A., El-Haram, M., & Horner, M. (2008) A critical review of reductionist approaches for assessing the progress towards sustainability. *Environmental Impact Assessment Review*, 28, 286–311.

Hak, T., Kovanda, J., & Weinzettel, J. (2012) A method to assess the relevance of sustainability indicators: Application to the indicator set of the Czech Republic's Sustainable Development Strategy. *Ecological Indicators*, 17, 46–57.

Hak, T., Janouskova, S., & Moldan, B. (2016) Sustainable development goals: A need for relevant indicators. *Ecological Indicators*, 60, 565–573.

Hanley, N., Dupuy, L., & McLaughlin, E. (2014) *Genuine savings and sustainability. Discussion papers in environmental economics*. Paper 2014-09. University of St Andrews.

Heink, U. & Kowarik, I. (2010) What are indicators? On the definition of indicators in ecology and environmental planning. *Ecological Indicators*, 10, 584–593.

Helm, D. (2015) *Natural Capital. Valuing our Planet*. New Haven, CT and London, Yale University Press.

Holden, E. (2007) *Achieving Sustainable Mobility: Everyday and Leisure-time Travel in the EU*. Aldershot, Ashgate.

Holden, E. & Linnerud, K. (2007) The sustainable development area: Satisfying basic needs and safeguarding ecological sustainability. *Sustainable Development*, 15(3), 174–187.

Holden, E., Linnerud, K., & Banister, D. (2013) Sustainable passenger transport: Back to Brundtland. *Transportation Research Part A: Policy and Practice*, 54, 67–77.

Holden, E., Linnerud, K., & Banister, D. (2014) Sustainable development: 'Our Common Future' revisited. *Global Environmental Change*, 26, 130–139.

Holden, E., Linnerud, K., & Banister, D. (2016) The imperatives of sustainable development. *Sustainable Development*, DOI: 10.1002/sd.1647.

Lafferty, W. M. & Langhelle, O. (eds) (1999) *Towards Sustainable Development: On the Goals of Development and the Conditions of Sustainability*. London: Palgrave Macmillan.

Lancker, E. & Nijkamp, P. (2000) A policy scenario analysis of sustainable agricultural development options: A case study for Nepal. *Impact Assessment and Project Appraisal*, 18(2), 111–124.

Langhelle, O. (2016) Sustainable development: Linking environment and development. In: Meadowcroft, J. & Fiorino, D. (eds) *Conceptual Innovations in Environmental Policy*. Cambridge, MA, MIT Press, pp. 234–260.

Leach, M., Scoones, I., & Stirling, A. (2010) *Dynamic Sustainabilities: Technology, Environment, Social Justice*. London and Washington, DC, Earthscan.

Lindblom, C. E. (1973) The science of 'muddling through'. In: Faludi, A. (ed.) *A Reader in Planning Theory*. Oxford, Pergamon Press, pp. 151–169.

Linnerud, K. & Holden, E. (2016) Five criteria for global sustainable development. *International Journal of Global Environmental Issues*, 15(4), 300–314.

Maffettone, S. (2010) *Rawls: An Introduction*. Cambridge, UK and Malden, MA, Polity Press.

Maslow, A. H. (1943) A theory of human motivation. *Psychological Review*, 50, 370–396.

Max-Neef, M. A. (1991) *Human Scale Development: Conceptions, Applications and Further Reflections*. New York and London, The Apex Press.

MEA (2005) *Ecosystems and Human Well-being: Synthesis*. Millennium Ecosystem Assessment. Washington, DC, Island Press.

Meadowcroft, J. (2012) Pushing the boundaries: Governance for sustainable development and a politics of limits. In: Meadowcroft, J., Langhelle, O., & Ruud, A. (eds) *Governance, Democracy and Sustainable Development: Moving Beyond the Impasse*. Cheltenham, UK and Northampton, MA, Edward Elgar, pp. 272–296.

Meadowcroft, J., Farrell, N., & Spangenberg, J. (2005) Developing a framework for sustainable governance in the European Union. *International Journal for Sustainable Development*, 8(1&2), 3–11.

Momete, D. C. (2016) Rational development as a sustainable progress welfare vector: A cross-country analysis. *Sustainable Development*, DOI: 10.1002/sd.1645.

Morse, S. (2015) Developing sustainability indicators and indices. *Sustainable Development*, 23, 84–95.

Neumayer, E. (2013) *Weak and Strong Sustainability: Exploring the Limits of Two Opposing Paradigms*. 4th edition. Cheltenham, UK and Northampton, MA, Edward Elgar.

Nussbaum, M. (2000) *Women and Human Development: The Capabilities Approach*. Cambridge, Cambridge University Press.

OECD (2002) *Indicators to measure decoupling of environmental pressure from economic growth*. SGSD (2002)1/final. Paris, The Organisation for Economic Co-operation and Development.

OECD (2010) *A framework to measure progress of Societies*. Working paper No. 34, STD/ DOC(2010)5. Paris, The Organisation for Economic Co-operation and Development.

Pearce, D., Barbier, E., & Markandya, A. (1990) *Sustainable Development: Economics and Environment in the Third World*. Cheltenham, UK and Northampton, MA, Edward Elgar.

Pigou, A. C. (1932) *The Economics of Welfare*. 4th edition. London, Macmillan.

Pindyck, R. S. (2007) Uncertainty in environmental economics. *Review of Environmental Economics and Policy*, 1(1), 45–65.

Rametsteiner, E., Pülzl, H., Alkan-Olsson, J., & Frederiksen, P. (2011) Sustainability indicator development: Science or political negotiation? *Ecological Indicators*, 11(1), 61–70.

Rawls, J. (1999) *A Theory of Justice* (revised edition). Cambridge, MA, Belknap Press.

Robeyns, I. (2011) The capability approach. *The Stanford Encyclopedia of Philosophy*. Available from: http://plato.stanford.edu/archives/sum2011/entries/capability-approach/.

Rockström, J., Steffen, W., Noone, K., Persson, Å., Chapin, F. S. III, Lambin, E. F., Lenton, T. M., Scheffer, M., Folke, C., Schellnhuber, H. J., Nykvist, B., de Wit, C. A., Hughes, T., van der Leeuw, S., Rodhe, H., Sörlin, S., Snyder, P. K., Costanza, R., Svedin, U., Falkenmark, M., Karlberg, L., Corell, R. W., Fabry, V. J., Hansen, J., Walker, B., Liverman, D., Richardson, K., Crutzen, P., & Foley, J. A. (2009) A safe operating space for humanity. *Nature*, 461(24), 472–475.

Sachs, J., Schmidt-Traub, G., Kroll, C., Durand-Delacre, D., & Teksoz, K. (2016) *SDG Index and Dashboards – Global Report*. New York, Bertelsmann Stiftung and Sustainable Development Solutions Network.

Sandel, M. K. (2009) *Justice: What's the Right Thing to Do?* New York, Farrar, Straus and Giroux.

Sandhu, S., McKenzie, S., & Harris, H. (eds) (2014) *Linking Local and Global Sustainability.* Dordrecht, Heidelberg, New York, London, Springer.

Sen, A. (1987) The standard of living. In: Sen, A., Muellbauer, J., Kanbur, R., Hart, K., & Williams, B. (eds) *The Standard of Living: The Tanner Lectures on Human Values.* Cambridge, Cambridge University Press.

Sen, A. (2009) *The Idea of Justice.* London, Penguin.

Singh, R. K., Murty, H. R., Gupta, S. K., & Dikshit, A. K. (2007) Development of composite sustainability performance index for steel industry. *Ecological Indicators,* 7(3), 565–588.

Singh, R. K., Murty, H. R., Gupta, S. K., & Dikshit, A. K. (2012) An overview of sustainability assessment methodologies. *Ecological Indicators,* 15, 281–299.

Spangenberg, J. H. (2002) Environmental space and the prism of sustainability: Frameworks for indicators measuring sustainable development. *Ecological Indicators,* 2, 295–309.

Steffen, W., Richardson, K., Rockström, J., Cornell, S. E., Fetzer, I., Bennett, E. M., Biggs, R., Carpenter, S. R., de Vries, W., de Wit, C. A., Folke, C., Gerten, D., Heinke, J., Mace, G. M., Persson, L. M., Ramanathan, V., Reyers, B., & Sörlin, S. (2015) Planetary boundaries: Guiding human development on a changing planet. *Science,* 347, 736–746.

Stiglitz, J. E., Sen, A., & Fitoussi, J-P. (2010) *Mismeasuring Our Lives: Why GDP Doesn't Add Up.* The report by the Commission on the Measurement of Economic Performance and Social Progress. New York, The New Press.

Sutton, P. (2004). What is sustainability. *Eingana: The Journal of the Victorian Association for Environmental Education,* 1–7.

Turner, R. K. (1993) Sustainability: Principles and practise. In: Turner, R. K. (ed.) *Sustainable Environmental Economics and Management: Principles and Practise.* New York and London, Belhaven Press, pp. 3–36.

UN (1992a) *The Rio Declaration on Environment and Development.* The United Nations Conference on Environment & Development. Rio de Janeiro, Brazil, 3–14 June 1992. Available from: www.unesco.org/education/nfsunesco/pdf/RIO_E.PDF.

UN (1992b) *Agenda 21.* United Nations Conference on Environment & Development. Rio de Janeiro, Brazil, 3–14 June 1992. Available from: https://sustainabledevelopment. un.org/content/documents/Agenda21.pdf.

UN (2007) *Indicators of Sustainable Development: Guidelines and Methodologies.* 3rd edition. New York, The United Nations Commission on Sustainable Development.

UN (2015) *Transforming Our World: The 2030 Agenda for Sustainable Development.* Resolution adopted by the General Assembly on 25 September 2015, A/RES/70/1. United Nations General Assembly.

UNDP (2015) *Work for Human Development.* Human Development Report 2015. New York, United Nations Development Programme.

UNECE, OECD, Eurostat (2008) *Measuring Sustainable Development: Report of the Joint Working Party on Statistics for Sustainable Development.* New York and Geneva, United Nations.

UNEP (2007) *Global Environmental Outlook.* Geneva, United Nations Environmental Programme.

UNESC (1995) *Indicators of sustainable development.* Commission on Sustainable Development, 3rd Session, United Nations Economic and Social Council. New York, 11–28 April [E/CN, 17/1995/32].

Wackernagel, M. & Rees, W. (1994) *Ecological Footprints and Appropriated Carrying Capacity.* Washington, DC, Island Press.

WCED (1987) *Our Common Future.* World Commission on Environment and Development. Oxford, Oxford University Press.

Weitzman, M. (2009) On modelling and interpreting the economics of catastrophic climate change. *The Review of Economics and Statistics*, 91(1), 1–19.

Wildavsky, A. (1973) If planning is everything, maybe it's nothing. *Policy Sciences*, 4(2), 127–153.

World Bank (2017) *Monitoring Global Poverty: Report of the Commission on Global Poverty.* Washington, DC, World Bank, DOI: 10.1596/978-1-4648-0961-3.

Wright, L., Kemp, S., & Williams, I. (2011) 'Carbon footprinting': Towards a universally accepted definition. *Carbon Management*, 2(1), 61–72.

6
FACTS AND FIGURES

This award is not just for me.
It is for those forgotten children who want education.
It is for those frightened children who want peace.
It is for those voiceless children who want change.
Malala Yousafzai at age 17 in her Nobel lecture 2014

In her Nobel acceptance speech, Malala Yousafzai raised her voice to remind us of those who are voiceless but who have as much to say as any other citizen of the world. She continues to ask questions and demand answers, and she dedicates her creativity and capacity to change the world. 'The world we want' is the slogan of the United Nation's sustainable development goal campaign, but what is it that we want? And are we on a good path to achieve our dreams?

The following chapter complements the normative model of sustainable development presented in chapter 5 by building a bridge from words to numbers. In the next two chapters, we add facts and figures to our verbal interpretation of 'The world we want'. We do not do this because we believe in the beauty of mathematics (which we do) nor because we adore raw figures (which we do not). Instead, we do this because we recognize that quantified goals expressed by indicators and related thresholds are useful for taking stock and shedding light on whether the right paths are being taken to achieve our desired goals. It is probably not an exaggeration to say that data can create a momentum of accountability, which is critical when it comes to lifting sustainable development from a buzzword to an applied policy framework.

Yet, the usefulness of numbers rises and falls with their quality and reliability, a topic we already pondered in chapter 5. What we need is good data, sober number-crunching methods, and indicators that allow meaningful interpretations (i.e., indicator reliability). This means that we must prioritize indicators that do not overlap, but instead separate the various key themes to the largest extent possible. For example, we do not open with a discussion of fairness or historic responsibility when choosing an indicator for the key theme 'mitigating climate change' because both topics are clearly tackled elsewhere. This clear distinction is also a prerequisite of our statistical analysis in chapter 7, for which the key theme indicators need to be as uncorrelated as possible.

We are attempting to measure the world, but where do we start and where do we end? The challenge is that the problem of interest is complex and interwoven in time and space. What happened yesterday has repercussions tomorrow. What occurs in one place may change things on the other side of the world. All of this is contained in the data we mine, and we can only try our best to reveal the stories the numbers have to tell us.

This brings up a question that was not discussed in chapter 5 (but was mentioned in chapter 1) – what is the 'right' scale of indicators and thresholds? Humans are part of the global nature–human system whose parts interact in complex ways. Thus, sustainable development must be addressed globally, while simultaneously addressing local boundaries as well as regional interlinkages. National territories, economies, and societies constitute only one level of system organization, and the boundaries of many system-relevant scales differ from politically chosen borders. An obvious example is the natural subsystem, where relevant system boundaries can be as small as a pond.

We believe that the national scale is most relevant to convey our results to academia and practitioners (see chapter 8 for a discussion of this topic). One reason to focus on the national scale has to do with political feasibility because governance and its institutions are presently strongest at this level. Hence, the national scale currently offers the best opportunities to discover dead ends and reveal alternative pathways for the desired shaping of our societies. It is also an entry point to revise national policies. A second reason has to do with data quality. The best and most complete data are available from national sources. Moreover, since the establishment of national accounting systems, countries have started and continue to harmonize their methods of collecting and processing data, fostered by international organizations such as the United Nations. Only harmonized data-handling methods enable us to carry out transparent and comparative analyses across countries from which we can also draw global conclusions. We can link to the global scale by translating existing global and local sustainability thresholds to national thresholds to the largest extent possible and vice versa. A fallback option for deriving national thresholds is to apply the precautionary principle, which establishes the wisdom that safety 'guardrails' must be sufficient to avoid inaction that may lead to irreversible damages (Saunier & Meganck, 2009, p. 229).

Here we present options to measure the essence of the six key themes. As elaborated in chapter 5, the six key themes provide the foundation for the fulfilment of the three imperatives that guide our model of sustainable development, i.e., respecting environmental limits, ensuring social equity, and satisfying human needs. We primarily examine country-level data for each of the key themes and discuss the reasons for preferring one indicator over various alternatives. We also provide the rationale for drawing threshold values for each indicator to determine where each country is located in relation to the sustainable development space.

Eradicating extreme poverty

A poor person is a person deprived in her basic needs such as not having sufficient access to safe food and water, sanitation, education, health, and shelter. The key theme 'eradicating extreme poverty' focuses on people who are severely deprived. A frequently used monetary red line to signal extreme poverty is the equivalent of $1.90 per day and person, which is given in purchasing power parity of 2011. We hereafter call this 'international $1.90 (2011) per day and person'. This is considered the minimum amount needed to cover basic expenses. This international poverty line (IPL)[1] represents an average of the national poverty lines of the 15 poorest countries, all of which have a very low threshold for the standard of living. The countries are Malawi, Mali, Ethiopia, Sierra Leone, Niger, Uganda, The Gambia, Rwanda, Guinea-Bissau, Tanzania, Tajikistan, Mozambique, Chad, Nepal, and Ghana. Although the methods used to derive national poverty lines differ, they are all based on economic welfare theory and require a normative definition of a basic needs bundle for food and energy intake. The cost of the bundle is then estimated at a current price level, also reflecting national, climatic and/or geographic characteristics in more or less detail (cf. Ravillion, 2016). The threshold of international $1.90 (2011) per day and person is well established. It is also used as one of the indicators to track the first of the UN's sustainable development goals, which targets to end 'poverty in all its forms' (UN, 2015a).

Using this international poverty line, how many people are classified as extremely poor? The most comprehensive answer currently available can be drawn from PovcalNet, a global poverty data bank maintained by the World Bank that covers the years 1981–2013 for most developing countries (Ferreira *et al.*, 2015). According to PovcalNet, about 897 million people were statistically counted as extremely poor in the year 2012 (12.7 per cent of the total population). Three decades ago, there were twice as many people counted as extremely poor. Development efforts in East Asia and the Pacific have been comparatively successful in alleviating extreme poverty, notably in China and India, where the numbers of extreme poor dropped from 878 million (1981) to 150 million (2010) and 403 million (1983) to 264 million (2011), respectively. In sub-Saharan Africa, however, this trend has not been observed. Instead, the number of extremely poor people has remained constant at about 380 million since the start of the new millennium. Looking at country-level data, the global divide becomes even more apparent. The countries suffering most from very high shares of extreme poverty are Madagascar (81 per cent in 2010), Burundi (78 per cent in 2006), Democratic Republic of the Congo (77 per cent in 2012), Malawi (71 per cent in 2010), and Mozambique

(69 per cent in 2008), all of which are located in sub-Saharan Africa, which makes the region a focus area for poverty reduction.

These are what we have called 'raw' figures, but how are these numbers obtained and what do they reveal? These poverty estimates are based on more than a thousand surveys carried out at the household level. One way to obtain this type of information is to record a household's consumption and the other is to measure its income. These surveys are conducted on a regular basis in each country, and a number of households representing different income groups are selected to be interviewed. These data samples are then extrapolated to the underlying population and commonly linked to a nationwide or global poverty line such as the threshold value of international $1.90 (2011) per person and day. Apart from methodological differences and varying survey frequencies from one country to the next, several remarks need to be made about the quality of data, as well as their comparability within and across countries. An important point, however, is that a single measure is insufficient to capture the multidimensional problem of poverty.

One concern is that the disposable income of a household only reflects the *opportunity* to achieve a certain living standard at a given price level. In other words, it is only a proxy for the living standard *actually* achieved. Also, a household may be able to consume in ways that are not reflected by purchases at market prices. For example, food can be borrowed from a neighbour, firewood can be collected from common property, or a person can be employed in the informal sector. Therefore, consumption-based surveys are considered superior over income surveys, but unfortunately they are less readily available. Indeed, in Latin America, employment surveys are virtually the only type of surveys regularly carried out. Also, any survey requires a huge effort and hence they are not conducted every year. To fill in the blanks in the time series, survey data are occasionally supplemented by national account statistics deploying, for example, GDP per capita. In this way, differences between population groups may be lost. In addition, the two types of data are blended to give one overall result. Another problem is the distortion of datasets by less frequent but weighty effects. For example, very wealthy people are less likely to be interviewed and thus prone to falling through cracks. As a response to such criticism, the World Bank is pursuing 'twin goals', that is, to supplement the international poverty line data with the shared prosperity indicator (World Bank, 2014). This additional indicator focuses on the income growth of the poorest 40 per cent within a country. Because this indicator is closely related to the key theme 'ensuring fair distribution', we discuss this topic in that section.

World Bank indicators have been criticized because they oversimplify the complex poverty phenomenon.[2] One alternative is the multidimensional poverty index (MPI) published for the first time in 2010 by Oxford University (Alkire *et al.*, 2015). This composite index draws from household surveys as does the IPL, but the MPI specifically collects data for ten different sub-indicators quantifying a household's simultaneous deprivation in education (schooling years, attendance), health (nutrition and child mortality), and living standards (access to electricity, improved sanitation, improved drinking water, flooring, cooking fuel, assets ownership). For example, an adult household member is deprived in nutrition if she is severely undernourished (body mass index < 18 kg/m²), or a household member is deprived in sanitation if she has no access to a flush-toilet, latrine, ventilated improved pit or composting toilet. It is not sufficient if she can share such a facility with other households. However, the MPI's sublevel thresholds are arbitrary. In the case of the IPL, at least democratically legitimized institutions set the bundle of basic needs that in turn defines the threshold for extreme poverty. The overall MPI threshold is also arbitrary: people deprived in more than one-third (half) of the indicators are counted as (severely) poor.

What can be learned from the most recent MPI data and how they compare to the IPL? The latest MPI report discloses 1.6 billion people as multidimensionally poor, of whom 787 million are severely poor (Alkire et al., 2016). Although the total numbers are not directly comparable, the World Bank's count of the extreme poor reached 897 million in 2012. A close look at the national level is more instructive. Ethiopia is an example that particularly sticks out because the two methods of measuring poverty draw very different pictures. About 34 per cent of Ethiopians did not possess at least a daily equivalent of international $1.90 (2011), a finding that was reported to be robust to a sensitivity analysis of 2011 estimates (Hill & Tsehaye, 2015). Although this is still a high share, it was 55 per cent in 2000. The MPI from 2011 found much higher shares of poor (87 per cent) and severely poor (71 per cent) people, and 38 per cent of the population were deprived in all ten MPI indicators simultaneously in 2011. Why is the difference so large, from 78 million people who were considered to be multidimensionally poor (and 64 million severely poor) in the MPI to 'only' 29 million (extremely poor) with the IPL? A closer look into the development of Ethiopia in the period 2000–2011 is necessary to better understand the explanatory power of the poverty measures. For the following discussion, we also draw from two additional sources, the Demographic and Health Survey for Ethiopia (DHS Ethiopia, 2012) and the country briefing for Ethiopia by the Oxford Poverty and Human Development Initiative (CB Ethiopia, 2013).

As pointed out above, a strength of the MPI is the possibility of disaggregating data into separate dimensions of deprivation. The data for Ethiopia show comparatively good progress with respect to education and health dimensions. From 2000 to 2011, each improved by 34 per cent and 18 per cent, respectively, whereas the progress regarding living standards was a rather modest 8 per cent (Hill & Tsehaye, 2015). In fact, CB Ethiopia (2013) found that 76 per cent of the total population in 2011 were simultaneously deprived with respect to cooking fuel, flooring, sanitation, electricity access, and asset ownership. Thus, it is not surprising that almost half of Ethiopia's multidimensional poverty in 2011 is explained by the high number of people being deprived in just one dimension, but it is one that contains six out of ten indicators (Hill & Tsehaye, 2015).

As shown in figure 6.1, this finding is generalizable for most of the 20 poorest countries as determined by the IPL.[3] With the exception of Burkina Faso and Senegal, living standards make the largest contribution to the MPI. In the case of

Ethiopia, as Hill and Tsehaye (2015) point out, the cut-off for living standards considered by the MPI is simply too high to show any progress that has been made. For example, Ethiopian households without access to a toilet dropped substantially from 82 per cent to 38 per cent by 2011, but only 'improved' toilets are counted for the purpose of the threshold. Another problem is that Ethiopia's specific conditions are not well reflected in the assets considered for the MPI. For example, in Ethiopia, agricultural assets such as livestock are very important, particularly in the poorest rural areas – indeed, they are much more valuable than the possession of a bicycle in mountainous areas. The latter is counted in the multidimensional poverty index, however, but the former is not. In fact, one of the key drivers of progress in poverty reduction in Ethiopia has been the sustained growth in agriculture in addition to growth in services and public investment (Hill & Tsehaye, 2015).

In conclusion, what is the better indicator and threshold to measure the performance in the key theme 'eradicating extreme poverty'? We chose the IPL for several reasons. First, it relates directly to the group of extreme poor who are our focus. Second, it is also used for monitoring sustainable development goals, and hence, it allows us to directly compare our model of sustainable development with the progress recorded by UN targets. Third, it has better geographic and time-series coverage. Finally, although the MPI allows a decomposition into different dimensions of poverty, the insights may be limited for two main reasons. First, they are not always able to reflect the specific conditions in a country as we have

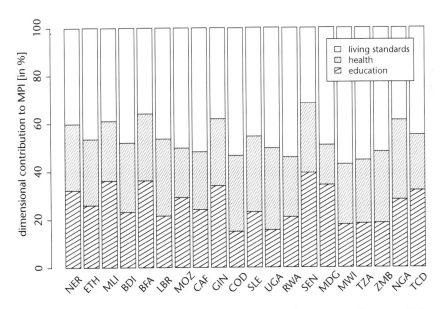

FIGURE 6.1 Share of three poverty dimensions in the multidimensional poverty index (MPI) for the 20 poorest countries (sorted according to the international poverty line). See appendix for country codes.

Source of data: Alkire *et al.* (2016), World DataBank (2016).

illustrated for the example of Ethiopia. The second argument limiting its use for our purpose is that we cover some of the dimensions of multidimensional poverty in other key themes, notably the development in health and education, which are part of the key theme 'enhancing human capabilities'. In this way, we avoid double counting and reduce built-in correlation among the key themes.

Enhancing human capabilities

Human wellbeing is linked to the capability of an individual to make choices in her social environment, so that she can pursue a fulfilling, long, and creative life, while being knowledgeable of and having access to necessary resources (see chapter 3 for the normative arguments). Therefore, the indicator on human capabilities needs to assess if the conditions are such that they enable an individual to seize and realize her opportunities.

A widely used indicator in this respect is the human development index (HDI) developed by the Pakistani economist Mahbub ul Haq and the Indian economist Amartya Sen. A 'long and healthy life' is measured by life expectancy, the capability of a person to attain knowledge is measured by years of schooling, and the assessment of a 'decent standard of living' is related to gross national income. It is a composite index with values from 0 to 1 and ranks countries according to their human development. In 2010, the HDI was revised so that the geometric mean of the three dimensions replaced the arithmetic mean, implying imperfect substitutability among the three.

The UN's 2015 report on human development covers 188 countries (UNEP, 2015a). It is not very surprising that African countries score remarkably lower relative to the rest of the world, with Niger at the bottom. The African continent is behind across all three dimensions, but the low number of years of education particularly stands out. Just five African countries achieve more than 7.5 years of schooling. Even in Asia, the continent with the second highest deficit in education, most young people spend much longer in school. The continent with the highest human development is Europe, where all countries, except Moldavia, score at least 0.7, categorizing them as countries with at least 'high human development'. The existing spread in values of human development across Europe is primarily driven by differences in gross national income, which is understandable because life expectancy and years of schooling are already close to their ceiling levels of 12 years for most Europeans.

Despite being a common index, measuring human development based on the HDI has drawn criticism since its first use. One of the most severe shortcomings is its failure to capture rapid changes in a society. A drastic example is the case of Syria whose current HDI hardly reflects the disastrous situation of its ongoing civil war. Although the HDI has decreased from 0.66 to 0.59 (10 per cent) since 2009, the country is still placed in the group of countries with medium human development. Moreover, despite the ongoing war, the current HDI of Syria continues to be higher than it was in 1990. Such inertia has to do with the stock and flow variables used in the index. Indeed, these different types of data are mixed when composing the HDI, because life expectancy and education are stock values whereas income is a flow. If, for example, yearly enrolment ratios were used instead of mean years of schooling, the breakdown of institutions caused by the civil war would have an immediate effect on the HDI. Of course, the same criticism applies to constructive and hopeful developments. The effects of current policies (e.g., education efforts in developing countries) are not seen immediately. In this light, it is not very surprising that a government's spending on education and the performance of the country in the HDI ranking are not well correlated with each other.[4]

The importance of education cannot be stressed enough to overcome poverty and achieve at least a decent standard of living (Lutz *et al.*, 2014). Otherwise, even the bottom rung of a person's ladder of lifetime possibilities is simply out of reach. It is particularly important to close the gender gap that exists in many countries. Indeed, the high correlation between female education and fertility rates is empirically well-established. For example, the Demographic and Health Survey in Ethiopia (DHS Ethiopia, 2012) found that a woman without formal education gives birth to an average of 5.0 children, whereas the number drops to 3.4 children for women who have completed a secondary education (similar figures are associated with women of very low or rather high wealth as well).

The HDI is certainly not a perfect measure of a person's capabilities, but the categories of education, health, and living standards are without doubt relevant to assessing the set of opportunities available to an individual. The main problem is that education measured in school years says little about the actual level of education attained or whether it is suitable from the perspective of a country's economic and social development. Similarly, health measured by life expectancy does not reveal much about the quality of life someone can attain. The practice of equating a person's living standard with per-capita gross national income has long been criticized. Given long-term established national accounting systems, this proxy is comparatively well-standardized across the various countries, but it only measures economic activity. Although the set of opportunities increases with greater possibility to be economically active, a wide range of factors is outside of a person's economic sphere, such as reliable governmental institutions and functioning infrastructure. Furthermore, the 'average' person does not always well represent the diversity between inhabitants in a country.

An alternative is to ask an individual about her own perception of how she is endowed with opportunities. One such option is the happy planet index (Abdallah *et al.*, 2012; Helliwell *et al.*, 2015). This composite indicator draws from the World Gallup Survey, where a person is asked to self-evaluate her life opportunities today and five years from today on a scale from zero (worst possible life) to ten (best possible life). The results are ranked as a life ladder poll. The happy planet index then combines the poll data with life expectancy data to compute the happy life years.

In figure 6.2 we compare the human development index (HDI) and the happy life years (HLY).[5] Countries that are italicized in figure 6.2 are Costa Rica (CRI), Mexico (MEX), Venezuela (VEN), Israel (ISR), New Zealand (NZL), Australia

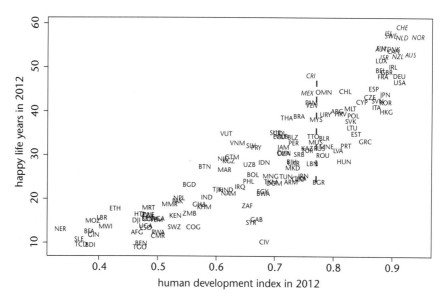

FIGURE 6.2 Human development index compared with the happy life years in 2012. See appendix for country codes.

Source of data: Helliwell *et al.* (2015), UNEP (2015a).

(AUS), Austria (AUT), Canada (CAN), Denmark (DNK), Finland (FIN), Switzerland (CHE), Iceland (ISL), Netherlands (NLD), Norway (NOR), and Sweden (SWE). All of them score at least seven out of ten points in the life ladder poll; that is, they have an optimistic outlook on their futures. The correlation between HDI and HLY is notably high, underlining that per-capita gross national income can very well serve as a proxy for living standards. However, for a given value of the HDI (especially the higher values), the number of happy life years varies. An example cross-section is highlighted in the figure by the vertical dashed line at the HDI of 0.77 from Bulgaria (BGR: 24 happy life years and 4.2 on life ladder poll) to Costa Rica (CRI: 48 happy life years and 7.3 points on the life ladder scale). At the same time, 'happy' Costa Rica is on a par with countries such as Great Britain or the USA, which exhibit the same HLY but a much higher HDI. Comparing the HDI components for the USA and Costa Rica, one finds that their inhabitants can enjoy similarly long lives, whereas the number of years of education and the per-capita yearly income differ, at 12.9 (8.4) years and US$53,000 (13,000) for the USA (Costa Rica).[6] Despite these differences, Costa Rican people consider themselves as happy as their US counterparts do. This may have to do with their long-term satisfying experience of a stable democracy and its institutions, but also with the fact that the market basket of goods making Costa Rican people happy differs from that making Americans happy. In the end, perceived happiness is a subjective measure with generally low comparability across countries and time periods, so we consider HDI to be the more suitable indicator.

The choice of a threshold for the HDI cannot be backed up by theory, however. The common grouping of countries into 'very high human development' (greater than 0.8 HDI) and 'low human development' (less than 0.55) is purely based on statistical considerations. That said, the threshold of 0.8 appears to be a good choice from the perspective of HPY (the dashed line in figure 6.2 is at 0.77). Apart from Hungary, all countries above this value enjoy at least 30 happy life years.

How do these findings compare to the sustainable development goals? Individual categories of the HDI play a crucial role in many of the goals, but the related indicators only specify certain aspects of the broader categories. For example, among the sustainable development goals there is no indicator measuring life expectancy, but there are indicators for child and maternal mortality, epidemics, injuries, accidents, drug misuse, and health coverage (goal no. 3 'education and well-being'). Similarly, goal no. 4 ('quality education') targets a 'completed, equitable, and quality primary and secondary education' by 2030 for all girls and boys. Additionally, youths and adults should have 'relevant skills, including technical and vocational skills, for employment, decent jobs and entrepreneurship'. The goal most closely related to economic endowment is goal no. 8 ('decent work and economic growth'). Its aim is to 'sustain per capita economic growth in accordance with national circumstances and, in particular, at least 7 per cent gross domestic product growth per annum in the least developed countries'. While this goal guarantees a catch-up period in the less developed world, it does not directly translate into a numeric value for per-capita gross national income itself.

To sum up, the choice to use the HDI to measure the capability of inhabitants is guided by its widespread use, its comparatively strong explanatory power across countries, and because it is complementary to what we measure in the other key themes (see following discussion). Namely, the poverty indicator is about the satisfaction of basic needs on a personal level, whereas the inequality measure adds the social dimension about the fair distribution of resources, and finally, the indicator for capability assesses if a society uses its resources to foster human development. A missing element in judging the social dimension of sustainable development is the role of institutions and political stability of a country. This topic is addressed in the next section.

Ensuring rich participation

The possibility for any citizen to participate and influence shaping the society she lives in constitutes the heart of civil rights and democracy. We refer to this as 'rich participation' in chapters 3 and 5. There are plenty of useful ways to conceptualize and measure the extent to which this can be achieved. The challenge is to enable comparisons across countries and time periods, which is necessary because societal changes such as institutional change (whether good or bad) may not be immediately visible. The political empowerment of women in society is an example of such a slow change – it took more than five decades from the first introduction of universal suffrage for women in Finland in 1903 to the actual first election of a female head of government (in Sri Lanka).

A recently developed and promising approach to measure the possibilities to participate and shape society is the Varieties of Democracy Project, co-hosted by the Department of Political Science at the University of Gothenburg, Sweden and the Kellogg Institute at the University of Notre Dame, USA. This project not only offers good discriminatory power across its indicators, but also provides a consistent method that allows it to be easily linked to other common democracy indicators and background variables (Coppedge *et al.*, 2011). Most importantly, it currently provides the largest dataset on democracy and related issues.

The project distinguishes among seven principles of democracy: electoral, liberal, participatory, majoritarian, consensual, deliberative, and egalitarian. Five related indices evaluate to what extent the principle's ideal has been reached. In all of them, the electoral principle is a 'must-have'; hence, the electoral indicator is a component of all other indicators. The principle most closely related to our key theme 'ensuring rich participation' is the participatory principle, which tests whether ordinary citizens have an active role in political processes. Covering electoral and non-electoral elements, the participatory democracy index (PDI) punishes the delegation of authority to representatives, preferring direct rule by citizens. The data to compute this and the other indicators are drawn from extensive questionnaires that are evaluated by a theory-based, standardized procedure with the help of a pool of country experts and under the guidance of program managers. This makes the program's approach qualitatively different from that of other approaches, where the dataset is created by only a handful of experts. Here, we use data of the Varieties of Democracy Project, Version 6.1 (Coppedge *et al.*, 2016).

The top three countries offering the most participatory elements to their citizens over an extended period of time are Switzerland (CHE), Uruguay (URY), and New Zealand (NZL). The surprising occurrence of Uruguay is driven by the strong power of regional elected governments in Uruguay and the deep participation of residents in civil society, which prompted the *New York Times* to call Uruguay a 'quiet democratic miracle' (*New York Times*, 2014). Uruguay's success story seems deeply rooted in the history of the country's liberal traditions. At the bottom are Lao People's Democratic Republic (LAO), People's Republic of Korea (PRK), and Saudi Arabia (SAU).

Although the participatory democracy index (PDI) of the Varieties of Democracy Project is suitable for our purposes, the question remains about how to choose the threshold for the key theme. To do this, we compared the PDI with the democracy index of the *Economist* Intelligence Unit (EIUDI), which is another widely used democracy indicator (*Economist* Intelligence Unit, 2016). This index groups countries into four regime types: full democracies, flawed democracies, hybrid regimes, and authoritarian regimes. Both indicators exhibit a strong positive correlation, as shown in figure 6.3. However, in comparing the PDI and EIUDI indicators, different conclusions can be drawn for some nations. For example, countries falling into the category of 'flawed democracies' (6<EIUDI<8) rank

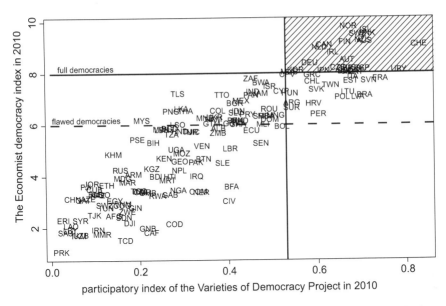

FIGURE 6.3 The participatory democracy index of the Varieties of Democracy Project versus *The Economist*'s democracy index (EIUDI) for 2010. See appendix for country codes.

Source of data: Coppedge *et al.* (2016), *Economist* Intelligence Unit (2016).

is considered to be rather close to the ideal of a participatory democracy. Looking relatively high according to the PDI and vice versa. France is one example of a flawed democracy, but it scored 0.75 on the PDI in 2010. With that value, France into the details of the French EIUDI, it is clear that deductions from the ten-point maximum score are mostly due to a relatively low score in relation to the direct popular vote index, whereas the power of local and regional governments are evaluated to be strong. This is, in fact, similar to the observations in the PDI, where the democratic shortcomings of France are noted as a widespread distrust of the national government and the immense power of the French president to overrule regional decisions. In the end, the labelling of a democracy as 'flawed' as distinct from 'full' is at least partially an arbitrary decision, but both categories at least approach the democratic ideal. We chose a threshold of 0.52 for the PDI because it ensures that no country from a lower category according to the EIUDI enters the group of countries passing, while at the same time, all countries evaluated as 'full democracies' are included.

Ensuring participation is also a relevant topic in the UN's sustainable development agenda. The goal most closely related to our key theme is sustainable development goal no. 16, which is 'to promote peaceful and inclusive societies for sustainable development, provide access to justice for all and build effective, accountable and inclusive institutions at all levels'. At this point, however, only one indicator has been proposed to measure progress for this goal. It is an important,

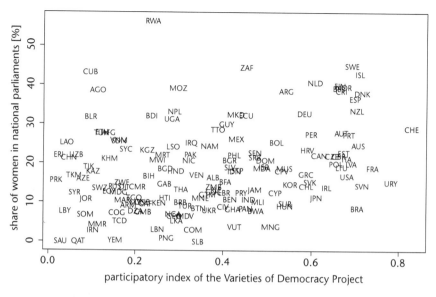

FIGURE 6.4 Share of women in national parliaments versus the participatory democracy index of the Varieties of Democracy Project for 2010. See appendix for country codes.
Source of data: World DataBank (2015), Coppedge *et al.* (2016).

but rather specific indicator, which measures the percentage of seats held by women and minorities in a national parliament and/or subnational elected office according to their respective share of the population. Thus, instead of measuring how *any* citizen potentially can participate in her society, the focus is on a *specific* group. Such indicators tell the very relevant but complementary story of societal discrimination. However, they fail as a proxy indicator that captures progress towards ensuring participation *in general*. Moreover, the indicator only looks at one level of political participation, that is, the share in national parliaments, whereas the PDI is much more comprehensive. Finally, given the current poor empowerment of women (or low-income groups) across countries in the world, it is also not surprising that there is hardly any correlation between the indicator for sustainable development goal no. 16 and the PDI (figure 6.4). For this reason, we consider the PDI to be the best choice.

Ensuring a fair distribution

In chapter 3, we looked into different philosophical concepts that address various approaches to achieve a fair society. Then, in chapter 5, we concluded that ensuring a fair distribution constitutes a cornerstone of our sustainable development model. The indicator for this key theme addresses three choices: the society we live in needs to decide *who* gets *what* and whether the distribution can be called *fair*. Its translation into measurable quantities requires answers to the following questions.

The first choice concerns the perspective from which the analysis is taken: *Who* should be in the spotlight? Do we look at the situation from the perspective of a world citizen? Or do we focus on a person in a specific country or do we consider social status? The second question relates to *what* is being distributed: Is it the distribution of welfare, resources, income, or more generally, utility or opportunity? This question is more quickly answered, because the coverage of wealth data in contrast to income at the country level is insufficient for our intended statistical analysis. Thus, at this point, our choice is limited to an analysis of the distribution of income, but refer to chapter 3 for a brief discussion of the wealth–income debate. The third question tackles the problem of the underlying *fairness concept* (see chapter 3 about Rawls' contribution to this debate): Is a distribution 'fair' if the same amount is allocated to everybody (equal division)? Or is it fairer if each person perceives her share as desirable as that of someone else (no-envy distribution)? Or should the change in allocation affect everybody in the same way? Alternatively, should the less capable be preferred, thereby allowing them to catch up?

A starting point for coming up with answers to these questions is to review how progress towards the UN sustainable development goals is measured. The fact that this remains an ongoing discussion shows that the choice of a useful measure is not straightforward. Sustainable development goals no. 10 and no. 17 are related to this key theme. The former targets the reduction of inequality *within* and *among* countries. To date, a list of possible indicators has been drafted and a few quantified targets have been chosen (UN, 2016; United Nations Economic and Social Council, 2016). A striking fact is that none of the targets addresses inequality *across* countries and generations; that is, none looks at inequality from the perspective of a world citizen. Goal no. 17 aims to revitalize global partnerships for sustainable development.

Of the long list of possible indicators, the most interesting one for our purpose is the 'shared prosperity index', which focuses on the income distribution of the poorest 40 per cent in a country (World Bank, 2014). The target is that income growth in this group should be sustained at a higher rate through 2030 relative to a country's average rate of income growth. Note that the required data come from national income and/or consumption surveys, whose background has already been discussed in relation to the key theme 'eradicating extreme poverty', where we concluded that income surveys have better coverage, and hence provide a more comprehensive dataset.

Figure 6.5 presents the most recent World Bank estimates for the shared prosperity index for 94 countries. A general finding is that annual growth in average income is highly correlated with growth in the income of the bottom 40 per cent. This implies that a growing average income can improve the situation for those earning less than average. However, only countries that are situated below the diagonal line in the figure are currently on track to achieve the target, so only these countries would deserve the label 'fair' when it comes to the distribution of income. By this standard, distribution is not fair in 38 out of the 94 countries (40 per cent) for which data were available. Among them are countries that differ

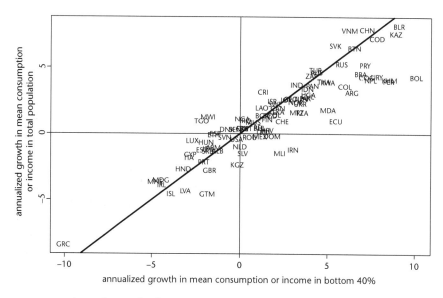

FIGURE 6.5 Annual growth of a country's average income compared to growth for the poorest 40 per cent for the most recent available combination of years. See appendix for country codes.

Source of data: World DataBank (2015).

greatly in their economic power, such as Malawi, Vietnam, Luxembourg, and Greece. At this point, we would argue that the world community still has a long way to go with respect to actually ensuring a fair distribution of income. Surprisingly, the inequality measure with the best coverage in terms of space and time – the Gini coefficient – was dropped from the list of proposed indicators for sustainable development goals. Its value can range from 0 per cent where income is equally distributed to 100 per cent where there is a maximum unequal distribution of income across all groups (Gini, 1909). The interpretation of the Gini coefficient is not straightforward, but a Gini of 60 per cent has an easily understood interpretation: it roughly implies that the richest 20 per cent own about 80 per cent of the wealth. But what is a 'fair' value? A priori, there is no threshold above which a Gini coefficient would be called unfair. The only judgement inherent to its definition is the equal division of income (i.e., a Gini of 0 per cent). The choice of any other threshold is purely normative. Yet, one guideline that is often deployed is that a Gini coefficient of more than 40 per cent is considered unfair (United Nations Research Institute for Social Development, 2013).

What does the Gini coefficient add to the picture obtained thus far with the help of the shared prosperity index? According to the World Bank's most recent data, the five countries with the highest Gini coefficients are Cape Verde, South Africa, Seychelles, Comoros, and the Federal States of Micronesia. Among the countries with the fairest distribution of income are Norway, Switzerland, and the Netherlands. How then does a *change* in the Gini coefficient over time compare with the shared prosperity index? This dynamic comparison is shown in figure 6.6 which additionally highlights countries in italic with a Gini coefficient of lower than 40 per cent.

What do we find? First, we observe the measures are strongly correlated.[7] Second, almost all countries fall into either the upper left rectangle or the lower right one. These two areas represent opposite views of the world, and the view is influenced by both indicators. In other words, the achievement of the shared prosperity target overwhelmingly coincides with a decreasing Gini coefficient over time. Likewise, it is not fulfilled if the Gini coefficient increases with time. Notably, there are only five countries where this general finding does not hold, Bhutan (BTN), South Africa (ZAF), China (CHN), Slovakia (SVK), and Hungary (HUN). Putting Bhutan aside (because both indicators are in fact so close to zero that they can be ignored), all of the counterexamples are located in the lower left rectangle. This location implies that the distribution of income became fairer in these countries (as shown by the decrease in the Gini coefficient), but the income growth rate of the bottom 40 per cent was lower than that of higher income groups.

A disadvantage of a dynamic inequality measure (like the shared prosperity index) is that knowing the trend of a country does not help to understand its starting point. Figure 6.6 adds to this information by additionally highlighting those countries with Gini coefficients below 40 per cent at the end of the

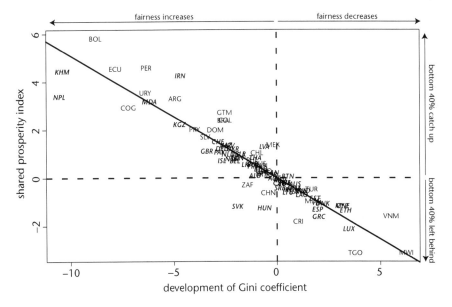

FIGURE 6.6 Change in the Gini coefficient with time compared to the shared prosperity index for the most recently available combination of years. Countries in italic exhibit Gini coefficients lower than 0.4 at the end of the observation period. See appendix for country codes.

Source of data: World DataBank (2015).

observation period (in italic). Many of those not highlighted are from Latin America. Their Gini coefficients remain very high even though many of these countries have made improvements with respect to the shared prosperity index. Thus, they fulfil the criteria for the shared prosperity index but they do not pass the threshold for the Gini coefficient. Our conclusion is that the Gini coefficient has a twofold advantage. First, it captures *actual* conditions. Second, observing change in the Gini coefficient over time overwhelmingly equates with what can be learned from the shared prosperity index. In chapter 7, we will be evaluating different time steps for our cross-country analysis, and the Gini coefficient is suggested as the best indicator.[8]

Next, we move away from a national focus. Will the world also appear to become fairer when moving the spotlight from nations to the world as a whole (or the world citizen) by looking into global interpersonal inequality? A major step forward in this direction was recently achieved by Lakner and Milanovic (2015) who argue that it is pivotal

> to recognize the increasing role played by international organizations, and that the cosmopolitan view is the only one consistent with their [the international organizations] constitutions. One might also have an instrumental concern for global interpersonal inequality if extreme global inequality leads to increased international tension, conflict or large scale migration.
>
> (ibid.)

They compare the development of different equality measures at the global and regional level for the period 1988–2008.[9] With values in the 70.5–72.2 per cent range, the global Gini coefficient is very high over the whole period. Remarkably, it is much higher than the Gini coefficient constructed from most national data, where South Africa (67 per cent) and Cape Verde (73.5 per cent) exhibit the highest values. We take a closer look at this below, but this finding deserves to be stressed because it implies that the focus on nations as opposed to world citizens creates a much more optimistic picture about the fair distribution of income in the world.

How does the Gini coefficient compare with other inequality measures from a global perspective? In contrast to other indicators, Lakner and Milanovic (2015) find that the world Gini coefficient did not vary considerably over the two decades. This seems to point to an often stressed weakness of the Gini coefficient – it is more sensitive to the middle income group and less so to small income changes in the bottom income group (Ryu, 2013). Indeed, the strongest changes of inequality from the cosmopolitan perspective are observed when using generalized entropy indices weighing the lowest and highest income groups.[10] Inequality in the lowest income groups of the world decreased during 1988–2008 by 10 per cent, whereas inequality in the higher income groups increased by 15.9 per cent. A strong advantage of the generalized entropy indices is that they allow decomposition into contributions from inequality within and inequality between countries. According to Lakner and Milanovic (2015), more than 70 per cent of the global inequality index originates from inequality between countries. In other words, the cosmopolitan perspective has to be part of any sustainability narrative.

A weakness of all of the single-number indicators discussed so far is that they do not provide the means to capture the *dynamics* of income mobility across all groups. Such insights can be generated with the help of kernel density estimates. Lakner and Milanovic (2015) show such estimates for the income distribution of five different macro regions, which have been adjusted to reflect the share in population of each region relative to the world population (figures 6.7 and 6.8, adapted from ibid.). Remarkably, the world income distribution in 1988 had a bimodal structure,[11] with a larger peak in the lower income group (dominated by India, China, and the less wealthy parts of the 'rest of the world') and a lower peak (mostly formed by the rich 'mature economies'). After 20 years, the distribution is hinting towards the emergence of a 'global middle class' (mainly due to a wealthier China). Other countries also show some signs of convergence towards higher income, but much less so for sub-Saharan Africa. On the other hand, its growth in population shows up in its much stronger influence on the global distribution by 2008. The smallest change between the income distributions in 1988 and 2008 is observed for mature economies.

What can we conclude from this chapter's discussion? First, there is no best indicator, because inequality cannot be boiled down to a single number. Rather, it is connected with a distribution *function*. Also, the picture of inequality in the

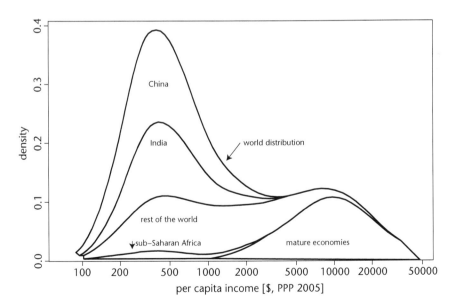

FIGURE 6.7 Distribution of world income in 1988 with regional contribution (stacked). Adapted from: Lakner and Milanovic (2015).

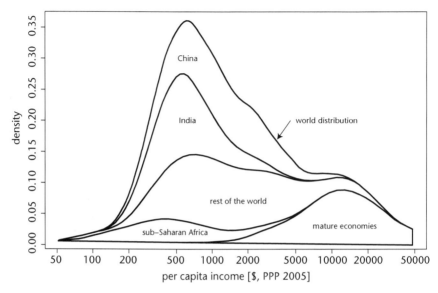

FIGURE 6.8   Distribution of world income in 2008 with regional contribution (stacked). Adapted from: Lakner and Milanovic (2015).

world depends on the perspective taken. We have exemplified the differences when taking a national and a cosmopolitan perspective, with the latter being much less optimistic. We note that accounting for these weaknesses comes at the expense of drastically increasing the number of indicators. For these reasons, we will use the national Gini coefficients in combination with an alert line of 0.4 (United Nations Habitat, 2012), which is further complemented by the dynamic insights that are discussed in chapter 7, where we analyse how the indicators change over time.

Mitigating climate change

Despite the common practice of expressing anthropogenic climate change by an increase in the global average temperature, the effects of climate change materialize at the regional and local levels. Climate change is about changes in sea levels, precipitation patterns, and the occurrence of extreme weather events. Seen from a human perspective, it can be harmful in some places, but it can also improve living conditions in others. Also, the climate system is part of our global dynamic system and, as such, it undergoes natural changes. The question is then, at which level does climate change become a problem that we cannot or can barely handle? It becomes a global sustainability problem if phenomena such as large-scale seasonal wind patterns in the Asia-Australian monsoon system permanently change. This type of change is what Article 2 of the United Nations Framework Convention on Climate Change refers to as 'dangerous anthropogenic interference' (UNFCCC, 1992). We will utilize this intergovernmental interpretation to derive the threshold for the key theme 'mitigating climate change', but how can it be operationalized?

According to the fifth assessment report of the IPCC, the confidence across research communities is high that an 'additional global warming of 1°C by the end of this century increases the number of unique ecosystems and cultures under severe threat', and furthermore, that an 'additional warming of 2°C puts many more under severe stress' (IPCC, 2014a). In other words, if humanity wants to avoid an unsustainable pathway, the continued increase of the average global temperature should be halted by the end of this century to avoid *at least* an increase of more than 2°C. The political recognition of such a temperature threshold took place at the negotiations of the UNFCCC in Paris in 2015. In the 21st Conference of the Parties, it was decided to

> address the significant gap between the aggregate effect of Parties' mitigation pledges in terms of global annual emissions of greenhouse gases by 2020 and aggregate emission pathways consistent with holding the increase in the global average temperature to well below 2°C above pre-industrial levels and pursuing efforts to limit the temperature increase to 1.5°C above pre-industrial levels.
>
> (UNFCCC, 2015)

Note that the 'pre-industrial level' is a reference to the period 1850–1900.

Uncertainties around future emission pathways are, however, high. Even so, the *range* of projected pathways allows us to connect the 2°C target with an estimate of how much can still be emitted into the atmosphere. This is commonly referred to as the global carbon budget, and it amounts to roughly 1000 $GtCO_2eq$[12] (Rogelj et al., 2016). That is about as much as the world has been emitting between 1990 and 2012, and most of these emissions originate from the fossil fuel and industry sectors. Half of the emissions are from just five countries/regions: the USA (18 per cent), China (17 per cent), the 28 members of the European Union (14 per cent), the Russian Federation (6 per cent), and India (5 per cent).

Assessing whether the world is on track to achieve the 2°C target is difficult, but a precondition is a worldwide standardized accounting and monitoring system. In this respect, the establishment of the protocol of the UNFCCC since the Kyoto treaty in 1992 was a tremendous step forward. It obliges participating countries to submit yearly, detailed greenhouse gas inventories. By now, different institutions have been set up to check the quality of the data submitted and also to provide alternative estimates when deemed necessary. Examples of monitoring systems are the Emissions Database for Global Atmospheric Research (EDGAR) published by the Joint Research Centre of the European Commission and the Carbon Dioxide Information Analysis Centre (CDIAC) run by Oak Ridge National Laboratory.

The next challenge is to translate the global carbon budget of roughly 1000 $GtCO_2eq$ into national carbon budgets. Different allocation schemes are being discussed, ranging from the establishment of a single global per-capita limit to distribution methods that account for historic responsibilities in various ways. An example is the suggestion of 'greenhouse gas development rights' as put forward by the Stockholm Environment Institute.[13] The idea is that all countries with a yearly income below international \$7500 (2011) per person are granted a free development threshold until they cross this income level. Richer countries, on the other hand, are obligated to reduce their combined emissions correspondingly.

Besides choosing an allocation of a spendable carbon budget among countries, a decision must also be made on how to distribute it across time through 2100. This is not an easy task because the unknown future is part of the equation. As a matter of scientific principle, there is no alternative but to utilize scientific consensus found with the help of a multitude of models, scenario projections, and rigorous statistical analyses (Schwanitz, 2013).

Given this background, what are the steps forward to derive the threshold for the climate mitigation indicator? We start by taking 2030 as the reference year because it is the point most often referred to (UNEP, 2015b). Next, we collect information on the pathways that are consistent with the 2°C target, which specify to what extent emissions need to be lowered by 2030. Figure 6.9 shows 116 scenarios from 247 model runs that have been submitted to the 5th Assessment Report of the IPCC Working Group III (IPCC, 2014b).[14] The figure also provides estimates for the global carbon budget (2011–2100). The estimates range between 630 and 1180 $GtCO_2eq$ (IPCC, 2014a; Rogelj et al., 2016). This range is calculated from the paths that lie within the 10–90 per cent range (see the funnel in figure 6.9 depicted by the shaded area). The highlighted path is the so-called representative concentration pathway (RCP) 2.6. This pathway suggests one of the estimates for a waypoint indicating the necessary cut in greenhouse gas emissions (Van Vuuren et al., 2007). It implies that emissions need to be 22 per cent lower relative to 2010 (equalling those in 1990). The two other waypoints depicted in figure 6.9 are taken from Meinshausen et al. (2015; refer to the circles) and the Emission Gap Report (UNEP, 2015b; see the triangles). Including the uncertainty ranges from the waypoints suggests that emissions should not exceed 31–44 $GtCO_2eq$ in 2030. This value accounts for all greenhouse gases and emissions from land use, land-use change, and forestry. The range of uncertainty for the latter is particularly large.[15] A common trend, however, is that net zero emission needs to be achieved before the end of this century (figure 6.9).

Looking first at the global level, can we say that the world is on track to fulfil the target of limiting global warming below 2°C by the end of this century? Figure 6.9 also shows the range of emission estimates for the year 2030 that results from all countries implementing the pledges made at the Conference of the Parties in Paris 2015 (UNEP, 2015b). Given these estimates, there is a gap with respect to achieving the 2°C target ranging between 10 and 17 $GtCO_2eq$ (accounting for the uncertainty ranges related to unconditional as well as conditional commitments).

Next, we look at the national level. For this analysis, we first need to derive national thresholds. To do so, we take the lower bound of the range of the global 2030 waypoints. By choosing 31 $GtCO_2eq$, we apply the precautionary principle. Utilizing the medium-variant projection of the United Nations World Population Prospects (UN, 2015b), there will be about 8.5 billion people living on the planet

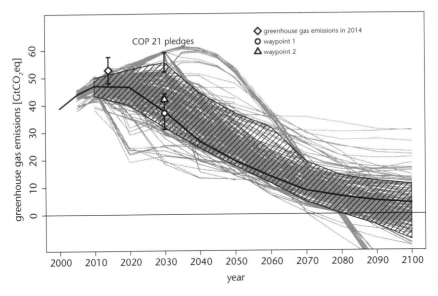

FIGURE 6.9 Greenhouse gas emission pathways compatible with a 2°C target.

Source of data: IPCC (2014b), Meinshausen *et al.* (2015), UNEP (2015b).

in 2030. Therefore, each person would need to emit less than 3.6 tCO$_2$eq annually. Looking at current data for population and greenhouse gas emissions, we can calculate for 2010 how close to or far away countries were from their 2030 targets. It is obvious from the data shown in figure 6.10 (note the logarithmic scale) that the majority of developed countries are following the wrong path. The worst 'offenders' are Kuwait, Brunei, and Qatar, with emissions of an order of magnitude higher than those set by the threshold.

The per-capita approach suggests itself from a global perspective because it assigns the same responsibility to each person in the world (cosmopolitan view). There are, however, alternative allocation schemes. Meinshausen *et al.* (2015) compare the per-capita approach with two other schemes to obtain country-level carbon budgets. One approach accounts for historic responsibility by accumulating greenhouse gas emissions from 1990 onwards. The other approach grants development rights as suggested by the Stockholm Environment Institute.[16] The difference between the three approaches can be substantial, and we show examples of the effects for the top five emitters on the right side of figure 6.10. Compared with the per-capita approach, the cumulative approach can move countries by about 20 per cent in either direction (figure 6.10). In particular, the currently rapidly developing India and China would profit, whereas some mature industrialized economies (e.g., Russia and the USA) would face more stringent targets. Taking the development rights perspective, India would not profit whereas China would. The penalty for the USA and the European Union (28 members) would be substantially higher.

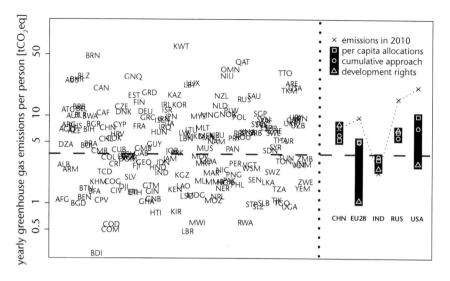

FIGURE 6.10 Per-capita greenhouse gas emissions in 2010 for 190 countries. The dashed line at 3.6 tCO$_2$eq marks the per-capita milestone for 2030 to achieve the 2°C target.

Note the logarithmic scale to differentiate countries. China, EU28, India, Russia, and the USA are shown in the right part to additionally illustrate the consequences of different allocation schemes. See appendix for country codes. Source of data: Emission Database for Global Atmospheric Research (2016).

Despite the important implications of these corrective approaches, we argue here to keep the simple per-capita threshold of 3.6 tCO$_2$eq derived from the global greenhouse gas emission budget. Given the high uncertainties around future mitigation pathways and the difficulty in agreeing to and specifying commitments in the international political negotiation process, this threshold is most likely the most objective measure from the perspective of a global citizen. Indeed, experience shows that political reality leads to overcomplex protocols that pose serious challenges to any monitoring system – even though the introduced complexity may be put in place for very good reasons, such as to open up opportunities for flexibility. Yet, the more sophisticated any approach behind a protocol becomes, the more it endangers effective enforcement. In other words, at this point, we can only hope that the follow-up to the Kyoto Protocol also refers to mechanisms that ensure justice.

The Green Climate Fund is an example that was set up to support adaptation measures and technology transfer. The target for the fund is to distribute $100 billion annually by 2020. Unfortunately, the global community is currently far from an agreement regarding actual national thresholds. Such issues are left for upcoming conferences of the parties, which eventually also may find their way into the sustainable development agenda. However, at the end of the day, there is no way around achieving actual reductions. Therefore, we have chosen to treat every global citizen in an equal way and establish the threshold level for this theme at 3.6 tCO_2eq per person.

Safeguarding biosphere integrity

This key theme has to do with the capacity of our global biosphere to resist fundamental changes (regime shifts) and to maintain its essential system functions. In other words, passing thresholds or tipping points leading to irreversible changes is not environmentally sustainable. Since the biosphere consists of multiple ecosystems of different scales across space and time, various thresholds exist, but not all are of global relevance. For example, if a smaller river (e.g., the Nysa) crosses a tipping point because it is overloaded with agricultural fertilizers that accumulated over past decades, its parent stream (the Oder, bordering Germany and Poland) may still be able to digest the polluted water coming from the Nysa. But if many rivers around the Baltic States are affected (which is indeed the case), then the large-scale ecosystem of the Baltic Sea may tilt. In other words, the integrity of the global biosphere depends on the overall health of its parts, and the higher the number of ecosystems affected, the larger the risk of infection. Also, the stronger a system's ties with other systems, the more important it becomes from a global perspective. At the same time, it is quite difficult to isolate the causes leading to a troubled system. As a consequence, the overall health of an ecosystem can hardly be described by any one aspect, and most importantly, by a single indicator. Moreover, going back to the above example, which of the Baltic countries is responsible for the environmental state of the Baltic Sea and by how much?

The difficulty – if not impossibility – of measuring the integrity of the global biosphere is a result of this complexity (see Mace *et al.*, 2014). In essence, human forces are causing perturbations in the balance in and between multiple systems of the biosphere. These factors include population growth, production, and consumption of resources (energy, food, and materials) and transformation of habitats and their fragmentation. These perturbations lead to measurable deviations from the dynamic behaviour of a system without the interference of human activities (cf. Spears *et al.*, 2015). For example, we are observing accelerated desertification; accumulation of nitrogen, phosphorus, and other chemicals in soil and water systems; oceans acidification; and an overall decrease in biodiversity.

As mentioned in chapter 4, the planetary boundary concepts have recently attracted substantial attention in the scientific and popular media (Rockström *et al.*, 2009; Steffen *et al.*, 2015). However, there is currently no agreement on how to derive global indicators and to determine their critical thresholds. The same is true for the establishment of guidelines at national level. Indeed, many doubt that it will be possible *at all* to derive meaningful and precise multi-scale operable indicators and thresholds given the fundamental uncertainties involved (cf. Groffmann *et al.*, 2006; Brook *et al.*, 2013; Galli *et al.*, 2016). The principle difficulty originates from the fact that our biosphere's integrity concerns the whole globe which is a complex system of interacting components at multiple scales of which we have insufficient knowledge. Having said this, we foreclose already now our choice for the indicator to measure the integrity of our biosphere in advance of our discussion of the pros and cons of various indicators. Due to the impossibility of deriving a single ecosystem-based indicator that reflects the necessary level of complexity, we do not choose an ecological indicator but opt for a political indicator. We are choosing a single indicator that measures the *actual dedication* of a country to secure our nature while at the same time reflecting the specific conditions of the country. But before we describe this indicator, we discuss various ecosystem-based indicators to assess the state of the environment. *Together* they provide a comprehensive view of the state of the biosphere's integrity.

Generally, the task of measuring the integrity of the global biosphere from a natural science perspective[17] boils down to not only quantifying the biosphere (e.g., by counting the number of trees, the number of birds, the area covered by forests, etc.), but also to assessing its quality, for example, to distinguish between healthy and non-healthy trees, to count the number of endangered birds, or to analyse the speed of deforestation. After such measurement, the local quantity and quality indicators need to be aggregated and compiled into a global indicator. Obviously, such a task not only requires long-term, high-quality data, but also a level of understanding of the functional relationships of different parts in the biosphere, both of which are not available. This is why commonly used indicators such as the red list are insufficient for our purpose.

One common practice to fill knowledge and data gaps is to use proxy indicators as well as simulations from various types of integrated assessment models. Three key approaches stand out in the literature because they can be operationalized at different geographic scales. The first approach is connected to Earth's productivity (e.g., accumulation of biomass or the provision of other ecosystem services), the second approach relates to its biodiversity (e.g., richness and abundance of species), and the third approach links to topography (e.g., land-use patterns and fragmentation). In the following, we briefly discuss the advantages and disadvantages of each approach and why we choose none of them as an indicator.

The ecological footprint issued by the World Wildlife Fund (Wackernagel *et al.*, 1997; Mancini *et al.*, 2016) is the best known example for the first approach. Its intriguing purity is an advantage – the footprint that people leave originates from our demand to use land and to produce food, fibre, and fuel. If the demand is higher than the productive capacity of the biosphere, a threshold is crossed. Trends for biocapacity and the footprint are presented in figure 6.11, from pre-industrial times through the present. Clearly, demand began to exceed supply in about 1970.

The disaggregation of global data depicted in figure 6.12 further shows that almost all continents overshoot their capacities, in particular Europe and Asia-Pacific, with the exception of Latin America, which is still well below its regional buffer. This is not surprising given that Latin America is endowed with the Amazon forest, one of the world's largest bio-productive areas. Yet, its intrinsic value for the integrity of the biosphere is certainly beyond its provisioning capacity for the human race. It is, for example, invaluable for the functioning of the global climate

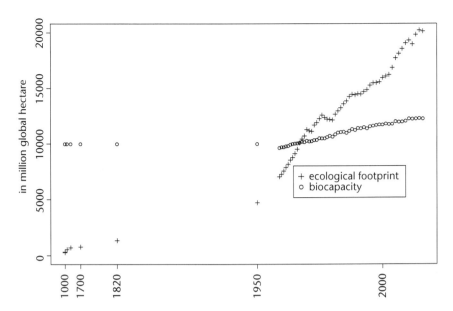

FIGURE 6.11 Global ecological footprint versus global biocapacity from 1000 to 2012. Source of data: World Wildlife Fund (2014), Tóth and Szigeti (2016).

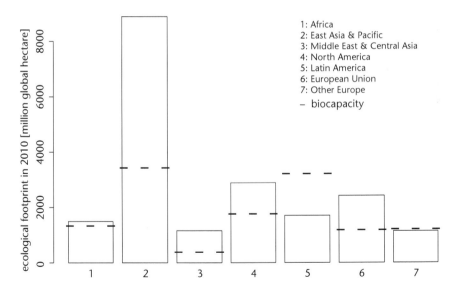

FIGURE 6.12 Ecological footprint in 2012 for different world regions. The dashed lines indicate the biocapacity of the regions.

Source of data: World Wildlife Fund (2014).

sytem and is a prime biodiversity hotspot. The advantages and disadvantages of the footprint indicator are outlined by Van den Bergh and Grazi (2013, 2014) and Galli *et al.* (2016), who conclude that the environmental footprint falls short on providing insights on why we are over-exploiting the planet.

The idea of biodiversity hotspots (i.e., threatened regions that are of high endemic importance) goes back to Myers *et al.* (2000). Up to now, 35 hotspots have been identified, most of which are near the equator and on isolated islands such as Japan, Australia, and New Zealand[18] (Mittermeier *et al.*, 2004; Williams *et al.*, 2011). In total, they account for about 44 per cent of the world's plants and 35 per cent of terrestrial vertebrates. Compared to the original area they covered, almost 85 per cent of the land has been lost, implying that many functions that support the resilience of the related ecosystems are endangered (see Sloan *et al.*, 2014). Among these are plants known as hyper-accumulators that are able to absorb enormous amounts of pollution. Another example is the indispensable function of bees for pollination.

Figure 6.13 shows the recent status of the 35 biodiversity hotspots using three measures: species abundance and richness (both obtained from a combination of observations and model simulations, see Newbold *et al.*, 2016), and the index of natural intact vegetation (NIV). The latter is defined as the share of 'mature vegetation in its natural state having minimal signs of human perturbation' (Sloan *et al.*, 2014). The situation is quite alarming, especially when an NIV ratio threshold of at least 20 per cent is applied (see the lowest dashed line in each panel in figure 6.13). This threshold implies that 24 of 34 hotspots have already passed the threshold. A similar warning sign is found inspecting the abundance of species and their richness. When establishing a safe limit of 90 per cent for the former and 80 per cent for the latter (the higher two dashed lines in each panel), 22 and 30 hotspots, respectively, do not meet the threshold (Newbold *et al.*, 2016).

Although the focus on biodiversity hotspots is relevant, the importance of other parts of the world for the biosphere's integrity is ignored using only this measure. It is important to stress that most biodiversity hotspots are located in a few countries around the equator. For them, national thresholds could be established, but how could thresholds for other countries be set? Therefore, we take the idea of natural intactness and apply it to national boundaries.

Specifically, we look into each country's proportion of vegetation that can be regarded as natural. Figure 6.14 presents the results from satellite data (scale: 500 m × 500 m; Friedl *et al.*, 2010). We aggregated the 14 land-use categories available for each country into four categories: (1) natural vegetation (including non-vegetated land such as deserts); (2) urban and built-up areas; (3) croplands; and (4) crop-land in combination with natural vegetation mosaics. Although this type of snapshot provides interesting insights, an indicator such as the relative share of natural vegetation linked to a certain threshold also has severe drawbacks because the specific circumstances of every country have to be accounted for.

For example, the Ukraine served for centuries as Europe's main granary. The assessment of the current and future state of environmental sustainability in the Ukraine should therefore aim at capturing whether this agrarian country is able to a) conserve the remaining natural areas or b) to what extent they can restore natural

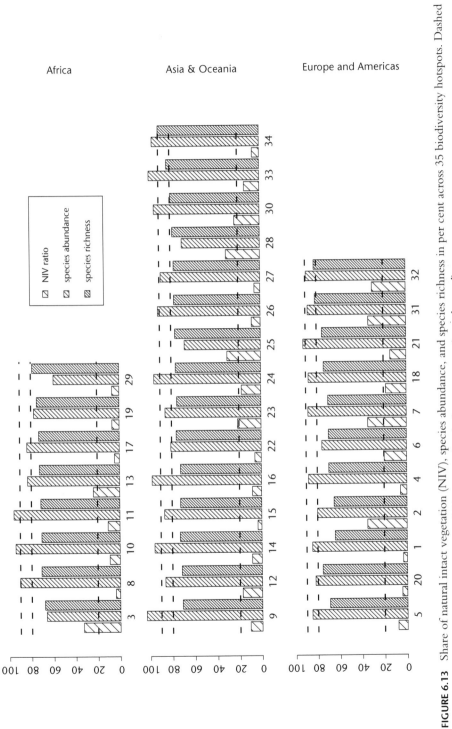

FIGURE 6.13 Share of natural intact vegetation (NIV), species abundance, and species richness in per cent across 35 biodiversity hotspots. Dashed lines indicate 20 per cent, 80 per cent, and 90 per cent levels (bottom to top in each panel).

Source of data: Sloan *et al.* (2014), Newbold *et al.* (2016).

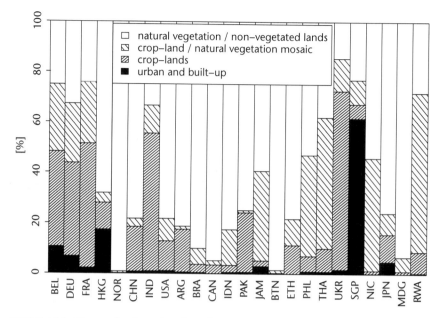

FIGURE 6.14 Current land use in selected countries. See appendix for country codes. Source of data: Friedl *et al.* (2010), Channan *et al.* (2014).

a) conserve the remaining natural areas or b) to what extent they can restore natural land. Yet, these are not part of the snapshot indicator. For economically strong Belgium, on the other hand, a country with high population densities and a large share of built-up land (figure 6.14), the country's responsibility for the biosphere's integrity rests little upon environmentally friendly food production. Instead, it is more about the country's ability to green its cities or to support other countries by providing financial support to protect their natural vegetation. Such historical issues, however, cannot be assessed by only looking at land-cover data. Again, as with the geographical approach,[19] finding an appropriate indicator that suits all countries is currently not feasible.

To summarize, all three general approaches to measure the biosphere's integrity reveal alarming signs about the state of our environment. However, we also have to conclude that a satisfactory *single* measure is not at hand, and none of them allow us to define national thresholds at this point. On the other hand, we need a single indicator for this key theme to be on the same footing with the other key themes. Therefore, we choose a somewhat surprising compromise. We propose the use of one of the biodiversity targets adopted at the 10th Conference of the Parties to the Convention on Biological Diversity, in Nagoya, Japan, in 2010; that is, we suggest using Aichi goal no. 17, which is in fact not related to any environmental attribute. Instead, it measures the actual dedication of a country to *safeguard* the biosphere today and in the future.

Specifically, the goal states, 'By 2015, each Party has developed, adopted a policy instrument, and has commenced implementing, an effective, participatory and updated national biodiversity strategy and action plan.'[20] The advantage of using this indicator is twofold. First, each country's goals, measures, and biodiversity hotspots can be specified to a satisfactory level reflecting the complexity of its environment. Second, national commitments are assessed through a transparent international monitoring process. The review and assessment process of the National Biodiversity Strategies and Action Plans is in the hands of the Convention on Biological Diversity, a supranational body established under the Nagoya Protocol. According to its last status report in November 2016,[21] 185 of 196 parties have developed plans, but few actually have achieved the 'adopted' status, and none of them has officially started implementation. In other words, all countries have failed to achieve the goal set for 2015. This clearly resonates with the alarming signs revealed by the selected environmental indicators discussed above.

This chapter complements the normative model of sustainable development presented in chapter 5 with the choice of key theme indicators and their national thresholds. Table 6.1 provides an overview of each. In addition, we also show how our threshold choices are linked to goals of the sustainable development agenda for each of the key themes (UN, 2015a). Although this chapter has focused on each of the key themes separately, the next chapter will assess all key themes at the same time to obtain a comprehensive picture of a country's performance in relation to a sustainable pathway. We furthermore extend the dynamic perspective by looking into the period from 2000 to 2010. This will allow us to provide a comprehensive picture about Earth's current state and also to elicit what needs to be changed to achieve sustainability.

TABLE 6.1 Final choices of indicators and thresholds for key themes and their links to sustainable development agenda goals. Table is the work of the authors.

Key theme	Indicator and threshold	Sustainable development goal
Eradicating extreme poverty	No person below the international poverty line of $1.90 (2011)	Identical to no. 1 'End poverty in all its forms, everywhere'
Enhancing human capabilities	Human development index reaching 0.8 or higher	Related to no. 3 'Education and well-being', no. 4 'Quality education', and no. 8 'Decent work and economic growth'
Ensuring rich participation	Participatory index of the Varieties of Democracy Project of at least 0.52	Related to no. 16 'Promote peaceful and inclusive societies ...'
Ensuring fair distribution	Gini coefficient below 0.4	Related to no. 10 'Reduced inequalities'
Mitigating climate change	Limiting yearly greenhouse gas emissions to less than 3.6 tCO_2eq per capita	Related to no. 13 'Take urgent action to combat climate change and its impacts'
Safeguarding biosphere integrity	Fulfilment of goal no. 17 of the Aichi biodiversity targets	Related to no. 14 'Life below water' and no. 15 'Life on land'

Notes

1 Here we follow the recommended nomenclature in the recent report, 'Monitoring Global Poverty: Report of the Commission on Global Poverty' (World Bank, 2017).

2 Recently, a high-level commission led by Anthony Atkinson along with an advisory board of 23 internationally renowned economists finalized their recommendations on how to go forward with measuring extreme poverty. The comprehensive report provides an excellent summary on the subject (World Bank, 2017).

3 Angola is not covered by the multidimensional poverty index.

4 The adjusted R-squared is 7 per cent using data from the World DataBank for 2010, that is, expenditure on education as a percentage of total governmental expenditure versus HDI.

5 Note that the ranking of countries by the HDI and the HPI differ strongly, and this can largely be attributed to the ecological footprint of the HPI (Otoiu *et al*,, 2014; Bondarchik *et al.*, 2016). For this reason, we only look at the sub-indicator 'happy life years'.

6 Measured in purchasing power parity of 2011.

7 The adjusted R-squared is 78 per cent. Excluding Bulgaria (BGR), it increases to 84 per cent (there likely are data issues with Bulgaria for 2007).

8 Note that values for the Gini coefficient are taken from the World DataBank as well from Branko L. Milanovic, *All the Ginis Dataset*, World Bank Group. Available from: http://data.worldbank.org/data-catalog/all-the-ginis [Accesssed on 20 November 2016].

9 The data are constructed from a mix of 565 national household surveys of income and consumption. Data are corrected for inflation within a country and converted to 2005 purchasing power parities. For China, India, and Indonesia, differences in price level for urban and rural areas are accounted for (Lakner & Milanovic, 2015).

10 The Theil and Atkinson indices show similar behaviour but not as pronounced. Both capture changes in the bottom and top income groups in a more sensitive way similar to the Gini (Lakner & Milanovic, 2015). Recently, the Palma Index was suggested as a replacement for the Gini coefficient (Palma, 2011). This index compares the ratio of the income share of the top 10 per cent to that of the bottom 40 per cent of the population. However, it is strongly correlated with the Gini coefficient (94 per cent), and thus adds little information for our purpose.

11 Compare also to the famous twin peaks observed first by Quah (1997).

12 $GtCO_2eq$ is the unit used to measure the sum of all greenhouse gases. Non-carbon dioxide greenhouse gases are converted into carbon dioxide equivalents using 100-year global warming potentials as shown in the 2nd Assessment Report of the IPCC (IPCC, 1995).

13 More information about the Greenhouse Gas Development Rights initiative: http://gdrights.org/.

14 The scenarios in figure 6.9 are those classified as 'climate category 1' in IPCC (2014b), implying a radiative forcing of 430–480 ppm CO_2eq with a full anthropogenic forcing equivalent of 2.3–2.9 Watt per square metre (IPCC, 2014b, Annex 10). The chance of limiting global warming in these pathways is larger than 66 per cent.

15 Emissions from land use, land-use change, and forestry can be positive (e.g., deforestation) and negative (afforestation). The Emission Gap Report 2015 estimates the maximum technical potential for yearly negative emissions to be up to 9 $GtCO_2$ in 2030 (UNEP, 2015b).

16 Refer to the data for the 'Greenhouse Gas Developments Rights' approach collected from www.mitigation-contributions.org/ [Accesssed on 20 December 2016].

17 For a discussion of approaches taken by other disciplines, see chapter 4.

18 Biodiversity hotspots: Africa: 3 – Cape Floristic Region, 8 – Coastal Forests of Eastern Africa, 10 – Eastern Afromontane, 12 – Guinean Forests of West Africa, 14 – Horn of Africa, 18 – Madagascar and the Indian Ocean Islands, 20 – Maputaland-Pondoland-Albany, 30 – Succulent Karoo, Asia & Pacific: 9 – East Melanesian Islands, 13 – Himalayas, 15 – Indo-Burma, 16 – Irano-Anatolian, 17 – Japan, 23 – Mountains of Central Asia, 24 – Mountains of South-West China, 25 – New Caledonia, 26 – New Zealand, 27 – Philippines, 28 – Polynesia-Micronesia, 29 – South-west Australia, 31 – Sundaland, 34 – Wallacea, 35 – Western Ghats and Sri Lanka, America & Europe: 1 – Atlantic Forest, 2 – California Floristic Province, 4 – Caribbean Islands, 5 – Caucasus, 6 – Cerrado, 7 – Chilean Winter Rainfall-Valdivian Forests, 19 – Madrean pine-oak woodlands, 21 – Mediterranean Basin, 22 – Mesoamerica, 32 – Tropical Andes, 33 – Tumbes-Chocó-Magdalena.

19 A promising approach is to measure and assess the change of fragmentation in the landscape over time in a country. However, the data demand is high and currently under development with a common methodology for European countries (cf. projects led by the European Environmental Agency, available from: www.eea.europa.eu/publications/landscapefragmentation-in-europe [Accessed on 20 December 2016].

20 Aichi Biodiversity Targets can be found at www.cbd.int/sp/targets/ [Accesssed on 20 December 2016]. For the protocol see United Nations Nagoya Convention (2010).

21 Available online: www.cbd.int/nbsap/about/latest/default.shtml [Accessed on 20 December 2016].

References

Abdallah, S., Michaelson, J., Shah, S., Stoll, L., & Marks, N. (2012) *The Happy Planet Index: 2012 Report: A Global Index of Sustainable Well-being.* London, New Economics Foundation (NEF).

Alkire, S., Foster, J., Seth, S., Santos, M. E., Roche, J. M., & Ballon, P. (2015) *Multidimensional Poverty Measurement and Analysis.* Oxford, Oxford University Press.

Alkire, S., Jindra, C., Robles, G., & Vaz, A. (2016) *Multidimensional Poverty Index 2016: Brief methodological note and results.* OPHI Briefing 42, University of Oxford.

Bondarchik, J., Jabłońska-Sabuka, M., Linnanen, L., & Kauranne, T. (2016) Improving the objectivity of sustainability indices by a novel approach for combining contrasting effects: Happy Planet Index revisited. *Ecological Indicators*, 69, 400–406.

Brook, B. W., Ellis, E. C., Perring, M. P., Mackay, A. W., & Blomqvist, L. (2013) Does the terrestrial biosphere have planetary tipping points? *Trends in Ecology & Evolution*, 28, 396–401.

CB Ethiopia (2013) *Ethiopia Country Briefing.* Oxford Poverty and Human Development Initiative. Multidimensional Poverty Index Data Bank. OPHI, University of Oxford.

Channan, S., Collins, K., & Emanuel, W. R. (2014) *Global mosaics of the standard MODIS land cover type data.* University of Maryland and the Pacific Northwest National Laboratory, College Park, Maryland, USA.

Coppedge, M., Gerring, J., Altman, D., Bernhard, M., Fish, S., Hicken, A., Kroenig, M., Lindberg, S. I., McMann, K., Paxton, P., Semetko, H. A., Skaaning, S. E., Staton, J., &

Teorell, J. (2011) Conceptualizing and measuring democracy: A new approach. *Perspectives on Politics*, 9, 247–267.

Coppedge, M., Gerring, J., Lindberg, S. I., Skaaning, S. E., Teorell, J., Altman, D., Bernhard, M., Fish, M. S., Glynn, A., Hicken, A., Knutsen, C. H., Marquardt, K., McMann, K., Miri, F., Paxton, P., Pemstein, D., Staton, J., Tzelgov, E., Wang, Y., & Zimmermann, B. (2016) V-Dem [Country-Year/Country-Date] Dataset v6.1. Varieties of Democracy (V-Dem) Project. Available from: www.v-dem.net/en/data/data-version-6-1/.

DHS Ethiopia (2012) *Ethiopia Demographic and Health Survey 2011.* Central Statistical Agency, ICF International, Addis Ababa, Calverton.

Economist Intelligence Unit (2016) *Democracy Index 2015: Democracy in an age of anxiety.* EIU. Available from: www.eiu.com/public/democracy_index.aspx.

Emission Database for Global Atmospheric Research (2016). European Commission, Joint Research Center. Available at: http://edgar.jrc.ec.europa.eu/.

Ferreira, F. H. G., Chen, S., Dabalen, A., Dikhanov, Y., Hamadeh, N., Jolliffe, D., Narayan, A., Prydz, E. B., Revenga, A., Sangraula, P., Serajuddin, U., & Yoshida, N. (2015) A global count of the extreme poor in 2012 data issues, methodology and initial results. *Policy Res. Work. Pap.* 7432.

Friedl, M. A., Sulla-Menashe, D., Tan, B., Schneider, A., Ramankutty, N., Sibley, A., & Huang, X. (2010) MODIS Collection 5 global land cover: Algorithm refinements and characterization of new datasets. *Remote Sensing of Environment*, 114, 168–182.

Galli, A., Giampietro, M., Goldfinger, S., Lazarus, E., Lin, D., Saltelli, A., Wackernagel, M., & Muller, F. (2016) Questioning the ecological footprint. *Ecological Indicators*, 69, 224–232.

Gini, C. (1909) Concentration and dependency ratios (in Italian). English translation in *Rivista di Politica Economica*, 87 (1997), 769–789.

Groffman, P. M., Baron, J. S., Blett, T., Gold, A. J., Goodman, I., Gunderson, L. H., Levinson, B. M., Palmer, M. A., Paerl, H. W., Peterson, G. D., Poff, N. L., Rejeski, D. W., Reynolds, J. F., Turner, M. G., Weathers, K. C., & Wiens, J. (2006). Ecological thresholds: The key to successful environmental management or an important concept with no practical application? *Ecosystems*, 9, 1–13.

Helliwell, J. F., Layard, R., & Sachs, J. (2015) *World Happiness Report 2015.* New York, Sustainable Development Solutions Network. Available from: www.unsdsn.org/happiness.

Hill, R. & Tsehaye, E. (2015) *Ethiopia Poverty Assessment.* Washington, DC, World Bank Group. Available from: http://documents.worldbank.org/curated/en/356111468021623080/Ethiopiapoverty-assessment.

IPCC (1995) *Climate Change 1995: A Report of the Intergovernmental Panel on Climate Change*, 2nd Report, IPCC. Available from: www.ipcc.ch/pdf/climate-changes-1995/ipcc-2ndassessment/2nd-assessment-en.pdf.

IPCC (2014a) *Climate Change 2014: Synthesis Report.* Contribution of Working Groups I, II, and III to the Fifth Assessment Report of the Intergovernmental Panel on Climate Change [Core Writing Team, R. K. Pachauri and L. A. Meyer (eds)]. Geneva, Switzerland, IPCC, 151 pp.

IPCC (2014b) *Climate Change 2014: Mitigation of Climate Change.* Contribution of Working Group III to the Fifth Assessment Report of the Intergovernmental Panel on Climate Change. Edenhofer, O., Pichs-Madruga, R., Sokona, Y., Farahani, E., Kadner, S., Seyboth, K., Adler, A., Baum, I., Brunner, S., Eickemeier, P., Kriemann, B., Savolainen,

J., Schlomer, S., von Stechow, C., Zwickel, T., & Minx, J. C. (eds) Cambridge, UK and New York, Cambridge University Press.

Lakner, C. & Milanovic, B. (2015) Global income distribution: From the fall of the Berlin Wall to the Great Recession. *World Bank Economic Review*, 30, 203–232.

Lutz, W., Butz, W. P., & KC, S. (2014) *World Population and Human Capital in the Twenty-First Century*. Oxford, Oxford University Press.

Mace, G. M., Reyers, B., Alkemade, R., Biggs, R., Stuart Chapin III, R., Cornell, S. E., Diaz, S., Jennings, S., Leadley, P., Mumby, P. J., Purvis, A., Scholes, R. J., Seddon, A. W. R., Solan, M., Steffen, W., & Woodward, G. (2014) Approaches to defining a planetary boundary for biodiversity. *Global Environmental Change*, 28, 289–297.

Mancini, M. S., Galli, A., Niccoluccia, V., Lin, D., Bastianonia, S., Wackernagel, M., & Marchettinia, N. (2016) Ecological footprint: Refining the carbon footprint calculation. *Ecological Indicators*, 61, 390–403.

Meinshausen, M. J. L., Guetschow, J., Robioudu Pont, Y., Rogelj, J., Schaeffer, M., Hohne, N., den Elzen, M., Oberthur, S., & Meinshausen, N. (2015) National post-2020 greenhouse gas targets and diversity-aware leadership. *Nat. Clim. Chang.*, 1306, 1–10.

Mittermeier, P. R. G., Hoffman, M., Pilgrim, J., Brooks, T., Mittermeier, C. G., Lamoreux, J., & da Fonesca, G. A. B. (2004) *Hotspots Revisited*, Mexico City, CEMEX.

Myers, N., Mittermeier, R. A., Mittermeier, C. G., da Fonseca, G. A. B., & Kent, J. (2000) Biodiversity hotspots for conservation priorities. *Nature*, 403, 853–858.

New York Times (2014) Uruguay's quiet democratic miracle, by Uki Goňi. Available from: www.nytimes.com/2016/02/10/opinion/uruguays-quiet-democratic-miracle.html.

Newbold, L. N. H., Arnell, A. P., Contu, S., De Palma, A., Ferrier, S., Hill, S. L. L., Hoskins, A. J., Lysenko, I., Phillips, H. R. P., Burton, V. J., Chng, C. W. T., Emerson, S., Gao, D., Pask-Hale, G., Hutton, J., Jung, M., Sanchez-Ortiz, K., Simmons, B. I., Whitmee, S., Zhang, H., Scharlemann, J. P. W., & Purvis, A. (2016) Has land use pushed terrestrial biodiversity beyond the planetary boundary? A global assessment. *Science*, 353, 288–291.

Otoiu, A., Titan, E., & Dumitrescu, R. (2014) Are the variables used in building composite indicators of well-being relevant? Validating composite indexes of well-being. *Ecological Indicators*, 46, 575–585.

Palma, J. G. (2011) Homogeneous middles vs. heterogeneous tails, and the end of the 'inverted-U': It's all about the share of the rich. *Dev. Change*, 42, 87–153.

Quah, D. (1997) Empirics for growth and distribution: Stratification, polarization, and convergence clubs. *Journal of Economic Growth*, 2, 27–59.

Ravillion, M. (2016) *The Economics of Poverty: History, Measurement, and Policy*. Oxford, Oxford University Press.

Rockström, J., Steffen, W., Noone, K., Persson, A., Chapin, F. S., Lambin, E. F., Lenton, T. M., Scheffer, M., Folke, C., Schellnhuber, H. J., Nykvist, B., de Wit, C. A., Hughes, T., van der Leeuw, S., Rodhe, H., Sorlin, S., Snyder, P. K., Costanza, R., Svedin, U., Falkenmark, M., Karlberg, L., Corell, R. W., Fabry, V. J., Hansen, J., Walker, B., Liverman, D., Richardson, K., Crutzen, P., & Foley, J. A. (2009) A safe operating space for humanity. *Nature*, 461, 472–475.

Rogelj, J., Schaeffer, M., Friedlingstein, P., Gillett, N. P., van Vuuren, D. P., Riahi, K., Allen, M., & Knutti, R. (2016) Differences between carbon budget estimates unravelled. *Nat. Clim. Chang.*, 6, 245–252.

Ryu, H. K. (2013) A bottom poor sensitive Gini coefficient and maximum entropy estimation of income distributions. *Econ. Lett.*, 118, 370–374.

Saunier, R. E. & Meganck, R. A. (2009) *Dictionary and Introduction to Global Environmental Governance.* 2nd edition. London, Earthscan.

Schwanitz, V. J. (2013) Evaluating integrated assessment models of global climate change. *Environmental Modelling & Software,* 50, 120–131.

Sloan, C. N. J., Joppa, L. N., Gaveau, D. L. A., & Laurance, W. F. (2014) Remaining natural vegetation in the global biodiversity hotspots. *Biological Conservation,* 177, 12–24.

Spears, B. M., Ives, S. C., Angeler, D. G., Allen, C. R., Birk, S., Carvalho, L., Cavers, S., Daunt, F., Morton, R. D., Pocock, M. J. O., Rhodes, G., & Thackeray, S. J. (2015). Effective management of ecological resilience: Are we there yet? *Journal of Applied Ecology,* 52, 1311–1315.

Steffen, W., Richardson, K., Rockström, J., Cornell, S. E., Fetzer, I., Bennett, E. M., Biggs, R., Carpenter, S. R., de Vries, W., de Wit, C. A., Folke, C., Gerten, D., Heinke, J., Mace, G. M., Persson, L. M., Ramanathan, V., Reyers, B., & Sorlin, S. (2015) Planetary boundaries: Guiding human development on a changing planet. *Science,* 347, 1–17.

Tóth, G. & Szigeti, C. (2016) The historical Ecological Footprint: From over-population to overconsumption. *Ecological Indicators,* 60, 283–291.

UN (2015a) General Assembly resolution 70/1, *Transforming Our World: The 2030 Agenda for Sustainable Development,* A/RES/70/1 (21 October 2015). Available from: undocs. org/A/RES/70/1.

UN (2015b) United Nations, Department of Economic and Social Affairs, Population Division (2015). *World population prospects: The 2015 revision, key findings and advance tables.* Working paper no. ESA/P/WP.241.

UN (2016) *The Sustainable Development Goals Report 2016.* Available from: http://unstats. un.org/sdgs/report/2016/.

UNEP (2015a) *Human Development Report 2015 – Work for Human Development.* New York, UN Development Programme (UNEP). Available from: http://hdr.undp.org/en/2015-report/download.

UNEP (2015b) *The Emissions Gap Report 2015.* United Nations Environment Programme (UNEP), Nairobi. Available from: http://web.unep.org/emissionsgapreport2015.

United Nations Economic and Social Council (2016) *Report of the Inter-Agency and Expert Group on Sustainable Development Goal Indicators,* E/CN.3/2016/2 (17 December 2015). Available from: http://unstats.un.org/unsd/statcom/47th-session/documents/2016-2-IAEG-SDGs-E.pdf.

United Nations Framework Convention on Climate Change (1992) FCCC/INFORMAL/84 GE.05- 62220 (E) 200705. Available from: https://unfccc.int/resource/docs/convkp/conveng.pdf.

United Nations Framework Convention on Climate Change (2015) Adoption of the Paris Agreement. FCCC/CP/2015/L.9/Rev.1. Available from: https://unfccc.int/resource/docs/2015/cop21/eng/l09r01.pdf.

United Nations Habitat (2012) *State of the World's cities.* 2012/2011, UN-HABITAT. Available from: www.unhabitat.org/documents/SOWC10/R8.pdf.

United Nations Nagoya Convention (2010). Available from: www.cbd.int/abs/doc/protocol/nagoya-protocol-en.pdf.

United Nations Research Institute for Social Development (2013) *Inequalities and the post-2015 development agenda – a concept note,* 1–5. Available from: www.un.org/en/development/desa/policy/untaskteam_undf/groupb_unrisd_inequality.pdf.

Van den Bergh, J. C. J. M. & Grazi, F. (2013) Ecological Footprint policy? Land use as an environmental indicator. *Journal of Industrial Ecology,* 18, 10–19.

Van den Bergh, J. C. J. M. & Grazi, F. (2014) Response to Wackernagel. *Journal of Industrial Ecology*, 18, 23–25.

Van Vuuren, D., den Elzen, M., Lucas, P., Eickhout, B., Strengers, B., van Ruijven, B., Wonink, S., & van Houdt, R. (2007) Stabilizing greenhouse gas concentrations at low levels: An assessment of reduction strategies and costs. *Climatic Change*, 81, 119.

Wackernagel, M., Onisto, L., Linares, A. C., Falfan, I. S. L., Garcia, J. M., Guerrero, A. I. S., & Guerrero, M. G. S. (1997) *Ecological footprint of nation: How much nature do they use? How much nature do they have?* Toronto, International Council for Local Environment Initiatives, Commissioned by the Earth Council for the RIO +5 forum.

Williams, A. F., Rosauer, D., De Silva, N., Mittermeier, R., Bruce, C., Larsen, F. W., & Margules, C. (2011) Forests of East Australia: The 35th biodiversity hotspot. In: Zachos, F. E. and Habel, J. C. (eds) *Biodiversity Hotspots: Distribution and Protection of Conservation Priority Areas*. Berlin, Springer-Verlag, pp. 295–310.

World Bank (2014) *Ending Poverty and Boosting Shared Prosperity, Development Goals and Measurement Challenges*. Policy Research Report. Washington, DC, World Bank.

World Bank (2017) *Monitoring Global Poverty: Report of the Commission on Global Poverty*. Washington, DC, World Bank.

World DataBank (2016) *The World DataBank*. Washington, DC, World Bank (producer and distributor). Available from: http://databank.worldbank.org/.

World Wildlife Fund (2014) *Living Planet Report 2014: Species and Spaces, People and Places*. McLellan, R., Iyengar, L. Jeffries, B., & Oerlemans, N. (eds). Gland, Switzerland, WWF.

7

AN ANALYTIC NARRATIVE FOR SUSTAINABLE DEVELOPMENT

If you can't do it yourself –
Just don't, but cooperate.
Help each other
And life goes on.

Do not rejoice, when you possess
Do not cry, when it's gone.
Whether it's good or bad
Is only settled later.

Be humble when you are satisfied.
Mind the value of being modest.
The boughs that bear most
Hang lowest.

Folk song from Okinawa, Tinsagu nu hana (verses 7–9)

The entry point for this chapter is the wisdom revealed by an Okinawan folk song passed on orally through generations among the inhabitants of the Ryūkyū archipelago. This song's view on the relationship between humans and nature is simple, but it shows a strikingly deep understanding about sustainable development. The song 'Balsam flower' teaches the value of cooperation, the need for adaptive learning, and the necessity for respecting our natural environment. It even suggests that human wellbeing best originates from modesty and the appreciation of less materialistic lifestyles. Indeed, the insights from this song, with its roots in Confucianism, are close to the essence of the sustainable development narrative for our modern world, as we will elicit and discuss in this chapter. The novelty of the narrative lies in the holistic approach of combining a normative model with multidimensional data analysis to ultimately derive storylines.

Our understanding and operationalization of the term 'narrative' broadly follows the idea outlined in Roe (1991) of structuring a narrative's storyline into three parts, which are: (1) recognition of the problem, (2) conceptualization of the solution, and (3) arrival at the envisaged goal. All three parts draw from the outcomes of the data-driven assessment whose foundation has been laid in the previous chapters (see chapter 5 for an overview on the normative model of sustainable development and chapter 6 for the rationales behind choosing indicators and national thresholds for six key themes). By complementing words with numbers, we literally make the numbers part of the story, which is why we refer to our narrative as 'analytic'.

The focus of the quantitative narrative that we develop in this chapter is on the provision of a positive outlook on how to achieve sustainable development. We emphasize the value of learning from experience. The need for such 'narratives of change' has more recently been expressed by Costanza (2014), Costanza and Kubiszewski (2014), Ostrom (2014), and the International Council for Science and International Social Science Council (2015). Positive narratives are the opposite of 'crisis narratives', whose primary aim is to bring attention to the possibility (or in some cases to the fact) that wrong routes may have been taken. Although it is important to observe and point out alarming signs, some sort of action must also follow. So a next step concerns decisions about and departure to an alternative route. One could say that this step is about 'planetary opportunities' (DeFries *et al.*, 2012) and much less about 'planetary boundaries' (Rockström *et al.*, 2009; Steffen *et al.*, 2015).

To make our point, it is illustrative to think of a ship cruise from years past. It is the job of the look-out to shout a warning when observing a signal of danger or distress. After having understood that navigation to less troublesome waters is necessary, the captain and ship's crew need to have an idea where to turn instead. Indeed, it no longer matters, for example, exactly how high the approaching dangerous wave is or how large the iceberg. Instead, it is enough to have a common understanding that the ship is under threat and that action is demanded. Precious time will be lost if the crew ponders the wave's height. What matters is that the crew is clear about what to do next, which starts with avoiding the obvious and stop moving towards the threat. The earlier the crew starts to act and the better the crew members cooperate, the smoother the ship can be steered to safe waters – even if visibility is low. Moreover, following a precautionary pathway allows the crew members to fine-tune their way out of the stormy water, stroke by stroke. Admittedly, this is a simple illustration, but it helps to motivate the intention of this chapter. By shifting the focus away from the alarming voice and towards a constructive approach, we embrace the concept of adaptive narratives. Such narratives are not written in stone and evolve over time. That is, they adapt as we learn how to steer into calmer waters.

In this chapter, we depart from the recognition of the problem (step 1). We evaluate whether the development of countries has taken place inside the sustainable development space as defined in chapter 6 and whether the thresholds for the six key theme indicators have been approached or even crossed. The six indicators are:

1   *Eradicating extreme poverty:* In each country, no person is below the international poverty line, i.e., having less than international $1.90 per day in purchasing power parity (2011).

2   *Enhancing human capabilities:* Each country achieves 'high human development', implying a human development index above 0.8.

3   *Ensuring rich participation:* For each country, the participatory index of the Varieties of Democracy Project is larger than 0.52.

4   *Ensuring fair distribution:* The Gini coefficient in each country is below the alert line of 0.4.

5   *Mitigating climate change:* National yearly per-capita emissions do not exceed 3.6 tCO$_2$eq per person.

6   *Safeguarding biosphere integrity:* Each country has developed, adopted and begun implementing National Biodiversity Strategy and Actions plans by 2015 (Aichi target no. 17).

The multidimensional country-level data analysis based on the above key themes and thresholds leads to a grouping of countries relative to their performance over time. Namely, we analyse the full set of data for the years 2000, 2005, and 2010 for about 100 countries. Deploying cluster algorithms used in artificial intelligence, we depart from the common grouping into developing countries, developed countries, and countries in transition – a division criticized as largely being biased towards the currently dominant narrative of economic development (cf. Rodrik, 2003; International Council for Science and International Social Science Council, 2015). Instead, we identify groups of countries that tell similar stories of modern societal evolution, equally accounting for all of the three imperatives of sustainable development (i.e., satisfying human needs, ensuring social justice, and respecting environmental limits as detailed in the previous chapters). From data crunching, we derive insights about attention points for sustainable development. These characteristics form the cornerstones for the conceptualization of a solution to the problem, on which we will build by further deploying background data such as urbanization and population trends, economic development, energy demand, and land-use changes. To close the narrative, we finally look into the future to envisage the desired goal that is achieving sustainable development. Before we can move towards an interpretation of the numbers, however, and ultimately tell the narrative of sustainable development, we need to technically examine the trends and correlations among the key theme indicators.

Trends and correlations among key themes

A high correlation between two key themes suggests that one of the key themes is obsolete, that basically the same issue is being measured, just with a different name or using a different metric. We want to carry out a cluster analysis of our country-level dataset on relatively independent dimensions, with as little redundancy as possible. Thus, choosing among the possible headline indicators noted in chapter 6 required us to prioritize indicators that do not overlap. For example, choosing an indicator for the key theme 'mitigating climate change' could include notions of fairness or historic responsibility. However, when deriving the thresholds we have excluded both, because these topics are already tackled in other theme indicators.

In examining binary correlations between all combinations of key themes for the years 2000, 2005, and 2010, we find that only two key themes exhibit a correlation coefficient with an absolute value of higher than 0.5 (i.e., they are either highly positively or negatively correlated). The first is the strong negative correlation between the key themes 'eradicating extreme poverty' and 'enhancing human capability'; the binary correlation coefficient was −0.81 for 2000 and 2010 and −0.89 for 2005. The second is the modest positive correlation between 'enhancing human capability' and 'ensuring rich participation', where the binary correlation coefficient was 0.61 in 2000, 0.57 in 2005, and 0.56 in 2010.

The strong correlation between the human development index and the international poverty line is not surprising: people in extreme poverty (less than international $1.90 per day) are primarily also those who suffer from low life expectancy, poor education, and low per-capita gross national income. In other words, and as is also discussed in chapter 6, people in extreme poverty are generally deprived in several other dimensions as well. Does the high negative correlation thus imply that one of the key themes is obsolete for the cluster analysis? We argue that this is not the case because data on extreme poverty as measured by the international poverty line generally focus on poor economies and therefore often do not include data from countries with more prosperous economies, which can exaggerate the correlation. Moreover, if we just consider those countries for which the relevant surveys were carried out in the particular years, the sample of our dataset would be limited to only 33–35 countries. To overcome these shortcomings, we augment the data sample intended for the cluster analysis by adding data for countries whose inhabitants have an income of at least international $18,000 per year (in 2011 purchasing power parity). Assuming that the amount of extreme poverty in these countries is comparatively small, we set the percentage of the population below the international poverty line to zero, implying that the countries fulfil the threshold. We are aware that there are extremely poor people in richer countries (e.g., the USA), but we can justify the assumption because the spread of economic income within a country is tackled in key theme 'ensuring fair distribution'.

The modest correlation of about 0.6 between the key themes 'enhancing human capability' and 'ensuring rich participation' is also not of great concern for the cluster analysis. This correlation disappears when we take a subsample of countries that are outside of the sustainable development space with regard to both key theme thresholds (to about 0.18). This may indicate an important first point for sustainable development: the simultaneous fulfilment of the thresholds of both key themes seems important. Figure 7.1 plots the human development index versus the participatory democracy index. As can be inferred from the figure, countries fall into two groups: either they are within the sustainable development space for both

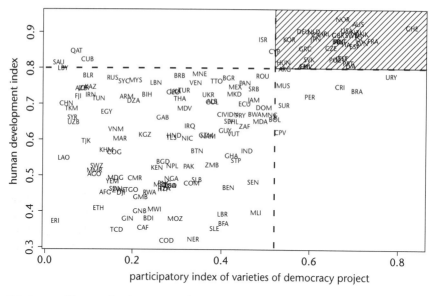

FIGURE 7.1 Human development index against the participatory democracy index of the Varieties of Democracy Project for 2010. See appendix for country codes. Figure is the work of the authors.

key theme indicators (the shaded area) or they are in neither. Out of 161 countries whose data were available for the year 2010, only a dozen were not in one of these two groups (and most of those were close to being in one of the groups). It is remarkable that our chosen thresholds so clearly delineate these two classes of countries. Seemingly, a fundamental change is occurring when a country transitions from the lower to higher level in both indicators. This is a useful insight for the development of a quantitative narrative because it allows the identification of countries that are about to reach their turning points towards a sustainable development pathway. These features were similar in 2000 and 2005.

There are other interesting examples from the binary analysis. For example, in 2010, none of the 179 countries fulfil the threshold for the key theme 'enhancing human capabilities' without also crossing the line for per-capita greenhouse gas emissions (i.e., the 'mitigating climate change' theme indicator). This also holds true for 2000 (153 countries) and 2005 (168 countries). The main driver behind this finding is sustained economic growth enabling high human development. Given the considerable carbon intensity of developed economies, this is clearly in conflict with the mitigation of greenhouse gas emissions. Furthermore, from these two headline indicators alone, it can be inferred that no country is located within the sustainable development space as of 2010. The key for countries with current low human development, therefore, is the development of a low carbon economy in coming years.

Furthermore, the relationship between the climate change indicator and the indicator for 'ensuring rich participation' is enlightening. Only four smaller

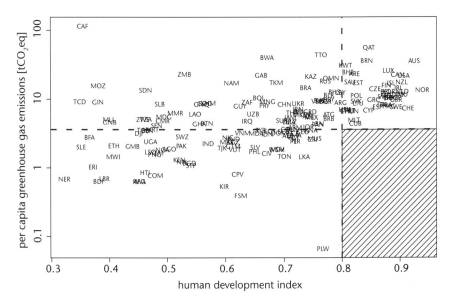

FIGURE 7.2 Per-capita greenhouse gas emissions against the human development index for 2010. See appendix for country codes. Figure is the work of the authors.

countries (Costa Rica, Mauritius, Peru, and Cape Verde) out of 158 countries pass both thresholds in 2010 (in 2000, it was only Mauritius and Costa Rica and 2005 added Peru). All other countries with strong participatory elements in their democracies are above the threshold for greenhouse gas emissions. This again hints at the important role of economic growth at present: countries with strong economic growth may possess the means to successfully push participatory elements as part of that growth. Again, with the few exceptions mentioned, all countries are outside of the sustainable development space.

In general, observing development from 2000 to 2010, we find that the trends for some of the key themes are clearly pointing in the right direction, so that there is good reason to believe that the thresholds can be met in the near future. In particular, the human development index ('enhancing human capability') is increasing for the majority of countries. The eradication of extreme poverty is also making notable progress. The trends are not as pronounced but still positive for 'ensuring rich participation' and 'ensuring fair distribution'. The key themes regarding the biosphere's integrity and mitigation of climate change are the most problematic because trends in the related indicators are moving further away from the sustainable development space for most countries. Just as important, the reversion in greenhouse gas emission trends that can be observed for some high-income countries is not strong enough to achieve the thresholds in the near future. Furthermore, many lower income countries appear to be on the path to following historic carbon-intensive pathways of economic development.

Grouping countries by cluster analysis

We now turn from a binary to a cluster analysis of all six themes. For the comparison, we extend the dataset by using linear interpolation and (limited) extrapolation for some countries. For example, if a survey was conducted in 2009 and 2011 and if the corresponding data entries appear smooth, we interpolate between the two values to obtain a value for 2010. We also used extrapolation in a similar manner, but never for more than one year ahead. The extended dataset generated through using the interpolation and extrapolation procedures is only used for the cluster analysis. The final set of data contains entries for 79–100 countries in the years 2000, 2005, and 2010 and covers all six key themes. The intersection between 2000 and 2010 will be used in the cluster analysis.

The first step in the cluster analysis is the normalization of indicators, so that they range from zero to one, ensuring that all indicators are comparable. Five of the indicators naturally range between a minimum and a maximum value, but greenhouse gas emissions are not limited in such a way. Therefore, the normalization of the emissions indicator is arbitrary. Our choice for the scaling of this indicator is a normalization to the per-capita emissions of Australia, because it had the highest emissions in 2000 of all the countries for which data on all six key themes were available.

The second step is clustering the full dataset for a given year. The clustering is done by the K-means procedure employing the Hartigan–Wong Algorithm (Hartigan, 1975; Hartigan & Wong, 1979). The K-means algorithm is a popular way to perform unsupervised learning in artificial intelligence; that is, no further information is given for the learning steps. The K-means procedure partitions data into k groups of countries by minimizing the within-cluster sum of squares. The basic idea is to choose cluster membership by finding the shortest distances between the pairs in the data. Note that the number of groups is given in the algorithm as a parameter. Furthermore, the cluster algorithm is set up such that it does not consider how many people live in a country, thereby treating countries as equal entities. Interestingly, the K-means algorithm can also be considered as a discrete version of principal component analysis (Ding & He, 2004), and a principal component step can be used as an initial guess for the cluster grouping.

A quality measure for clustering is the ratio of the between-cluster-distance to the total sum of distances. The closer it is to 100 per cent, the better the separation works, but there is a trade-off. On one hand, the quality measure generally increases if more groups are included. On the other hand, the higher the number of clusters, the more difficult it is to elicit common features, so this trade-off needs to be balanced. For example, in 2010, our six-dimensional dataset consists of 107 countries for which we consider a grouping into 5–13 clusters. We found that the optimal cluster size for this dataset and particular year is seven. The measure of separation for this cluster size is 82 per cent. A smaller number of clusters come at the expense of a lower percentage (e.g., a cluster size of five: 78 per cent). The gain from going to more clusters, however, does not substantially improve the quality measure, but it does create groupings with very few members. In this sense, a cluster size of seven provides the best balance.

The choice for clustering into seven groups of countries can additionally be motivated by the following theoretical consideration. Assume that only high- and low-value entries exist for each of the key themes. For example, there are only countries with high or low human development. In the case of the key theme 'biosphere integrity', all entries are low because no country complies with the threshold. Having said this, there remain 2^5 (i.e., 32) combinations between the five remaining indicators. As we have seen in the binary analysis in the previous section, some combinations exclude each other. For example, a high value of human development always coincides with a high value of societal participation. The same holds for human development and the reduction of extreme poverty, as well as the amount of greenhouse gas emissions. Thus, the number of possible combinations decreases to six clusters assuming strictly binary entries, which is close to the choice of seven clusters for the continuous dataset. The clustering by the algorithm is a result of a minimization procedure in a high dimensional space. Care must be taken, therefore, to ensure the algorithm always finds the absolute minimum, which is done by performing a large number of runs.

There is no reason, however, to observe the same clustering in different years because countries can develop in various directions. Cluster changes over time can provide interesting dynamic insights, which we explore further in our later discussion. Here, we provide only a technical description of the clusters. Figure 7.3

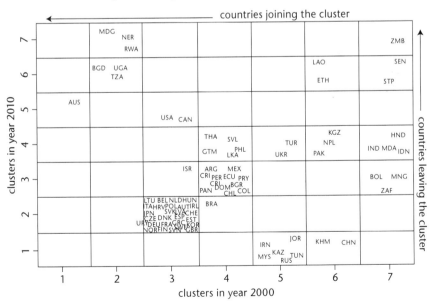

FIGURE 7.3 Cluster membership changes between 2000 and 2010 (based on a joint intersection of 79 countries). Refer to the text for details. See appendix for country codes. Figure is the work of the authors.

shows the creation and dissolution of the seven clusters. Notably, cluster 3 (entry 3 on the x-axis) is the most stable over time with only Israel (ISR), Canada (CAN), and the USA leaving the cluster in 2010 and Brazil (BRA) joining. Cluster 4 in the year 2000 dissolves into two larger clusters, which become clusters 3 and 4 in 2010. The new cluster 3 comprises mostly Latin American countries such as Costa Rica (CRI), Mexico (MEX), and Chile (CHL). The most dynamic cluster is cluster 7 in 2000. From there, countries follow very different pathways and are spread over clusters 3, 4, 6, and 7 in 2010.

Characterization of the different clusters

Next, we discuss the characteristic features that distinguish the clusters from each other. We do this for each of the six dimensions. Specifically, we analyse whether the country clusters are located above or below the thresholds of the indicators. Data from 95 countries are available for the year 2010 covering 86 per cent of the world's population (6.9 billion people). Final energy consumption of all countries in the dataset amounts to 87 per cent, and they were responsible for 85 per cent of global greenhouse gas emissions in 2010. Thus, the dataset provides a good global coverage. Applying the cluster algorithm, we obtain a grouping of countries relative to the sustainable development space established with the six thresholds.

Table 7.1 presents an overview of how the different clusters perform across the key themes. The seven clusters are characterized by their status quo in 2010, as well as by their stylized decadal trends between 2000 and 2010 (refer to the upward, downward, and horizontal arrows in table 7.1). The ordering of the clusters from A to G is based on the share of each cluster in the world population. This information, as well as additional background data, is provided in table 7.2. Other additional data used are the predicted population shares of different clusters in the year 2050 (as published by the United Nations World Urbanization Prospects in 2014); the level of urbanization in 2010;[1] the number of average happy life years in 2012 (Jeffrey *et al.*, 2016); each cluster's share in world final energy consumption and greenhouse gas emissions for 2010; the percentage of population with access to electricity; a list of countries that qualify as mega-diverse[2] (i.e., they are of high global endemic importance); and each cluster's environmental footprint in 2012, covering agricultural area, forests, fisheries, and built-up land (Global Footprint Network, 2016). Note that the environmental footprint is not the same as the commonly published total ecological footprint, which combines these factors with a country's carbon footprint. The performance of the countries regarding greenhouse gas emissions is covered in key theme 5. If not stated otherwise, data are taken from World DataBank (2016).

What can we infer from the cluster analysis? For a start, we clearly see that the world is currently not even coming close to a sustainable development path, because none of the clusters is fully located inside the sustainable development space. Notably, it is not key theme 6 alone (i.e., safeguarding the biosphere's integrity) that is signalling this alarming state of our planet. Instead, either the

TABLE 7.1 Performance of different clusters of countries across the six key themes.

The key themes: 1 – Eradicating extreme poverty, 2 – Enhancing human capabilities, 3 – Ensuring rich participation, 4 – Ensuring fair distribution, 5 – Mitigating climate change, and 6 – Safeguarding biosphere integrity. Legend: '+' – threshold met in 2010, '−' ('− −') undershooting by less (more) than 10 per cent. For key theme 6, '+' requires that most countries in a cluster have adopted their national biodiversity strategy and action plans. A mixed tendency within a cluster is indicated by '+/−', whereby the dominant statistic is indicated first. Dynamic trends in 2000–2010 focus on countries located outside of the sustainable development space: '↑' indicates a positive trend, '↓' notes unsustainable trends, and '→' symbolizes stagnation. Mixed trends are given by '↑↓'. 'n.a.' is 'not announced', and 'n.c.' means 'not considered'. Table is the work of the authors.

Cluster	Countries[1] belonging to cluster in 2010		Row 1: Status in 2010 — Row 2: Trends 2000–2010 — Key theme indicators					
			1	2	3	4	5	6
A 'Space for overall considerable improvements, but yet a relatively small carbon footprint'	BTN, GEO, GTM, HMD, IDN, IND, KGZ, LKA, MDA, NPL, PAK, PHL, SLV, THA, TUR, UKR	Status	−/−	−/−	+,−/−	−	+,−/−−	−
		Trends	↑	↑→	↑→	↑↓	↑	n.c.
B 'Moderate human development with a participatory deficit'	ARM, BLR, CHN, IRN, JOR, KAZ, KHM, MYS, RUS, SYC, TUN, VNM	Status	−/−	−/−	−−	+/−	−/−	−−
		Trends	↑	↑	→↑	↑↓	↑→	n.c.
C 'High to very high societal development at high environmental costs'	AUT, BEL, BRA, CHE, CYP, CZE, DEU, DNK, ESP, EST, FIN, FRA, GBR, GRC, HRV, HUN, IRL, ISL, ITA, JPN, KOR, LTU, LVA, NLD, NOR, POL, PRT, SVK, SVN, SWE, URY	Status	+/−	+/−	+	+/−	−	−−
		Trends	↑	↑	↑	↑	↑↓	n.c.
D 'Towards a better societal development; current front runner'	ARG, BGR, BOL, CHL, COL, CRI, DOM, ECU, ISR, MEX, MNG, PAN, PER, PRY, ZAF	Status	−/−	−/−	+,−/−	−/−/+	−,−/+	−
		Trends	↑	↑	↑↓	↑	→↑	n.c.
E 'Very high societal development at very high environmental costs'	AUS, CAN, USA	Status	+	+	+	+/−	−−	−−
		Trends	n.a.	↑	↑	→↑	↑	n.c.
F 'Rural countries struggling with societal development'	BGD, COG, ETH, GIN, LAO, SEN, STP, TZA, UGA	Status	−−	−−	−−	+/−	−/+	−
		Trends	↑	↑	→	↑	→↑	n.c.
G 'Rural countries struggling with extreme poverty'	LSO, MDG, MWI, NER, NGA, RWA, ZMB	Status	−−	−−	−−	+/−	+/−	−
		Trends	↑↓	↑	↑↓	↑↓	↑→	n.c.

1 See appendix for country codes.

TABLE 7.2 Key characteristics across clusters, taken from various 2010 background data sources. Sources: United Nations World Urbanization Prospects (2014), Global Footprint Network (2016), World DataBank (2016), and author calculations.

Cluster	A	B	C	D	E	F	G
Share in world population in 2010 in %	29	25	13	5	5	5	3
Share in world population in 2050 in %	29	19	9	5	5	7	7
Average share of urban population in 2010 in %	45 (17–71)	59 (20–82)	75 (50–98)	73 (59–92)	83 (80–89)	36 (14–63)	28 (16–43)
Average happy life years in 2012	27 (20–39)	29 (18–38)	45 (29–59)	35 (19–53)	51 (47–54)	16 (12–23)	14 (12–17)
Share in world final energy consumption in 2010 in %	11	28	22	4	20	1	1
Percentage of population with access to electricity	89 (72–100)	94 (31–100)	100 (98–100)	93 (80–100)	100 (100–100)	38 (15–66)	18 (9–48)
Share in 2010 global GHG emissions in %	11	31	19	4	16	2	2
Mega-diverse countries in cluster	MYS, IDN, IND, PHL	CHN	BRA	COL, ECU, MEX, PER, ZAF	AUS, USA	COG	MDG
Average ecological footprint w/o carbon footprint in 2012 in gha[1]	1.1 (0.4–4.2)	1.3 (0.9–2.5)	2.5 (1.0–6.9)	1.6 (0.7–3.2)	3.3 (2.3–4.5)	1.0 (0.5–1.3)	1.0 (0.7–1.5)

1 Includes the cropland footprint, grazing footprint, forest product footprint, fish footprint, and built-up land, based on www.footprintnetwork.org/ecological_footprint_nations/index.html, accessed on 27 December 2016.

countries in a cluster lack the societal development described by key themes 1–4 or the progress in the related indicators comes at the expense of violating the threshold for the mitigation of climate change (in addition to the problem with key theme 6).

This violation is very pronounced in clusters C and E. Accordingly, we label them as 'high to very high societal development at high environmental costs' and 'very high societal development at very high environmental costs', respectively. Even though these two clusters made up only 18 per cent of the global population in 2010, they consumed more than 40 per cent of the world's final energy and had an ecological footprint that is 2–3 times higher than that of the other clusters. Moreover, they were responsible for about 35 per cent of the world's greenhouse gas emissions in 2010. In addition, the trends show only modest progress in these areas in recent years, and these first signs of trend reversals with respect to the environmental key themes are still too slow to say that the countries in clusters C and E are role models for transitioning towards sustainable pathways. Therefore, it is clearly time to 'stop celebrating the polluters' (Togtokh, 2011).

Two decisive differences between clusters C and E are the substantially higher per-capita greenhouse gas emissions and the large spread in the Gini coefficients of Australia, Canada, and the USA (cluster E). Indeed, cluster C is the only cluster that is homogeneous in the Gini coefficient, whereby all members are fulfilling the threshold that ensures a fair distribution of income and wealth in society. Members of cluster C are mainly European countries but also Japan, Korea, and Uruguay. Brazil joined this group in 2010. The primary reason for the two Latin American countries being a part of cluster C is their good performance regarding human capabilities and, particularly, their strong participatory democracies.

The countries of cluster D are close to also achieving these two thresholds (themes 2 and 3). Indeed, one could think of this cluster as currently being closest to reaching the sustainable development space in the future. Cluster D comprises countries such as Argentina, Bulgaria, Peru, and Costa Rica. For many countries belonging to this cluster, societal development trends are pointing in the right direction, and thresholds (including those for environmental key themes 5 and 6) are not too far out of reach (e.g., the relatively positive status quo of cluster D in 2010 and the upward trends for many of the key themes). This surprising finding is further confirmed by taking a look at other background data (table 7.2). For example, the average number of happy life years in 2012 was relatively high (35), and the ecological footprint of cluster D was relatively low (1.6 global hectares). Also, many mega-diverse countries can be found in this cluster, such as Colombia, Peru, Ecuador, Mexico, and South Africa. In other words, cluster D countries currently have a unique chance to continue their progress while avoiding the past mistakes made by many OECD countries. Countries in this cluster could provide evidence that high societal development can be compatible with respecting environmental limits.

Countries in cluster B (e.g., Armenia, China, Iran, Malaysia, Vietnam, and Russia) stand in stark contrast to those in cluster D. Although these countries have achieved a moderate to high level of human development, they clearly lack elements of participatory democracy and their shares in final energy consumption and greenhouse gas emissions substantially exceed the group's share in world population. With respect to these key themes, cluster B is behind the countries of cluster A, to which Guatemala, Turkey, Thailand, and Indonesia belong. Their deficit, in turn, is their modest progress in enhancing human capabilities. At the same time, cluster A performs much better with respect to the mitigation of climate change as compared to cluster D, but the other decisive element is that cluster D is ahead of cluster A in terms of social development.

Clusters F and G contain countries that struggle most with respect to societal development. Many of the member countries are from sub-Saharan Africa and South East Asia. Both clusters face challenges with very high levels of extreme poverty. About 40 per cent of the population is extremely poor in cluster F, and the share is as high as 60 per cent on average for countries belonging to cluster G. The situation is also clearly compounded by the substantially lower number of happy life years, which is smaller by a factor of 2–4 as compared with the other clusters. However, during the last decade, substantial progress has been made in reducing the number of extreme poor. Furthermore, most of the trends for the other key themes are also pointing in more promising directions, so that there are good reasons to believe that these countries will be able to catch up with the rest of the world in the near future.

It is worth taking a closer look at the projected clustering by the key themes 'eradicating extreme poverty' and 'ensuring fair distribution'. Figure 7.4 shows the dynamic trends (2000–2010) for clusters A, D, F, and G, confirming that substantial progress has been made during the past decade in lowering the number of extremely poor people, with the exception of Zambia and Madagascar (cluster G, see ZMB and MDG). Most countries in clusters A and F either have small enough Gini coefficients to fulfil the threshold (marked by the solid vertical line) or they do not undershoot the threshold by more than 10 per cent (the dashed vertical line). On the contrary, there is no clear trend regarding the Gini coefficient that is true for all of the clusters (apart from cluster C). China and South Africa are notable because both countries progressed substantially with respect to the reduction of extreme poverty (see CHN around 40–40 and ZAF around 55–35), but the distribution of income in their societies has become much less fair over the last decade. Indeed, a fair distribution is not automatically associated with higher human development. Rather, the achievement of the threshold for a fair distribution needs to be made a separate target in society.

The cluster analysis can be combined with a relative weighting of clusters reflecting their percentage shares in the world population. Notably, clusters A, B, and C together represent about 67 per cent of the global population in 2010. Given their population shares of 29 per cent and 25 per cent, respectively, the future pathways of clusters A and B are central from a global sustainability perspective. A key element here is whether these countries will be able to avoid carbon-intensive technology lock-ins when catching up with the highly

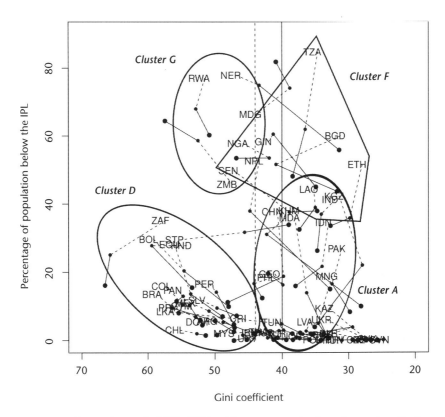

FIGURE 7.4 Dynamic trends 2000–2010 with respect to the key themes 'eradicating extreme poverty' and 'ensuring fair distribution' for countries of clusters A, D, F, and G. The threshold of the former is zero and the threshold of the latter is indicated by the vertical solid line, and the dashed vertical line indicates undershooting the target by 10 per cent. A country's code marks its position in the year 2000, the dashed line indicates the transition to the year 2005 (a small dot), and the solid line shows the direction to which the country continued its development to 2010 (the large dot). See appendix for country codes. Figure is the work of the authors.

industrialized world or whether they follow existing material- and energy-intensive economic growth patterns. The necessity to transition towards low-carbon economies and avoid unsustainable technology lock-ins will be even more urgent as the world population increases. Over the next 40 years, the population is projected to increase by 40 per cent, reaching about 9.6 billion (UN Medium Population Projections, 2016). The population in countries from sub-Saharan Africa, South East Asia, and Latin America are projected to experience strong growth. Yet, these countries are among the poorest in the world today, and no time should be lost in enabling their societal development.

Three major challenges are connected to the findings from the cluster analysis: (1) substantially slowing down population growth, (2) further reducing the absolute number of extremely poor people in societies, and (3) replacing the developmental blueprint deployed by the highly industrialized countries in the past since the development of those countries has come at the expense of the environment. Indeed, as we learned from assessing the key themes related to the state of nature shown in chapter 6, a population of roughly one billion people (of the economically strong countries in North America, Europe, Australia, and East Asia) was sufficient to drive the globe to its limits.

One example illustrating the principle problem is the generation of municipal waste (which does not include industrial waste or sewage sludge). In Norway, a country ranking high on many different lists when it comes to societal development as well as an abundance of natural environments, the urban population was about 3.6 million people in 2000 and they generated an average of 2.8 kg of municipal waste per person per day (World Bank, 2012). This amount placed Norway among the top three per-capita waste producers out of 161 countries (if small islands are ignored). In 2025, the amount is projected to decrease to 2.3 kg per day per person (which is still above the world average of 1.2 kg in 2001). What would happen if the rest of the world took Norway as a role model for municipal waste? In 2025, global urban society would generate 11 million tonnes of municipal waste per day (4.9 billion people × 2.3 kg/person/day), which represents a 150 per cent increase in municipal waste as compared to that generated at the beginning of the millennium.

Obviously, to sustainably support the world's expected 9.6 billion people in 2050 demands completely new concepts. We need to proclaim unprecedented global solidarity if we want to avert losing the progress made over the last decade in lifting millions of people out of extreme poverty. Shifting the focus away from societies that have already achieved high societal development according to the set thresholds is not only a matter of ethics and moral responsibility but also a matter of efficiency from a global perspective. People in highly developed countries are already endowed with enhanced human capabilities, and their rich participation in society, as well as the fair distribution of income is ensured. The individuals living in those countries therefore have both the ability and responsibility to use their capabilities and participative opportunities to shape their societies as they want.

Even so, we are talking about minor adjustments with respect to key themes 1–4 in economically strong countries. Substantially more resources (including intellectual resources) could be freed in their societies to support countries that are strongly lagging behind. However, major adjustments are needed in countries with high societal development when it comes to the environment. We need to decouple societal prosperity from unsustainable energy and material consumption if we want to support high-quality lifestyles for everybody on the globe. We need to secure the resilience of natural systems if we want to keep nature intact. In particular, remaining biodiversity hotspots have to be secured and ways have to be found to increase dedicated refuge areas to strengthen the biosphere's resilience.

The data presented in tables 7.1 and 7.2 reveal possible actions that can promote sustainable development. The provision of access to electricity and clean energy, as well as the utilization of urbanization trends can have positive outcomes. Lower numbers of extremely poor people are observed in clusters coinciding with higher shares of urban population and higher shares of the population having access to (clean) energy sources (table 7.2). In fact, only clusters F and G can be characterized as rural, and in both, the inhabitants struggle with very high shares of extreme poverty. Clusters A–E, on the other hand, have already reached or are close to a 50 per cent urban share in the total population. Hence, making the design and development of sustainable cities a worldwide focus is a key point of departure from current unsustainable pathways. The cluster analysis furthermore shows that countries performing best in enhancing human capabilities feature societies that are endowed with rich participation. Another point of attention is, thus, to further elaborate on how societies can foster participatory elements and improve the democratic literacy of their inhabitants. These points form the cornerstones for working out a conceptualized narrative that tells how the transition to a sustainable development space can be achieved.

Sustainable development narrative – the ways forward

Problem statement. In the nineteenth century, it was not clear that the Industrial Revolution, with its marvellous acceleration of economic growth starting in Europe and eventually spreading to many more places, would become the origin of problems in the twenty-first century. Though the Industrial Revolution enabled the creation of great inventions such as internal combustion engines, modern medicine, mass produced automobiles, waterproof fabrics, aeronautics, modern communications, and semiconductors, they came at the expense of the integrity of our biosphere because the carbon and material footprints of modern societies are exceeding environmental limits by far (see key themes 5 and 6 and chapter 4). Moreover, more than 897 million people – about 13 per cent of the global population in 2012 (Ferreira *et al.*, 2015) – are not profiting from economic growth and technological progress, but are suffering from extreme poverty and are deprived in multiple dimensions, including access to healthy food, energy sources, education, and modest accommodations (see key theme 1 and chapter 2). Although, in absolute terms, huge progress has been made to enhance worldwide human capabilities, the gains are unevenly spread among countries. Some countries have achieved the thresholds for key theme 2 (see chapter 3), but human development is lagging behind in many others.

At about the same time as the start of the Industrial Revolution, the French Revolution ignited social transformation by opening the door to empowering ordinary people and breaking the centuries-long hegemony of the nobility. Stimulated by both revolutions, the world also saw the introduction of universal suffrage, a burst of democracy, the birth of international governmental and non-governmental institutions such as the League of Nations (later, the United Nations), the International Committee of the Red Cross, Amnesty International, and Greenpeace. Even so, there are many countries where rich citizen participation in society is not ensured (key theme 3). At the beginning of the twentieth century, the Russian Revolution marked another important attempt to change the world into something better. This was followed by movements in other Eastern European, African, Latin American, and Asian countries after WWII, with the goal of establishing socialist societies based on a fair distribution of income and wealth. But these movements ended in failure. Today, the distribution of income and wealth across the world is not sustainable. Having summarized the overall underperformance of nations with respect to the thresholds of our normative model of sustainable development (see chapter 5), the need for transitioning to a sustainable development space becomes obvious (see chapter 6 and previous sections in this chapter).

The ways forward. The cluster analysis revealed four pivotal points that offer guidance on how to bring about a sustainable development path. These are:

1 Reducing population growth
2 Proclaiming unprecedented global solidarity
3 Decoupling of societal prosperity from unsustainable energy and material consumption
4 Securing the resilience of the natural system.

In the following, we briefly describe (partly novel) concepts that were inspired by the numerical analysis for each of these attention points.

Reducing population growth

Projections of demographic growth depend on several parameters, such as fertility rates, death rates, and child mortality. Indeed, estimates of the number of people living on the planet in 2050 range between 8.5 and 12 billion people (Lutz *et al.*, 2014 and United Nations Medium Population Projections, 2016). If the smaller number is assumed, the world population in 2100 is projected to be even lower than it is today. The difference between these projections is largely due to changes in fertility rates, which are strongly driven by women's education (KC & Lutz, 2017). Women with education wish to have fewer children, and they also have better opportunities to actively plan the desired size of their families. A clear empirical finding of KC and Lutz (2017) is that fertility rates fall substantially when women attain primary as well as secondary education. The Wittgenstein Centre of Demography in Austria predicts that the global proportion of people with higher education will increase considerably in the next several decades (KC & Lutz, 2017). The global mean years of schooling of the total adult population will exceed 11 years by about 2050, which is about the current level in Europe and North America. In other words, 40 years from today, the global population might be as well educated as people in Europe today. It is quite likely that people will then also experience the positive opportunities that are associated with higher education. Most importantly, the gender gap in education could be closed by then, easing the growth of population in Africa, Asia, and Latin America. For example, the increase in population in Africa could be less than a factor of two to about 1.8 billion people instead of 2 billion people in the year 2050 according to one optimistic projection (Lutz *et al.*, 2014). To achieve this outcome, programmes need to be established, strengthened, and financed in countries where the education of women, in particular, is poor. Yet, how realistic is this imperative? The Republic of Korea provides an excellent example showing that large advances in attaining nation-wide education are possible within a short time. Within only two generations, the country (then a country struggling with extreme poverty) improved from being twenty-third in an OECD education study to being one of the top performers in 2012 (OECD, 2014).

Proclaiming unprecedented global solidarity

Sustainable development goal no. 17 is about the 'revitalization of the global partnership for a sustainable development' (UN, 2015). The targets are to increase official development assistance by collecting 0.7 per cent of gross national income from developed countries and transferring those resources to developing countries while at the same time securing 0.2 per cent for the least developed countries (ibid.). The alarming signals from the key theme indicators relate to the underperformance of large parts of the world regarding societal development and demonstrate that the global community has a long way to go in this area. A substantial increase is needed in funding, as well as the search for creative and collaborative ways on how to solve persisting problems. A benchmark achievement of successful solidarity is whether the threshold for the key theme 'eradicating extreme poverty' is achieved in all countries.

Two opportunities for alleviating poverty were striking when analysing the different country clusters: a low share of population with access to electricity coincides with high numbers of people in extreme poverty. The same holds true for high shares of rural population. Indeed, access to electricity and other affordable clean energy sources is necessary for health, food security, and income generation (Global Energy Assessment, 2012, Ch. 2). Simple and cheap technologies can already substantially improve this situation (e.g., solar lighting and cooking instead of kerosene lamps and cow dung ovens). When it comes to urbanization, we need to specify that it is not just the obvious search for opportunities that makes people leave rural areas even though they do indeed have better chances to overcome poverty. It is also the quality of the urban environment they find when they arrive. Thus, said more generally, extreme poverty can be reduced via rural diversification by town development as well as by metropolitanization (for further discussion of this concept, see Christiaensen *et al.*, 2013).

Improving education in low-income countries is a third major factor, as the following empirical examples show (Global Partnership for Education, 2016). The health situation in extremely poor countries improves significantly with higher levels of education. For example, child vaccination rates in Indonesia increased by a factor of three when mothers finished at least secondary education, and 66 per cent fewer malaria deaths occurred in Zambia thanks to specifically trained health workers. Furthermore, in instances of extreme poverty, average income increased by about 10 per cent with each year of additional education. The question arises then, how much extra money is needed to provide the poor with primary and secondary education? According to the Global Partnership for Education,[3] an average of just $1.18 per day is needed to educate a child in a developing country, and the daily funding gap amounts to only 14 cents.

Even though this number is surprisingly low for education, substantial investments are needed to finance all three major avenues for improvement, including related infrastructure, equipment, and workplaces. For example, it is estimated that about 1.9 million additional teachers are needed (UNESCO, 2016).

Where then would the necessary resources come from? One starting point would be for those with more than enough to learn to desire less or find other ways to satisfy their wishes. For example, it might be personally very tempting for someone living in Europe to own a second, third, or even fourth special-purpose bicycle. However, many poor families do not have even a single simple bicycle, which – if possessed – could change their life dramatically by providing transportation and a basis for a decent income. In this case, the European could instead donate the money not spent to purchase the extra bicycle – and many good initiatives to channel this money effectively already exist – and this type of simple change would not mean a dramatic curtailment in one's own quality of life. It is indeed not only ancient wisdom that the possession of too much distracts from one's purpose of life, but it is also an empirical fact that people do not gain much additional daily emotional wellbeing from a certain level of income onwards (Kahneman & Deaton, 2010). There are many examples of people practising solidarity in this way, ranging from donations in offertories, to volunteering or financing to build schools. A pledge campaign is an example where wealthy people commit themselves to practise solidarity through giving. Global solidarity only needs to become a more common and widespread practice. For example, why not establish an obligatory payment of 1 per cent of people's income who already enjoy a high level of human development?

In addition to promoting solidarity at the individual level, wealthy countries, institutions, and corporations have the opportunity to share more of their financial and/or intellectual resources. Indeed, three countries (Sweden, the United Arab Emirates, and Norway) currently donate more than 1 per cent of their gross national income (2015) to overseas development (OECD, 2016). Examples at the corporate level also show that commercial interest and philanthropy can go together; for example, the biotech company Gilead Science supported the building of health facilities in India in 2015 (Gilead, 2015). The United Nations and other institutions could also take easy actions. Instead of making it the norm to contract companies or consultants to 'polish' publications with expensive designs and layouts that in most cases provide little added value to the much more important contents, the same funds could be used for much better purposes. Again, we ask, why not establish a worldwide solidarity corporation and institutional tax of 1 per cent in countries where a high level of societal development has already been achieved?

Decoupling societal prosperity from material and energy consumption

The transition towards the sustainable development space is a global goal implying the achievement of high societal development everywhere while at the same time respecting environmental limits. The ways forward cannot be achieved without a focus on the economic catching-up of countries that are lagging behind (and whose share of world population is large and drastically increasing), as well as without behavioural changes, especially in societies whose citizens already enjoy high-quality lifestyles. It is particularly necessary that countries with low and medium economic development 'leapfrog' to where more highly developed countries have slowly started to move towards. Finances could be provided by a generously endowed green development fund. Technologies have to be transferred and adapted to meet local needs through collaborative efforts. A mutual adaptive learning process has to be ignited. For example, Norway could learn from Uruguay how to reduce municipal waste drastically. At the same time, both countries are forerunners in producing electricity from renewable energy sources – both countries currently produce over 90 per cent of power from renewable sources. A country such as Poland could learn from these experiences. Eastern European countries, on the other hand, have long-term experience in finding alternative materials and substantially extending the lifespan of products. Indeed, people worldwide are creative regardless of their income, for example, the bamboo bike initiative in Ghana.[4] The needed paradigm shift is sometimes called a 'green shift' or moving 'towards a zero emission society'. All of this implies that the prosperity of humanity needs to be decoupled from material and energy consumption, but how can this be achieved?

Starting at the individual level, this calls for reflection. We need to seriously ask ourselves what it is that makes us happy and content with our lives. Indeed, there might be some truth in the example provided in chapter 6 that similar levels of happiness are achieved in Costa Rica and the USA despite the quite different economic power of the two nations (see Helliwell et al., 2015 and UNEP, 2015). We need to make a habit of asking whether and why we are in need of a product before we purchase it. Almost certainly, in many cases, the actual possessing of the product could be replaced by simply renting the services that it was meant to deliver. For example, instead of owning a car, a book, or a home, it could be rented or shared when needed. It could also be purchased second hand, and in many cases we could easily do without the product at all.

At the regional and national level, it might be a timely idea to replace gross domestic product as one of the main indicators measuring overall success in societal development. An alternative already in place is the gross national happiness index, which is the main target indicator of Bhutan (Zurick, 2006). The task at the political level is to provide the right incentives to change individual behaviour.

One example is broadcast licences in many countries such as Japan, Norway, Germany, Namibia, and Ghana, where everybody is obligated to pay for broadcast services whether or not he or she actually uses them. Why not create public transport licences, so that everybody pays to finance a well-functioning public transportation system (with no extra payments for tickets when one uses the service)? Nations could also introduce different tax levels, differentiating whether products are new, second-hand (or repaired), or cause comparatively high ecological footprints. Such product-specific taxes already exist and the schemes could be simplified and revised. For example, many countries have special taxes on food and luxury goods. Meat products, which have a large ecological footprint, could easily be included in this type of scheme. Governments could also declare tax exemptions or tax cuts when taxpayers make financial efforts to offset their carbon or material footprints. Governments could support local production (including agriculture) while at the same time taxing remote (long-distance) production. All of these measures should be complemented by adaptive learning approaches, implying that care is exercised with regard to the problems of unintended consequences and unmet expectations. The locking-in of good practices is what can stimulate worldwide societal change.

Apart from providing incentives that push demand towards sustainable consumption patterns, governments can also ban the obvious as they do with hazardous items. When it comes to greenhouse gas emissions, it is most efficient to ban the burning of lignite and coal for providing heat or generating electricity. It would not only substantially lower greenhouse gas emissions but also improve air quality (IPCC, 2014). In this way, Australia could become a role model by demonstrating how to move away from the dependence on the worst of the fossil fuels. National and regional governments could also demand that companies conduct energy and material flow analysis before starting new production lines. Material saving and waste handling standards could be introduced as it has been done with energy saving and standards. For example, in the design of new public buildings, energy use and safety must be considered, but minimization of the use of construction materials is not yet a requirement. This issue could be addressed via regulations regarding design codes or could be made part of the selection criteria of public procurement. There could also be more restrictions on advertisements, as done successfully with tobacco products and alcohol. Why not extend the idea to products that attempt to raise levels of consumption for the sake of consumption? For example, why not ban 'buy one and get one free' campaigns? Finally, governments are one of the main sponsors of research and development activities. Key technologies should be supported that boost a circular economy where reduction, recycling, and reuse become the norm. Other key technologies are energy storage technologies, renewable energies with recyclable rare-earth components, and biofuels for international transport, as well as techniques that largely can replace non-biodegradable plastics, cement, and other energy- and material-intensive products.

Securing the resilience of the natural system

To keep the natural system intact is in our own interest, because we are not separate from but an integral part of nature. Acknowledging the services nature provides, it is straightforward to extend the idea of universal human rights to the universal rights of all living beings. This idea is not utopian and is at least partly grounded in reality in law in the USA. A prominent example is a white oak tree in Athens, Georgia, which owns itself and, hence, streets need to circumvent its property.[5] In a way, the consequence is to extend the concept of the key theme 'ensuring rich participation' beyond humanity to also include nature. The fulfilment of this threshold is a prerequisite to shape our world in the way we want it to be and to eliminate step-by-step what takes us further away from a sustainable pathway. Rich participation in our societies means that society should develop and nourish empathy for each other (humans and nature alike) and individuals should become actively involved in transformation processes. We need to enhance our participative literacy, which means become trained in listening, teamwork, and collaboration. Inspiration can be gained from 'manifold initiatives', which for example, are run under the 'transition network'.[6]

Ways forward also include a variety of other activities, including the extension of active voting rights to children and teenagers, the introduction of an obligatory double citizenship (with the idea of adopting a brother/sister country in the spirit of the 9th Symphony of Ludwig van Beethoven/Friedrich Schiller), the custom of celebrating a social and/or ecological year (as is already done in Austria and Germany), and the general introduction of political co-chairs with the aim of ensuring the participation of minority groups (including women, indigenous groups, elderly people, and others, depending on local circumstances).

Our ecological footprints need to become much smaller and nature needs more space to recover its resilience. This space will be horizontal as well as vertical, and it includes primal natural as well as cultural landscapes. We have to make it a principle to give back what we receive. This could range from the reinvention of rural sustainable concepts in agriculture (e.g., the sato-umi and sato-yama traditions in Japan) to actual payments for ecosystem services (e.g., establishing a fund to finance nature conservation). It could also mean establishing default environmental standards, such as building wildlife crossings on highways or fulfilling one's 'tree-duty' when erecting new buildings, as suggested by the Austrian artist and architect Friedensreich Hundertwasser. In fact, this and similar ideas (e.g., urban gardening and building of communities with aquaponic systems) could be further developed making use of the global mega-trend of urbanization.

Many advantages come with urbanization, for example, the provision and optimization of public transport and healthcare. The cultural density of cities is also attractive to many people. Urbanization may allow us to find the necessary natural recovery space if most people live in medium to larger size cities endowed with large parks and green spaces for quietness, relaxation, and greenhouse gas fixing. The cities could then be surrounded by rural rings acting as environmental buffer zones, followed by mostly human-empty natural areas. If currently available third generation biofuels become available for air and sea transportation, the number of new highways and other transportation structures could be kept to a minimum, and some could even be removed. Indeed, reducing the number of highways is a key to stopping the fragmentation of our landscape, which means reducing the number of meshes while at the same time increasing their size. For example, regions in the north of France have as many as 128 meshes per 1000 square kilometres, whereas the Covasna region in Romania has a mesh density of just 0.30 meshes per 1000 square kilometres (European Environmental Agency, 2011).

We currently still have relatively little knowledge about the actual fragmentation of our landscape and how it is connected to the resilience of our natural surroundings. A detailed fragmentation atlas is being created as part of a study by the European Environmental Agency (2011). We need to continue to increase our environmental literacy, beginning with gardening and eco-lessons in schools and kindergartens (such as the obligatory programme in schools in the German Democratic Republic), and continuing with the funding of research programmes and the establishment of environmental citizen science. A great example from the Congo Basin involving people with no or limited literacy into scientific activities is the establishment of environmental monitoring via so-called 'Community Memories' to collect data about the state of the environment and the relationship people have with it.[7] Finally, we have to start systematically accounting for the services provided by Earth's ecosystems and the damages done to them (cf. Millennium Ecosystem Assessment, 2005).

This chapter identified four pivotal points and ways to approach them. First, a key way to reduce population growth is to raise the levels of primary and secondary education among women and others worldwide. Second, an unprecedented level of global solidarity must be exercised by individuals, institutions, nations, and corporations to join in the effort to eradicate extreme poverty across the globe. A default contribution of 1 per cent from each person's income could, among other things, be channelled to poorer countries to encourage access to healthy energy sources, invest in rural and urban infrastructure, and support the improvement of educational attainment levels. Third, decoupling of societal prosperity from material and energy consumption requires a 'leapfrogging' to green technologies for those who are lagging behind in economic development and a behavioural shift for those who already enjoy high-quality lifestyles. Fourth, all of these changes need to be complemented by broad efforts – involving everybody from children to governments – to increase environmental literacy because we only care about what we know. It is crucial to account for the services nature provides as well as for the damage we do. There is no way around necessary behavioural changes. The mostly individual perspective taken in this chapter will be enlarged by looking into the local scale in chapter 8 and political dimensions in chapter 9.

Finally, we are brought back to where we began the chapter. The ancient folk song from the Ryūkyū Islands teaches us that the power to change is in ourselves, and it is the appreciation of modesty, cooperation, and the respect of our natural environment that will lead to sustainable development.

Notes

1   If not stated otherwise, data are taken from World DataBank (2016).
2   Criteria for a mega-diverse country: The principle criterion is endemism, first at the species level and then at higher taxonomic levels such as genus and family. To qualify as a mega-diverse country, a country must: (1) have at least 5000 of the world's plants as endemics; and (2) have marine ecosystems within its borders. Mega-diverse countries not included in the dataset: Papua New Guinea and Venezuela. See: www. biodiversitya-z.org/content/megadiverse-countries.
3   See www.globalpartnership.org/funding/education-costs-per-child. In total, the funding gap amounts to about $21 billion per year (UNESCO, 2011, 2016).
4   Refer to http://ghanabamboobikes.org/ for more inspiration.
5   See https://en.wikipedia.org/wiki/Tree_That_Owns_Itself.
6   Find great ideas for and lessons learnt from changing your environment at https:// transitionnetwork.org/.
7   More information and links to scientific publications about the project can be found at: www.ucl.ac.uk/excites/projects/excites-projects/intelligent-maps/intelligent-maps.

References

Christiaensen, L., De Weerdt, J., & Todo, Y. (2013) Urbanization and poverty reduction: The role of rural diversification and secondary towns. *Agricultural Economics*, 44, 435–447.

Costanza, R. (2014) A theory of socio-ecological system change. *Journal of BioEconomics*, 16, 39–44.

Costanza, R. & Kubiszewski, I. (2014) *Creating a Sustainable and Desirable Future: Insights from 45 Global Thought Leaders*. Singapore, World Scientific.

DeFries, R. S., Ellis, E. C., Chapin III, F. S., Matson, P. A., Turner II, B. L., Agrawal, A., Crutzen, P. J., Field, C., Gleick, P., Kareiva, P. M., Lambin, E. Liverman, D., Ostrom, E., Sanchez, P. A., & Syvitski, J. (2012) Planetary opportunities: A social contract for global change science to contribute to a sustainable future. *BioScience*, 62, 603–606.

Ding, C. & He, X. (2004) K-means clustering via principal component analysis. Appearing in Proceedings of the 21st International Conference on Machine Learning, Banff, Canada. Available from: http://ranger.uta.edu/~chqding/papers/KmeansPCA1.pdf.

European Environmental Agency (2011) *Landscape fragmentation in Europe*. EEA Report No. 2/2011, Copenhagen. Available from: www.eea.europa.eu/publications/ landscapefragmentation-in-europe.

Ferreira, F. H. G., Chen, S., Dabalen, A., Dikhanov, Y., Hamadeh, N., Jolliffe, D., Narayan, A., Prydz, E. B., Revenga, A., Sangraula, P., Serajuddin, U., & Yoshida, N. (2015) A global count of the extreme poor in 2012 data issues, methodology and initial results. *Policy Res. Work. Pap.* 7432.

Gilead (2015) *Gilead, Gilead Sciences Annual Report 2015*. Available from: www.gilead.com/ ar2015/assets/img/Gilead_2015_Annual_Report.pdf.

Global Energy Assessment (2012) *Global Energy Assessment: Toward a Sustainable Future*. Cambridge, UK and New York, Cambridge University Press and Laxenburg, Austria, the International Institute for Applied Systems Analysis.

Global Footprint Network (2016) National global footprint data from public data package of footprint calculations. Available from: www.footprintnetwork.org/en/index.php/GFN/page/public_data_package.

Global Partnership for Education (2016) Data available from: www.globalpartnership.org/.

Hartigan, J. A. (1975) *Clustering Algorithms*. New York, John Wiley & Sons, Inc.

Hartigan, J. A. & Wong, M. A. (1979) Algorithm AS 136: A k-means clustering algorithm. *Applied Statistics*, 28, 100–108.

Helliwell, J. F., Layard, R., & Sachs, J. (2015) *World Happiness Report 2015*. New York, Sustainable Development Solutions Network. Available from: www.unsdsn.org/happiness.

International Council for Science and International Social Science Council (2015) *Review of the Sustainable Development Goals: The Science Perspective*. Paris, International Council for Science (ICSU). Available from: www.icsu.org/publications.

IPCC (2014) *Climate Change 2014: Mitigation of Climate Change*. Contribution of Working Group III to the Fifth Assessment Report of the Intergovernmental Panel on Climate Change [Edenhofer, O., Pichs-Madruga, R., Sokona, Y., Farahani, E., Kadner, S., Seyboth, K., Adler, A., Baum, I., Brunner, S., Eickemeier, P., Kriemann, B., Savolainen, J., Schlomer, S., von Stechow, C., Zwickel, T., & Minx, J. C. (eds)], Cambridge, UK and New York, Cambridge University Press.

Jeffrey, K., Wheatley, H., & Abdallah, S. (2016) *The Happy Planet Index: 2016. A Global Index of Sustainable Well-being*. London, New Economics Foundation.

Kahnemann, D. & Deaton, A. (2010) High income improves evaluation of life but not emotional wellbeing. *Proceedings of the National Academy of Sciences of the United States of America*, 107, 16489–16493.

KC, S. & Lutz, W. (2017) The human core of the shared socioeconomic pathways: Population scenarios by age, sex and level of education for all countries to 2100. *Global Environmental Change*, 42, 181–192.

Lutz, W., Butz, W. P., & KC, S. (eds) (2014) *World Population and Human Capital in the Twenty-First Century*. Oxford, Oxford University Press.

Millennium Ecosystem Assessment (2005). *Ecosystems and Human Well-being: Synthesis*. Washington, DC, Island Press.

OECD (2014) *Lessons from PISA for Korea, Strong Performers and Successful Reformers in Education*, Paris, OECD Publishing.

OECD (2016) Net ODA (indicator). Available from DOI: 10.1787/33346549-en.

Ostrom, E. (2014) Do institutions for collective action evolve? *Journal of Bioeconomics*, 16, 3–30.

Rockström, J., Steffen, W., Noone, K., Persson, A., Chapin, F. S., Lambin, E. F., Lenton, T. M., Scheffer, M., Folke, C., Schellnhuber, H. J., Nykvist, B., de Wit, C. A., Hughes, T., van der Leeuw, S., Rodhe, H., Sorlin, S., Snyder, P. K., Costanza, R., Svedin, U., Falkenmark, M., Karlberg, L., Corell, R. W., Fabry, V. J., Hansen, J., Walker, B., Liverman, D., Richardson, K., Crutzen, P., & Foley, J. A. (2009) A safe operating space for humanity. *Nature*, 461, 472–475.

Rodrik, D. (2003) *In Search of Prosperity: Analytic Narratives on Economic Growth*. Princeton, NJ, Princeton University Press.

Roe, E. M. (1991) Development narratives, or making the best of blueprint development. *World Development*, 19, 287–300.

Steffen, W., Richardson, K., Rockström, J., Cornell, S. E., Fetzer, I., Bennett, E. M., Biggs, R., Carpenter, S. R., de Vries, W., de Wit, C. A., Folke, C., Gerten, D., Heinke, J., Mace, G. M., Persson, L. M., Ramanathan, V., Reyers, B., & Sorlin, S. (2015) Planetary boundaries: Guiding human development on a changing planet. *Science*, 347, 1–17.

Togtokh, C. (2011) Stop celebrating the polluters. *Nature*, 479, 269.

UN (2015) General Assembly resolution 70/1, *Transforming Our World: The 2030 Agenda for Sustainable Development*, A/RES/70/1 (21 October 2015). Available from: https//undocs.org/A/RES/70/1.

UNEP (2015) *Human Development Report 2015 – Work for Human Development*. New York, UN Development Programme. Available from: http://hdr.undp.org/en/2015-report/download.

UNESCO (2011) *Education Counts: Towards the Millennium Development Goals*, Paris, United Nations Educational, Scientific and Cultural Organization. Available from: http://unesdoc.unesco.org/images/0019/001902/190214e.pdf.

UNESCO (2016) *Global Education Monitoring Report 2016, Education for People and Planet: Creating Sustainable Futures for All*, Paris, United Nations Educational, Scientific and Cultural Organization. Available from: http://unesdoc.unesco.org/images/0024/002457/245752e.pdf.

United Nations Medium Population Projections (2016) Available from: www.un.org/en/development/desa/population.

United Nations World Urbanisation Prospects (2014) *World Urbanisation Prospects: The 2014 Revision*. Available from: https://esa.un.org/unpd/wup/publications/files/wup2014-highlights.Pdf.

World Bank (2012) *WHAT A WASTE: A Global Review of Solid Waste Management*. Available from: http://siteresources.worldbank.org/INTURBANDEVELOPMENT/Resources/336387-1334852610766/What_a_Waste2012_Final.pdf.

World DataBank (2016) *The World DataBank*. Washington, DC, World Bank (producer and distributor). Available from: http://databank.worldbank.org/.

Zurick, D. (2006) Gross national happiness and environmental status in Bhutan. *Geographical Review*, 96, 657–681.

8

LOST IN TRANSLATION?

Scene 1: On a holiday stroll through a charming coastal village in western Scotland I noticed a sign announcing a 'sustainable fashion show' in the village the following week. I left before the show. Back in Norway I couldn't stop wondering: What on Earth is a sustainable fashion show?

Scene 2: On a cold, rainy day in the spring of 1998, backed by the school orchestra, the young mayor enthusiastically announced that his municipality had turned its back on unsustainability. It would now aim for a sustainable development to ensure quality of life and livelihoods for today's and future generations. More importantly, the municipality would seek to make its activities environmentally sustainable both locally and globally, to reduce resource use and environmental impact.[1] Since 1998, an increasing number of mayors worldwide have made similar enthusiastic announcements. Whenever I hear a school orchestra playing I wonder: Can a municipality ever become sustainable?

Scene 3: Bored while flying to an international conference on sustainable mobility (oh, the irony), I browsed the airline's annual report. The smiling CEO, shirt sleeves rolled up, announced that the three pillars of sustainability were cornerstones of the company's business model, that the company's decisions and practices would support the world and its people. No less. He closed by announcing that their commitment to a sustainable future was evidenced by their corporate responsibility efforts. Looking at the heavy exhaust stream from the plane's engines, I wondered: Can a firm ever become sustainable?

Scene 4: *Director* [in Japanese, to the interpreter]: The translation is very important, OK? The translation. *Interpreter* [in Japanese, to the director]: Yes, of course. I understand. *Director* [in Japanese, to Bob]: Mr Bob. You are sitting quietly in your study. And then there is a bottle of Suntory whisky on top of the table. You understand, right? With wholehearted feeling, slowly, look at the camera, tenderly, and as if you are meeting old friends, say the words. As if you are Bogie in *Casablanca*, saying, 'Here's looking at you, kid' – Suntory time!

Interpreter [In English, to Bob]: He wants you to turn, look in camera. OK? *Bob*: … Is that all he said?

Lost in Translation (2003)²

Many important points can be made from the scenes above (the first three from the life of one of the authors). The first three show that the sustainable development concept is now universal. As Lafferty and Langhelle pointed out 18 years ago, 'the idea of a nonsustainable society is simply not on' (Lafferty & Langhelle, 1999, p. 1). Clearly, for an increasing number of local actors – fashion shows, municipalities, and firms – the idea is still not on.

According to the global network Local Governments for Sustainability (ICLEI), more than 1500 cities, towns, and regions in more than 86 countries are committed to building a sustainable future. ICLEI has instigated a movement of about 10,000 local governments that have engaged their citizens in local sustainability work. Moreover, ICLEI has created a network of more than 1000 cities that have undertaken climate action planning and set voluntary targets for reducing greenhouse gas emissions, which could lead to an annual emission reduction of more than 60 million tons of CO_2eq.³

In their *International Corporate Responsibility Reporting Survey 2011*, KPMG revealed a significant increase in sustainability reporting, with 95 per cent of the world's 250 biggest firms disclosing sustainability performance information in 2011 (compared to 80 per cent in 2008). This increase, KPMG claims, suggests a shift in which sustainability reporting is now becoming the norm for large firms and that 'corporate responsibility reporting' (where sustainability performance normally is reported) has become the *de facto* law for business.⁴ According to McKinsey Group, 43 per cent say their firms seek to align sustainability with their overall business goals, mission, or values (up from 30 per cent in 2012).⁵

Researchers too have embraced the local dimension of sustainable development. A search on Google Scholar gives some 2.2 million results on 'local sustainable development' and 'local sustainability', respectively. A further 2 million results appear for 'sustainable development and firms'.

Cities, towns, regions, firms, and researchers have the following approach to develop plans for local sustainable development (from now on referred to as local sustainability). First, they start with a global understanding of sustainable development by referring to *Our Common Future*'s authoritative definition (see chapter 1). Second, they translate the authoritative definition to fit their own understanding of local sustainability. A closer study of varieties of local sustainability shows that a significant amount of creativity is allowed for in that approach. Indeed, important parts of sustainable development easily get lost in that translation, which leads us to scene 4 above.

Bob Harris, an ageing American movie star, meets Charlotte, a young college graduate, at a Tokyo hotel. Both, sleepless due to their respective personal crises, are lost in several senses. First, to Bob the meaning and detail of the director's words get lost in translation. For the interpreter, the director's lengthy, impassioned directives in Japanese are too time consuming and cumbersome to translate. This is a relevant point when translating the global imperatives of sustainable development to local sustainability. It is often too time consuming and cumbersome to properly translate sustainable development's moral imperatives to local sustainability. Second, Bob and Charlotte get lost in the alien Japanese culture. Likewise, it is easy to get lost when trying to translate global sustainable development to (alien) local conditions. The culture to which one would like to translate matters. Different cultures would choose different pathways, as described in chapter 7. Third, Bob and Charlotte get lost in their own lives, a feeling amplified by their displaced location, which leads to their blossoming friendship and growing connection. Here, too, there is relevance to translating sustainable development. At some point we got lost in a displaced, non-sustainable society, a place we should not have been visiting. Making sense of our lives in that displaced location can pave the way for achieving sustainable development. Thus, being in an unsustainable place could stir our sense of sustainability.

In chapters 1–5, we developed a global model for sustainable development. Now we translate this model to the local level. But how do we know if what we are doing locally is actually sustainable globally? How can we be sure that the global imperatives of sustainable development do not get lost in translation? Indeed, can we *think* globally while simultaneously *acting* locally? Yes, we think we can by distinguishing between two different approaches to local sustainability: comprehensive and comparative sustainability. Before presenting the two approaches, we will reflect upon why it is important to simultaneously think globally and act locally, and will also say something about how *Our Common Future* treats local sustainability.

A conceptual clarification seems necessary. When we refer to local sustainability, we mean sustainability at *any other scale than global and national*. Thus, local sustainability means translating the global model onto a variety of scales, including municipalities, cities, communities, societal sectors, firms, programmes, products, projects, and individuals. Importantly, local sustainability does not, as often portrayed in the literature, solely apply to local authorities such as municipalities and cities. We do not intend to develop detailed indicators and thresholds at each scale. Rather, using the moral imperatives of sustainable development and using theories fundamental to understanding those imperatives, we present principles for achieving local sustainability at different scales.

'Think globally, act locally'

The maxim 'think globally, act locally' has been a mantra of sorts in environmental policy for the last four decades. It has also been referred to often in numerous research studies (more than 250,000 results on Google Scholar). The maxim focuses on the impasse between simultaneously thinking about global environmental challenges and taking necessary actions locally to face those challenges. Thus, it urges actors to consider the entire planet's health when taking action in their own communities and cities. No longer, therefore, is it sufficient to address environmental issues only locally, like noise and municipal waste (though these are still important). Rather, one must take action locally that considers the entire planet's health.

This maxim was not used in either *Our Common Future* or Agenda 21 (we return to Agenda 21 shortly). Its use is often linked to the French environmentalist Rene Dubos, who used it in an unofficial background report to the UN's first Conference on the Human Environment, in Stockholm in 1972 (Dubos & Ward, 1972). The maxim was also used by many of the crucial social movements that emerged in post-war Europe and the United States, including the peace movement, the solidarity movement, and the environmental movement (O'Connor, 1992). These movements worked to solve global challenges through local actions, and therefore had to think globally and act locally. We must, however, go back to 1915 to find the first use of the maxim in an environmental policy context. The maxim was originally formulated by the Scottish biologist, sociologist, and urban planner Patrick Geddes (Stephen *et al.*, 2004). In his book of 1915, *Cities in Evolution: An Introduction to the Town Planning Movement and to the Study of Cities*, Geddes launched a planning concept that included the maxim of thinking globally and acting locally. He supported a planning concept where the nature and the countryside (in this context, the 'global') must be brought to the city (the 'local').

Why is it so important to think globally about sustainable development? First, as we have argued in this book, it is an inherently global concept. The issue is the future of our planet and the species inhabiting it. More than anything, *Our Common Future* has warned us about the challenges facing 'the Earth', 'our world', 'the entire humanity', 'our fragile planet', and 'the global community'. Thus, we agree with John Whitelegg (1993, p. 11) that 'there can be no understanding of sustainability at any level other than global'. Thus, the challenges we face, such as mitigating climate change, fighting against loss of biosphere integrity, eradicating extreme poverty, and promoting social justice, are global and must be understood as such. Acting locally, without understanding and thinking of these global challenges, would not give the results that are imperative to achieve sustainable development. Thinking globally does not, however, mean that local issues are unimportant, such as noise and local pollution. Focusing on such local issues in isolation would, however, not address global challenges of sustainable development.

Second, we should think globally about sustainability issues to avoid the danger of parochialism. Amartya Sen sees non-parochialism as a requirement of promoting social justice; in fact, he claims that 'assessment of justice demands engagement with the "eyes of mankind"' (Sen, 2009, p. 130).[6] He gives four reasons for this claim, which we find similarly relevant in achieving sustainable development. First, we must avoid parochialism because we often identify with others elsewhere and not just with our local community. Many people are truly concerned about acute poverty in areas far from their own local community. Many people are truly concerned about the loss of biodiversity in distant locations, such as the destruction of tropical rainforests in Brazil or desertification of grassland in Africa. Showing these concerns by thinking globally, which many people actually do, is vital to address global sustainability challenges – this is engagement. Second, we must avoid parochialism because our (local) actions may affect the lives of others both near *and* far. The barbarity of 9/11 in New York and the assassination of Archduke Franz Ferdinand of Austria on 28 June 1914 in Sarajevo are prominent examples of local actions that had far-reaching consequences. As for the environment, climate change will have far-reaching consequences. Although greenhouse gas emissions from private cars do not necessarily pose a threat locally, the accumulated emissions from many cars can pose a serious threat globally by causing climate change – this is interconnectivity. Third, avoiding parochialism prevents us from being locked up in lazy acceptance of strongly manifest values, custom, habits, and presumptions in the local community. Because of such acceptance, we miss other people's perspectives that may help us overcome our own parochialism. Surely, Europeans can learn from Africans and vice versa. A part of this reasoning is to avoid the influence of vested local interest, which often could lead to short-term, one-sided solutions. Allowing for perspectives from outside the local community can reduce the influence of vested interest – this is learning. Fourth, and finally, is the danger of intellectual parochialism. Simply adhering the issues and solutions of sustainable development to a single scientific discipline would be highly inadequate. Rather, a truly interdisciplinary approach is necessary, including important contributions from ecology, sociology, psychology, political science, and others – this is complexity.

Thinking globally is important, but why should we act locally? For several reasons. First, and most obvious, is that almost all action takes place locally. Although actions' consequences can be distant in time and space, all action is here and now.

Second, local authorities and other actors possess many means to follow up and implement national (and global) sustainability policies. There is only so much that national governments (or the United Nations) can do. The main implementation is left to actors at local scales, not only because actions take place locally, but also because we find locally many means that can promote sustainability. Governments can use national economic measures (for example introducing a CO_2 tax) or make national laws (for example banning the sale of diesel cars). Local authorities are responsible for land-use planning with consequences for transport and housing, businesses make decisions about building factories and making products, and individuals decide whether to travel in private cars or by public transport. Thus, many important actions are carried out at local scales. That is what is meant by 'act locally'.

Third, we usually find the best solutions locally. Therefore, regarding finding the proper means by which to achieve sustainability goals, some parochialism should be allowed for. The historical, geographical, and cultural contexts make some means more efficient than others. If a municipality must work to ensure participation in decision-making, surely it is best situated to find ways to do so (though it probably needs a little push from the national government). If a company must reduce its CO_2 emissions by 80 per cent, surely it must be allowed to use its employees' creativity to find ways to do so (though its efforts probably need to be followed up by the national government). If an individual seeks ways to live more sustainably, surely she should be allowed to find her own ways of doing so (though she probably needs information about how to do so). Thus, creativity in finding the best means by which to achieve the goals flourishes locally. That creativity cannot, though, be used to set the goals as we often see in so-called 'stakeholder approaches' to sustainable development (see chapter 1).

Fourth, ownership of solutions matters. Allowing for some parochialism in finding the best ways to achieve a goal increases the chances that local actors will comply. If someone commands me to do something I am not keen to do, the chances that I comply are much greater if I can choose for myself how to comply. I am not very happy with reducing my CO_2 emissions by 50 per cent, but wait, let me see what I can do. Most likely, I will find a way, but it will be *my way*. This is not as naïve as it sounds. A recent study of European households' ability and willingness to reduce their CO_2 emissions, appropriately called HOPE,[7] tells us so. In an experiment, households could choose from a large menu of measures that would potentially reduce their emissions. The measures included general consumption (for example, electronic devices and clothing), food, transport, and housing. The study found that households voluntarily reduced their emissions by 30 per cent and, given the requirement that they *must* reduce their emissions by 50 per cent, had little trouble finding measures to reduce further (Feidje *et al.*, 2016). The most interesting finding, however, was that households' 'package of measures' varied significantly. They all found their own way of halving their emissions. Allowing for some parochialism is thus likely to increase the chances of actually achieving objectives. Thus, the chances that sustainability goals will be achieved are much greater when local actors feel they have found their own ways of achieving them.

Fifth, local actors (e.g., local authorities or firms) can act as 'test sites' for developing new innovative policy approaches and measures (Aall & Skarbø, 2014). When the national government is unsure about the most efficient way to guide a municipality or a firm towards sustainable development, and the municipality and the firm are correspondingly unsure how to proceed, together they can always try something and see how it works. There are numerous examples of such test sites, and the Fredrikstad Declaration already mentioned is one (see note 1). The advantage of using test sites is twofold. First, on an overall level, it tells us if the test is successful in achieving the goal. Does the test work? If not, we are back to square one. Second, engagement on a more detailed level gives us information about why things do not work and how we can make them work. Why does the test not work? Can we do something to make it work? This is probably how we all go about living our lives anyway. We try something to achieve something, and if unsuccessful, we try something else. If we find something that works, we stick to it.

Sixth, we should act locally because sometimes national governments are unwilling to take the necessary actions to achieve sustainable development. When such unwillingness appears, local actors can go further. Local authorities (because they lack proper signals from their national governments), firms (probably to make more money or to attract skilled and motivated workers), and individuals (because they are fed up with passive and incompetent national politicians), might want to go further. Local authorities, firms, and individuals cannot and will not wait for national governments to sort out their priorities. Rather, local actors take independent policy initiatives and send political signals that national governments' actions are inadequate. They could also 'interfere' in policy areas that normally fall under the national government's responsibility (ibid.).

Of course, such local interference is a double-edged sword. On the one hand, such disobedience, impatience, and creativity are good and indeed a part of the reasoned scrutiny that Sen (2009) calls for. We need to act now, and not sit endlessly waiting for others to act. Thus, creativity is essential to local solutions. On the other hand, local interference creates opportunities for various interpretations of the goal and, moreover, of whether the goal is worth working towards at all. Although we argue that people should always debate the normative foundations of society, sustainable development nevertheless demands some imperatives that must be respected.

Our Common Future and local sustainability

Our Common Future said little about local sustainability. Though it acknowledged that 'ecology and economy are becoming ever more interwoven locally, regionally, nationally, and globally into a seamless net of causes and effects' (WCED, 1987, p. 5), it provided little guidance about how to facilitate local sustainability. That came shortly afterwards. *Our Common Future* recommended that

> within an appropriate period after the presentation of the report to the General Assembly, an international Conference could be convened to review progress made and promote follow-up arrangements that will be needed over time to set benchmarks and to maintain human progress within the guidelines of human needs and natural laws.

(ibid., p. 343)

The General Assembly did as told. A conference was arranged in Rio de Janeiro in 1992[8] and an agenda – Agenda 21 – was launched (UN, 1992).

Agenda 21 is a non-binding, voluntarily implemented UN action plan regarding sustainable development. It is an action plan for the UN, other multilateral organizations, and individual governments worldwide that can be executed at local, national, and global levels. (The '21' in Agenda 21 refers to the 21st century – which, even if we lack progress in many areas, still gives us some time!) Agenda 21 has been affirmed and is, with minor modifications at subsequent UN conferences, still valid. At the 2012 United Nations Conference on Sustainable Development, the attending members reaffirmed their commitment to Agenda 21 in *The Future We Want* (UN, 2012). In 2015, the UN's General Assembly presented a new agenda named *Transforming Our World* (UN, 2015), which included 17 global sustainable development goals. The new agenda reaffirms all the principles of the 1992 Rio Declaration on Environment and Development and the spirit of Agenda 21 is clearly embedded in the sustainable development goals.

Agenda 21 gives some guidance about how to translate global imperatives of sustainable development to local conditions (UN, 1992). In section III (*Strengthening the role of major groups*), women, youth, indigenous people and their communities, non-governmental organizations, local authorities, workers and their trade unions, businesses and industry, and farmers all get the UN's attention. Regarding translating from global to local sustainable development, chapter 28, *Local authorities' initiatives in support of Agenda 21*, is particularly relevant. The chapter, often referred to as Local Agenda 21 (LA21), has become the touchstone for most theoretical approaches to local sustainability. Its practical importance is no less. In most countries, LA21 is the preferred strategy and action programme for implementing sustainable development locally.

Thus, it is worthwhile scrutinizing section III in Agenda 21, and LA21 particularly. In section III's preamble, it is stated that 'critical to the effective implementation [of sustainable development goals] will be the commitment and genuine involvement of all social groups' (ibid., §23.1). Thus, we need everyone to agree to the proposed changes and to be actively involved. All groups must participate as 'one of the fundamental prerequisites for the achievement of sustainable development is broad public participation in decision-making' (ibid., §23.2). Passive forms of participation, like showing up for balloting every fourth year, are not enough for achieving local sustainability, as

> the need for new forms of participation has emerged. This includes the need of individuals, groups and organizations to participate in environmental impact assessment procedures and to know about and participate in decisions, particularly those which potentially affect the communities in which they live and work.
>
> (ibid.)

These new forms of participation require that individuals, groups, and organizations have access to all relevant information held by national authorities. Such information includes the environmental impacts of products and activities, and the measures that can alleviate these impacts.

Notwithstanding the importance of actions taken by firms, local organizations, and individuals, LA21 acknowledges local authorities as crucial to achieving local sustainability:

> Because so many of the problems and solutions being addressed by Agenda 21 have their *roots in local activities*, the participation and cooperation of local authorities will be *a determining factor in fulfilling its objectives*. Local authorities

construct, operate and maintain economic, social and environmental infrastructure, oversee planning processes, establish local environmental policies and regulations, and assist in implementing national and subnational environmental policies. As *the level of governance closest to the people*, they play a vital role in educating, mobilizing and responding to the public to promote sustainable development.

(ibid., §28.1, italics added)

LA21 does not give many substantial recommendations regarding what actions need to be taken. Nowhere are to be found recommendations like advanced renewable energy schemes, ambitious low-carbon vehicles programmes, or radical sustainable land-use planning programmes. Rather, the agenda focuses on building a 'local green-consciousness' which, eventually, could lead to necessary actions. The objectives are basically to 'undertake consultative processes with local groups', to 'implement plans for increased participation' and to 'achieve consensus on a local Agenda for the community' (ibid., chapter 28).

Thus, except for securing the involvement of 'women and youth' (objective 'd' in §28.2), the objectives of LA21 are primarily procedural. In contrast to many of the objectives in other chapters of Agenda 21, the LA21 objectives are quite *specifically* procedural (Lafferty & Eckerberg, 1997). Lafferty and Eckerberg interpret this as 'omission by design: rather than trying to outline in detail the content areas of a preordained plan or programme, the chapter [28] leaves this open' (ibid., p. 3). The message is clearly 'that it is up to the local authorities to take responsibility for initiating and co-ordinating the dialogue among the local groups, which is necessary to determine *the form and content of their specific Local Agenda 21 initiative*' (ibid., p. 3, italics in original). Therefore, at the most ambitious level, Lafferty and Eckerberg see the task of implementing local sustainability as one of interpreting and 'relativizing' sustainable development to suit local conditions and problems. The underlying logic of implementation task, they argue, 'implies a process whereby *local authorities function as responsible disseminators and facilitators of the Local Agenda 21 idea*' (ibid., p. 4, italics in original).

The logic of the task is an expression of underlying general assumptions about what actions are necessary to achieve local sustainability. Lafferty and Eckerberg argue that in LA21 the goals are the processes themselves, that is, the processes deemed necessary to bring sustainable development down to local actors. Moreover, the processes acknowledge that local communities will vary considerably regarding which aspects of the action plan are most relevant for moving the community towards sustainable development. Conditions of regional location, geography, demography, and most importantly, the nature of the local economy, will all affect the interpretation and application of the plan. Surely, Amartya Sen would have approved.

We do not question that raising awareness, building consensus, and fostering networks are important. Nor do we question the important role of local authorities and the fact that local conditions should play a role when translating sustainability locally. There is a flip side to the coin though. Being too 'relative' and opening for too many local 'adaptations' may well cause local actors to lose sight of the global imperatives of sustainable development. Surely, sustainable development is something that should not – and cannot – easily be 'relativized' away.

Two approaches to local sustainability: Rawls versus Sen

Arguing for the three imperatives of sustainable development is an unpleasant task. Few will agree, and many more will probably disagree. Translating these imperatives to local conditions is an even more unpleasant task. It is like entering a minefield: a mine (that is, a *major* objection to how the translation has been done) is likely to explode anytime. And the more concrete one is in translating themes, indicators, and thresholds, the closer one gets to an exploding mine. No wonder that many approaches to local sustainability, including LA21, leave it to local stakeholders to interpret and implement!

Amartya Sen (2009) argues that the natural starting point for developing a theory of justice is to focus on the questions to be answered. One could ask: What would be perfectly just institutions? One could also ask: How would justice be advanced? Each starting point leads to different approaches of justice. The distance between the two approaches is, according to Sen, 'quite momentous'. As chapter 3 showed, taking different starting points and approaches has dramatic implications for the resulting theory.

A starting point for finding approaches to local sustainability could be to ask the same types of questions as Sen does for finding approaches to justice. One could ask: What would be perfect local sustainability? or How would local sustainability be advanced? Inspired by Sen's terminology, the first question points at an approach to local sustainability that we call 'comprehensive sustainability' and the second question points at an approach we call 'comparative sustainability'.

We will present the two approaches shortly, but first let us make some comments regarding them. Sen uses the term 'transcendental institutionalism' for efforts by scholars seeking perfectly just institutions, which, according to their view, subsequently would influence political regulation and guide appropriate behaviour. This 'contractarian' way of thinking was initiated by Thomas Hobbes and further argued by John Locke, Jean-Jacques Rousseau, and Immanuel Kant. Some of these scholars, in their search for perfectly just institutions, have also presented analyses of moral or political imperatives regarding socially appropriate behaviour. This applies, according to Sen, particularly to Immanuel Kant and John Rawls, both of whom have participated in transcendental institutional investigations, but also have provided far-reaching analyses of behavioural norms. Thus, their analyses can be seen more broadly as an 'arrangement-focused' view of justice. According to this view 'justice should be conceptualized in terms of organizational arrangements – some institutions, some regulations, some behaviour rules – the active presence of which would indicate that justice is being done' (ibid., p. 10). Sen contrasts this 'arrangement-focused' view to that of a 'realization-focused comparison' view.

Should we really, he asks, be satisfied with getting the institutions, regulation, and behaviour right? Should we not also have to examine 'what emerges in the society, including the kind of lives that people can actually lead, given the institutions and rules, but also other influences, including actual behaviour, that would inescapably affect human lives?' (ibid., p. 10). Indeed, Sen insists, we should.

Comprehensive sustainability: Rawls' 'social ideal'

The starting point for the comprehensive approach to local sustainability is to translate sustainable development (as defined in chapter 5) locally. The three imperatives of satisfying human needs, ensuring social justice, and respecting environmental limits, guide the translation. The starting point leads us to Sen's transcendental, or arrangement-focused approach. The approach is 'ideal' in the sense that local sustainability goals align with the goals derived from the global imperatives. It is 'perfect' in the sense that it perfectly achieves the goals. Thus, we use the term 'comprehensive sustainability' to acknowledge the ideal and perfect nature of the approach. It is the preferred approach to local sustainability and should apply whenever appropriate.

To some extent comprehensive sustainability is a Rawlsian approach. Not necessarily in the contractarian sense but in the sense that it begins with the ideal theory, which provides the 'only basis for the systematic grasp of these more pressing problems' (Rawls, 1999, p. 8). Rawls' pressing problem is the lack of social justice, ours is the lack of sustainable development. Moreover, Rawls assumes that 'a deeper understanding [of these more pressing problems] can be gained in no other way, and that the nature and aims of a perfectly just society is the fundamental part of the theory of justice' (ibid., p. 8). Rawls' ideal theory is derived from what he calls 'strict compliance theory', one which is opposed to 'partial compliance theory' (ibid., p. 8). The latter theory resonates with Sen's realization-focused view and with our own comparative sustainability to be presented in the next section.

Rawls focuses on social justice. To Rawls, the primary subject of social justice is the way in which major social institutions, that is, the basic structure of society, distribute fundamental rights and duties and determine the division of advantages from social cooperation. The basic structure is Rawls' primary subject of justice because its effects on people's life prospects are so profound and present from the start. He argues that a convincing account for his principles of justice is the 'first objective of justice as fairness' (ibid., p. xii). Our focus in this book is not on the basic structure of society and the major social institutions as such. Nor is it on how individuals and organizations cooperate and behave. Rather we focus on presenting the 'first objectives of sustainable development', that is, on the moral imperatives of sustainable development and the key themes derived from those imperatives. The first objectives constitute comprehensive sustainability, a state of affairs that ultimately should guide institutions, regulations, and behaviour.

We argue in this book that achieving sustainable development represents different challenges for different countries. In this sense, it could be argued that different countries, given their present sustainable state of affairs, conform to a 'narrow' sustainability requirement. By narrow sustainability, we mean that the challenge of achieving sustainable development is reduced to one or a few key themes supposedly more important than others. According to Asheim *et al.* (2001), sustainable development is primarily an equity concept that should be linked to justice between generations. Others, like the Norwegian philosopher Arne Næss (1993), argue that sustainable development is primarily a matter of staying within environmental limits. Our position is that countries face different sustainability challenges because of historical and economic necessities, not by choice. A country's historical and economic background conditions point at the key sustainable themes that must be addressed, *not its preference for or choice of themes.*

An important point: countries with great resources economically, have a twin responsibility in achieving sustainability. First, they have a responsibility to achieve sustainable development at home. Second, they simultaneously have a responsibility to help low-resource countries to achieve sustainable development. The latter responsibility applies whether or not the resource-rich countries conform to a particular sustainability threshold. The low-resource countries have responsibilities too. They cannot work to reduce poverty or to increase the capabilities for their inhabitants endlessly if that means they are eventually trespassing environmental limits.

What has been said here about countries' challenges and responsibilities is equally true at the local level. Municipalities, firms, and individuals are not free to choose sustainability themes, indicators, and thresholds. Resource-rich municipalities, firms, and individuals have a responsibility towards municipalities, firms, and individuals lacking in resources.

What does it all come down to regarding comprehensive local sustainability? We claim that the following principles apply:

- All six key themes described by the global model of sustainable development must be assessed.
- All six thresholds specified in the global sustainable development model must be met.
- All six thresholds are equally important, no trade-offs are allowed for.
- All actors have a twin responsibility to meet the thresholds in their own locality (e.g., municipality) while simultaneously supporting other localities (e.g., other municipalities) to meet their thresholds.

A final comment on the challenge of finding data. Whereas data about human development, the Gini coefficient, and per-capita CO_2 emissions are readily available at the country level (see chapters 6 and 7), such data about the local level can be hard to obtain. Nevertheless, achieving comprehensive sustainability requires such data. Thus, a process for finding and collecting existing or new data is necessary.

Comparative local sustainability: Sen's 'actual lives'

At some levels, it would be difficult, meaningless, or even impossible to apply the principles of comprehensive sustainability. It is, for example, difficult to apply the principles of comprehensive sustainability for projects such as railway bridges or office buildings. It is, likewise, close to meaningless, if not impossible, to apply the principles of comprehensive sustainability for products such as diapers and plastic bottles. In such cases, a second-best approach to local sustainability is needed. Comparative sustainability is that second-best approach. Nevertheless, we must stress, applying principles of comprehensive sustainability is always the first-best approach.

An alternative to a second-best approach to local sustainability, that is comparative sustainability, could be to abandon the idea of sustainable development on the local level. One could, for example, argue that sustainability has no place at the local level, and that traditional local policies for protecting the environment, securing social welfare, and ensuring fair distribution of goods are sufficient. It would, however, be a mistake to abandon the idea of sustainable development on the local level for two reasons. First because *Our Common Future*, Agenda 21, and the UN's recently adopted sustainable development agenda all urge us to think globally about all sustainable actions at the local level. Second, because sustainable development bears with it an idea of commitment in time (to future generations) and space (to unprivileged people elsewhere in the world) that should not be taken lightly. The very term 'sustainability' reminds us so, and it would be a mistake if that reminder were to become lost in local policies and local actions.

Why do we have to stick to the second-best choice of comparative local sustainability? (Amartya Sen would probably not agree with our portraying comparative sustainability as a second-best choice; rather, he would portray it as realism-based sustainability on a par with comprehensive sustainability.) The reasons have everything to do with the issues of feasibility, redundancy, and the actual conditions under which real actors live. Here, however, one must tread carefully. Sen refers to the issue of feasibility as one where there 'may be no reasoned agreement at all on the nature of the "just society"' (Sen, 2009, p. 9). Correspondingly, there may be no reasoned agreement at all on the nature of sustainable development, so why indeed keep looking for it? We disagree with Sen here. We think that the sustainable development space presented in this book, with its basis in three moral imperatives, forms a reasoned agreement on the nature of a sustainable development. Of course, we can always reject the idea of sustainable development. That is a choice. But as long as we commit ourselves to achieving sustainable development (remember the fresh commitment made by the Heads of State and Government and High Representatives), what we are committing to is pretty clear: we need to stay within the sustainable development space.

Moreover, Sen refers to the issue of redundancy as one where we, rather than seeking perfect solutions (that we by the way, according to Sen, would not agree upon anyway), need to seek the best possible solutions, taking into account alternatives actually available. These alternatives can be found in 'the lives that people manage – or do not manage – to live' (ibid., p. 18). This means *advancing* justice, or sustainability, rather than finding perfect justice, or perfect sustainability. The goal, according to Sen, is to remove injustice whenever we see it rather than waiting for the perfect solution. We go, he claims, 'as far as we reasonably can' (ibid., p. 401).

We largely agree with Sen's argument about redundancy. In certain cases, we can be satisfied by advancing sustainability rather than waiting for the perfect solutions (that is comprehensive sustainability). But the reason we settle for the second-best option is because that is what we *can do* in the actual situation, not, as we understand Sen, because we *should* accept to settle for less. Actually, Sen regards his 'as-far-as-we-possibly-can approach' to justice as his first-best option (or at least at the same level as perfect justice).[9] Sen uses the same approach to sustainable development (ibid., pp. 248ff). To us, that would be a descriptive approach and not a normative one. It would indeed have been a great achievement to halve extreme poverty and to reduce the world's expected temperature increase to 3°C, but it would be wrong to call it comprehensive sustainability.[10]

The case for comparative sustainability, we argue, is grounded on two conditions: relevance and availability. The first condition is somewhat related to Sen's concept of feasibility, but departs from his understanding in the sense that we mean feasibility of relevant choices rather than preference choices. Thus, we prefer to use relevance rather than feasibility. The second condition is broadly equal to Sen's concept of redundancy.

The condition of relevance implies that in some cases all three imperatives of sustainable development, and the respective key themes, simply are not relevant to promote local sustainability. When assessing a product's sustainability (e.g., a plastic bottle), it is not very relevant to assess how producing the bottle would eradicate extreme poverty or enhance human capabilities. How can that possibly be done? When assessing a project's sustainability (e.g., a railway bridge in a developed country), one must work hard to see the relevance to the goal of ensuring rich participation.[11] When assessing a company's sustainability (e.g., a car manufacturer), the relevance to the goal of ensuring fair distribution in society is not obvious. When assessing a social welfare programme's sustainability, the relevance to mitigating climate change and safeguarding biosphere integrity is somewhat tangential. Nevertheless, as we have argued, it is important to perform some sorts of sustainability assessments of the bottle, the bridge, the company, and the welfare programme. We need to be 'thinking global' whenever we produce, build, manufacture, or plan. At a minimum, every actor should have to justify omitting key themes from the assessment.

An important part of the relevance condition is that of not having proper means to act on a relevant theme. According to the Tinbergen Rule, every policy target (for example, a key sustainability theme's threshold) must be accompanied by at least one policy tool (a means). If one does not possess the proper means, one is unlikely to reach the target.[12] In many cases, an actor does not possess the means by which he or she can make necessary changes towards sustainability. If the bottle manufacturer would like its new zero-carbon emissions bottle to be cheaper than traditional bottles, some sort of tax relief may be necessary. The bottle manufacturer is unable to introduce tax relief (although they can apply political pressure for achieving it), and so they must rely on the national government to do so. Likewise, if a municipality finds yearly elections to be an important means to ensure participation, they would probably find it hard to get support from the national government to do so. The municipality lacks the necessary (in this case legal) means to implement their desired way to promote sustainability.

The condition of availability implies that in some cases the perfect choice of comprehensive sustainability is simply not available. One must make the best possible choice from the alternatives available. When assessing the plastic bottle's sustainability, what would be the comprehensive (or perfect) solution for the relevant themes? Obviously, mitigating climate change is a relevant theme. Comprehensive sustainability would require the following setting: The plastic (and possibly other materials) is part of a zero-carbon material system of extracting, distributing, and processing products. The factory is part of a zero-carbon building system for material use, construction, and operation. The energy used at all stages in the system is part of a zero-emission energy system of renewable energy. It is highly unlikely that this setting will exist now or even in the near future. Meanwhile, the bottle manufacturer must design a sustainable product. In the contemporary material, building, and energy systems, the manufacturer's choices are indeed limited. Nevertheless, the manufacturer must perform as well as possible, taking into account the available solutions. In such a setting, the lowest possible CO_2 emissions would be the sustainable goal.

Comparison is crucial here. The bottle manufacturer, the car manufacturer, the bridge builders, and the planners of the social welfare programme cannot work endlessly to achieve comprehensive sustainability. Comprehensive sustainability might be neither relevant nor available. Rather, comparative sustainability requires comparing realistic alternatives and choosing the best alternative available for the relevant theme(s). When subjected to comparative rationality, decision-makers seek a satisfactory solution rather than an optimal one. Thus, local actors can make a valid contribution to the agenda of global sustainability, without needing to make an overall assessment of their contribution to that agenda (Sandhu et al., 2014).[13]

What does it all come down to regarding comparative local sustainability? Comparative sustainability creates possibilities to exclude key themes from the assessment (because they are not relevant) and to not meet the thresholds fully (because the necessary means to do so are unavailable). The following principles apply:

- All relevant key themes should be assessed. The reasons for judging a theme not relevant must be given.
- All relevant key themes are equally important, no trade-offs are allowed.

- For each relevant key theme, use available means to choose the solution that gives the greatest progress towards the global threshold for that theme while simultaneously not negatively affecting other relevant themes.

Concerning the comparative sustainability approach, it would be wrong to see *any* action regarded as relevant as being one leading to sustainable development. Accepting that comparative sustainability can be argued for in some cases does not mean that we should lose sight of the overall goal of comprehensive sustainability. Losing sight of that overall goal opens up for what we call a 'stakeholder approach' to sustainability. A stakeholder approach loosely follows four steps. Step one is to gather a group of stakeholders that somehow have a stake in, or are influenced by, a plan or a project. Step two is to quickly introduce them to the inherently open-ended three-pillar model of sustainable development (see chapter 1 for details on the three-pillar model). Step three is to encourage them to define the problem and moreover to make their own sustainability goals, indicators, thresholds, and solutions. Step four is to balance the consequences (a requirement of the three-pillar model) however they think best.

Surely, the underlying logic is that the chances of success are greater if people affected by the consequences of a plan or an action can find their own solutions and their own ways of dealing with the consequences. They know the problem and are therefore best suited to find a viable solution. However, the three-pillar model opens up a view on sustainability reflecting how stakeholders 'want sustainability to be perceived' and 'what groups and individuals want it to mean on the day' (Sandhu *et al.*, 2014). Indeed, we agree that sustainability certainly is 'more than a blanket term for anything that seems like a "good idea"' (ibid., p. 31).

A final note on the comparative sustainability approach: Does such an approach lead to weak or insufficient action towards sustainable development? Surely, merely advancing sustainability is not good enough? Well, no. But sometimes one must do the best one can with the available means. Acknowledging that some local actors cannot go all the way towards achieving sustainable development underscores the important role of national governments and intergovernmental institutions (for example, the UN). They possess the means to coordinate the numerous (insufficient) actions at local levels, which in sum result in comprehensive sustainability.

Comparative sustainability at the national scale?

Is the distinction between comprehensive and comparative sustainability relevant only when assessing local sustainability? Is the distinction not similarly relevant on a national scale? There are four reasons, we argue, that the answer to that question is 'no'. The first reason is that of *appropriateness*. We used global moral imperatives to develop the global model presented in chapter 5. Ultimately, sustainability should be addressed globally. However, although national territories, economies, and societies constitute only one level of system organization, it is perhaps the most significant level because governance is presently strongest at the national level

(Dahl, 2012). National governments thus possess the most significant means and the capacity to use them to address all relevant imperatives of sustainable development.

The second reason is that of *responsibility*. Although there are strong grounds to argue that every actor at every level should voluntarily comply with the moral imperatives of sustainable development, national governments have a particular responsibility to ensure that they do comply. Agenda 21 acknowledged this particular responsibility almost three decades ago: 'its [that is, sustainable development's] successful implementation is first and foremost the responsibility of Governments' (Agenda 21, §1.3). The UN reaffirms this responsibility in its new sustainable development agenda: 'Our Governments have the primary responsibility for follow-up and review, at the national, regional and global levels, in relation to the progress made in implementing the goals and targets over the coming fifteen years' (UN, 2015, §47).

The third reason is that of *commitment*. Those who committed themselves to a goal certainly have a special responsibility to achieve it. There can be no doubt that national governments have committed themselves to sustainable development:

> We, the Heads of State and Government and High Representatives, meeting at United Nations Headquarters in New York from 25 to 27 September 2015 as the Organization celebrates its seventieth anniversary, have decided today on new global Sustainable Development Goals.
>
> (UN, 2015, §1)

This is a bold commitment and one that is much welcome (and one, some would argue, that is long overdue). It is also one that the Heads of State do not take lightly: 'We commit ourselves to working tirelessly for the full implementation of this Agenda by 2030' (ibid., §2). It is equally bold that they commit themselves on our behalf: 'On behalf of the peoples we serve, we have adopted a historic decision on a comprehensive, far-reaching and people-centred set of universal and transformative goals and targets' (ibid., §2). Surely, committing oneself on behalf of someone else gives one a particularly important responsibility.[14]

The fourth reason is that of *allocation*. The imperative of, for example, respecting environmental limits can be hard to translate to the local level. There can be good reasons for a national government to allocate CO_2 emission targets to the transport sector that are different from those it allocates to the agriculture sector. It can be more efficient (for example, cheaper) to reduce emissions in one sector than in another. So why not do that? We think that nations can, and indeed should, allocate according to their preferences and conditions as long as they stay within the sustainable development space.

Should nations be allowed to allocate emissions between them? Why not allow Norway to exceed the CO_2 threshold by X tonnes as long as it contributes to more than X tonnes reductions in another country? We believe this should not be allowed, first, because of the inherent difficulties in demonstrating the efficiency of such allocation, and second, because rich countries would be accused (rightly) of buying themselves out of their moral responsibility. Thus, the global imperatives of sustainable development apply at a national level without exemption. All imperatives and key themes are equally relevant. At a local level, however, some sort of comparative sustainability can be allowed for.

Sustainability and scale

Two dimensions are essential when translating global sustainability to local sustainability: approach and scale. We have presented two main approaches. The first is comprehensive sustainability, which is comprehensive in the sense that one must address all six key themes from the global model and that the suggested thresholds must be met for each theme. The second approach is comparative sustainability, which is comparative in the sense that not all key themes from the global model are relevant and that we can settle on the best available solution. Scale varies from the global level to the local level. Figure 8.1 shows the relationship between approach and scale.

We would like to make two comments about figure 8.1. First, the term 'local' does not refer to sustainability solely at the municipality or city level. Rather, 'local' also refers to a single product or a single action by an individual. Second, the downward line indicates that there is a sliding transition between comprehensive and comparative sustainability. Sustainability at a country level calls for comprehensive sustainability, whereas local sustainability opens up for comparative sustainability. There is no telling at exactly what scale the one approach is more appropriate than the other.

Although we do not intend to develop a blueprint for sustainability at all scales (the principles must do), we will nevertheless end this chapter by making a few

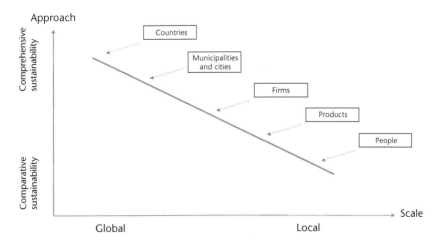

FIGURE 8.1 Approaches to sustainable development at different scales. Various actors are shown on the figure. Figure is the work of the authors.

comments on local sustainability at the municipality and city levels. This is the domain of LA21 and is the 'special responsibility of the local authorities'. Local authorities are a part of the basic structures in society that profoundly affect groups and individuals. Thus, we regard actions taken at this level as a particularly important part of achieving local sustainability and subsequently global sustainable development.

A first step for local authorities is to provide the necessary data to find to what extent they comply with the requirements provided by the global model of sustainable development. These data will help identify the sustainability challenges they are facing. It is important to note that even if they comply with requirements of a particular key theme, they are not exempt from working on that theme beyond their territory. Likewise, if they fail to comply with requirements of a key theme, they are not solely responsible for taking the necessary steps to comply. Surely, they will need help in doing so, notably from national authorities.

All six key themes in the global model are relevant for local authorities because they possess the necessary means to find and implement solutions on all themes. As a starting point therefore, no less than opting for comprehensive sustainability would do at this level. Correspondingly, all thresholds must be met. However, they do not necessarily prevail over the *sufficient* means to meet all thresholds. Thus, some sort of 'comparativeness' is inevitable (as indicated in figure 8.1). They can contribute to complying with the thresholds, but obviously need help in doing so.

One example: Local authorities have a responsibility to reduce greenhouse gas emissions, and are also particularly well placed to do so through their regulatory and strategic functions. A report by the UK Committee on Climate Change[15] concluded that local authorities can contribute to significant reductions in emissions in residential buildings, non-residential buildings, surface transport, and waste management. Moreover, they also have an important role in supporting power sector de-carbonization through, for example, granting planning approval for onshore wind projects. In addition, local authorities can play a part through supporting investment in electric vehicle charging infrastructure, which likely will result in long-term emissions reductions. The report concludes that 'a failure to secure reductions across the areas where local authorities have significant influence would leave emissions above levels required to meet carbon budgets' (CCC, 2012, p. 9).

However, local authorities can do only so much. The report warns that there is a risk that local authorities will not develop and implement sufficient low-carbon plans unless the national government provides the necessary national guidelines and financial resources. Thus, the report recommends that the national government 'should seriously consider providing additional funding ... and/or introducing a statutory duty for local authorities to develop and implement low-carbon plans' (ibid.).

Another example: Local authorities have a responsibility to facilitate citizens' participation in actions that influence their lives. Such participation extends far beyond mere balloting every fourth year. Local authorities must facilitate public meetings, open seminars, and other activities that create dialogue and discussion among their constituents. Such activities are important for two reasons. First, as mentioned, they make it possible to find better solutions to specific sustainability issues. The creativity of a whole community is always greater than that of a few elected politicians and their bureaucracy. Second, and more importantly, such activities make possible an open-minded public dialogue, which inherently is part of a conception of justice (Sen, 2009). This dialogue is in turn part of the discussion about the moral imperatives of sustainable development. Through Sen's 'reasoned scrutiny', participation can facilitate the moral and political engagement needed to achieve sustainable development.

Why would one want to open up a discussion of the moral imperatives of sustainable development? Is not any notion of 'unsustainable development' a false view that one wishes to suppress? Is not sustainable development a truth? John Stuart Mill argues that we should definitely *not* suppress arguments that run against the common understanding of a truth. If we do not continuously challenge the truth, he argues, then 'however true it may be, if it is not fully, frequently, and fearlessly discussed, it will be held as a dead dogma, not a living truth' (Mill, 1859, p. 52). The danger here is that the real meaning of sustainable development might be lost or enfeebled if it is not constantly challenged and defended, and so becomes 'deprived of its vital effect on the character and conduct: the dogma becoming a mere formal profession, inefficacious for good' (ibid., p. 77). Thus, the robustness and reach of the sustainable development imperatives depend on contributions from discussion and discourse. But perhaps the greater danger is that when challenged by a sparkling presentation of unsustainable development, the champions of sustainability 'will be unable to defend themselves. Not only will they look foolish, but the false view may gain a popularity it does not merit, sometimes with disastrous consequences' (Wolff, 2006, p. 111).[16] Thus, the moral imperatives of sustainable development must be discussed and a thorough defence of them must be prepared. Indeed, we need sustainable development to be a living truth, not a dead dogma.

Throughout this book we have tried to present a consistent argument about the nature of sustainable development in a transparent and accessible manner. A main conclusion is that there are several pathways that can be followed by different countries to reach the elusive sustainable development space, and these will vary according to local circumstances, stages of development, and the particular time. This chapter has added a new dimension to the debates, by making a strong case for involving all actors at all levels in that discussion. Although the primary responsibilities and powers reside at the national level, where it is possible to promote comprehensive sustainable development, there are also equally important actions needed at all levels across the spectrum (figure 8.1). It is at the local level where even limited actions can improve sustainability in people's (and firms') immediate surroundings, and these actions can contribute to both local and global sustainable development in a more comparative perspective. The major concern here is the need for consistent actions across all sectors and all actors, at all levels of decision-making. It is only through such a comprehensive approach that real progress can be made on sustainable development, hence the need for commitment and a sharing of responsibilities. This in turn leads to the necessity for a continuous, open, and vibrant debate and discussion between all parties on sustainable development – the maxim is perhaps to think globally and locally, and to act locally and globally.

A second message that emerges throughout this book has been that sustainable development is not only an end in itself, but also a journey that can be followed in many different ways. The sustainable development space is not fixed, but both the measures and the thresholds may change over time, and over time the existing priorities may change, and new ones may emerge. The final chapter will attempt to suggest some next steps, through looking backwards (reflection) and forwards (anticipation). These final two chapters will make possible a full appreciation of both the complexity and the dynamics of sustainable development, and they provide the necessary background against which the continuing debate over sustainable development can be placed.

Notes

1 The municipality committed itself to 'the Fredrikstad Declaration', an invitation from the National Conference of Local Agenda 21 to all municipalities, communities, and organizations to contribute to sustainable development. The conference was held in Fredrikstad, Norway, 9–11 February 1998 and gathered over 700 participants from central government, municipalities, counties, and organizations. The Fredrikstad Declaration's main message is that municipalities now must take responsibility for starting a local Agenda 21 process.

2 Quote from Motoko Rich, 'What Else Was Lost in Translation', *The New York Times*, 21 September 2003.

3 www.iclei.org/.

4 www.kpmg.com/global/en/issuesandinsights/articlespublications/corporate-responsibility/pages/default.aspx.

5 www.mckinsey.com/business-functions/sustainability-and-resource-productivity/our-insights/sustainabilitys-strategic-worth-mckinsey-global-survey-results.

6 Sen draws heavily on Adam Smith's *The Theory of Moral Sentiments*. Smith sees 'the impartial spectator' as crucial to avoiding parochialism. Sen's 'open impartiality' (as opposed to Rawls' 'closed impartiality' uses much of Smith's thinking.

7 HOPE stands for Household Preferences for Reducing Greenhouse Gas Emissions in four European high-income countries. The partners in HOPE are the International Research Center on Environment and Development, TEC Conseil, Heidelberg Institute of Public Health, Umeå University Heidelberg Institute of Public Health, and Western Norway Research Institute.

8 The United Nations Conference on Environment and Development (UNCED), also known as the Rio de Janeiro Earth Summit, Rio Summit, Rio Conference, and Earth Summit, was a major United Nations conference held in Rio de Janeiro from 3 to 14 June 1992.

9 Sen argues that it is possible to have a theory of justice that includes both transcendental and comparative approaches to justice. That would be a 'conglomerate' theory, one that Sen does not support greatly. The two approaches, he argues, simply address different questions regarding justice. Sen would probably not approve of the distinction between comprehensive and comparative sustainability made here.

10 It could of course be a step towards sustainable development, but that is not, we think, what Sen means.

11 One could argue, though, that the bridge increases people's possibility to participate.

12 Jan Tinbergen (1903–1994) was a Dutch economist. He was awarded the Nobel Prize in Economics in 1969, which he shared with Ragnar Frisch for having developed and applied dynamic models for the analysis of economic processes.

13 Sandhu *et al.* (2014) acknowledge that for various reasons 'we cannot fully comprehend the ideal global end-state', and that it is therefore important to have 'appropriate local goals' (p. 226).

14 Though many actors at lower levels have made commitments to sustainable development, their commitments rest heavily on necessary action of national governments. Thus, it is very difficult, some would argue impossible, for a municipality or a firm to become sustainable in an unsustainable country.

15 The Committee on Climate Change (the Committee) is an independent statutory body which was established under the Climate Change Act (2008) to advise UK and Devolved Administration governments on setting and meeting carbon budgets, and on preparing for climate change.

16 This is all too apparent in TV debates on the causes of climate change. Naïvely leaning on the 'self-evident truths' of the IPCC reports, defenders of active climate policies are frequently defeated by well-prepared climate sceptics.

References

Aall, C. & Skarbø, K. (2014) When is change change? In: *Proceedings of Transformation in a Changing Climate*, 19–21 June 2013, Oslo, University of Oslo, pp. 53–61.

Asheim, G. B., Buchholz, W., & Tungodden, B. (2001) Justifying sustainability. *Journal of Environmental Economics and Management*, 41, 252–268.

CCC (2012) How local authorities can reduce emissions and manage climate risk. Committee on Climate Change, UK. Available at: www.theccc.org.uk/archive/aws/Local%20Authorites/1584_CCC_LA%20Report_bookmarked_1b.pdf.

Dahl, A. L. (2012) Achievements and gaps in indicators for sustainability. *Ecological Indicators*, 17, 14–19.

Dubos, R. & Ward, B. (1972) *Only One Earth: The Care and Maintenance of a Small Planet.* An unofficial report commissioned by the Secretary-General of the United Nations Conference on the Human Environment, prepared with the assistance of a 152-member Committee of Corresponding Consultants in 58 countries. London, André Deutsch.

Feidje, R. B., Johnsen, S. H., & Boge, B. O. (2016) *Household preferences for reducing greenhouse gas emissions – A theoretic and empiric study of households in Sogndal.* Bachelor thesis. Sogndal, Sogn and Fjordane University College.

Lafferty, W. M. & Eckerberg, K. (1997) The nature and purpose of 'Local Agenda 21'. In: Lafferty, W. M. & Eckerberg, K. (eds) *From Earth Summit to Local Forum. Studies of Local Agenda 21 in Europe.* Oslo, Program for Research and Documentation for a Sustainable Society, pp. 1–18.

Lafferty, W. M. & Langhelle, O. (eds) (1999) *Towards Sustainable Development: On the Goals of Development and the Conditions of Sustainability*. Basingstoke, UK, Palgrave Macmillan.

Mill, J. S. (1859) *On Liberty*. London, Penguin Books.

Næss, A. (1993) *Ecology, Community and Lifestyle: Outline of an Ecosophy* (reprint edition). Cambridge, Cambridge University Press.

O'Connor, J. (1992) Think globally, act locally? *Journal of Capitalism, Nature, Socialism*, 3(4), 1–8.

Rawls, J. (1999) *A Theory of Justice* (revised edition). Cambridge, MA, Belknap Press.

Sandhu, S., McKenzie, S., & Harris, H. (eds) (2014) *Linking Local and Global Sustainability*. New York and London, Springer.

Sen, A. (2009) *The Idea of Justice*. London, Penguin Books.

Stephen, W. M., Leonard, S. G., MacDonald, M., & MacLean, K. (2004) *Think Global, Act Local: The Life and Legacy of Patrick Geddes*. Edinburgh, Luath Press.

UN (1992) *Agenda 21*. United Nations Conference on Environment & Development. Rio de Janeiro, Brazil, 3–14 June 1992. Available from: https://sustainabledevelopment. un.org/content/documents/Agenda21.pdf.

UN (2012) *The Future We Want*. Resolution adopted by the general assembly on 27 July 2012, 66/288. United Nations.

UN (2015) *Transforming Our World: The 2030 Agenda for Sustainable Development*. Resolution adopted by the General Assembly on 25 September 2015, A/RES/70/1. United Nations General Assembly.

WCED (1987) *Our Common Future*. World Commission on Environment and Development. Oxford, Oxford University Press.

Whitelegg, J. (1993) *Transport for a Sustainable Future: The Case for Europe*. New York, Belhaven Press.

Wolff, J. (2006) *An Introduction to Political Philosophy* (revised edition). Oxford, Oxford University Press.

9

THE NEXT STEPS

> All nations will have a role to play in changing trends, and in righting an international economic system that increases rather than decreases inequality, that increases rather than decreases numbers of poor and hungry. ... The next few decades are crucial. The time has come to break out of past patterns.
>
> WCED (1987, p. 22)

As can be seen from the above quote, all nations have a responsibility to address issues of growth and inequality, together with strong actions on reducing the use of non-renewable resources and the human impact on the ecosystem. In the 30 years since the publication of *Our Common Future* (WCED, 1987), progress towards sustainable development has been painfully slow, and no country at present resides within the sustainable development space (chapter 7). Although one billion people have been taken out of poverty, the global population has increased by 1.3 billion people over this period (1987–2015),[1] global inequality has increased (World Bank, 2016), and we now need 1.6 planets to support current lifestyles and consumption patterns.[2] It is accepted that global (and national) policy action has been difficult to achieve, and substantial change has been hard to identify, and the most recent political changes and economic stagnation has meant that global action may become even more problematic in the future. But there may also be new opportunities.

The scope of the task confronting humanity in addressing sustainable development has been seriously underestimated, and it is only in the most recent past that some real progress has been made at the global level with the 17 Sustainable Development Goals (SDGs) (2015) and the Paris Agreement (2015). But even here, there is an increasing concern over whether the SDGs and the 2°C and 1.5°C goals are going to be seen as real targets to be achieved across all nations. Traditional growth models have been based on increasing levels of global trade, multinational companies, the free movement of labour and capital, and the increasing roles of technology and automation. This approach is now being questioned, as it primarily benefits the rich countries, and concentrates both income and wealth in the hands of the elite (Piketty, 2014). When the economic paradigm, which has provided huge benefits through increasing the levels of overall global wealth and at the same time reducing levels of global poverty, comes under investigation about whether it is sustainable, it is clear that new thinking and debates are needed. This new thinking must embrace the social and environmental imperatives, as well as those that determine the global economic model.

The issues of inequality and living beyond the global environmental limits have for too long not received sufficient attention, as narrowly defined economic growth has determined priorities. Yet all these factors are closely connected and each impacts on the other (Steffen *et al.*, 2007, 2015). It is clear that both wealth and income have become more concentrated in the rich countries and with the elites within those countries. Such a situation might have been tolerated in the past, but with global economic stagnation, it has become the focus for attention, as it has important social implications across the whole of the income spectrum with the growth in the 'squeezed' middle income groups. Thewissen *et al.* (2015) have found a significant negative association between changes in the Gini coefficient and median income across countries over time (since the 1980s), so direct measures of how these incomes are evolving need to be seen as part of inclusive growth. The World Bank has found that even though income inequality may have declined (1988–2013) between nations, it has increased within nations (World Bank, 2016). There are a range of social consequences apparent from this increase in inequality, including a slowing down of social mobility, greater inequality in opportunities, the weakening of social cohesion, and the growth in populism resulting from an alienation and a loss of trust between the people and politicians.

The fundamental question here is whether the relatively successful Western economic model can or should be applied globally so that it benefits the 7–10 billion and not just the one billion. Given the growth in inequality in many nations and the costs on the planet, there is also the supplementary question as to whether this model is still even appropriate for the rich countries. Indeed, the poorer countries may aspire to follow the same pathway as the rich countries have, namely one of economic growth and high levels of consumption. This is why clear leadership and action is necessary nationally and globally that embraces needs and justice related boundaries, as well as planetary limits.

In this book we have taken an explicitly ethical perspective on what can and should be done to address these three issues in a way that is fair to all people, as well as being fair to the planet. This is an essentially normative view about what should be done, but it is accepted that idealism needs to be moderated by realism. The means to measure the three imperatives of sustainable development is central to our thinking, bringing the more idealistic debates presented in the first five chapters together with the more pragmatic empirical material presented in the next three chapters. We accept that the approach presented simplifies complexity, but we argue that it is important to determine where, within a multidimensional space, each country can be located. This is achieved through the three theories (needs, justice, limits) and the means by which each can be assessed through two complementary measures. The intention is to give each theme equal weighting, and it follows the logic that society must ensure the basic needs for all people and seek to reduce levels of inequality within and between different societies. But at the same time equal weight should be given to the planet, as this constrains all activity and should protect future generations. It is in this way that the debate is reconfigured to cover the key dimensions of sustainable development.

Within this framing of sustainable development, we would emphasize that this is not an end but more of a journey that follows different pathways. This means that the sustainable development space is not fixed, as the thresholds can be changed over time as aspirations and expectations change (e.g., as thresholds for global quality increase), and as better measures (and data) become available. The concept of the sustainable development space suggests that there are potentially several combinations of our six headline indicators that can allow a country to be placed within the sustainable development space. It also suggests that there is no one pathway to sustainable development but many different pathways to follow, and some of these may be more suitable for particular countries than others. The means to reach the sustainable development space is flexible, but the conditions of entry at any one point in time are fixed. But, as noted in chapter 7, there is no country currently within the sustainable development space, even when some pairs of indicators are used, for example HDI and GHG emissions (figure 7.2).

There are two other comments that need to be reinforced. Throughout, we have emphasized the need for measurement, and we have not left this important issue open to interpretation. We have adopted such an approach as a basis for debate and discussion about how society can conceptualize the nature of sustainable development in a way that is meaningful and also helpful in understanding the scale and nature of achieving real progress towards the thresholds identified. Second, we have also introduced the concept of non-tradability between the thresholds identified. This means that none of them can be exchanged and that a country has to achieve the threshold levels for all six headline indicators to enter the sustainable development space. There is also no separate economic theme, as there are economic implications embedded in all pathways to be followed, and these need to be part of that debate. Although the main focus has been on the numerical measurement, and this has been carried out at the national level as this is where many of the critical decisions are taken by governments, the numbers only tell part of the story. The different narratives highlighted in chapter 7 provide an important set of pathways that can and have been followed by the different countries in the past, and the intention here is to learn from these experiences, both positive and negative.

Reflection – looking backwards

As noted above, this book has been divided into two parts, one more theoretical and the other more empirical. The first five chapters outline the justification for a moral perspective on sustainable development through setting the scene and through three more detailed interpretations of the sustainability themes. The basic argument presented (chapter 1) makes a strong case for a holistic approach to sustainable development that is built on a normative framework that can provide both the direction and the case for immediate strong action at all levels of governance. It also makes the argument for goals or thresholds that need to be set, rather than to rely upon the willingness of all to participate fully. The rationale here is twofold. One is that it is only through specific and precise measurement that a real debate and action can take place. Precision can lead to action, but vagueness does not. The second is that guidance is required so that we can see what works well and what does not work. The intention is not to be prescriptive, but to help decision-makers at all levels to realize their ambition in the move towards sustainable development. Chapter 1 is therefore opening up the imperatives for sustainable development to discussion and debate with all parties accepting moral responsibility for involvement and action.

This holistic perspective is then developed in much greater detail through the following three chapters, each of which is devoted to one of the three basic theories – needs, justice, and limits. In chapter 2, the issue of needs is addressed through balancing those concerns that affect individuals and those that are more societally based. It is here that Sen (2009) has articulated the importance of capabilities, or what opportunities are available to individuals, and their functionings, or what individuals actually choose to do. The complexities of meeting or satisfying needs are well known, and there are strong cultural and time-specific dimensions that form part of this picture. This more individualistic approach is contrasted in the next chapter on social justice that examines Rawls' (1999) thinking. His approach is more idealistic, arguing for societal-based forms of fairness and institutional justice. In both these chapters, the focus is on societal values and the importance of the individual, but the wider issues of sustainable development seem to get lost. There seems to be an implicit assumption that once needs and justice are met, then the environmental concerns will also be met. Such an approach is limited as there are strong interactions between people, societies, and the environment, to which must be added the time dimension, the importance of finite resources, and the moral responsibilities to others (including future generations).

It is in chapter 4 with the introduction of planetary boundaries that substantive arguments are provided for explicitly including environmental factors as an integral part of sustainable development. It should be noted that many of these environmental issues have only come to prominence over the last 20 years. The science of climate change is relatively new, but we have now exceeded one key threshold in 2016 (when global CO_2 levels have exceeded 400 ppm by volume[3]). This is the highest level of carbon dioxide emissions for 4 million years, and this predates humans.

Apart from global warming (primarily from carbon dioxide and methane), the science is now becoming clearer about the health effects of local pollutants, including the oxides of nitrogen and particulate matter. The two messages here are that as we learn more about the science, we also begin to understand the interconnectedness between the human and natural environments, and this strongly suggests that they must both be part of the debate – they cannot be separated. Second, there is a more conceptual question about whether people today should be responsible for the actions of past generations, when the science of global and local pollutants were not well known. However, there can be no doubt that we are responsible for future generations, as we cannot plead ignorance.

These three conceptual chapters have provided a strong foundation for the empirical part of the book. Chapter 5 presents the key arguments concerning the imperatives for sustainable development, as the concept of the sustainable development space is outlined as the means by which the three theories can be operationalized into a set of six key non-negotiable themes, indicators, and thresholds. There is a considerable debate over which thresholds should be used, and there is an acceptance that not all those used here are ideal. These issues are discussed in chapters 6 and 7. There are substantial data and measurement problems inherent in all transnational comparative research, but it is important to make the best use of available information so that the model can be used. Our thinking here builds on the SDGs, and links are drawn throughout, and part of the argument made here is that the 17 SDGs and the 169 indicators should be reduced to a more manageable set of headline indicators that can be investigated as a whole (rather than individually).[4] It is easy to reflect a complex reality through a complex approach, but it is far more useful to be able to provide a simplified and transparent reality. This objective has been central to our thinking.

To reiterate, our six key sustainability themes are designed to:

- eradicate extreme poverty;
- enhance individual capabilities;
- ensure a fair distribution of resources;
- encourage participation in society;
- contribute to climate change mitigation;
- maintain biodiversity.

All six key themes are important, all are non-negotiable, and all provide evidence of the scale of change needed at both the individual and the societal levels in patterns of consumption. The empirical evidence presented in chapters 6 and 7 illustrate what has happened over the last 30 years and the varied pathways that have been followed by different countries. It has also included a detailed discussion over the different measures that could have been used to measure sustainable development, and this data again help to indicate where progress has been realized, and where there has been no improvement and a move away from the thresholds set.

The empirical analysis presented in the book has been carried out in two stages. One examines the six sustainability themes over the three points in time across the whole database (about 100 countries) to establish patterns, and these have been commented upon (chapter 6) in terms of whether the thresholds set are (or have been) achieved. In contrast, chapter 7 takes the same data and subjects them to a bivariate and then a cluster analysis to establish similarities between the diversity inherent in each country over time. With no preconceptions about groupings, the cluster analysis provides an open process, trying to find countries with similar profiles, as measured by the thresholds identified in the sustainable development model. Seven different clusters are found and these are commented on, together with the changes over time (2000–2010). From this evidence, a pathway is described that would lead towards sustainable development, where important issues concerning population growth, the need for global action and solidarity, a decoupling and movement away from consumption-based lifestyles, and strong protection of the natural environment, are all elaborated. These themes are also taken up in this chapter.

As the scale of change required to move into the sustainable development space is so large, the responsibility for action resides at all levels of governance, from the global to the local. Although most discussion has taken place at the global and national levels, it is often at the local level that implementation actually happens. Chapter 8 examines the role that Agenda 21 has had in taking the debate to the most suitable level for effective action. Here it is argued that it is at the local level that specific actions are needed, and this is where monitoring, adaptation, and closeness to the problems are most relevant. It is also the level at which engagement and involvement cut across individual and societal interests, where ownership becomes central, and where positive outcomes can be 'locked in'. However, the local action focus requires action at other levels to provide the legal framework, the necessary powers, the skills, and the finance for effective implementation. Actors at all levels must be fully involved throughout the process. In addition, the international agencies and the multinational companies are all key players that have central roles to play. It is only through such engagement, commitment, and ownership of the issues relating to needs, justice, and limits, that progress can be made towards sustainable development, and all parties have a moral obligation to contribute fully.

Anticipation – looking forwards

Many people like to speculate about the future, and most perspectives are optimistic about the ability of 'humankind' to find ways through the most difficult problems, where those futures are probable, possible, or preferable (see chapter 7 and Adam, 2010). However, we also like to dwell on catastrophic or dystopian futures that could be based on de-growth[5] futures predicated on a powering down of the carbon intensity on a global scale and reducing demand (Urry, 2016, p. 177), or in futures with no oil, a surveillance society, an atomized and dispersed future, an over- or under-regulated society, one ruled by cyborgs, and even the empty earth.

In the end it is really about identifying what sort of future society actually wants, and how this can be achieved. Yet, at present the pathway being followed is one that continues current trends (business as usual), pursuing a set of interdependencies that are unsustainable.

In the 30 years since Brundtland (WCED, 1987), sustainable development has proved elusive, and although there have been substantial improvements in some areas (less poverty and better health), little has been achieved in others, such as the future of the planet and the inequalities that are now endemic in society. Looking forwards to 2050, certain trends are fairly clear and accepted. Principal here is the expected growth in global population to 9.7 billion people (UN, 2015), most of whom (70 per cent) will be living in urban areas, and much of this growth will take place in the developing world (e.g., Africa) (World Bank, 2016). These people (with a fair degree of certainty) will have better access to clean water, food, sanitation, education, health, and energy, as incomes rise in these countries. But the situation may be different in the developed countries, as economies may not grow, and as stagnation (and de-growth) takes place with the transition to a post-industrial society based on the service and information sectors. In addition, there may be other important factors at work (with an even less degree of certainty) that relate to levels of migration, fundamentalism, war and terrorism, cyber security, access to clean water and energy. For example, it is likely that much of the water will need to have been recycled and separated into drinking and grey water; and that more than half of the ever increasing demand for global energy will have to come from renewable sources.

Two different avenues are followed here in bringing together many of the ideas that have been raised in this book. One thinks through the implications of the sustainable development space that has formed the core conceptual basis behind operationalizing the concept of sustainable development in terms of the wider theoretical lessons that can be learned. The second returns to *Our Common Future* (WCED, 1987) to integrate the ideas presented here with those that prevailed in the 1980s, with commentary on their current relevance and on how they might be interpreted today. From these two avenues, there is then a discussion over a set of ideas that need to form a more central part of the debate in the future.

1. Sustainable development space: A common theme that has provided the starting point for much of our thinking has been social justice, and the theoretical and practical elements of this has provided much of the material outlined in the core chapters on satisfying human needs, ensuring social justice, and respecting environmental limits. From this starting point, six key sustainability themes have then provided the indicators (and determined thresholds) within which the sustainable development space has been defined. Key to this thinking has been that these boundaries cannot be traded between individuals, communities, or nations, and that all are equally important. Here, the purpose is to comment on some of the common issues and to outline ways forward. In this sense we are following Agyeman's (2005) case for a strong connection between the environmental and justice 'bridge' to one that can encompass 'just sustainable development'.

Apart from the three imperatives of sustainable development (needs, justice, and limits) that define the sustainable development space, there are a series of key concepts that cut across all of the imperatives, and it is these concepts that meet the requirements of the capability approach (chapters 2 and 3). The pluralistic framework developed by Davoudi and Brooks (2014) identifies four concerns of environmental justice as they relate to both needs and justice – they are recognition, participation, responsibility, and capability. One important message from the literature on environmental justice is that in the sustainable development debates there has been too much emphasis on the human and not enough on the non-human aspects (Agyeman, 2005), and this explains why the sustainable development space includes limits as one of its imperatives. Environmental justice has sought to extend the arguments to non-human nature, moving beyond the connections between climate justice and the distributive equity and fairness concerns through the disputes over the historical responsibilities, and restorative justice, to a fully integrative approach. It has long been recognized that environmental justice has a disproportionate effect on particular communities (and nations), and that there are benefits from cleaner industry, new technology, and renewable energy. But often these same communities were excluded from decision-making and experienced a worsening of their quality of environment (Schlosberg, 2013).

There are also the longer-term consequences over the availability of clean water, food (including protein), accessibility (to employment, education, and health), and housing that are all part of the SDGs. Most recently, adaptive capacity and resilience have become clear mechanisms by which the human and non-human elements of climate change are now being considered more holistically, so that these disadvantaged communities can be better supported. Environmental justice and sustainability need to be designed and implemented in more just and sustainable ways so that everyday practices can be made more resilient. Unsustainable practices and their reproduction should be changed as they lead to greater injustice. Practices need to address the issues of recognition, participation, and responsibilities, so that basic capabilities can be enhanced to become more just and inclusive, and such practices may require different or new institutional structures. As Schlosberg (2013, p. 44) comments, 'it is the disruption and increasing vulnerability of the integrity of ecosystems that is at the heart of the injustice of climate change'.

This discussion provides the means to draw together the three imperatives that define the boundaries of the sustainable development space, as an integrated concept that is internally consistent. The sustainable development space embraces the thinking of Sen (needs) and Rawls (justice), together with Steffen *et al.* (limits), and the six key themes identified (figures 5.5 and 5.6) relate to the pluralistic framework described here, as they cover poverty, capabilities, participation, fair distribution, recognition, together with the wider responsibilities. These wider responsibilities concern the planetary boundaries. It is this symbiotic relationship between humans and non-humans that has been given a heightened role here, as measured by climate change and biodiversity. Sustainable development cannot exclude the environment, and mankind's responsibility to safeguard the future of the planet, in a condition that is at least as good as it is now.

2. *Our Common Future* (WCED, 1987) was a landmark document that placed sustainable development on the global agenda. It put forward long-term environmental strategies that would create greater cooperation between all countries at different stages in social and economic development, and it was designed to lead to the achievement of 'common and mutually supportive objectives that take account of the interrelationships between people, resources, environment and development' (ibid., p. ix). This was a formidable agenda that has opened up a 30-year debate on global futures that has addressed common concerns, challenges, and endeavours, by mapping out in a comprehensive way the fundamental issues of poverty and development, but making it clear that these two issues must now be addressed within the 'changing productive potential of the ecosystem'. It is only when all three imperatives of sustainability are dealt with holistically that sustainable development can be achieved (ibid., p. 8):

1   Meet the basic *needs* of all and extending to all the opportunities to fulfil their aspirations for a better life;
2   The poor to get their 'fair share of the resources' arising from growth. This new allocation would be aided by political systems that secure effective participation in decision-making, and greater democracy in international decisions – *justice*;
3   Affluent to adopt lifestyles within the planet's ecological means – *limits*.

These three imperatives of sustainable development form the boundaries of the sustainable development space (figure 5.6). *Our Common Future* further qualifies the basic concept by suggesting that sustainable development can only be pursued if 'population size and growth are in harmony with the changing potential of the ecosystem' (ibid., p. 9). This clearly articulates the relationship between population growth and economic growth, and the difficulty of meeting all three imperatives under conditions of a rapidly increasing global population. To remain within the boundaries set, all members of 'rich' societies must reduce their consumption of resources and live within the environmental limits set.

Some of the thresholds in the sustainable development space are related to individuals and others to the distribution of individuals within countries. But as the global population increases, this means that if the total sustainable development space is not expandable, then the amounts available for any individual or country may have to decrease. This possibility is not addressed here, and the expectation in the future must be that the global population will stabilize. This was one of the main conclusions from chapter 7. But even if it does, life expectancy is increasing and this in turn places another set of constraints on the sustainable development space. The thresholds set may have to relate to 'lifetime' levels rather than daily or annual amounts. For example, the poverty income threshold should be related to the average lifetime earnings rather than a daily threshold. Similarly, the CO_2eq budget should relate to an individual over their lifespan, not to an annual threshold.[6] One of the clear lessons from *Our Common Future* is that sustainable development cannot be seen as a 'fixed state of harmony, but rather as a process of change in which the exploitation of resources, the direction of investments, the orientation of technological development, and institutional change are made consistent with future as well as present needs' (ibid., p. 9). This comment again suggests that the thresholds in the sustainable development space need to be tightened over time, as society is expecting an improvement in the quality of life and wellbeing, but at the same time moving towards sustainable development.

As with many of the seminal publications over the last 30 years, *Our Common Future*[7] strongly advocates immediate action, as the 'future is conditional on decisive political action now' (ibid., p. 1). But, there are now more hungry people, a widening of the gap between the rich and the poor, increasing land degradation, deforestation, desertification, and higher levels of pollution and climate change. To some extent the (wider) sustainable development has been subsumed in the (narrower) climate change debate, but even here there has been inactivity at the global level, at least until the recent COP21 meeting in Paris, where it was made clear that a net-zero carbon economy must be achieved this century (Stern, 2016).

However, Stern is critical of current climate change models that underestimate the potential impacts of global warming and the real benefits of transition to a low-carbon economy. He highlights the need for radical change in the assessment of the risks and costs of irreversible climate change, including the release of methane, large-scale migration, the shortage of clean water, sea level rise, and the increasing frequency and intensity of extreme weather events. The science and economics are important to our understanding of the problems, the potential impacts, and the huge costs of taking or not taking action now. But it is really the patterns of consumption and behaviour that are crucial, together with political leadership and decision-making. The Stern analysis is also extremely techno-optimistic, arguing (ibid., p. 409) that there is a huge potential for future technologies (unspecified) in driving change, and that such innovation should provide much better estimates of the benefits of different pathways, and the costs of action now rather than the much higher costs of actions delayed until later. His conclusion is that 'well-being and prosperity of future generations are worth more' (ibid., p. 409). This conclusion about the instrumental role of new technology in resolving issues of climate change is more optimistic than that of *Our Common Future*, where the focus is much more on increasing productivity and efficiency, and in looking at ways for existing best practices and technologies to be transferred between countries – this is more of a techno-realistic approach.

More generally, the seven messages from the *Our Common Future* model are still very relevant today, even though some of the issues have changed, the importance of each has also changed, and new issues (and thinking) have emerged. *Our Common Future* based its views on sustainable development on the *growth model*, arguing that poverty reduction and environmental improvement could not take place without global growth. But even then, it was acknowledged that for long-term sustainable growth, it would require 'far-reaching changes to produce trade, capital, and technology flows that are more equitable and better synchronised to environmental imperatives' (WCED, 1987, pp. 40–41). So the *quality of growth* element was designed to make growth less material and energy intensive, to ensure greater equity in its impact (including income distribution), and to maintain the stock of ecological capital. These issues are even more important today as levels of vulnerability increase (economic, social, and environmental), and as resilience becomes a new key determinant of sustainable development.

The third element was to meet *essential human needs*, principally by providing employment, but also including food (and protein) and reliable energy (for cooking). There were also comments made on housing (formal and informal), water supply, and sanitation. All these three elements were strongly related to a *sustainable level of population* that was at a level consistent with the productive capacity of the ecosystem, and to the huge growth in levels of urbanization that is taking place and threatening the quality of life.

The fifth element was to *conserve and enhance the resource base* to account for the moral obligations to others (human and non-human), and to future generations. This included the options for all to earn a sustainable livelihood, and the necessity to prevent the overuse of resources (in particular agriculture, fishing, and forestry). The sixth element called for a *reorientation of technology and management of risk* through a greater focus on environmental factors and through extending its relevance and capabilities to developing countries through appropriate legal and institutional mechanisms. The final element concerned the *merging of environment and economics in decision-making* arguing that the two must and should be seen as working together in the same direction.

The *Our Common Future* model provides a comprehensive and formidable agenda, and one that is still relevant today. It calls for a holistic view that moves away from technological optimism that assumes a strong role for innovation in finding solutions, to one that re-orientates societal values away from overconsumption towards one that is based on fairness and greater equality, and one that makes less demand on the finite resources of the planet. It also introduces the concept of intergenerational equity and the quality of life for future generations, commenting on the 'ignorance' of the distant consequences of today's decisions.

Four issues that will define sustainable development over the next 30 years

When thinking about sustainable development, there were two important conclusions reached by the Sarkozy Commission (Stiglitz *et al.*, 2010). One concerned the need to think about the future and to have a clear (if possible) set of projections that addressed technological and environmental interactions, but also took a view on socio-economic and political developments. The second concerned the need for a normative perspective on what will be really important tomorrow, and it builds on the four pivotal points raised in chapter 7. This perspective should address issues of population and economic growth, and equally issues relating to the distribution of wealth, income, and other less tangible aspects of quality of life, alongside the resource and environmental limits. It is in this spirit that four more normative future-oriented issues have been identified that cut across our three imperatives of sustainable development. All four are likely to be of instrumental importance in achieving sustainable development in the future.

1. Developing countries and urbanization

Over the last 30 years, global population and cities have grown at a phenomenal rate, particularly in developing countries, and with debates over carbon and increasing energy consumption, these issues provide a key issue that cuts across all three imperatives of sustainable development. It is clear that the global population will still be increasing to 2050, when there will be some 9.7 billion people on the planet, but after that it is expected that there will be some stabilization. At the same time life expectancy is also increasing, and so the net effects on total population will not be dramatic, and it is expected that global population will reach 11 billion by 2100 (World Bank, 2016).

Cities are undergoing a renaissance with a huge growth in urban population, and the emergence of the megacity (over 10 million population), the metacity (over 20 million population), and the megacity regions (with a total population over 80 million). Examples of metacity regions can be seen in Japan (Tokyo to Nagoya and Osaka), in China (Pearl River Delta), and in Brazil (São Paulo to Rio de Janeiro). In 1900, about 13 per cent of the global population was urban, but by 2000 this figure was 47 per cent, and the 50 per cent threshold was reached in 2007 when 3.3 billion people were 'urban'.[8] This enormous increase is being driven by population growth rates, longer lives, and migration into the city, and the structure of the urban population will also change as the newcomers tend to be young and active. Cities will provide the main sources of employment in manufacturing and service provision. But in addition, they will also provide the new growth in the knowledge economy and in the networked society. Cities are continuing to drive the global economy, as well as being centres of innovation, creativity, and wealth. As illustrated in chapter 7, cities are central to sustainable development, and cities must be made sustainable.

Looking back over the last 50 years, the growth in the number and size of urban areas was unimaginable. The number of megacities has grown from three (1965) to over 30 (2016), and this will increase further to 36 in 2020 and 41 in 2030 (UN, 2014 and table 9.1). By 2020, only three of the world's largest cities (>10 million) will be in Europe and two in North America, and of the remaining 31, three will be in Africa and four will be in Latin America. The majority will be in Asia (24), with seven in China and six in India, and two in Japan, with the remaining cities distributed around the larger Asian countries. By 2030 over 60 per cent of the global population will be living in urban areas, and this figure is higher than the total global population in 1987, when *Our Common Future* was published.

TABLE 9.1 Growth in cities and in urban population

City size	Number of cities				Population in cities (millions)			
	1965	2010	2020	2030	1965	2010	2020	2030
>10 million	3	23	36	41	49	370	588	730
5–10 million	12	40	50	63	80	285	333	434
1–5 million	112	373	472	558	212	742	931	1128
500k–1 million	152	487	592	731	105	339	410	509
300k–500k	201	628	742	832	78	238	285	319
<300k	663	1607	1778	1922	660	1598	1791	1938
Total	1143	3158	3760	4147	1184	3572	4338	5058
Global population					3329	6916	7719	8321
Urban population					35.6%	51.6%	56.2%	60.8%

Source: UN (2014)

In the rapidly growing cities of the developing world, both the speed and scale of change are unprecedented, and this requires strong institutional and governance structures as well as substantial investment funds for housing, transport infrastructure, and other services (including energy, clean water, and sanitation). The traditional notions of work, as being construed by a 35-hour week and by 40 years of commitment to one employer, have already effectively been destroyed. The new forms of work are much more flexible with people moving around between different jobs, with hours to suit their own needs, and with time taken out to learn new skills or to raise a family. Gender barriers are being broken down and home working is becoming much more common, as both work and leisure are becoming increasingly organized around the internet in its many manifestations. The cities that adapt to this new knowledge- and network-based environment are the ones that will prosper, with tradition counting for little as labour becomes ever more mobile. In addition to being the centres of work, cities will retain their positions as centres of government, finance, education, and culture, as this is where key decisions will be made about the future of globalization.

Multinational companies may still influence many aspects of life, but this is also likely to change, as decision-making revolves increasingly around the power of the internet, and coalitions that are formed to address particular challenges (e.g., climate change). Because of the greater transparency brought about by internet-based transactions, there is now much greater flexibility in decision-making and this could lead to a strong movement against big government (e.g., the occupy movements against various forms of inequality). It is unclear how many of these potential conflicts of interest between governments, multinational companies, and society in general will actually be resolved (Heck & Rogers, 2014), and whether globalization will continue to dominate, or whether global futures will become more fragmented as a result of populism and nationalism.

Urbanization will provide a major opportunity for sustainable development, as cities provide the most efficient locations for employment, and for the provision of housing, services and facilities, and for infrastructures (chapter 7). But it is the underlying population growth and the lack of universal education that creates most problems, as population stabilization depends on education, information, and health (chapter 7). However, it has been argued (Abel *et al.*, 2016) that the SDGs have indicators that address future demographic trends, and this means that sustainable development can lead to lower (and stable) levels of global population growth. The levels projected in their multidimensional model of population growth point towards a 2100 global population of between 8.2 and 8.7 billion, far less than the official forecasts mentioned here of 11 billion (UN, 2015), but still 13 per cent more than today.

The levels of future global population have substantial impacts on the levels of needs, justice, and limits as combined in setting the boundaries for the sustainable development space, and the clear conclusion here is that sustainable development can be more easily achieved with lower levels of population growth. Population growth makes it much harder to achieve sustainable development, unless everyone accepts limits and lower material levels of growth. Even before *Our Common Future* (WCED, 1987), Commoner (1971) and Ehrlich and Holdren (1971) were making this point, namely that impact was a function of population, affluence (consumption), and technology. Since that time most of the discussion has been focused on the affluence and technology dimensions of that relationship, but it is important that population growth is addressed as an issue that is instrumental in achieving sustainable development. It cannot be ignored, and it may be true that sustainable development can only be achieved when population growth becomes an explicit and integral part of the debate.

2. Resource efficiency and technology

Levels of consumption of all resources are increasing in absolute terms as population grows, and in relative terms on a per-capita basis – this covers food, water, materials, and energy (UNEP, 2016). Although new resources and materials may reduce shortfalls in each of these over the short term through increases in yields, through desalination, and through shale gases, there remains the underlying question about whether this can continue at current rates, or at increased (or decreased) rates. This continuation depends on the costs of innovation, extraction, refining or processing, and transport to the final user, as well as the impacts on the ecosystem. There are also considerable uncertainties over the costs and benefits globally and locally of following different pathways, and the implications for equity and the environment. Underlying much of the debate are the political uncertainties about investments in renewable energy sources, in measures to encourage the circular economy, the means to eliminate the waste culture, and the effective pricing of carbon. For example, over a third of all food produced globally is wasted,[9] and this amounts to 1.3 billion tonnes. This is split roughly half and half between developed ($680 billion by value) and developing countries ($310 billion by value). In short, there seems to be reluctance about changing existing practices, and the speed and scale of change required to address the potential shortage of resources. Such thinking is well illustrated by the continued subsidies to the fossil fuel industry, estimated to be about $5.3 trillion (2015) annually (Coady *et al.*, 2015).

As presented in chapters 6 and 7, resources are not being used sustainably, and their distribution between countries is unequal. In addition, there is a lack of integration between the sectors, resulting in low levels of knowledge sharing and a lack of understanding of best practice. Food production provides a good example of these problems. Food is a major producer of greenhouse gases (about 16 per cent of the total), and as more land comes under cultivation more carbon is released, but agriculture also consumes 75 per cent of global water and directly impacts on global biodiversity. The efficiency of food production needs to be increased, with significantly less waste, and clear incentives to produce for local consumption rather than global markets with long supply chains (UNEP, 2016). Technology can help increase yields, and Genetic Modification (GM) has potential here but at present it does not have the public's confidence. As with many resources, sufficient food is available to feed the global population, but it requires careful husbandry that raises the quality as well as the yields, and most important the need to reduce waste – this is a 'quick hit'.

There is still a strong underlying dynamic that promotes a narrow view of economic growth, as measured by GDP, and the continued view that more growth is better. For example, this growth argument is reflected in much of the current thinking, such as the Global Commission on the Economy and Climate (2014), where an optimistic view is presented that permits a harmonious symbiosis between economic growth and carbon reduction, provided that the pricing mechanism is working efficiently. If the prices are correctly set, all major sectors of the economy will work efficiently, but this narrow view only addresses economic efficiency and not sustainable development.

Urban areas provide the potential for more sustainable futures, but the growth in the urban population makes this difficult. Cities account for 75 per cent of global energy consumption, and nearly 80 per cent of greenhouse gas (GHG) emissions come from cities burning fossil fuels (UN Habitat, 2013). For example, about 44 million people are being added to Asia's urban population every year, and 80 per cent of new economic growth will be concentrated in cities, and the motorized vehicle fleet will double every 5–7 years (ADB, 2014[10]). This prospect is bleak, as levels of congestion and pollution will continue to increase, suggesting that the only way forwards is to look at the broader development objectives with less transport.

Absolute decoupling of energy growth from economic growth is crucial to sustainable development (Loo & Banister, 2016), but most countries have at best only achieved a relative decoupling. This argument has been highlighted in the UNEP (2016) report, where it has been concluded that:

> Decoupling of material use and related environmental impacts from economic growth is a strategy that will be instrumental for ensuring future human wellbeing based on much lower material throughput. Many regions and countries have embarked on a strategy to substantially increase the material efficiency of their economies and to reduce the overall level of material use. Many countries and regions, including the European Union, Japan and China among others, now have high-level policy frameworks and laws that support resource efficiency and guide investments into green sectors of the economy supported by sustainable consumption and production practices.
>
> (UNEP, 2016, p. 18)

There is considerable potential for greater efficiency in the use of resources, in reducing waste, and in looking at ways to promote output of all resources with less material (and energy) inputs. Such a framing promotes sustainable development and begins to tackle some of the root causes for overconsumption. A second set of opportunities are to make judicious use of new technologies to help promote efficiency, waste reduction, and decoupling. The optimism of many promoters of technology as the answer to the resource issues needs to be tempered with a realism that prioritizes innovations that help achieve this set of opportunities through the promotion of non-resource-intensive uses of energy and material across all sectors. This prioritization avoids the current lock-in to non-sustainable use of resources, and it explicitly encourages renewable energy, together with strategies that reduce, reuse, and recycle all goods. It must be realized that new technologies tend to work with existing technologies rather than replace them. This means that it is market enhancing and encouraging more use of resources – this is not a pathway to sustainable development.

3. Healthy people and healthy planet

Apart from the concerns over climate change and the global pollution issues, much greater interest is now being placed on local pollution, particularly in cities. This is a new element in the debate over sustainable development, and it is important as it affects many of the largest cities in the world, and it is spread across both developed and developing countries. It is also an issue that directly affects the health and wellbeing of the population, and it can be seen as being important in gaining public support for immediate strong measures to reduce these levels of pollution. It cuts across some of the key sustainability themes, but is picked up indirectly through poverty, HDI, and GHG emissions.

More than 80 per cent of people living in urban areas that monitor air pollution are exposed to air quality levels that exceed World Health Organization (WHO) limits.[11] While all regions of the world are affected, populations in low-income cities are the most impacted, as 98 per cent of cities in low- and middle-income countries with more than 100,000 inhabitants do not meet WHO air quality guidelines. In high-income countries, that percentage decreases to 56 per cent. In the past two years, the WHO database – now covering 3000 cities in 103 countries – has nearly doubled, with more cities measuring air pollution levels and recognizing the associated health impacts. As urban air quality declines, the risk of stroke, heart disease, lung cancer, and chronic and acute respiratory diseases (including asthma), all increase for the residents.

The WHO (2016) has compared a total of 795 cities in 67 countries for levels of small and fine particulate matter (PM_{10} and $PM_{2.5}$) during a five-year period (2008–2013). PM_{10} and $PM_{2.5}$ include pollutants such as sulphate, nitrates, and black carbon, which penetrate deep into the lungs and into the cardiovascular system, posing the greatest risks to human health.

The four main conclusions are:

1   Global urban air pollution levels increased by 8 per cent, despite improvements in some regions.
2   Ambient air pollution, made of high concentrations of small and fine particulate matter, is the greatest environmental risk to health – causing more than 3 million premature deaths worldwide every year.
3   Most sources of urban outdoor air pollution are well beyond the control of individuals and demand action by cities, as well as national and international policymakers to promote cleaner transport, more efficient energy production, and better waste management.
4   WHO's air quality guidelines offer global guidance on thresholds and limits for key air pollutants that pose health risks. The guidelines indicate that by reducing particulate matter (PM_{10}) pollution from 70 to 20 micrograms per cubic metre ($\mu g/m^3$), air pollution-related deaths could be reduced by roughly 15 per cent.

The WHO (2016) lists cities by $PM_{2.5}$ annual mean concentration measurement, where the levels are greater than or equal to the air quality guidelines value of $10\,\mu g/m^3$ (2008–2013). Air quality in the database is represented by the annual mean concentration of particulate matter (PM_{10} and $PM_{2.5}$ relate to particles smaller than 10 or 2.5 microns in diameter). There are 38 cities with $PM_{2.5}$ levels over 100 (ten times the guidelines above); 18 of these are in India, six in China, three in Saudi Arabia, two in Pakistan and Iran, and one in Cameroon, Bangladesh, and Uganda.

In addition, air pollution is linked directly with diseases that kill. It has been estimated by UNICEF that in 2012 air pollution was linked with one out of every eight deaths, globally – or around 7 million people. Around 600,000 of those were children under five years old, and almost one million children die from pneumonia each year, more than half of which are directly related to air pollution (UNICEF, 2016). As well impacting on youth deaths, air pollution also affects health throughout an individual's life, making them more susceptible to growth and educational attainment. Globally, some 300 million children live in areas where the outdoor pollution levels exceed WHO guidelines by at least six times, and some 2 billion are subject to annual levels of $PM_{2.5}$ of 10 $\mu g/m^3$, the level that constitutes a long-term hazard (ibid.).

These levels are high and increasing, and demonstrate the links between the different aspects of the sustainable development space, as it is those in poorer countries and in the poorer parts of the city that suffer most from pollution, and they are also probably those people that do not produce the pollution (Kjellstrom *et al.*, 2007). The imperative of growth has been more important than the health of those people who are meant to benefit from that growth. In the future it is likely that the growth imperative will change with a fundamental move towards sustainable development, and the health of the planet and the people would seem to be key reasons for such a change.

4. Governance – engagement and participation

Governance is an essential part of sustainable development, and the appropriate institutions need to be seen as an integral part of the debate on the pathways forwards. There are questions about the scale and rate of change, and the speed at which the political and planning systems can adapt to the requirements that are now being placed on it. The demands for flexibility at the national and city levels mean that decisions need to be taken quickly, but more important is that the new dimensions also need to be considered. It is not just the best value for money, but also whether other objectives can also be achieved. These include resilience to external factors (such as climate-related threats), improvements in the quality of the environment (reductions in air pollution and health-related factors), the availability of new opportunities that are open to all (reducing the levels of inequality), and a measurable improvement in the quality of life – and whether all of these objectives collectively can be achieved. The most attractive places are those that offer all of these tangible and less tangible qualities, and these are likely to be the most attractive places to live in the future. It is not only the wealth that matters, but the many other factors that contribute to quality of life.

Central to the realization of the potential is the need for strong governance and institutions that allow decisions to be taken that benefit all citizens, for principles relating to justice and fairness to be apparent, and for a clear system of accountability. This includes issues of development and land ownership, as well as transparent processes for implementation. Consultation and participation with all (public sector and private sector) stakeholders provide accountability and give the different parties responsibility and empower them to take action. Underlying real change is the need for leadership, political will, and trust between all the main stakeholders.

The Worldwide Governance Indicators (WGI[12]) use 350 variables across more than 200 countries to measure levels of governance over the period 1996–2015 for six dimensions of governance:

- voice and accountability
- political stability and absence of major violence and terror

- government effectiveness
- regulatory quality
- rule of law
- control of corruption.

Data from a variety of sources are combined with the views of enterprises, citizens, and expert survey respondents in developed and developing countries. These are important indicators, and it is incumbent on the global institutions to monitor these six dimensions across countries and over time. But this responsibility should also identify where there are shortcomings, and then to enter into discussions with those countries to address the means to improve the quality and effectiveness of governance. Guidance and transparency are two means by which institutional structures can be improved and stability introduced that in turn allows the implementation of policies to promote sustainable development. Such stability also encourages greater compliance from the private sector. All stakeholders have an interest in maintaining stability, and the achievement of longer-term goals rather than only concentrating on the immediate short term. Sustainable development requires the acceptance of longer-term responsibilities.

Underlying these possibilities and the new challenges is the importance of including all stakeholders in the process of understanding the importance of sustainable development in achieving high-quality (urban) environments. This means engaging stakeholders in that debate in ways that make sense to them. If it is accepted that change is necessary, then it must be realized that people (and policy) drive innovation. This engagement needs to take place at all stages in the decision processes and it is important to raise expectations and to deliver change in a positive way (see chapter 7). The internet and the social media in all their forms allow the full involvement of all parties in presenting issues, in providing evidence, and in giving them choices. Underlying this greater level of engagement is the requirement to find new ways of presenting the issues so that these 'new' narratives can raise levels of societal interest and involvement. For example, online voting may provide the next democratic revolution with 'people power' deciding outcomes on issues that affect and concern them.

5. Comment

These four issues are not new, but they have become central to the debate over the last 30 years since *Our Common Future* (WCED, 1987). For much of this time, population growth has not been discussed as it was seen to be a national issue and one that governments were quite naturally sensitive about. The time for such sensitivities has passed and limits to global population are important as less pressure is put on the planet and global resources. A stronger view (Abel *et al.*, 2016) would be that the SDGs are 'only' achievable with a stable global population. Apart from more people, society is becoming increasingly urban and this again provides huge opportunities for the most efficient means to provide people with more jobs, better housing, services and facilities, and high-quality accessibility to all of these. Concentrating people in the cities at higher densities means that there is more land available to support them and the opportunity to protect the quality of the natural environment.

The second cross-cutting set of issues relates to resources and the potential that technological innovation offers. It is argued that technology is extremely helpful if wisely used, but it does not necessarily lead to sustainable development. As custodians of resources, we should seek opportunities to reduce our use of them. This means finding the most efficient ways to produce goods and services, to reduce waste to a minimum, and to decouple society's wellbeing (and economic growth) from resource use (covered in chapter 7). The resource issue has been with us for more than 30 years, but the imperatives of sustainable development mean that society needs to face the resource challenge more effectively. The answer is not to find more resources, but to manage the available resources more effectively so that quality of life can be enhanced for all within planetary limits.

The healthy people and planet issue leads on directly from these comments, as pollution affects the planet and the people, both directly and indirectly. Global warming means that futures are becoming increasingly uncertain, as sea levels rise, as temperatures reach record levels, and as the patterns of rainfall and wind change. High levels of local pollution, particularly in cities, are causing disruption, illness, and premature death, and the longer-term effects on the young and old are not yet well understood. Certainly, the quality of life has deteriorated in many cities, and this is likely to continue as the globe becomes increasingly industrialized. Again, this suggests that clean technologies must be prioritized, but also that production processes need to consider the pollution and health effects of rapid growth and high levels of consumption.

The final issue addresses governance, together with engagement and participation. All society has a vested interest in achieving sustainable development, but successful implementation requires strong decision-making structures at all levels. Such a multilevel approach also needs to have an internal consistency across all levels, and it needs to be moving in the same (or at least complementary) direction. Top-down direction (e.g., SDGs and COP21) provides one element in that process, but most decisions are implemented by national and local governments. So a complementary bottom-up element is also required. In addition, businesses have a major role to play, together with strong action from NGOs, and from the population as a whole. It is important that there is a debate about the scale and nature of sustainable development, and the means by which each and every individual can contribute to this ambition. Engagement of all actors in the process, together with an acceptance of the need for change, both seem to be essential conditions. It is only through such an all-encompassing process that real progress can be made. The science and technology have important roles to play, but in the end it is the people that are the arbiters of whether the pathway being followed is towards sustainable development – we are all part of the problem and so we should also all be part of the solution.

Conclusions

The reader has been taken on a long journey through this book. We started with looking back at sustainable development from its genesis in *Our Common Future* (WCED, 1987), and we have consistently argued for a holistic perspective that brings together needs, justice, and limits. We have also argued for simplicity and transparency, so that there is clarity over the nature and scale of change needed to achieve sustainable development. This has in turn meant that there is a requirement for measurement, a decision on the best level for analysis (the country), the search for suitable indicators, and the setting of thresholds. All these thresholds have to be met to enter the sustainable development space. The contributions of this book are substantial and here we highlight the following nine, and they can be seen as complementary to and reflecting on the arguments raised in chapter 1:

1   There is an overriding need to get serious, as the speed and scale of change has been underestimated, and the actions being taken now do not address the severity of the original agenda on sustainable development or the more recent agenda on climate change. The sustainable development space combines both of these debates into one set of coherent indicators and thresholds.

2   There is a strong ethical dimension to sustainable development that has not been extensively discussed in the literature or by the main actors. This covers difficult legacy issues and current responsibilities, but equally important is the acceptance that effective action needs to be taken. There does seem to be an understanding and an increased engagement at the international and national levels, and many companies are now much more active in promoting sustainable practices. But there is a long way to go and time may be short.

3   The belief that technology will provide the solution to sustainable development is mistaken. Technology can help address some of the issues, but in many cases it also promotes less sustainable activities that increase rather than decrease levels of consumption. Society has to change and this more fundamental thinking underlies the normative perspective taken in the book.

4   There is the question about whether the consumption-based paradigm is still fit for purpose. Alternatives, such as de-growth (Latouche, 2009), the circular economy (Webster, 2015), the sharing economy (Botsman & Rogers, 2011), and prosperity without growth (Jackson, 2009) have all been offered. It is not our purpose here to give support to any one of these alternatives, or to propose our own solution. We would conclude that sustainable development does not work well with the current economic paradigm, and any alternative must consider the 6–7 billion poor people in the world as well as the 1 billion that have really driven the consumption paradigm.

5   Approaches to sustainable development should combine top-down and expert-driven thinking, together with the more interpretative bottom-up and people-driven perspectives. The experts should take consideration of the best scientific evidence, the range of principles to be used, and to some extent the

instrumental issues that must be addressed. These experts may also have new ideas and be key innovators, as restrictive and habitual thinking often reinforces existing injustices (Nussbaum, 2003). Similarly, having a local dimension means that the specific local factors can be accommodated, as the narrative used relates to a particular place at one point in time. It also reflects their priorities and values. Both perspectives should work together, and convergence in thinking and action should address what matters most to them, so that real change can be achieved.

6   All three of our theories (needs, justice, and limits) have to be considered together, as they are all connected and there are synergies between them. For example, high levels of urban pollution affect the health of residents, including the young and the elderly (limits), and as noted above this often impacts on the poor rather than the rich (justice), and these effects impact on people's long-term health and opportunities (e.g., childhood development or premature mortality) (needs). This means that improvement in one dimension can have positive impacts across other dimensions. The potential for improvement across all three theories presents attractive possibilities for decision-makers that can make the task of achieving sustainable development less difficult.

7   Throughout this book it has been emphasized that there is no single pathway to reach the sustainable development space, but there are a series of alternatives for each country and for each situation. The pathways are not prescriptive, and there are many lessons to be learned from the different experiences. The non-tradability of each threshold means that there is some flexibility, but it is also accepted that a strong performance on one indicator does not necessarily mean that movement towards the sustainable development space is guaranteed.

8   It is also accepted that the indicators and thresholds selected are not perfect, and that others may be as good or even better. In the future, this expectation will probably be true, as better measurement and data become available. Second, some of the thresholds used here may need to be tightened in the future. This requirement is partly driven by population growth. For example, as the planetary boundaries are limited, the per-capita levels (e.g., on carbon emissions) may have to be reduced. It is also driven by the understanding that quality of life should improve over time, so the thresholds set now may be raised in the future. Sustainable development is not a fixed ideal, but a concept that is flexible and robust – it will change over time.

9   Part of our thinking has been to open up a discussion and debate over the importance of sustainable development today and tomorrow. We see this book as a contribution to bringing the different parties, the different theoretical standpoints, and the different disciplines together to discuss our common future within a positive and creative framework. We do not see this book as the final word, but as part of the ongoing narrative over some of the great challenges facing society today.

Our great hope is that in 30 years' time (2048), society will have met the needs of all the global population in a way that is both fair and just, but at the same time accepts that we have to live within the finite limits of the planet. Embedded here is respect for ourselves, respect for others, and respect for nature – this is the moral responsibility that we as humans have to accept, so that prosperity and a high quality of life can be enjoyed by all.

Notes

1 Poverty is defined as under $1.25 per person per day (2005 PPP), raised to $1.90 per person per day (2011 PPP) in 2015. The global population in 1987 was 5.045 billion, of whom 1.72 billion (34.1 per cent) were in poverty. By 2005 the corresponding figures were 6.514 billion of whom 1.376 billion (21.1 per cent) were in poverty, and in 2015 the figures were 7.324 billion of whom 0.75 billion (10.0 per cent) were in poverty (Ferreira *et al.*, 2015).

2 See the Global Footprint Network at www.footprintnetwork.org/en/index.php/GFN/page/world_footprint/.

3 In September 2016 the 400 ppm CO_2 threshold had been exceeded for a whole year, meaning that it is deemed to be permanent. The safe level is 350 ppm, and above this level means that it is highly unlikely for a 2°C increase in global average temperature to be avoided. This might make the COP21 Paris Agreement (2015) aspiration to limit the increase to 1.5°C an impossibility.

4 This is not a question of big data analysis, but one of transparency, so that it is clear whether boundaries have been exceeded or not.

5 De-growth involves the reduction of the carbon intensity of the global economy, primarily through reducing levels of demand rather than using alternative sources of energy (Latouche, 2009).

6 These comments are theoretically sound, but in practical terms almost impossible to measure. The alternative would be to adopt lifetime averages to assess the performance of countries (and individuals), which in turn can be reflected in annual or daily averages.

7 *Our Common Future* laid the groundwork for the 1992 Earth Summit (Rio de Janeiro), and the adoption of Agenda 21 and the Rio Declaration. It also resulted in the setting up of the Commission on Sustainable Development that provided a high-level forum for debate and meetings on the implementation of Agenda 21, including the Climate Change conventions at Kyoto (1997) and elsewhere. The commission was replaced by a new high-level political forum on sustainable development in 2013.

8 There is no international definition of the term urban area (built-up urban area, urbanized area, or urban agglomeration), but it is a continuously built-up land mass of urban development that is within a labour market (metropolitan area or metropolitan region). In some nations, a population threshold is used to differentiate urban from rural (e.g., in England and Wales where the threshold is 10,000) (http://demographia.com/db-define.pdf).

9 www.fao.org/save-food/resources/keyfindings/en/, accessed 24 December 2016.

10 www.adb.org/sectors/transport/key-priorities/urban-transport.

11 WHO Ambient Air Quality Guidelines:

$PM_{2.5}$ 10 µg/m³ annual mean   25 µg/m³ 24-hour mean
PM_{10} 20 µg/m³ annual mean   50 µg/m³ 24-hour mean.

12 http://info.worldbank.org/governance/wgi/index.aspx#home.

References

Abel, G., Barakat, B., Samir, K., & Lutz, W. (2016) *Meeting the Sustainable Development Goals leads to lower world population growth.* PNAS Early Edition, p. 6. Available from: www.pnas.org/cgi/doi/10.1073/pnas.1611386113.

Adam, B (2010) History of the future: Paradoxes and challenges. *Rethinking History,* 14, 361–378.

ADB (2014) *Urban Transport.* Asian Development Bank. Available from: www.adb.org/sectors/transport/key-priorities/urban-transport.

Agyeman, J. (2005) *Sustainable Communities and the Challenge of Environmental Justice.* New York, New York University Press.

Botsman, R. & Rogers, R. (2011) *What's Mine Is Yours: How Collaborative Consumption is Changing the Way We Live.* London, Harper Collins.

Coady, D., Parry, I., Sears, L., & Shang, B. (2015) *How large are global energy subsidies?* International Monetary Fund Working Paper 15/105, Washington, DC.

Commoner, B. (1971) *The Closing Circle: Nature, Man, and Technology.* New York, Random House.

Davoudi, S. & Brooks, E. (2014) When does unequal become unfair? Judging claims of environmental injustice. *Environment and Planning A,* 46, 2686–2702.

Ehrlich, P. & Holdren, P. (1971) Impact of population growth. *Science,* 171(3977), 1212–1217.

Ferreira, F., Chen, S., Dabalen, A., Dikhanov, Y., Hamadeh, N., Jolliffe, D., Narayan, A., Prydz, E., Revenga, A., Sangraula, P., Serajuddin, U., & Yoshida, N. (2015) *A global count of the extreme poor in 2012: Data issues, methodology and initial results.* Policy Research Working Paper WPS 7432. Washington, DC, World Bank Group.

Global Commission on the Economy and Climate (2014) *Better Growth, Better Climate: The New Climate Economy Report.* London.

Heck, S. & Rogers, M. (2014) *Resource Revolution: How to Capture the Biggest Business Opportunity in a Century.* Seattle, Amazon Publishing.

Jackson, T. (2009) *Prosperity without Growth: Economics for a Finite Planet.* London, Earthscan.

Kjellstrom, T., Friel, S., Dixon, J., Corvalan, C., Rehfuess, E., Campbell-Lendrum, D., Gore, F., & Bartram, J. (2007) Urban environmental health hazards and health equity. *Journal of Urban Health,* 84(1), 86–97.

Latouche, S. (2009) *Farewell to Growth.* Cambridge, Polity.

Loo, B. & Banister, D. (2016) Decoupling transport from economic growth: Extending the debate to include environmental and social externalities. *Journal of Transport Geography,* 57, 134–144.

Nussbaum, M. (2003) Capabilities as fundamental entitlements: Sen and social justice. *Feminist Economics,* 9(2/3), 33–59.

Piketty, T. (2014) *Capital in the Twenty-First Century.* Cambridge, MA, Belknap.

Rawls, J. (1999) *A Theory of Justice.* Oxford, Oxford University Press.

Schlosberg, D. (2013) Theorising environmental justice: The expanding sphere of a discourse. *Environmental Politics,* 22(1), 37–55.

Sen, A. (2009) *The Idea of Justice.* London, Penguin.

Steffen, W., Crutzen, P., & McNeill, J. (2007) The Anthropocene: Are humans now overwhelming the great forces of nature? *Ambio,* 36(8), 614–621.

Steffen, W., Richardson, K., Rockström, J., Cornell, S. E., Fetzer, I., Bennett, E. M., Biggs, R., Carpenter, S. R., de Vries, W., de Wit, C. A., Folke, C., Gerten, D., Heinke, J., Mace, G. M., Persson, L. M., Ramanathan, V., Reyers, B., & Sörlin, S. (2015) Planetary boundaries: Guiding human development on a changing planet. *Science*, 347, 736–746.

Stern, N. (2016) Current climate models are grossly misleading. *Nature*, 530, 407–409.

Stiglitz, J. E., Sen, A., & Fitoussi, J-P. (2010) *Mismeasuring Our Lives: Why GDP Doesn't Add Up*. The report by the Commission on the Measurement of Economic Performance and Social Progress. New York, The New Press.

Thewissen, S., Kenworthy, L., Nolan, B., Rosera, M., & Smeeding, T. (2015) *Rising income inequality and living standards in OECD countries: How does the middle fare?* INET Oxford Working Paper no. 2015-01, Employment, Equity and Growth Programme.

UN (2014) *World urbanisation prospects: 2014 revisions*. Paper 352. United Nations Department for Economic and Social Affairs, Washington, DC.

UN (2015) *World Population Prospects*. Washington, DC. Available from: www.un.org/en/development/desa/news/population/2015-report.html.

UNEP (2016) *Global Material Flows and Resource Productivity*. Assessment report for the UNEP International Resource Panel, UNESCO.

UN Habitat (2013) *Planning and Design for Sustainable Urban Mobility*. Global Report on Human Settlements 2013. London, Routledge.

UNICEF (2016) *Clear the air for children: The impact of air pollution on children*. The United Nations Children's Fund. Available from: http://weshare.unicef.org/Package/2AMZIFKPWU1.

Urry, J. (2016) *What is the Future?* Cambridge, Polity.

WCED (1987) *Our Common Future*. World Commission on Environment and Development. Oxford, Oxford University Press.

Webster, K. (2015) *The Circular Economy: A Wealth of Flows*. Cowes, Isle of Wight, Ellen MacArthur Foundation Publishing.

WHO (2016) *Global Urban Ambient Air Pollution Database*. Geneva, World Health Organization. Available from: www.who.int/phe/health_topics/outdoorair/databases/cities/en/.

World Bank (2016) *Poverty and Shared Prosperity*. Available from: www.worldbank.org/en/publication/poverty-and-shared-prosperity.

Appendix
COUNTRY ABBREVIATIONS IN ALPHABETICAL ORDER

ABW	Aruba
AFG	Afghanistan
AGO	Angola
AIA	Anguilla
ALA	Aland Islands
ALB	Albania
AND	Andorra
ARE	United Arab Emirates
ARG	Argentina
ARM	Armenia
ASM	American Samoa
ATA	Antarctica
ATF	French Southern Territories
ATG	Antigua and Barbuda
AUS	Australia
AUT	Austria
AZE	Azerbaijan
BDI	Burundi
BEL	Belgium
BEN	Benin
BES	Bonaire, Sint Eustatius and Saba
BFA	Burkina Faso
BGD	Bangladesh
BGR	Bulgaria
BHR	Bahrain
BHS	Bahamas
BIH	Bosnia and Herzegovina

BLM	Saint Barthelemy
BLR	Belarus
BLZ	Belize
BMU	Bermuda
BOL	Bolivia, Plurinational State of
BRA	Brazil
BRB	Barbados
BRN	Brunei Darussalam
BTN	Bhutan
BVT	Bouvet Island
BWA	Botswana
CAF	Central African Republic
CAN	Canada
CCK	Cocos (Keeling) Islands
CHE	Switzerland
CHL	Chile
CHN	China
CIV	Cote d'Ivoire
CMR	Cameroon
COD	Congo, the Democratic Republic of the
COG	Congo
COK	Cook Islands
COL	Colombia
COM	Comoros
CPV	Cabo Verde
CRI	Costa Rica
CUB	Cuba
CUW	Curacao
CXR	Christmas Island
CYM	Cayman Islands
CYP	Cyprus
CZE	Czechia
DEU	Germany
DJI	Djibouti
DMA	Dominica
DNK	Denmark
DOM	Dominican Republic
DZA	Algeria
ECU	Ecuador
EGY	Egypt
ERI	Eritrea
ESH	Western Sahara
ESP	Spain
EST	Estonia

ETH	Ethiopia
FIN	Finland
FJI	Fiji
FLK	Falkland Islands (Malvinas)
FRA	France
FRO	Faroe Islands
FSM	Micronesia, Federated States of
GAB	Gabon
GBR	United Kingdom
GEO	Georgia
GGY	Guernsey
GHA	Ghana
GIB	Gibraltar
GIN	Guinea
GLP	Guadeloupe
GMB	The Gambia
GNB	Guinea-Bissau
GNQ	Equatorial Guinea
GRC	Greece
GRD	Grenada
GRL	Greenland
GTM	Guatemala
GUF	French Guiana
GUM	Guam
GUY	Guyana
HKG	Hong Kong
HMD	Heard Island and McDonald Islands
HND	Honduras
HRV	Croatia
HTI	Haiti
HUN	Hungary
IDN	Indonesia
IMN	Isle of Man
IND	India
IOT	British Indian Ocean Territory
IRL	Ireland
IRN	Iran, Islamic Republic of
IRQ	Iraq
ISL	Iceland
ISR	Israel
ITA	Italy
JAM	Jamaica
JEY	Jersey
JOR	Jordan

JPN	Japan
KAZ	Kazakhstan
KEN	Kenya
KGZ	Kyrgyzstan
KHM	Cambodia
KIR	Kiribati
KNA	Saint Kitts and Nevis
KOR	Korea, Republic of
KWT	Kuwait
LAO	Lao People's Democratic Republic
LBN	Lebanon
LBR	Liberia
LBY	Libya
LCA	Saint Lucia
LIE	Liechtenstein
LKA	Sri Lanka
LSO	Lesotho
LTU	Lithuania
LUX	Luxembourg
LVA	Latvia
MAC	Macao
MAF	Saint Martin (French part)
MAR	Morocco
MCO	Monaco
MDA	Moldova, Republic of
MDG	Madagascar
MDV	Maldives
MEX	Mexico
MHL	Marshall Islands
MKD	Macedonia, the former Yugoslav Republic of
MLI	Mali
MLT	Malta
MMR	Myanmar
MNE	Montenegro
MNG	Mongolia
MNP	Northern Mariana Islands
MOZ	Mozambique
MRT	Mauritania
MSR	Montserrat
MTQ	Martinique
MUS	Mauritius
MWI	Malawi
MYS	Malaysia
MYT	Mayotte

NAM	Namibia
NCL	New Caledonia
NER	Niger
NFK	Norfolk Island
NGA	Nigeria
NIC	Nicaragua
NIU	Niue
NLD	Netherlands
NOR	Norway
NPL	Nepal
NRU	Nauru
NZL	New Zealand
OMN	Oman
PAK	Pakistan
PAN	Panama
PCN	Pitcairn
PER	Peru
PHL	Philippines
PLW	Palau
PNG	Papua New Guinea
POL	Poland
PRI	Puerto Rico
PRK	Korea, Democratic People's Republic of
PRT	Portugal
PRY	Paraguay
PSE	Palestine, State of
PYF	French Polynesia
QAT	Qatar
REU	Reunion
ROU	Romania
RUS	Russian Federation
RWA	Rwanda
SAU	Saudi Arabia
SDN	Sudan
SEN	Senegal
SGP	Singapore
SGS	South Georgia and the South Sandwich Islands
SHN	Saint Helena, Ascension and Tristan da Cunha
SJM	Svalbard and Jan Mayen
SLB	Solomon Islands
SLE	Sierra Leone
SLV	El Salvador
SMR	San Marino
SOM	Somalia

SPM	Saint Pierre and Miquelon
SRB	Serbia
SSD	South Sudan
STP	Sao Tome and Principe
SUR	Suriname
SVK	Slovakia
SVN	Slovenia
SWE	Sweden
SWZ	Swaziland
SXM	Sint Maarten (Dutch part)
SYC	Seychelles
SYR	Syrian Arab Republic
TCA	Turks and Caicos Islands
TCD	Chad
TGO	Togo
THA	Thailand
TJK	Tajikistan
TKL	Tokelau
TKM	Turkmenistan
TLS	Timor-Leste
TON	Tonga
TTO	Trinidad and Tobago
TUN	Tunisia
TUR	Turkey
TUV	Tuvalu
TWN	Taiwan, Province of China
TZA	Tanzania, United Republic of
UGA	Uganda
UKR	Ukraine
UMI	United States Minor Outlying Islands
URY	Uruguay
USA	United States of America
UZB	Uzbekistan
VAT	Holy See (Vatican City State)
VCT	Saint Vincent and the Grenadines
VEN	Venezuela, Bolivarian Republic of
VGB	Virgin Islands, British
VIR	Virgin Islands, U.S.
VNM	Viet Nam
VUT	Vanuatu
WLF	Wallis and Futuna
WSM	Samoa
YEM	Yemen
ZAF	South Africa
ZMB	Zambia

INDEX

Page numbers in *italics* denote figures, those in **bold** denote tables. End of chapter notes are indicated by a letter n between page number and note number.

2030 Agenda for Sustainable Development *see Transforming Our World*

Aerosol Optical Depth (AOD) 82
agency-sensitive capability approach 50
Agenda 21 97, 106–7, 201, 204–5, 206, 214; *see also* Local Agenda 21 (LA21)
aggregation of capabilities 50–1, 54n18
Agyeman, J. 16, 227
Aichi Biodiversity Targets 164–5, **165**
air pollution 236–8, 240
Alexander, Ernest 114
Alkire, S. 12, 46, 50, 115
American Declaration of Independence 72
Amnesty International 77n16, 187
analytic narrative 172–95; cluster analysis of key themes 178–87, *179*, **181**, **182**, *185*; decoupling prosperity from material consumption 191–2, 235–6; global solidarity 189–91; problem statement 187–8; reducing population growth 188–9; resilience of natural systems 193–4; trends and correlations among key themes 174–7, *176*, *177*
Anderson, E. 50
Aristotle 57

Arrow, K. 95
Asheim, G. B. 209
Atkinson, Anthony 166n2
atmospheric aerosol loading 82
authoritarian regimes 146
autonomy 43, 44, 45
axiological human needs 38

ballots 75, 116–17
Banfield, Edward 111, 112
Bangladesh 237
Ban Ki-moon 107
basic capabilities 48
basic needs theories 37–45, 47, 115
Belgium 164
Bentham, Jeremy 60, 61, 70, 76n7
Bhutan 191
biocentric perspective 85
biodiversity hotspots 162, *163*, 167n18
biodiversity loss 29, 67, 79, 81, 95
biosphere integrity **26**, *28*, 78, 81, 83, 119, *120*; indicators and thresholds 159–65, *161*, *163*, *164*, **165**, 167n18; and neoclassical economics 89–90; trends 177; *see also* cluster analysis of key themes

Bishop, R. C. 96
'The Blue Marble' (photo) 78
Borowy, I. 11
bottom-up approach to indicator
    development 109
Brazil 232
Brecht, Bertolt 39
broad sustainability 19
Brooks, E. 228
Brundtland, Gro Harlem 1, 15, 97
Burundi 138
businesses 22, 233; sustainability reporting
    199; triple bottom line accounting
    framework 97

Cameroon 237
capabilities *see* human capabilities
capability approach 45–53, 54n13, 115–16
cap-and-trade system 89
Caradonna, J. L. 72, 77n17
carbon budgets 155–6
carbon dioxide emissions *see* greenhouse
    gas emissions
Carbon Dioxide Information Analysis
    Centre (CDIAC) 155
chemical pollution 82
Chesterton, G. K. 105
child mortality 16
children: and air pollution 237; sense of
    injustice 57
China 138, 153, *153*, *154*, 157, 232,
    237
Christen, M. 110
chronological unfairness 67
Cichetti, C. J. 94
civil and political rights 45
Clausen, Alden Winship 10, 30n1
climate change 11–12, 23, 29, 67, 78, 83,
    96, 202, 230; planetary boundary 81
climate change mitigation **26**, *28*, 119,
    120; correlations with other themes
    176–7, *177*; indicators and thresholds
    154–9, *157*, *158*, **165**, 166n12, 176–7,
    177; local authorities 199, 216; and
    neoclassical economics 89; trends 177;
    see also cluster analysis of key themes
closed impartiality 74

cluster analysis of key themes 178–87, *179*,
    181, **182**, *185*
Cobb, J. 88
Cobb-Douglas production function
    100n9
Cocoyoc Declaration 19, 31n7
*Collapse: How Societies Choose to Fail or
    Succeed* (Diamond) 59
command-and-control policies 89
Committee on Climate Change, UK 216,
    219n15
Commoner, B. 234
comparative approach to social justice 70
comparative sustainability 29–30, 207,
    210–15
composite-sustainability indexes 122–4
comprehensive sustainability 207, 208–9
Conference of the Parties, Paris (2015) 155,
    156, *157*, 221, 230, 243n3
Conference of the Parties to the
    Convention on Biological Diversity,
    Nagoya, Japan 164–5
consequentialism 59; *see also* utilitarianism
constrained optimum 44
constraints on human behaviour 4, 7–8, 13,
    18–19, 52, 80, 97
contractarian approach to social justice
    61–8, 69, 70–1, 96, 116–17, 207, 208
Convention on Biological Diversity 99n7,
    165
conversion factors 47–8
Costanza, R. 173
Costa Rica 144, 191
cost–benefit analysis 90, 92, 95, 119
critical natural capital 92–3, 119
Crocker, D. A. 50
cultural imperialism 41
Czech Republic 111

Dahl, A. L. 110, 121
Daly, Herman E. 2, 8n2, 22, 88, 92, 113
Davoudi, S. 228
decoupling prosperity from material
    consumption 191–2, 235–6
deliberative democracy 50
democracy 45, 59, 74–5; deliberative 50;
    see also rich participation

Democratic Republic of the Congo 138
Demographic and Health Survey, Ethiopia
140, 143
desires 35–6
Diamond, Jared 59
Dickens, Charles 57
difference principle 64, 65, 66, 68, 69, 116,
117
Dostoyevsky, Fyodor 35–6
Doyal, L. 39, 40, 41–5, 115
draft exemptions 64
drinking water 16
Driver, J. 61
drivers, needs as 39–41
Dubos, Rene 201

Eagles 36, 57, 78
Earth Summit *see* Rio Summit (1992)
Eckerberg, K. 206
ecological constraints 44
ecological economics 85, 89, 119
ecological footprint 93, 122, 160–2, *161*
ecological sustainability 19
Ecological Sustainability Index 93
economic growth 22–4, 25, 97–8, 230–1,
238
Economics of Ecosystems and Biodiversity
99n7
Economics of Welfare, The (Pigou) 89
economic sustainability 91
Economist Intelligence Unit index
(EIUDI) 146–7, *147*
ecosystems *see* biosphere integrity
ecosystem services 83–5, 92, 99n7
Ecosystem Services Partnership (ESP)
99n7
education: and extreme poverty eradication
189–90; gender gap 143, 188–9; years
of schooling 142–3, 188
egoism 61
Ehrlich, P. R. 22, 234
EIUDI *see* Economist Intelligence Unit
index (EIUDI)
Ekins, Paul 84, 87, 90, 92, 93, 100n12
elections 75, 116–17
Elkington, John 97
Emission Gap Report 156, *157*

Emissions Database for Global Atmospheric
Research (EDGAR) 155
energy resources 79
environmental conversion factors 48
environmental economics 84–5, 89, 90–3,
118–19
Environmentalist, The 10
environmental justice 228
environmental limits 4, 16, 17–18, *18*,
78–101, 118–19; ecological economics
85, 89, 119; and economic growth 23,
97–8; ecosystem services 83–5, 92,
99n7; environmental economics 84–5,
89, 90–3, 118–19; irreversibility, risk,
and uncertainty 93–7; natural capital
approach 84–5, 90–3, 118–19; and
neoclassical economics 85, 86, 88–90,
118; non-renewable natural resources
91–2; *Our Common Future* on 17,
79–80; planetary boundaries 17, 78,
80–3, 118, 159; renewable natural
resources 92–3, 191; substitutability of
natural capital 85–8, 93, 118; *see also*
biosphere integrity; climate change
mitigation
environmental literacy 194
environmental movement 201
Environmental Performance Index (EPI)
100n13
environmental space 19, 31n84
environmental sustainability 19, 90, 92
environmental sustainability index (ESI) 93,
100n13
EPI *see* Environmental Performance Index
(EPI)
equality 16–17, 73; *see also* fair distribution;
inequality
equality of opportunity *see* fair opportunity
principle
equity *see* social justice
ESI *see* environmental sustainability index
(ESI)
ESP *see* Ecosystem Services Partnership
(ESP)
esteem needs 40
ethical individualism 51, 52
ethical pronouncements 71–3, 77n16

ethical statement of sustainable
    development 4, 11–13, 21–2, 71,
    105–6
Ethiopia 140–1, 143
European Environmental Agency 194
European Union 157; Biodiversity Strategy
    99n7; Eurostat 107
existential human needs 38
expert knowledge 105–6
extended-sustainability-theme indexes 122,
    123
extreme poverty eradication **26**, *28*, 116,
    120; correlations with other themes
    175; and global solidarity 189–91;
    indicators and thresholds 138–42, *141*,
    165, 166n2, 175; trends 177; *see also*
    cluster analysis of key themes

fair distribution **26**, *28*, 117, *120*, 188;
    indicators and thresholds 148–54, *150*,
    151, *153*, *154*, **165**, 166n10; trends
    177; *see also* cluster analysis of key
    themes
Fairfield Osborn Memorial Lecture in
    Environmental Science 10
fair opportunity principle 64, 65–6, 116
feasibility 70, 210, 211
fertility rates 143, 188–9
finite biosphere 85
Finnis, John 50
Fisher, A. C. 94, 95
flawed democracies 146–7, *147*
food production 234–5
fragmentation of landscape 167n19, 194
France 147, 194
Fredrikstad Declaration 203, 218n1
freedoms 45, 47, 48, 60, 64, 69, 72; *see also*
    liberty principle
Freeman, A. M. 94
Free to Choose (Friedman) 58
French declaration of the rights of man 72
French Revolution 187
freshwater cycle 82
Friedman, Milton 58
full democracies 146–7, *147*
functionings 46–7, 48, 49
Future We Want, The 205

Galli, A. 162
game theory 95–6
Geddes, Patrick 201
gender gap in education 143, 188–9
generalized entropy indices 152–3
Genetic Modification (GM) 235
genocide 59
genuine saving indicator 88, 91, 93,
    122
Ghana 191
Giddings, B. 2
Gilead Science 190
Gini coefficient 150–2, *151*, 154, **165**,
    166n10
global average temperature 154, 155, 156,
    157
Global Biodiversity Outlook 99n7
global carbon budget 155
Global Environmental Outlook 107
global ethic 15
global freshwater use 82
global hydrological cycle 82
global justice 69–73
Global Partnership for Education 190
global solidarity 189–91
goals, needs as 39, 41–5
Gough, I. 39, 40, 41–5, 115
governance 238–9, 240
government by election 75
Gray, Rob 22
Grazi, F. 162
Green Climate Fund 158
greenhouse gas development rights 155–6,
    157
greenhouse gas emissions 23, 29, 89, 96,
    119, 192, 202, 243n3; allocation
    between countries 214–15; cities 235;
    indicators and thresholds 155–9, *157*,
    158, **165**, 166n12, 176–7, *177*; local
    reductions 199, 216; planetary boundary
    81
Greenpeace 187
green shift 191
green technology 23, 189, 191, 192, 230,
    234–6, 240
gross domestic product 122
groups, and capability approach 52

Hak, T. 121, 122
happiness 60–1
happy life years (HLY) 143–4, *144*
happy planet index 143
Haq, Mahbub ul 142
Hartigan–Wong Algorithm 178
Hartwick, John 86, 91
Hartwick–Solow rule 86, 91
HDI *see* human development index
 (HDI)
headline indicators 120–5, *125*, 136–67,
 165; for biosphere integrity 159–65,
 161, *163*, *164*, **165**, 167n18; for climate
 change mitigation 154–9, *157*, *158*,
 165, 166n12, 176–7, *177*; for extreme
 poverty eradication 138–42, *141*, **165**,
 166n2, 175; for fair distribution 148–54,
 150, *151*, *153*, *154*, **165**, 166n10; for
 human capabilities 142–5, *144*, **165**,
 175–6, *176*, 177; for rich participation
 145–8, *147*, *148*, **165**, 175–7, *176*;
 trends and correlations among key
 themes 174–7, *176*, *177*; *see also* cluster
 analysis of key themes
health, and air pollution 237–8, 240
heavy metal compounds 82
Heink, U. 110–11
Helm, Dieter 91, 92, 93
Herzen, Alexander 67
hierarchy of needs theory 39–41, 42
higher and lower pleasures 60–1
highways 194
Hill, R. 141
HLY *see* happy life years (HLY)
Hobbes, Thomas 14–15, 70, 207
Holdren, P. 234
HOPE study 203, 218n7
Hopwood, B. 2
human capabilities **26**, *28*, 47, 48, 49, 69,
 116, *120*, 187; aggregation of 50–1,
 54n18; correlations with other themes
 175–6, *176*, *177*; indicators and
 thresholds 142–5, *144*, **165**, 175–6,
 176, 177; selection of 49–50; trends
 177; *see also* cluster analysis of key
 themes
human development 46, 67

human development index (HDI) 54n17,
 122, 142–5, *144*, **165**, 175–6, *176*, 177,
 177
Human Development Report 15–16, 36, 46,
 52, 142
human dignity 60, 61
human diversity, and capability approach
 48
human needs 4, 15–16, 18, *18*, 35–55,
 115–16; basic needs theories 37–45,
 47, 115; capability approach 45–53,
 54n13, 115–16; and economic growth
 23; *Our Common Future* on 15, 36,
 45–6, 53, 115; *see also* extreme
 poverty eradication; human
 capabilities
human rights 12, 21–2, 27, 71, 72, 77n16
Human Rights Watch 77n16
human-scale development theory 37–8
Hundertwasser, Friedensreich 193
hybrid regimes 146
hydrological cycle 82

ICLEI *see* Local Governments for
 Sustainability (ICLEI)
ICSU *see* International Council for Science
 (ICSU)
Idea of Justice, The (Sen) 68–75
idleness 53n6
impartiality 74
income inequality 17, 18, 23, 222; *see also*
 difference principle; fair distribution
inconvenient choices 7–8, 13, 52, 80
Index of Sustainable Economic Welfare
 (ISEW) 88
India 138, 153, *153*, *154*, 157, 190, 237
indicanda of sustainable development
 110–11, 113
indicators *see* headline indicators;
 sustainability indicators
*Indicators of Sustainable Development:
 Guidelines and Methodologies* 121
individual freedom 60
individualism, and capability approach
 51–2
Indonesia 189
Industrial Revolution 187

inequality 17, 18, 23, 222; *see also* difference principle; fair distribution

inequality-adjusted human development index 122

injustice: and poverty 58–9; sense of 57; *see also* social justice

institutions 69, 71; Rawls' theory of justice 59, 61–8, 69, 70

intellectual parochialism 202

intergenerational justice 16, 66–8, 76n12, 209; and environmental limits 86, 90, 91–2

Intergovernmental Panel on Climate Change (IPCC) 155, 156

Intergovernmental Platform on Biodiversity and Ecosystem Services (IPBES) 99n7

intermediate needs 43–5

International Committee of the Red Cross 187

International Corporate Responsibility Reporting Survey 2011 199

International Council for Science (ICSU) 25, 173

international poverty line (IPL) 138–9, 140, 141, **165**, 175

International Social Science Council (ISSC) 25, 173

intragenerational justice *see* social justice

intuition-based morality 61

IPCC *see* Intergovernmental Panel on Climate Change (IPCC)

IPL *see* international poverty line (IPL)

Iran 237

irreversibility 93–7, 101n16

ISEW *see* Index of Sustainable Economic Welfare (ISEW)

ISSC *see* International Social Science Council (ISSC)

Jacobs, M. 2

Japan 232

just savings principle 64, 66–8, 76n12

just sustainability 16, 122

Kant, Immanuel 10, 67, 70, 207

Kassar, I. 95

KC, S. 188

Kellogg Institute 146

kernel density estimates 153

key sustainability themes 21–2, 26–7, **26**, *28*, 113–19, *120*; cluster analysis of 178–87, *179*, **181**, **182**, *185*; trends and correlations among key themes 174–7, *176*, *177*; *see also* headline indicators

Khalid, Mansour 1–2

K-means algorithm 178

Knight, F. H. 93

Kowarik, I. 110–11

KPMG 199

Krutilla, J. V. 94

Kubiszewski, I. 173

Kyoto Protocol 155, 158

LA21 *see* Local Agenda 21 (LA21)

Lafferty, W. M. 10–11, 19–20, 31n6, 199, 206

Lakner, C. 152, 153

Lancker, E. 126

land preservation 94–5

landscape fragmentation 167n19, 194

land-system change 81–2, 162–4, *164*, 167n19, 194

Langhelle, O. 10–11, 19–20, 31n6, 199

Lasserre, P. 95

League of Nations 187

Leviathan 14–15

lexical ordering 26, 64, 76n13, 113–14

liberty principle 64–5, 66, 69, 116–17

life expectancy 142–3, 229, 232

life ladder poll 143

Lindblom, Charles 112

Local Agenda 21 (LA21) 28, 205–7, 216, 218n1

local authorities 28–9, 199, 202, 204, 205–7, 216

local environmental policy 29

Local Governments for Sustainability (ICLEI) 199

local sustainability 3–4, 28–30, 198–219; availability 30, 212; comparative approach 207, 210–15; comprehensive approach 207, 208–9; *Our Common Future* on 28, 201, 204–7; reasons for

acting locally 202–4; relevance 30, 211–12; scale 200, 215–17, *215*; thinking globally 28–9, 200–2
Locke, John 70, 207
love needs 40, 54n8
Lutz, W. 188

McKinsey Group 199
MacNeill, Jim 1–2, 3, 7, 10, 17
Madagascar 138
Maffettone, S. 64, 116
Malawi 138
manufactured capital 86–7
market-based approach *see* neoclassical economics
Marx, Karl 70
Maslow, Abraham Harold 39–41, 42, 54n8, 115
material preconditions for optimal need-satisfaction 45
maximax rule 95
maxmin rule 95–6
Max-Neef, Manfred 37–8, 40, 41, 53n6, 115
MDGs *see* millennium development goals (MDGs)
MEA *see* Millennium Ecosystem Assessment (MEA)
Meadowcroft, J. 117
means and ends 47
megacities 232, **233**
megacity regions 232
Meinshausen, M. J. L. 156, 157, *157*
methodological individualism 51–2
Methods of Ethics, The (Sidgwick) 61
Milanovic, B. 152, 153
Mill, John Stuart 60–1, 70, 217
Millennium Assessment Reports 83–4
millennium development goals (MDGs) 107
Millennium Ecosystem Assessment (MEA) 81
minimax regret 96
minimum optimorum levels 44
monetary sustainability gaps 93, 100n11
monsoon system 154
moral entitlements 50

moral imperatives 4, 14–20, *18*, 21, 27, 111–12, *111*, 229; *see also* environmental limits; human needs; social justice
moral responsibilities 44–5, 80
Morse, S. 110
motivation theory 39–41, 42
Mozambique 138
MPI *see* multidimensional poverty index (MPI)
Mridha, Debasish 45
multidimensional country-level data analysis 178–87, *179*, **181**, **182**, *185*
multidimensional poverty index (MPI) 139–42, *141*
multinational companies 233
municipal waste 186, 191
Myers, N. 162

Næss, Arne 19, 209
Nagel, Thomas 69
Nagoya Protocol 164–5
narrow sustainability 19, 209
National Biodiversity Strategies and Action Plans 165
national scale 213–15
natural capital: critical 92–3, 119; substitutability of 85–8, 93, 118; *see also* environmental limits
natural capital approach 84–5, 90–3, 118–19
Natural Capital: Valuing the Planet (Helm) 91, 92, 93
natural intact vegetation (NIV) 162, *163*
natural systems, resilience of 193–4
negative freedom 45
neoclassical economics 85, 86, 88–90, 118
Neumayer, Eric 86, 87
New Right 41
New York Times 146
Nijkamp, P. 126
nitrogen cycle 81
NIV *see* natural intact vegetation (NIV)
non-renewable natural resources 91–2
normative model of sustainable development 105–31; step 1: moral imperatives 111–12, *111*; step 2:

theories 112, *113*; step 3: key
sustainability themes 113–19, *120*; step
4: headline indicators 120–5, *125*; step
5: thresholds 125–8, *127*
North–South issues 16
Norway 91, 186, 190, 191
Nussbaum, Martha 46, 48, 49–51, 115–16

Obama, Barack 7
ocean acidification 82
OECD *see* Organisation for Economic
Co-operation and Development
(OECD)
official development assistance 189, 190
Okinawan folk song 172
On Liberty (Mill) 60
ontological individualism 51–2
open impartiality 74
Opschoor, Hans 31n84
options theory 94–5, 119
Organisation for Economic Co-operation
and Development (OECD) 107
O'Riordan, T. 2
Ostrom, E. 173
Our Common Future 1, 10, 11, 12–13, 18,
20, 72, 108, 126, 229–31, 243n7; broad
sustainability 19; definition of
sustainable development 1, 2–3; on
economic growth 23, 97, 230–1; on
environmental limits 17, 79–80; on
human needs 15, 36, 45–6, 53, 115;
inconvenient choices 7–8, 13, 52, 80;
on local sustainability 28, 201, 204–7;
on social justice 16, 17, 53, 58–9, 117
Oxfam 17
Oxford Poverty and Human Development
Initiative 140
ozone depletion 82

Pakistan 237
Palma Index 166n10
Pareto principle 88, 100n10, 118
Paris Agreement (2015) 155, 156, *157*,
221, 230, 243n3
parochialism 29, 69, 201–3
Parsons, Talcott 15
partial compliance theory 208

participation 59, 64–5, 75, 116–17, 238–9,
240; *see also* rich participation
participatory democracy index (PDI)
146–7, *147*, 148, *148*, **165**, 175–7, *176*
particulate matter pollution 237
paternalism 49
pathways to sustainable development 21
pay-off matrix 95–6
PDI *see* participatory democracy index
(PDI)
peace 12
peace movement 201
Perman, R. 94, 96
personal conversion factors 47–8
phosphorus cycle 81
physical health 43, 44
physical sustainability gaps 93
physiological needs 39
Pickett, K. 17
Pigou, Arthur Cecil 89
Pigovian tax 89, 118
Pillarisetti, R. 93
Pindyck, R. S. 95, 119
planetary boundaries 17, 78, 80–3, 118,
159
Plato 57
Policy Sciences 114
political liberties 64–5, 75, 116–17
pollution: air 236–8, 240; chemical 82
population growth 188–9, 221, 227, 232,
234, 239–40, 243n1; and thresholds
229–30
positive freedom 45
poverty 15–16, 18, 23, 36, 38, 48, 221,
243n1; and injustice 58–9; *see also*
extreme poverty eradication
poverty line *see* international poverty line
(IPL)
practical reasoning approach 50
precautionary principle 96–7, 99, 119, 137,
156
primary goods 63, 66, 69, 91, 115, 117
prism of sustainability 19
procedural preconditions for optimal need-
satisfaction 45
production function 85, 89–90, 100n9
proxy indicators 160

public reasoning 50, 74–5

radioactive materials 82
Rametsteiner, E. 110
Rawls, John 14, 26, 44, 58, 59, 61–8, 69, 70, 76n10, 76n12, 76n13, 96, 115, 116–17, 207, 208
Raworth, Kate 19
realization-based comparison 70
reasoned scrutiny 13, 72, 73–4, 109, 204
Red Cross 77n16, 187
redundancy 71, 210–11
relativist positions on human needs 41
renewable natural resources 92–3, 191
Republic of Korea 189
resilience of natural systems 193–4
resource-based approaches 47
resources: energy 79; non-renewable natural 91–2; renewable natural 92–3, 191; resource efficiency 234–6, 240; *see also* environmental limits
rich participation **26**, *28*, 116–17, *120*, 187–8, 193; correlations with other themes 175–7, *176*; indicators and thresholds 145–8, *147*, *148*, **165**, 175–7, *176*; local authorities 216–17; trends 177; *see also* cluster analysis of key themes
right to vote 64–5, 75, 116–17
Rio Declaration on Environment and Development 96, 97, 101n15, 101n18, 119, 205
Rio Summit (1992) 28, 97, 101n15, 106–7, 204, 218n8
risk 93–7, 101n16
risk aversion 94, 96
Robeyns, I. 50, 51, 52, 54n14
Rockström, J. 80–1, 93
Roe, E. M. 173
Romania 194
Rousseau, Jean-Jacques 70, 207
Russian Revolution 188
Rwanda 59

safe minimum standard of conservation (SMS) 96
safety needs 40

Sandel, M. K. 60, 61, 63, 65
Sandhu, S. 57, 125–6, 213
sanitation facilities 16
Sarkozy Commission 231
satisfiers 37–8, 43
Saudi Arabia 237
Schlosberg, D. 228
Schmidt, S. 110
Scholz, R. W. 21
scrutiny, reasoned 73–4
SDGs *see* sustainable development goals (SDGs)
selection of capabilities 49–50
self-actualization 40
self-esteem needs 40
self-respect 76n10
Sen, Amartya 12, 13, 14, 17–18, 29, 45, 46, 47, 48, 50, 51–2, 53, 54n13, 54n14, 54n17, 68–75, 77n16, 109, 115, 117, 128, 142, 201, 207–8, 210–11, 219n9
sense of injustice 57
sense of sustainability 14–15
serial ordering *see* lexical ordering
sexual needs 54n8
shared prosperity index 139, 149–50, *150*, 151–2, *151*
Sidgwick, Henry 61
Smith, Adam 70, 74
SMS *see* safe minimum standard of conservation (SMS)
social contract 14–15, 61–8, 69, 70–1, 96, 116–17, 207, 208
social conversion factors 48
socialist societies 188
social justice 4, 16–17, 18, *18*, 57–77, 116–17; and economic growth 23; between generations 16, 66–8, 76n12, 209; *Our Common Future* on 16, 17, 53, 58–9, 117; Rawls' theory of justice 59, 61–8, 69, 70, 96, 116–17, 207, 208; Sen's idea of justice 68–75; utilitarianism 59–61, 63–4, 66–7; *see also* fair distribution; rich participation
social movements 201
social realizations 70
social structures, and capability approach 52

societal preconditions for optimal need-satisfaction 41, 44–5
solidarity movement 201
Solow, Robert 86, 91
South Korea 189
Spangenberg, Joachim 19
specialist's expert knowledge 105–6
species abundance and richness 162, *163*
species extinctions 81, 95, 96
Stafford-Smith, M. 2, 8n3
stakeholder approach 21–2, 203, 213
Steffen, W. 81, 82–3
Stern, Nicholas 11, 14, 230
Stockholm Environment Institute 80, 118, 155–6, 157
Stockholm Resilience Centre 80, 118
Stokstad, E. 2, 8n3
stratospheric ozone depletion 82
strict compliance theory 208
strong sustainability 86–8, 93, 96
substitutability of natural capital 85–8, 93, 118
sustainability gaps 21, 93, 100n11
sustainability indicators 27, 88; bottom-up approach 109; composite-sustainability indexes 122–4; criteria for 120–1; critique of 109–11; extended-sustainability-theme indexes 122, 123; global solidarity 189; history of 106–9; and natural capital approach 93; sustainability-theme indexes 122, 123; three-pillar-model indicators 121–2, 123; top-down approach 109; *see also* headline indicators
Sustainability: Principles and Practice (Turner) 86
sustainability reporting 199
sustainability-theme indexes 122, 123
sustainable development: critique of 2–3; defining 1, 2–3; as goal or process 108–9, 125–7
sustainable development goal index 123–4
sustainable development goals (SDGs) 2, 19, 24–5, 107, 109, 121–2, 221; for biosphere integrity **165**; for climate change mitigation **165**; composite index of 123–4; economic growth 23, 25; for

extreme poverty eradication 138, 141, **165**; for fair distribution 149, 150, **165**; for human capabilities 145, **165**; irreversibility, risk, and uncertainty 97, 101n16; for rich participation 147–8, **165**
sustainable development space 4, 18, *18*, 19, 21, 27, *28*, 108, 128–9, *129*, 227–9
sustainable growth 8n2, 22–4
sustainable thinking, history of 10, 72, 77n17
Sutton, P. 126
Sweden 190
synthetic organic pollutants 82
Syria 142

Tällberg Foundation 80, 118
taxes 192; Pigovian 89, 118
technology 23, 189, 191, 192, 230, 234–6, 240
temperature, global average 154, 155, 156, *157*
test sites 203
Thatcher, Margaret 51, 55n19
Theory of Human Need, A (Doyal & Gough) 39, 40, 41–5
Theory of Justice, A (Rawls) 59, 61–8, 96
Theory of Moral Sentiments, The (Smith) 74
Thewissen, S. 222
thinking globally 28–9, 200–2
three-legged stool model of sustainable development 24, 123
three-pillar-model indicators 121–2, 123
three-pillar model of sustainable development 18, 23, 24, 25, 97
thresholds 20, 27, 93, 108, 125–8, *127*; for biosphere integrity 159–65, *161*, *163*, *164*, **165**; for climate change mitigation 154–9, *157*, *158*, **165**, 166n12, 176–7, *177*; for extreme poverty eradication 138–42, *141*, **165**, 166n2, 175; for fair distribution 148–54, *150*, *151*, *153*, *154*, **165**, 166n10; for human capabilities 142–5, *144*, **165**, 175–6, *176*, 177; and population growth 229–30; for rich participation 145–8, *147*, *148*, **165**, 175–7, *176*

top-down approach to indicator development 109
Town Planning Review 114
Townsend, K. N. 2, 8n2
tradable emissions permits 89
trade-offs: capabilities 50–1, 54n18; composite-sustainability indexes 123–4
transcendental institutionalism 70–1, 207
Transforming Our World 2, 7, 11, 13, 15, 23, 80, 205
triple bottom line accounting framework 97
Tsehaye, E. 141
Turner, Kerry R. 86

Uganda 237
Ukraine 162–4
UNCED *see* United Nations Conference on Environment and Development (UNCED)
uncertainty 93–7, 101n16
UNCSD *see* United Nations Commission on Sustainable Development (UNCSD)
UNCTAD *see* United Nations Conference on Trade and Development (UNCTAD)
UNDP *see* United Nations Development Programme (UNDP)
UNEP *see* United Nations Environment Programme (UNEP)
UNFCCC *see* United Nations Framework Convention on Climate Change (UNFCCC)
UNICEF 237
United Arab Emirates 190
United Nations 187; General Assembly 1, 2, 20, 204, 205; Universal Declaration of Human Rights 12, 72; World Population Prospects 156–7; *see also Our Common Future*; sustainable development goals (SDGs)
United Nations Commission on Sustainable Development (UNCSD) 107, 121, 243n7
United Nations Conference on Environment and Development

(UNCED) 28, 97, 101n15, 106–7, 204, 218n8
United Nations Conference on Sustainable Development 80, 204–5
United Nations Conference on the Human Environment 201
United Nations Conference on Trade and Development (UNCTAD) 31n7
United Nations Development Programme (UNDP) 46; *see also Human Development Report*
United Nations Environment Programme (UNEP) 31n7, 107, 156, *157*
United Nations Framework Convention on Climate Change (UNFCCC) 154, 155
United States 144, 157, 191
Universal Declaration of Human Rights 12, 72
University of Gothenburg, Sweden 146
University of Notre Dame, USA 146
urban air pollution 236–8, 240
urbanization 189, 193–4, 232–4, **233**
Uruguay 146, 191
utilitarianism 47, 54n14, 59–61, 63–4, 66–7
Utilitarianism (Mill) 60–1

values and norms 15
van den Bergh, J. C. J. M. 93, 162
Varieties of Democracy Project 146–7, *147*, 148, *148*, **165**, 175–7, *176*

Ward, Barbara 10
waste 186, 191, 234–5
WCED *see* World Commission on Environment and Development (WCED)
weak sustainability 86–8
Weak versus Strong Sustainability (Neumayer) 86, 87
wealth inequality 17, 18, 23; *see also* difference principle; fair distribution
weighting of capabilities 50–1, 54n18
Weisbrod, B. A. 94
Weiss, Edith Brown 17
Weitzman, Martin 96, 119

WGI *see* Worldwide Governance Indicators (WGI)
Whitelegg, John 201
WHO *see* World Health Organization (WHO)
Wildavsky, Aaron 114
wilderness amenity services 94–5
Wilkinson, R. 17
Wittgenstein Centre of Demography 188
Wolff, J. 65, 217
women: education 143, 188–9; political empowerment of 145–6, 148, *148*
World Bank 10, 11, 30n1, 88, 91, 93, 115, 121, 138, 139, 140, 149–50, *150*, 222

World Commission on Environment and Development (WCED) 1–2, 11, 15, 20; *see also Our Common Future*
World Conservation Strategy 19
World Gallup Survey 143
world government 69
World Health Organization (WHO) 236–8
world income distribution 153, *153*, *154*
Worldwide Governance Indicators (WGI) 238
World Wildlife Fund 160–2, *161*

Yousafzai, Malala 136

Zambia 189–90

Taylor & Francis eBooks

Helping you to choose the right eBooks for your Library

Add Routledge titles to your library's digital collection today. Taylor and Francis ebooks contains over 50,000 titles in the Humanities, Social Sciences, Behavioural Sciences, Built Environment and Law.

Choose from a range of subject packages or create your own!

Benefits for you

» Free MARC records
» COUNTER-compliant usage statistics
» Flexible purchase and pricing options
» All titles DRM-free.

REQUEST YOUR FREE INSTITUTIONAL TRIAL TODAY

Free Trials Available
We offer free trials to qualifying academic, corporate and government customers.

Benefits for your user

» Off-site, anytime access via Athens or referring URL
» Print or copy pages or chapters
» Full content search
» Bookmark, highlight and annotate text
» Access to thousands of pages of quality research at the click of a button.

eCollections – Choose from over 30 subject eCollections, including:

Archaeology	Language Learning
Architecture	Law
Asian Studies	Literature
Business & Management	Media & Communication
Classical Studies	Middle East Studies
Construction	Music
Creative & Media Arts	Philosophy
Criminology & Criminal Justice	Planning
Economics	Politics
Education	Psychology & Mental Health
Energy	Religion
Engineering	Security
English Language & Linguistics	Social Work
Environment & Sustainability	Sociology
Geography	Sport
Health Studies	Theatre & Performance
History	Tourism, Hospitality & Events

For more information, pricing enquiries or to order a free trial, please contact your local sales team: www.tandfebooks.com/page/sales

 Routledge
Taylor & Francis Group

The home of
Routledge books

www.tandfebooks.com